BEHIND THE SCENES IN

American Government

Peter Woll   BRANDEIS UNIVERSITY

BEHIND THE SCENES IN

American Government

Personalities and Politics

Sixth Edition

LITTLE, BROWN AND COMPANY
Boston   Toronto

Library of Congress Cataloging-in-Publication Data

Behind the scenes in American government.

Includes bibliographical references.
1. United States — Politics and government — 20th
century. 2. Politicians — United States. 3. Statesmen —
United States. I. Woll, Peter, 1933–
JK271.B533 1987 320.973 86-21444
ISBN 0-316-95177-3

Library of Congress Catalog Card No. 86-21444

ISBN 0-316-95177-3

9 8 7 6 5 4 3 2

MV

Published simultaneously in Canada
by Little, Brown & Company (Canada) Limited

Printed in the United States of America

For Jill,
politician extraordinaire

PREFACE

This book is designed as a supplementary text for introductory American government courses. It is also an exciting complement to a wide range of courses that analyze parties and political campaigning, interest groups and lobbyists, the media and political consultants, the presidency, Congress, the courts, and the bureaucracy.

Politics is, by any measure, fascinating. But this fascination is not often conveyed to students because many books and courses concentrate on structures and processes at the expense of the individuals who constitute the lifeblood of politics. And it is, after all, the people in politics who shape its character, just as they themselves are shaped by it. This book illustrates how character and personality influence politics, and the ways in which political institutions and processes, such as the presidency and political campaigning, affect the personalities and actions of those who are directly, and sometimes indirectly, involved. Vignettes of famous politicians, pressure group leaders, journalists and political consultants, members of Congress, White House staffers and presidential advisers, Supreme Court justices, and top-level bureaucrats comprise the book. By introducing students to the colorful and powerful personalities who are to be found in politics, I hope to make American government the lively subject that it should be.

The sixth edition, just off the press as the 1988 presidential contest begins to heat up, presents fresh profiles of leading contenders for the presidential nominations of both parties. Included in this volume are the most popular political profiles from previous editions that have, according to user surveys, riveted student attention and helped to give a sense of the excitement of politics through the firsthand accounts of participants and close observers.

New to the sixth edition are portrayals of vice-president and presidential hopeful George Bush, who early in the contest was a front runner for his party's nomination because of his position and the political ties he developed while in office. Lively accounts of Congressman Jack Kemp's run for the presidency and Mario Cuomo's political career and possible bid for the Democratic nomination also have been added.

In a fresh selection in Chapter 2, on pressure groups and lobbyists, *Time* cover-story writer Evan Thomas depicts influence peddling in the nation's capital. He portrays the colorful personalities and styles of the many lobbyists who prowl the corridors and inner offices of power in the city on the Potomac. Also new to the chapter is Tom Watson's account of PACs, and the PAC pilgrimages that all political candidates must make.

A number of fresh profiles highlight chapter 3 on the media and political consultants. Bill Peterson describes the political consultants who orchestrated the hotly contested Florida campaign for the United States Senate seat between Republican incumbent Paula Hawkins and Democratic Governor Bob Graham. ABC network's top White House correspondent Sam Donaldson gives *his* side of the story in a candid interview that describes both the exhilarating and frustrating aspects of his work. And a *Washington Monthly* account of the capital's reporters — the new Washington elite — winds up this completely revamped chapter on the media.

Chapter 4 on the presidency continues to be one of the most popular in the book. Stephen Weisman's piece on Ronald Reagan's presidential style, which readers of the last edition thoroughly enjoyed, introduces the chapter. Political scientist James David Barber provides new insights into the Reagan presidency, focusing upon the character, style, and performance of one of the most popular presidents in our history. Another new profile describes Treasury Secretary Jim Baker's political machinations in support of the president. *Washington Post* writer Lois Romano's account of women in the Reagan White House suggests that sexism was alive and well, and in this respect the Reagan administration differed little from its predecessors.

New accounts of Georgia's Democratic Senator Sam Nunn, and House Democratic Whip and possibly soon-to-become Majority Leader Tom Foley, open chapter 5 on the Congress. And the individualistic and aggressive style of Republican Senator Phil Gramm is the subject of another addition to the chapter.

In chapter 6 on the courts, *New York Times* correspondent Stuart Taylor, Jr., describes the conflict between Attorney General Edwin Meese and Supreme Court Justice William J. Brennan over how the Constitution should be interpreted. Retained is Bob Woodward's and Scott Armstrong's inside account of the "Brethren" and the 1973 abortion decision.

Chapter 7 on the bureaucracy begins with Sanford J. Unger's popular portrayal of "The King" — the late and greatly feared FBI Director J. Edgar Hoover. Jonathan Alter's close look inside the bureaucracy at the top-level bureaucrats whose consummate but different political skills enable them to maintain and expand their power over changing presidential administrations, ends the book on a lively and interesting note.

I would again like to thank Editor John Covell of Little, Brown and Company for his expert advice and assistance in planning the new edition. Cynthia Chapin oversaw the book's production, along with Melinda Wirkus. They skillfully guided the book through the many steps required before publication. Over the years Neil Sullivan and Rochelle Jones have taken an interest in the book and made many valuable suggestions for articles to be included. Also greatly appreciated are the comments of many others, both instructors and students, who have used the text. Finally, the manuscript could not have been completed without the help of Elaine Herrmann and Lisa Carisella, who kept the computers whirring as they transcribed my comments onto the word processor.

CONTENTS

Chapter Three
THE MEDIA AND POLITICAL CONSULTANTS   127

plots of voter attitudes shape his tactical advice. He was a major force behind Gary Hart's strong bid for the presidential nomination in 1984, and will undoubtedly influence future candidate selections.

Chapter Five
THE CONGRESS

Chapter Seven
THE BUREAUCRACY 327

POLITICAL PARTIES AND POLITICIANS

Chapter One

In classical democratic theory, political parties are supposed to bridge the gap between people and government. They are to be the principal policymakers, presenting contrasting choices to the electorate so that, by voting, people can participate in the choice of government programs. It is important that a political party have control over its candidates and office holders, because a party that has a majority in the legislature and controls the executive will then be able to carry out its platform.

Although political parties in an ideal situation are suited to presenting meaningful and realistic policy choices for the electorate, they also serve the personal goals of their active members, which may have nothing at all to do with implementing one public policy instead of another. Roberto Michels, the great European political sociologist of the early twentieth century, draws from German sociologist Max Weber to define the political party as:

> A spontaneous society of propaganda and of agitation seeking to acquire power, in order to procure thereby for its active militant adherents chances, ideal and material, for the realization of either objective aims or of *personal advantages*, or of both. Consequently, the general orientation of the political party, whether in its personal or impersonal aspect, is that of *machtstreben* (striving to power).[1]

In this chapter we will be concerned with the personal motives of active party members. These motives affect the organization and orientation of political parties at national, state, and local levels. The drive for power may completely overshadow party policy. American party leaders are more interested in power than in ideology, and therefore will often shape their policy promises in accordance with the wishes of the majority of the electorate. And, in the absence of any clear electoral desires, which is a common situation, party leaders themselves must determine their actions, which are usually directed toward expanding their power and status in both the party and the government. Their personalities often determine the kinds of decisions they will make, and the way in which they conduct their offices. At the lower levels of parties, particularly in city party machines, the orientation of adherents is often economic security as much as a drive for power. Policy is almost completely irrelevant at these lower echelons.

---

[1]Alfred De Grazia, trans., Roberto Michels' *First Lectures in Political Sociology* (Minneapolis: University of Minnesota Press, 1949), p. 134. Italics added.

THE 1988 PRESIDENTIAL RACE began almost as soon as the results were in on President Ronald Reagan's overwhelming 1984 electoral victory. Because Reagan was prevented from serving a third term by the Twenty-second Amendment, the Republican race was immediately open, and several contenders — including then Senate Minority Leader Howard Baker of Tennessee and Congressman Jack Kemp — began to test the political waters. But Vice President George Bush had the inside track simply by virtue of his position which gave him high visibility, staff, organizational and logistic support, and the fund-raising capabilities that his competitors could not match. The following selection describes how the vice president is using his position to launch a campaign that he hopes will not only enable him to capture his party's nomination, but also the most cherished political prize of all — the presidency.

1

Gerald M. Boyd
THE FRONT RUNNER

In the evening darkness, with his latest mission for President Reagan behind him, George Bush stares across his private cabin aboard Air Force Two as its four powerful engines roar in the background. The vice president has the wary look of a marathon runner just before the biggest race of his life. Though the primaries are two years off, Mr. Bush is clearly running for his party's nomination, and the words that tumble out of his mouth — like his expression — reinforce the notion.

After five years in Ronald Reagan's shadow, Mr. Bush has launched a drive to succeed the president, and he has done it with intensity. For the record, Mr. Bush is playing it close to the vest because he officially becomes a candidate only when he declares. But no one should get the impression that he doesn't want to be president.

"America faces many challenges," he says, sounding very much like a campaigner. "So long as I may be considered qualified to meet those challenges I am eager to do so. It's just as simple as that."

Mr. Bush, party insiders say, is the clear front runner for the Republican nomination. "Right now, it's his to lose," says an aide to President Reagan. It is also clear Mr. Bush is determined to hold that position. He is gathering a trusted and savvy staff around him, has formed a political action committee to raise money and spread the word, has installed operatives in key primary states, and in the last few months has gone on a vigorous speech-making offensive aimed at broadening his support in the Republican Party's conservative ranks.

The vice president has also furthered his cause by serving the president with unflagging loyalty and energy. He has logged more than 750,000 miles preaching the Reagan gospel, and has taken it upon himself to defend his boss's most controversial actions — for instance, Mr. Reagan's visit last year to a German cemetery where SS officers are buried. White House officials say that Mr. Reagan would anoint Mr. Bush without hesitation as the one most suited to carry his conservative revolution into the next decade, were it not for the president's role as party leader and his desire to stay above the political fray.

It is clear that Mr. Bush has made inroads into the party's conservative factions, which have in the past regarded him with suspicion. In fact, several recent surveys by Republican organizations showed that he is the first choice of party conservatives, that he is preferred by more Republicans than the combined percentage of those likely to oppose him in a primary, and that he is also rated above any of the most frequently mentioned Democratic contenders.

Sitting in the cabin of his plane after discarding his dark business-suit jacket for the more personal flight jacket (with "George Bush Vice President" on it), Mr. Bush told a visitor: "I feel fairly comfortable with where I stand. That isn't to say that I can't do better personally or I can't pick up support in one area or another where I might not have it right now. But I'm relaxed with myself."

Within the political community, however, a suspicion lingers that Mr. Bush, who lost when he sought the Republican nomination for president in 1980, and was a loser twice while running for the United States Senate from Texas, stands to become the Walter F. Mondale of 1988. That is, the party front runner with the money and organization, but without a message that voters are seeking.

Beyond support for the Reagan agenda, in fact, it is unclear exactly *what* Mr. Bush's message is. Both the vice president and his aides concede this, but contend that Mr. Bush most definitely *has* a message. But to spell it out now would risk upstaging Mr. Reagan, they say.

What is more, in an apparent attempt to be all things to all Republicans, Mr. Bush has created an identity problem. In one recent week, for example, despite the concerns of some conservative supporters, he joined civil-rights leaders for an emotional tribute to the Rev. Martin Luther King Jr. at the Ebenezer Baptist Church in Atlanta, joining in their cry of "We Shall Overcome." Three days later, he was among several hundred cheering at a dinner of the New York State Conservative Party. The day after that, he appeared in Washington before the Liberty Federation and praised its founder, the Reverend Jerry Falwell, for his "moral vision" for America.

What is clear in any detailed assessment of his chances to hold the lead, is that his most formidable opponent is not necessarily one of scattering potential challengers, but George Herbert Walker Bush himself.

The journey that the sixty-one-year-old vice president has embarked upon, at perhaps the most critical point in his career, is being taken without a complete road map. The strategy that he and his aides have devised involves a series of tactics rather than a detailed plan.

"The two major elements of the strategy in 1979 were to build upon George Bush's broad government experience, experience in Republican politics, and to concentrate on early and in-depth organizational efforts in the early primary and caucus states," says Treasury Secretary James A. Baker 3d, who was then Mr. Bush's campaign manager.

This time, aides believe that Mr. Bush can garner the nomination on the strength of an appeal to all elements within the Republican Party, and then win the general contest with a similar multifaceted approach. Moreover, they believe that Mr. Reagan's policies, and Mr. Bush's strong identification with them, will provide an important election benefit.

"Front runner is a very precarious situation, but if you know how to proceed, it's the best place to be," said Lee Atwater, the director of Mr. Bush's political action committee and a former top political adviser to Mr. Reagan.

Mr. Bush's plans call for following the script he used in the 1982 midterm elections, when he traveled the country vigorously campaigning for Republican candidates, and served as Mr. Reagan's stand-in. About 150 such trips are planned this year — roughly the same number taken four years ago.

On the advice of Mr. Baker, one of a small core of behind-the-scenes advisers for the vice president, (and other strategists who are publicly working for Mr. Bush), some other tactical decisions have been made. Gone, for example, are most of those who served in staff positions during Mr. Bush's first term as vice president, such as retired Admiral Daniel J. Murphy, his chief of staff; Peter Teeley, press secretary, J. Steven Rhodes, chief domestic policy adviser.

They have been replaced by a team operating out of two locations: Craig L. Fuller, who worked for Mr. Reagan, now serves as the vice president's chief of staff in the Executive Office Building, and Marlin Fitzwater, another Reagan staff alumnus, is press secretary. There is also a group of strategists at Mr. Bush's political action committee that includes Mr. Atwater, Helen Cameron — who was in charge of voter registration in the 1984 Reagan campaign — and Ron Kaufman, special assistant to Mr. Atwater. Mr. Bush also receives advice from such longtime associates as the poll-taker Robert Teeter; Dean Burch, a former chairman of the Republican National Committee, and Nicholas Brady, a former New Jersey Senator.

The forward-sounding Fund for America's Future has its headquarters on the third floor of a Washington office building eight blocks from the White House. Large color pictures of Mr. Bush dot the walls, and about 20 paid staff members and numerous volunteers are hard at work there.

Since its creation by Mr. Bush last May, the fund, which has representatives in each of the 50 states, has raised more than $3.9 million through direct-mail solicitations, contributions from supporters, and fund-raising events. The money is slated for the campaigns of Republican candidates in Senate, House, and state races this November. The vice president can expect this generosity to be repaid politically. The fund can also easily shift gears and raise money for Mr. Bush's own election.

Mr. Bush has taken other steps, including the establishment of an office in Michigan, and the dispatching of staff workers to New Hampshire and Iowa where key early primaries will be held. He has also visited Michigan, the site of precinct delegate contests that are viewed as the start of the primary process, five times since the 1984 election and plans another trip next month.

But the major tactic in Mr. Bush's quest for the nomination involves his relationship with Mr. Reagan. At almost every stop on his travels, this point is made in introductions of Mr. Bush: that he is loyal and that he is close to the president. The ability of Mr. Bush to present himself in such a manner has greatly enhanced his political standing, his aides say.

Although the relationship between the two men is largely private, aides for both say there is a genuine closeness, even affection, between them. Last February, Mr. Reagan, in what came close to an endorsement of Mr. Bush as his successor, called him the "finest vice president I ever have any recollection of."

"The president would endorse him in the minute," said one top Reagan aide, noting that he has a longstanding pledge against taking sides in intraparty contests.

Although interplay between the two men and the advice Mr. Bush provides in weekly lunches between the two and during daily national security briefings is secret, aides to the vice president point to several incidents to describe the relationship between him and the president. They tell of how genuinely upset Mr. Bush became last spring — the angriest they have ever seen him — when word leaked about his advice to the president on retaining special tax breaks for oil and gas exploration during the development of the tax-simplification plan later offered to Congress. Craig Fuller recalls, "He wanted the President to know that he wasn't going to suddenly start to find a way to put into print what he was recommending in small and private meetings."

Aides also mention Mr. Bush's decision to wade into the controversy last May surrounding the president's visit to Bitburg cemetery in West Germany. The vice president decided to act after his wife, Barbara, told him she had received criticism of the visit while speaking in New York. Marlin Fitzwater recalls that, "He said, 'I have been stewing at home and worrying about it and I'm damn tired of people not sticking up for the president.'" Mr. Bush then typed a speech in defense of the president that was later delivered, with few changes, to the United States Chamber of Commerce.

The relationship with Mr. Reagan has given Mr. Bush acceptance among Republican conservatives and hard-liners who, in recent years, have been the party's most active element. They range from Mr. Falwell and Congressman Robert K. Dornan of California on the far right, to Angela M. Buchanan Jackson, who served as treasurer of two Reagan presidential campaigns and is considered in the mainstream of the conservative ranks.

"George Bush has had a historical problem with the right wing of this party," says Mr. Atwater. "The type of problem that deprived Bush of being able to win in 1980 when he knocked Reagan down," he said, referring to Mr. Bush's upset victory in the Iowa primary. "That problem is by and large behind him."

But, the aide continued, "Is he the hero of the right or is he going to get a hundred percent?" The aide answered, "No," reflecting the prevailing view of the political community.

It is the potential candidacy of Representative Jack Kemp of New York, whom Mr. Bush refuses to criticize even in private, that generates the most concern within the vice president's camp. Some advisers believe that, unlike other possible challengers — such as Senator Bob Dole of Kansas or former Senator Howard H. Baker, Jr. of Tennessee — Mr. Kemp can mount a strong campaign as the ideological heir to the president, and also has a base on the right from which to launch an assault on Mr. Bush.

A desire to prove his conservative mettle was the prime motive for Mr. Bush's appearances at a number of conservative gatherings in recent months in which he promoted his credentials in sharp language. In a speech in New York, he blasted "every two-bit punk with a knife or a gun who mugs a cleaning lady." At a gathering of Mr. Falwell's Liberty Federation in Washington, he hailed the evangelist. "America is in crying need of the moral vision you will bring to our political life," the vice president told Mr. Falwell. In December, Mr. Bush even spoke at a tribute to the late William Loeb, the staunchly right-wing New Hampshire publisher who bitterly opposed him in the 1980 campaign.

These speeches have come at a critical period in which Mr. Kemp is seeking to gain a foothold of his own. The Bush plan is to cut off any possible confrontation with Mr. Kemp in the months ahead, focus instead on campaigning for Republicans, and serve as Mr. Reagan's surrogate.

But Mr. Bush has already run into a barrage of pointed — and unexpected — criticism. After the vice president's speech in New York, the conservative columnist George F. Will wrote, "The unpleasant sound Bush is emitting as he traipses from one conservative gathering to another is a thin, tinny 'arf' — the sound of a lap dog."

Mr. Bush said he was "surprised" by the personal nature of the Will attack. Aides say privately that they believe it was an isolated incident that will quickly be forgotten.

Yet it underscores the doubts some conservatives have with the vice president, and the danger that can occur to a politician, even when venturing into what appear to be safe waters.

"The lesson we learned is that we have to be careful and view all that the vice president does from the perspective of 1988," said Mr. Fitzwater.

Mr. Bush said recently of the speech: "Certainly, the people who were there for the most part seemed to think it was all right. But did it turn out the way I wanted? Obviously, no."

While not disputing the breadth of Mr. Bush's support within the Republican Party, strategists for some potential opponents question its depth. Moreover, they explain their main tactic for now is to depend heavily on Mr. Bush stumbling badly. "If this guy falters some place early, what does he fall back on?" said a top strategist for one rival, who did not want his name to be used.

As Mr. Bush discusses such a flap, the words that come out are not just defensive, they are downright exasperated. George Bush has grown weary of explaining his motives and his political philosophy. Any "fairminded" analysis of his record, Mr. Bush argues, would show him to be a conservative.

"In the first place, my appearances before the Conservative Party aren't something new," he says. "There seems to be a new focus on it in certain quarters, but I think that has to do with speculation about '88 and not the reality.

"Similarly, with Falwell," he says, "I've done events with Falwell. So what we are seeing is a continuation of what I've been doing, not just with the right wing but with other constituencies. What I say is

motives. Some assert that he is "mission-oriented," others cite a strong sense of public duty and patriotism. Still others point to a willingness to take risks and a strong sense of compassion. Mr. Teeley notes, for example, that as a child Mr. Bush's nickname was "Have-half," derived from his practice of sharing half of whatever he had with friends.

What perhaps makes Mr. Bush difficult to define is that he is a product of several vastly different experiences. He grew up in Greenwich, in an atmosphere that one aide described as "good family, good education, and good manners." He was the son of a United States Senator from Connecticut, Prescott Bush, and a student at Phillips Academy in Andover, Mass.

After World War II, from which he returned a decorated Navy pilot, Mr. Bush attended Yale, where he was captain of the baseball team, and graduated Phi Beta Kappa with a degree in economics. He then settled in Texas, where he became a self-made millionaire in the booming oil business.

In 1964, Mr. Bush, in effect, retired from business to pursue a career in politics and public service. He ran for the United States Senate that year and lost. He was elected to the House of Representatives in 1966 and 1968 before losing a second bid for the Senate in 1970. He subsequently served as chief United States delegate to the United Nations; as chairman of the Republican National Committee; as head of the United States liaison office in Peking, and as Director of Central Intelligence.

In public, Mr. Bush projects aspects of all three "lives." Privately, he shows a sensitivity to what he calls the "myths" that they have spawned, including the one he resents the most — that he is a preppy. When asked about where he buys his suits, he is quick to point out that they are not from Brooks Brothers, but from Arthur A. Adler in Washington, and Norton Ditto in Houston.

"You think of me as wearing button-down shirts," he said on a recent flight from Florida to Andrews Air Force Base. "Well, I haven't owned a button-down shirt in 10 years. You think of striped ties — I might have, I don't want to be going into much depth on my wardrobe but I'd say, 3, possibly 2 percent of the ties I've got are striped."

"Gucci shoes?" he asks, removing a shoe to read the label inside. "Is that your basic Gucci shoe? It's your basic 11D, very sensible-looking, Middle-American shoe."

Mr. Bush has other image problems. Unlike the president, he is not a man for the cameras. In front of them, he seems to lack assurance. When making a key point, his voice can rise to the point of shrillness, and occasionally — as in his debate with Geraldine Ferraro, when he appeared to be lecturing his opponent — he comes across as a bully.

While contending that it did him no lasting harm, Mr. Bush says now of his performance throughout the campaign: "Should I have been more pleasant? Yes. I should have continued to smile, and that's one of the things I would have done differently."

Aides have also begun working with Mr. Bush to overcome his habit of ad-libbing in speeches, a result of trying to maintain eye contact with the audience. In doing so, he often strays from the text and ends up paraphasing the words, thus losing some of their impact. In recent months, he has been using a Teleprompter and taking a larger role in the preparation of his speeches.

On the Bush staff there is no Michael K. Deaver, Mr. Reagan's much touted image man, who recently left the administration to start a public relations business. That role is largely Mr. Bush's own, although Mr. Fuller and Mr. Fitzwater provide advice. "I can't imagine Mr. Reagan without a Mike Deaver and I can't imagine Mr. Bush with a Mike Deaver," says one Bush adviser.

Sitting by a pool during a major Western swing that Mr. Bush made last fall, a senior adviser recalled how the vice president had once donned a pair of contact lenses and had rejected them with an "I can't live with them." "That's the way he is," the adviser said, "take it or leave it."

Mr. Bush enjoys verbal sparring with the press corps. Yet when he does, only a few insights emerge, a few pieces of a mosaic rather than a complete picture of the man. As a child, the vice president says, he had no interest in politics. As a young adult, fresh out of the Navy and Yale, he struggled on an income of $300 a month. But still he preferred taking his chances in the risky oil-field supply business in Texas to a more comfortable position in New York.

The Bushes—she, the daughter of the publisher of *McCall's* magazine; he, a Navy flier on leave — were married in 1945 in her hometown of Rye, New York. They have five children: George, 39, of Midland, Tex.; John 33, of Miami; Neil, 31, of Denver; Marvin, 29, of Alexandria, Va., and Dorothy Bush LeBlond, 26, who lives in Cape Elizabeth, Maine.

While Barbara Bush is influential in her husband's decisions, friends say, it is not in the manner of Rosalyn Carter, who served as an adviser to Jimmy Carter, or Nancy Reagan, who serves as a protector to her husband. Barbara Bush declines to discuss her views on key issues, saying that she is not the candidate. When asked if she would play a role in Mr. Bush's decision about his political future, she would only say: "It would not be a family war council that makes the key, or some of them, domestic decisions. They evolve."

The Bushes appear very much at ease together. While returning to Washington from a brief visit to Houston last fall, they sat comfortably on the vice president's plane, eating yogurt, trading good-natured banter. Has her husband changed over the years, Mrs. Bush is asked. "No, but I keep hoping," is the response — and they reminisced about their early, bittersweet days in Midland.

"Midland was new people, new faces, new ventures," said Mr. Bush. He had come to the west Texas town in 1948, fresh out of college. "I helped to start the YMCA, was a director of the bank, and helped raise money for a theater. We were participating in the wonderful expansion of a wonderful community. It was a tremendous experience."

But one of the Bushes' most difficult years occurred in that period, when their daughter Robin died of leukemia in 1953, at the age of three. "It was the most agonizing period of our lives," the vice president said, as tears formed in his wife's eyes. "But it drew us together."

"I remember going into the bank holding Robin's hand and they asked me where the little girl was who was sick," recalled Mr. Bush, who commuted from Texas to the Memorial Sloan-Kettering Cancer Center in New York while Mrs. Bush remained by their daughter's side. "And here she was, three months before her death. Today, given the advances of medical technology, she might still be alive."

"We couldn't understand why this child — we went through all of that as anybody does," the vice president said. "What's God's message? Why? We went through all of that and came out with a strong sense of faith. If the ending would have been different, it would have been the greatest experience of our lives."

As Air Force Two glides home from a more recent trip and Mr. Bush prepares for arrival in Washington and his next mission for Mr. Reagan, his thoughts are on the future.

His close identity with the president — now his strongest asset — could turn out to be a drawback as Mr. Reagan's budget and tax plans, as well as other policies, run into stiff opposition.

Mr. Bush concedes that "I am identified with the president's policies and will be identified with them and I am not going to change from being identified with them. If they are looking good, it will be an asset. If they are looking lousy, it will be a detriment."

And while no one would discount the impact of an endorsement from Ronald Reagan, tacit or otherwise, there is also the knowledge that the Reagan presidency is based more on his enormous personal popularity than it is on the strength of his policies. At this point, no one can predict how much of Mr. Reagan's glow will rub off on George Bush.

Yet friends and advisers to the vice president contend that he has the ability to be very much his own man. His experience in the 1980 campaign reinforced his resolve, they say. "It's as if someone says to you, you can't be the champ, but you say, 'Yeah, but I'm a better boxer,' " Mr. Teeley recalls of that year. "You feel that you are better and that you can win, and that you are being prevented from trying as hard as you possibly can."

Shirley Green, a longtime friend of Mr. Bush's who has served on his staff, says: "I would suspect that he probably feels that his whole life, or at least the last 15 years or more, has been one of preparation for the presidency. Not to aspire to it at this stage would be illogical based on the preparation he has had. It would be like a runner working up to a marathon and not doing it."

For now, Mr. Bush is content to strike a familiar note. "I want everybody to be for me that can be, absolutely," he says.

"More importantly, I want people who share my views more than any individuals. I disagree with Jerry Falwell on some things, just like I'm sure he disagrees with me on some issues. Of course, I want him for me. I've never been one who believed that you should start narrowing down your support," says Mr. Bush, who Mr. Teeter describes as "the one guy to keep all the Republicans in the tent."

"I could probably think of a group or two that I won't want support from," says the vice president. "But if it's under this broad umbrella that is the Republican Party, yes, I want it."

NEW YORK GOVERNOR MARIO Cuomo's keynote address to the Democratic National Convention in 1984 electrified the party faithful throughout the nation. Immediately a little-known governor outside of his state became a national figure, and increasingly was mentioned as a leading contender for his party's presidential nomination in 1988. Cuomo, obviously pleased by all the attention, proceeded cautiously, and did not announce plans to enter the race. On more than one occasion he stated flatly that he wanted to devote full time to his job as governor for the remainder of his term. The following likely account of Cuomo's colorful career highlights the possibilities and problems that a popular and skillful governor of one of the nation's largest states faces as he tentatively enters the national political ring.

2 Tom Morganthau and Larry Martz
WHAT MAKES
MARIO RUN?

He might. Or he might not.

So Mario Cuomo insists: as of now, he has no plans to run for president; and Cuomo is a truthful man. But the mere possibility that the New York governor might head the Democratic ticket in 1988 has pols in both parties sniffing the air and launching preemptive strikes. It is not just that Cuomo is the best known of a new crop of activist governors who are taking the play away from Washington these days, or that he was the keynote speaker who electrified the 1984 Democratic convention. What gives him an air of danger is that he is the most interesting and complex figure among the hopefuls, the one man nearly everybody wants to know more about.

He is undeniably tough, intelligent, competitive, and honest. But does his combativeness shade into hot-tempered vindictiveness? Do his old-fashioned Roman Catholicism and upright honor have an edge of sanctimony and priggishness? Is he a hard worker or a workaholic who can't delegate? Does his heritage as an immigrant's son make him thin-skinned and oversensitive to fancied slights? Will his quick wit and lawyerly love of debate lead him into blunders? And can his vision of the nation as a family really be translated into a political agenda to start the next decade?

Textured Paradox: Cuomo has supplied many of his own answers in an extraordinary pair of published diaries covering turning points in a public life that goes back 15 years. They show a richly-textured man who, at 53, can be deeply introspective, superficial, funny, intensely private, generous, stingy, sensitive, and sentimental to the brink of bathos. Defeated, he comes off the canvas to win; winning, he loses the savor of victory. But the enigma remains. There is no single key to Mario Cuomo, in the diaries or anywhere else.

He is governor of the second most populous state, a good political springboard, and it is a good time to be a governor. In the era of limits, when Ronald Reagan's military buildup and social cutbacks leave no room for major domestic initiatives from Washington, the states have had to find their own answers — and at least half a dozen activist governors are doing just that. "The federal government is just boring these days," says Hale Champion, executive dean of Harvard's John F. Kennedy School of Government. Cuomo himself says Washington "is trying to pull out of government altogether. We're trying to make it work better — and I'm talking about governors East and West, Democrat and Republican."

Cuomo is not the most innovative of the class nor the most admired among governors themselves — though a Gallup poll for *Newsweek* shows that Democratic governors think he could be the nominee in 1988. And he has yet to show that he can play effectively on the national and international stage. But his high profile on such issues as abortion and the deductibility of state and local taxes has already begun to nationalize his image. He is traveling selectively outside New York, and drawing fire from prospective rivals; Vice President George Bush recently criticized him so sharply that Bush in turn got a dressing-down from conservative columnist George F. Will. ("Bush should only do it every weekend," Cuomo says, grinning.) For the moment, he is playing a waiting game: he will run for a second term in Albany, and he hopes for a persuasive margin of victory. He isn't going to go away.

The Italian-American

"Let me tell you a speech I made and I'm very proud of it. Nobody heard it." Mario Cuomo, his pouched, mortician's eyes twinkling, his athletic six-foot frame fairly bursting across his office desk at Manhattan's World Trade Center, was recalling a lost but cherished moment in the 1982 gubernatorial primary campaign:

"Nineteen eighty-two, the end of the campaign, we wind up on Arthur Avenue in the Bronx. Incredibly beautiful place. All Italian . . . *And I said all the right things.* I have got my beautiful Sicilian wife and, hey, I mean it is terrific. All you have to do is press the button and they were going to explode. And then I said, 'Look, we're Italian, we're very proud of it . . . Wouldn't it be great if those of us who remember being called guineas and wops and dagos will now stop talking about people as spics and niggers? Wouldn't it be terrible if we did to the people that came after us what we think some people did to us? . . .' It was very well received, *very* well received."

It is all there: the passionate, humanist conviction along with the lawyer's calculation — the shrewd awareness that he has said "all the right things." In Mario Cuomo, the two are not so much contradictory as intriguingly intertwined. So, too, are other oddly assorted traits: the combativeness learned on the playing fields of his native Queens, N.Y., and the detachment that brought him his first fame as an arbitrator of neighborhood disputes.

"Swinging Doors": He can exude self-assurance to the point of arrogance and yet confide morose self-doubts in the diary he has kept, a shade too self-consciously, since his early days in politics. He can be sweetly reasonable and, by the testimony of those who have felt his sting, terrible tempered. In a less memorable political episode during his losing race for mayor in 1977, a frazzled Cuomo went after an obstreperous rival politician who had called him a liar at a Brooklyn high-school meeting. "Everybody has a temper, but I think he has more than most," the man says. "With both hands he grabbed me by my chest and flung me through the swinging doors." Later, after aides separated them, Cuomo apologized and the two shook hands.

In spite of his denials, the ethnic wound is there too; Cuomo has often told how he was refused entry to the best law firms because of his working-class Italian background, although he dismisses, with a characteristic effusion, any suggestion of lingering resentment: "I mean, I'm not maybe a typical case, but life has been so good to me and my family . . . The idea of resenting anything makes me feel so guilty that it worries me. I mean, look what I've got."

Life *has* been good to him. Born under the dark star of the Depression in 1932, he came of age in a postwar America rejoicing in its sense of might and mission. The country's mythology was working. Cuomo's father, Andrea, could offer his three children the example of an unschooled immigrant laborer who worked his way up from digging sewers to the proprietorship of a small grocery store in the polyglot Queens neighborhood of South Jamaica. It was a household, Cuomo's brother Frank remembers, where the idea of family was sacrosanct and work was something you did seven days a week. "He was our role model: 'You no fool with girls. You don't hurt anybody.' He was a Catholic, family-type guy."

Cuomo went to St. John's Prep in Brooklyn, to St. John's University and later its law school. For four years he juggled commuting to St. John's and playing basketball and sandlot baseball for Joe Austin's Celtics. "The center of our universe was sports, particularly baseball," says Vinny Vane, a teammate who hasn't seen Cuomo in at least 25 years. Covering centerfield for a semipro team one summer, Mario was signed by a big-league scout and sent to the Class D Brunswick (Ga.) Pirates. The scouting report was that he would run over anyone in his way. He likes to tell how he punched a catcher who called him "something unkind" — right in the face mask. But that may have been his hardest hit. His career was abbreviated by a bean ball that left him with a monthlong headache.

Street-Corner Kid: It was at St. John's that Cuomo met and married Matilda Raffa, a student in the teacher-education program. According to friends, she was the only real girlfriend Mario ever had. "He was not as aggressive in that arena as he was in sports," says Vane. His other arena was the street corner at Tiedermann's Ice Cream Parlor on Jamaica Avenue. From the end of grammar school through college, Mario and his buddies hung out there, hassling one another, arguing baseball. As much as anything, the street-corner jousting quickened his debating skill. "Mario was our designated lawyer," Vane recalls.

He was also the group's flaming liberal — even then a believer in unions and "the people" — and its most serious student, sharing first-place honors in his law school graduating class. In 1956, Cuomo got a clerkship with a New York State Court of Appeals judge. But despite that prestigious reference, he was turned down by the leading Manhattan law firms. "One of them came right out and told him they didn't hire Italians," says Fabian Palomino, a fellow clerk who is now his special counsel. Cuomo landed with a Brooklyn firm. Over 17 years he worked his way up to senior partner, distinguishing himself in appellate work. Always he made time for *pro bono* criminal defense, which he seemed to view as an obligation of Catholic conscience as well as an expression of solidarity with the underdog.

By then, the Cuomos had five children and a modest Cape Cod house in Holliswood, Queens — built for them by Mario's father — where they continued to live until they moved to the governor's mansion. Matilda, a slender, comely woman, had quit her job as a grammar school teacher and settled into the traditional role of homemaker and community do-gooder. The couple have taken only a single weeklong vacation in Rome since they married. But Mario almost always manages to set aside some weekend time for the children, relaxing with a round of basketball at the hoop attached to the garage. (There is an affectionate family complaint that Cuomo wins at games by playing dirty. "He cheats," says brother Frank.)

The family remains his bastion in a milieu where insult and injury are part of the game, and an Italian can still be felled by a bean ball. The charge is often made that Cuomo is too "insular," that he doesn't delegate beyond his inner circle. "What circle?" snorts his friend, columnist Jimmy Breslin. "There ain't enough people to form a circle."

Outside of his family and a very few friends, Cuomo is indeed a loner. He favors dark, relatively inexpensive suits, as if he were trying to avoid being conspicuous — a peculiar preference for a potential presidential candidate. He shows no interest in making money: under former Governor Hugh Carey he was the first state secretary to decline to continue private law practice.

There are, in any case, at least three Cuomos for the public to judge. There is the hothead, who last December blundered into an awkward debate with reporters over the existence of the "Mafia." There is the somberly reflective diarist, forever questioning his achievements, as in one 6 A.M. entry three years ago: "Has anything ever been so useless as the momentary acclaim of a world that does not know you, no matter how 'public'?" And there is the exuberant, irrepressible winner, celebrating his good fortune for the benefit of an interviewer last week, and implying he doesn't need anything more out of life: "I mean, look at what I have got . . . These kids are so nice, they are so perfect. But Matilda. (And) my mother! My mother forget about . . . I could write volumes about her. I am the governor of the State of New York, having a wonderful time."

The Catholic

Not since Eugene McCarthy's moral crusade for the presidency in 1968 has a political leader been so intellectually, self-consciously, even aggressively Roman Catholic as Mario Matthew Cuomo. And, paradoxically, no Roman Catholic politician — including John F. Kennedy — has done more to make the American Catholic bishops rethink the church's relationship to political issues.

Kennedy was Harvard, money and youth, Irish by birth and just Catholic enough to make his religion a troubling issue in 1960. He deftly defused it by declaring he would not as president take direction from his church. McCarthy went a step further by demonstrating that his Midwestern Catholicism was progressive — even radical — on issues like Vietnam. Now comes Cuomo from Queens borough, New York City, proudly ethnic in ways the patrician Kennedys never were and scrupulously Catholic in a manner alien to Midwesterners like McCarthy. But in his home town, Cuomo is confronted with Cardinal John J. O'Connor, whose instinct for politics is as pronounced as the governor's penchant for theological disputation. Each man has become a cross for the other to bear.

Cuomo is old enough to relish immigrant American Catholicism with its hushed Latin liturgy, neighborhood parishes and prickly consciences fine-tuned by zealous priests and nuns. But he is also young enough to appreciate the release that came with Vatican Council II. In parochial school, Cuomo's Italian sensibility was outfitted by parochial school nuns with an Irish conscience, and the tension between the two is evident in the published diary of his campaign for governor. "The whole religious experience of Catholics like myself in that time and place," he writes, "painted for us a world of moral pitfalls that needed to be avoided in order to earn an eternal peace." In conversation, that becomes a joke: "I mean, you're supposed to be unhappy!" Cuomo's turning point as a Catholic came in the early 1960s when he first read *The Divine Milieu*, a mystical meditation by the Jesuit paleontologist Pierre Teilhard de Chardin, which convinced Cuomo that Christians were called to embrace the world, not mistrust it. "We never heard that at St. John's Prep," he says of his Catholic high school.

Men of Values: Even so, Cuomo retained so many scruples about entering the messy world of politics that he sought the advice of Brooklyn's Bishop Francis Mugavero before agreeing to run for mayor of New York in 1977. The bishop told him that politics needs men of sound values, and ever since Cuomo has preached values as part of his politics. "What I believe as a Christian is totally compatible with what I believe as a Democrat," Cuomo insists. "Take the Sermon on the Mount. You could write a pretty good platform out of that, and it wouldn't have a single proscription in it."

In his own political sermons, Cuomo stresses love rather than prohibition, compassion rather than exclusion — and backs them up with tough political judgments: last week he endorsed New York City's proposed gay-rights bill against O'Connor's opposition. The two men remain at a cordial distance, but Cuomo considers O'Connor the nation's "most important cardinal" — a judgment that only a Catholic from New York would make.

Indeed, it was O'Connor who inadvertently helped propel Cuomo into his role as this decade's most influential Catholic politician. During the 1984 presidential campaign, O'Connor told reporters that he personally could not see "how a Catholic in good conscience can vote for a candidate who supports abortion." The archbishop's remark seemed aimed at vice presidential candidate Geraldine Ferraro, but it was Cuomo who was sufficiently offended to offer extended public rebuttal. He had been an altar boy and had graduated from St. John's University and its law school. Now, after two decades of service to Catholic institutions, of attending mass, and of raising five children in the faith, he found that the archbishop was questioning his Catholicism.

The issue was fully joined three months later when Cuomo went to the University of Notre Dame to deliver what he called the most important speech of his political life. He said he personally opposed abortion but that as a public servant he could not impose his personal morality on others. Lacking a public consensus to the contrary, he said, he must uphold the law.

After the speech, Notre Dame president Theodore M. Hesburgh proposed that 10 American Catholic politicians meet privately with an equal number of bishops to discuss the issues Cuomo had raised. Cuomo was willing but found little support among his peers, and at least two cardinals — O'Connor and Boston's conservative Archbishop Bernard Law — caustically rejected the idea.

Father Hesburgh believes that Cuomo the Catholic politician must be understood "in the context of New York State, New York City, and *The New York Times*; if he came from a prairie state, his personal and public stands on abortion might be more congruent." Cuomo disagrees. He believes that his views on abortion will be affirmed in the next presidential election, no matter who runs. He also thinks that publication of the Catholic bishops' pastoral letter on the American economy — which he supports — will help end what he calls the Republicans' six years of saying, "We can't take care of all those poor people." That's Cuomo's way of relating religion to politics. But the governor has yet to test whether it will play to a wider audience in which New York is just another state.

The Governor

He is known — affectionately — to his staff as "the Gorilla," and the Gorilla sits anywhere he wants. On a recent weekday morning in Albany, Governor Mario Cuomo is in a wicker armchair at the exact center of a long table surrounded by two dozen aides. The occasion is a regular weekly staff meeting, and Cuomo — brisk, demanding, occasionally curt and sometimes funny — is clearly in charge: there is no leeway for imprecision, no mercy for the unprepared. "When do I get a [briefing] paper from you?" he asks one participant. "You can't do it before Friday?" To another, he snaps: "It should have been done. Find out why it wasn't." The meeting is over in 90 minutes flat, and Cuomo heads for the door. "As governor, he's a hard taskmaster, and that can be a harsh experience," says one associate. "But from a presidential perspective, I'd rather have someone asking the hard questions when the Joint Chiefs and the CIA say we should invade Cuba."

The possibility of invading Cuba, or even Staten Island, has not arisen during Cuomo's three years in Albany — and in fact, there are those who suggest that his first term in office will be regarded as one of the more uneventful chapters in the history of the Empire State. Thanks in part to the nation's overall prosperity, New York's economy is on the mend — and the state government, which faced a $1.8 billion deficit when Cuomo took office, now enjoys a surplus estimated at up to $600 million. Cuomo can boast of lowering the state income tax, renovating the highway system, helping the homeless, and curbing crime; he has also taken the lead, in his typically combative fashion, at opposing key elements of Ronald Reagan's tax-reform bill. The consequence of all this is a job-approval rating that hovers over 70 percent and a consensus forecast that makes him a probable shoo-in for a second term.

Few in Albany would deny that Cuomo is one of the more articulate liberals around — but that does not mean that his first term is regarded as an unvarnished success. For one thing, even some Democrats regard the governor as a mediocre administrator. He is said to have assembled a staff that is more notable for its loyalty than its brilliance, and he is routinely criticized for his excessive reliance on a tiny coterie of advisers — his son Andrew, 28, chief among them. He is also criticized for refusing to delegate even the most picayune policy decisions — a charge he says is "kind of silly."

The more telling point is that Cuomo, despite his lofty rhetoric about the higher values of American society, has so far failed to advance a compelling vision of the future or to use the power of his office as an effective agent for change. In the words of one of Cuomo's harshest critics, William Stern, the Cuomo record is a "dismal" example of "business as usual — big spending [and]taking care of the boys." Stern, a former supporter who left the Cuomo administration in 1985, says Albany is saturated with pols who are "in government to make money for themselves" — and though no one doubts that Cuomo himself is impeccably honest, Stern says the governor has "no stomach" to clean up the system. As a result, Stern says, New York's economic future "is being held hostage by a public sector that seems incapable of fiscal responsibility." Some observers also speculate that New York City's current corruption scandal may ultimately spread to Albany as well, which could give Cuomo's opponents real ammunition. Cuomo seems alert to the risk: recently, he and Mayor Edward Koch announced the creation of a special commission to review the state's conflict-of-interest rules and come up with recommendations for reform.

Deeper and Bolder: Cuomo's first-term performance has been remarkable for its wary pragmatism. He has worked cautiously with the legislature and he has successfully defused the fiscal crisis he inherited. He has restrained Albany's annual "spring borrowing," a device by which his predecessors gradually expanded the state debt; this year he even proposed that the state make a modest down payment to reduce the accumulated deficit. But his critics argue that his tax cut could have been deeper and bolder: Cuomo, who proposed a $2.1 billion reduction in the state income tax, wound up assenting to Republican demands for a $3.2 billion cut and now claims credit for the biggest tax cut in New York's history. But New York's per capita state and local tax collections are still far higher than the national average, and Cuomo's current budget, at $41 billion, is 30 percent higher than his first-year budget. Others complain the governor has not pushed for fundamental reform in either welfare or education. He espouses a Democratic variant on workfare that is aimed at getting welfare clients private-sector jobs, and he has substantially increased state spending on teacher salaries. But as Cuomo himself observes, the dropout rate among New York City's minority students has reached catastrophic levels.

Cuomo meanwhile is inching his way into national politics — a combative, high-profile role he obviously enjoys, and one that in some respects has been forced on him. He sparred publicly with Vice President George Bush when Bush attacked him on a controversial parole case, and he has led the Democratic opposition to Ronald Reagan's tax-reform bill, which would eliminate the federal income-tax deduction currently allowed for state and local tax payments. That change would hit New York taxpayers hard, and it could ultimately force a radical restructuring of the state's high-tax fiscal policies. Cuomo, along with Democratic Senator Daniel P. Moynihan and Republican Senator Alfonse D'Amato, has campaigned against it — and though they won a partial victory when Reagan's bill was rewritten in the House, the battle is not over.

Stern sees Cuomo's recent yen for the national limelight as a ploy to distract the voters back home — which is probably unfair, since any New York governor would be compelled to oppose the Reagan tax plan. And yet, as Cuomo himself likes to say, "You campaign in poetry, you govern in prose" — which raises the question of whether the governor has already found Albany a bit prosaic.

The Candidate

For Mario Cuomo, it was the moral equivalent of spring training: a subway car repair yard on Coney Island, where he could slap shoulders and trade wisecracks with the mechanics while the transit officials, getting dust on their Florsheims, stood around with nervous smiles. Cuomo seemed to know every man he met, or at least his brothers or cousins. He had actually played on the same ball team with Dominic Depalo. He reminisced about McGuire's bar, where Richard Coyne hangs out on weekends. And when Anthony Aubert from Puerto Rico started in about why the state wasn't spending more on subways, Cuomo fended him off with a jokingly detailed quiz on the mambo.

He is a natural, "the best communicator in the business" according to political counselor David Garth, and he is tuning up for a political season that may not end short of the White House. Hardly anyone who knows him doubts that he wants to be president; his game now is a calculation that he can afford to wait and that there's no percentage in deciding too soon. Crinkly and direct, with an athlete's room-filling presence and a Neapolitan grin, Cuomo brings a lot to the game: wit and empathy in his one-on-one contacts, and passion and intensity in the kind of formal speech that launched him on the national scene at the Democratic National Convention in 1984. He has a long way to go and a lot to prove before he wins his party's blessing, but he has made a strong beginning. Among Democrats, he ranks second only to Gary Hart at this point in the 1988 race. And the Republicans, says Washington consultant Roger Stone, "are concerned about him for a very good reason. He could be a formidable candidate."

He learned it the hard way, with a string of tough losses and campaign debacles: first in the 1974 New York state primary, running for lieutenant governor against a Democratic hierarchy that thought he hadn't paid his dues, and then in 1977 in a mayoral race against Ed Koch. In his own glum postmortem reckoning, his campaigns were clumsy and disorganized. But his doggedness earned him Governor Hugh Carey's appointment as secretary of state and the lieutenant governor's slot in 1978. When Carey stepped down in 1982, Cuomo's chance to replace him looked good. But Koch, near the peak of his popularity, unexpectedly jumped into the race. Cuomo had to beat him in the primary — again without much help from his party — and go on to defeat a conservative millionaire, Lewis Lehrman, who outspent him $14 million to $4.8 million in the general election.

Cuomo's characterization of campaigning as the "poetry" of politics, while governing is merely "the prose," leads some rivals to suspect he prefers the poetry. But Cuomo himself insists it's the other way around. His friend and aide Fabian Palomino recalls his protest that glad-handing the voters is a kind of pandering: "The weight of my ideas should get me votes. Why should I have to shake their hands?" They want to feel they know you, Palomino replied; and Cuomo subsided, grumbling. But he still puts down campaigning as simplistic.

Bristly Reactions: Cuomo's own campaign poetry can be rough-hewn. His zeal for debate gets him into trouble; he winces at every reminder of his wisecrack last year that opponents of his mandatory-seat-belt law were like hunters who "drink beer, don't vote and lie to their wives about where they were all weekend." His temper is a problem: he once bolted from a parade to exchange harsh words with a bystander carrying an obscene poster. But he is trying to muffle his bristly reactions to unflattering media coverage.

He has still to prove whether he is a superb candidate of words or merely all talk. His keynote speech of 1984 was a triumphant reminder of the verities of the Democratic Party, but skeptics noted that nothing in it could not have been said four decades earlier: where were the new ideas? Cuomo protests that "to tell me I need a new political philosophy is ridiculous," and in truth he has been developing his central metaphor of the body politic as family since he first spoke it aloud at the New York State Fair in 1981. But its content is more soothing than specific. He clearly understands the blue-collar case against welfare, for instance; he is weaker when it comes to stating the rebuttal. In a speech at Princeton last month, he conceded that his promised agenda for fighting poverty in the age of limits was still "in preparation."

Cuomo's next hurdle will be his re-election campaign. On the face of it, that isn't much challenge: he already has an $8 million war chest, and his approval rating in New York City at last measuring was an astronomical 74 percent. The suburbs and upstate region — the areas he lost in 1982 — were behind him by 68.7 percent and 63.7 percent, respectively. His tactic is to nationalize the race; he insists straight-faced that he is an underdog against little-known Westchester County Executive Andrew O'Rourke, if only because the White House and the national GOP want him beaten. In fact, Vice President George Bush has delivered two personal attacks, one when Cuomo complained of media bias against Italian-Americans, and again after his granting of clemency to convicted cop-killer Gary McGivern. But it is clearly in Cuomo's interest to ward off overconfidence and lower the expectations of his national audience.

Beyond that election, Cuomo insists he has no "secret plans"; he is traveling a bit more these days, but the state plane, he jokes, is programmed so it can't fly over New Hampshire or Iowa. If he were running for president, he maintains, the right way to do it would be to leave office and run full time. In fact, a big New York win is probably his best chance, but political pros do agree that he should be more active: cultivating friends, setting up funding and polling, assembling a stronger staff, and visiting the early-primary states.

"The Pols Will Wait": It could indeed turn out that the waiting game is less a cool strategy than just a dither over a tough decision. But Cuomo's advisers seem comfortable with his role; they argue that his hot image conveys sincerity and that he has no need to overcome obscurity. "When other guys go out early, the question is, 'Who's he?'," says his friend Garth. "When Cuomo is coming, the question is, 'What size hall?' The pols will wait for him."

At his most candid, Cuomo says he won't finally decide until the field has shaken out a little more and his re-election is settled. If he does go for it, he will face a new set of hurdles: issues of his provincialism (he hasn't spent much time outside New York state and has been abroad only to Italy), his religion and Italian background, and the plain fact that many people fear and despise New York City. Cuomo acknowledges that John Kennedy may not have proved for all time that a Catholic can be elected, and he has gone to some lengths to point out that not all organized crime can be laid to the Mafia. But he scoffs at the other points. Was Abe Lincoln unfit to serve, he demands, because he hadn't been all over America? And regional prejudice, he maintains, is a straw man: "I don't think people are different. The things I said in the keynote were understood by everybody."

At bottom, presidential elections usually hinge on character — and Cuomo has almost too much of that. The problem is defining it and sharpening the image. If he has some of Ronald Reagan's common touch and moral authority, it is offset by arrogance and a kind of reverse snobbery; if there is a trace of Jimmy Carter in his workaholism and pietism, he also has the saving grace of humor. That could take him a long way. But for now, he chooses to wait.

I T SEEMS ONLY APPROPRIATE IN an era when professional football is beamed into every household from the time exhibition games start in August until the Super Bowl the following January, that a former pro-football quarterback for the San Diego Chargers and the Buffalo Bills, Jack E. Kemp, would become a leading contender for the presidency. But the political prominence Kemp was to achieve hardly seemed probable when New York's 38th Congressional district, which includes the Buffalo–Niagara Falls metropolitan area, elected the native Californian to Congress in 1970 by a narrow fifty-two — forty-eight percent margin.

By 1972 Kemp had solidified his constituency support — winning by a wide margin — and never again facing a serious electoral challenge at home. In Washington he was a strong player on the Republican-party team, consistently supporting the Nixon administration. A physical education major at Occidental College where he received his B.A. in 1957, the politician Kemp was both fascinated with and a serious student of economics. He became a leading advocate of "supply-side economics," a school of thought that proposed large tax cuts to boost consumption and investment on the theory that private sector demand, rather than government expenditures, produce prosperity.

At first Kemp was a lonely supply-sider in a world of doubtful politicians and economists. However, Ronald Reagan found the idea appealing, and based his entire economic program upon it, helping at the same time to boost Kemp's national reputation as a prescient politician. Whether or not Jack Kemp's style and politics make him Ronald Reagan's natural political heir is the subject of the following account of the New York Congressman's presidential bid.

3

Steven V. Roberts
CONGRESSMAN JACK KEMP'S RUN FOR THE PRESIDENCY

Jack Kemp is on his way to the White House. As he gets off the elevator in the Rayburn House Office Building on Capitol Hill, he sees a boy carrying a stack of boxes and gives the startled lad a playful cuff on the shoulder. Kemp does not walk to the car, he bounces toward it, emitting waves of restless energy the way a radiator spreads heat. The snazzy silver Thunderbird with the plush red seats is already at the garage door, and he is momentarily embarrassed by the automotive finery. It's leased, he protests, not owned. As the Thunderbird leaves Capitol Hill, Kemp recognizes a journalist in the car ahead. At the next red light, he lunges out the door and shouts at the reporter, "When are you going to interview me?"

During the drive up Pennsylvania Avenue, the talk turns to politics, and the Congressman from upstate New York says that he is glad now that he did not run for the Senate in 1980, or for Governor of New York in 1982. "To be frank," he says, "who has more influence over economic policy? A junior member of the Senate, or me?" Yes, he acknowledges, those unconsummated flirtations have left him with a reputation in the political community for indecisiveness, but he will probably make a firm decision by the end of this year whether to run for president in 1988.

Campaigning for the White House has turned into a four-year marathon, and potential candidates start lining up money and manpower for the next race even before a new president is inaugurated. Kemp knows that his friends will start drifting toward other candidates if he does not signal his intentions early on, and while he remains a bit coy on the subject, he is clearly ready to go. Those 50,000 names, stashed in his computer and waiting to be tapped for campaign cash, are not just a Christmas card list. "Am I interested?" he asks rhetorically. "The answer is yes."

The Thunderbird pulls up to the White House, where Kemp will join other House Republican leaders and President Reagan's advisers for a strategy session on the budget. The guard asks for identification, and Kemp expresses annoyance that he is not instantly waved through.

While his ID's are checked, Kemp's eyes eagerly roam the sidewalk and fasten on a familiar face. Kemp calls his friend over, and on his way the man tells the guard jokingly: "Let him through. He'll be president someday." When Kemp's friend mentions that his mother-in-law is in town from Montana, the Congressman practically shouts with delight: "Did you know that my mother is from Miles City, Montana?" As the guard waves the car through the gate, Kemp calls out, "Tell everyone in Montana hello."

When the Congressmen emerge an hour later, they strike a familiar tableau on the White House driveway: Kemp is talking, the others are listening. Now 49, the one-time quarterback of the Buffalo Bills retains the clean-jawed handsomeness of a football star posing for a Wheaties box. At 6 feet and 200 pounds, he has the burly shoulders that could propel a ball 70 yards down field. A reporter asks for a comment on proposed budget cuts, and Kemp answers: "Cuts have got to be part of an agenda for growth. . . . We can't just offer sacrifice . . . That's not what the President ran on. . . ."

An aide hauls the Congressman into the car before he launches into a full-dress speech, but the words linger in the nippy air as the Thunderbird edges through the evening traffic on its way back to Capitol Hill. Jack French Kemp has spoken those same phrases many thousands of times since coming to Washington 14 years ago as a freshman Congressman. He has marched through the land, proclaiming with evangelical earnestness that economic growth and expanding opportunity are the keys to the kingdom. It is a message made for the television age, upbeat as a beer commercial and easily marketed in a 30-second spot, and the old quarterback has used it to establish himself as a politician of all-pro caliber.

This week, as President Reagan delivers his State of the Union address and Congress gets down to business, Kemp will be starting the most important season of his political career. As the third-ranking Republican in the House, and as a senior member of the Budget Committee, he will be playing a leading role in the main debate facing the 99th Congress: how to reduce a Federal budget deficit that threatens to soar past $200 billion a year. He has already staked out his position, deriding fellow Republicans for their "hysterical" concentration on massive spending cuts, and insisting that economic growth will eliminate the need for painful budget surgery.

In fact, Kemp is the chief author of two bills designed to achieve that end. One would provide tax benefits for companies willing to invest in "enterprise zones" and create new jobs in declining regions of the country. The other bill would restructure the tax code by reducing and simplifying rates while eliminating many shelters and loopholes. Kemp's theory is that lowering the rates would give entrepreneurs more incentive to produce and earn, and that this rising tide of economic activity would lift all boats, so to speak, and fill the Treasury's depleted coffers. Some Republican leaders are skeptical that either bill will become law, though President Reagan expressed support for both concepts in his Inaugural address.

Kemp has a larger importance, however. His upbeat, positive message has inspired a whole new generation of lawmakers and helped spark the revival of the GOP as a party of ideas and innovation. Representative Newt Gingrich of Georgia calls him "the first Republican in modern times to show it is possible to be hopeful and conservative at the same time."

The beginning of the president's second term also marks the beginning of the post-Reagan era in American politics. The Republicans are already looking for a presidential candidate in 1988 who can carry on the "Reagan revolution" by continuing their drive to become the nation's dominant party. And to many strategists in both parties, the man who wants to say hello to all those good folks in Montana has a solid claim to being the president's legitimate heir.

More than any other potential nominee, they feel he has the sort of personal charm and appeal that has made Ronald Reagan so effective. And from a political viewpoint, he has the best chance of emulating the president's extraordinary ability to expand the Republican base and reach out to independent voters. In fact, the Inaugural address, with its evocation of an "American renewal," sounded very much like a speech Kemp could have delivered. Edward S. Rollins, who ran the president's last campaign, favors Vice President Bush for the nomination in 1988 but admits, "If the vice president chose to run, and asked me to run his campaign, the candidate I would least like to run against is Jack Kemp."

Yet for all of his potential, Kemp remains an untested and uncertain quantity. On the personal level, some politicians who know him well still view Kemp as an intellectual lightweight, a onetime jock with a good barber and a smooth tan, stuffed full of ideas that he does not completely understand. Dave Hoppe, his chief of staff, admits that the Congressman "comes on like a bulldozer" at times and "turns some people off" with his All-American ego.

On the political level, these qualities have brought Kemp his share of enemies. Moreover, many politicians still see the tax cut of 1981 — co-sponsored by Kemp and Senator William V. Roth, Jr., the Delaware Republican — as "voodoo economics," a wrong-headed plan that threatens eventually to swamp the recovery in a tidal wave of deficits. Kemp himself admits that his political future is "inextricably tied to the health of the economy."

In truth, Jack Kemp is a bit of a mystery, a blending of contradictory elements that defies an easy label, but that broadens his political appeal. He is a conservative WASP from Southern California who built his political career in Buffalo, a largely Catholic, blue-collar city; he believes in cutting taxes, but not in emasculating the government; he is cheered by business leaders in Dallas and by blacks at a memorial program for the Rev. Martin Luther King, Jr. in Atlanta

But the main reason Ed Rollins fears Jack Kemp is that the man possesses an extra dimension, an intangible but invaluable aura that touches only a few politicians in any generation. Part of it is that vitality that sends him bounding through life, cuffing shoulders and cadging converts as he goes. And part of it is that indelible image of the gallant gladiator, repeatedly facing danger as the screams of thousands echo through the bright Sundays of the past. As Lee Atwater, the deputy director of the 1984 Reagan campaign, noted, athletes might well be "the new American heroes who can transcend party loyalties." And Robert D. Squier, a Democratic consultant and filmmaker, adds: "Reagan, as the Gipper, only played a football player. Kemp really *was* a football player."

One night recently, Kemp was flying back to Washington from one of his frequent political forays into the hinterlands. The airline steward offered cocktails, but Kemp shook his head and explained that he and his wife, Joanne, were reared in strict religious homes and seldom drink more than a glass of wine. The Congressman is practically addicted to

Coca-Cola, though, and once he had one in hand, Kemp was ready to talk about his family and his early years.

His parents left the Midwest around 1920 and settled in Los Angeles, where his father ran a small trucking company and his mother was a social worker. They had four boys — Jack was the third — and in their comfortable, middle-class home, he recalled, "Everything was sports, sports, sports." Asked to write a school composition about a great invention, he chose the forward pass.

By his own admission, Kemp seldom cracked a book at Occidental College, a local school whose main attraction was a football squad with an offense that trained him for the pros. And after graduation in 1957, the Detroit Lions drafted him on the 17th round. "I had no doubt I'd play pro football," Kemp said. "I don't want to sound mystical, but I knew I'd play somewhere."

So the young hero married the girl from the sorority house next door and went off to fulfill his destiny. But he never made it with the Lions, or any other team in the National Football League, and when the American Football League started in 1960, Kemp jumped at the chance to play for the Los Angeles Chargers, who moved to San Diego the next year.

In those days, he recalled, the quarterback was really a "field general," reading the opposing team's defense and calling the plays on his own, and that taught him some useful lessons about leadership. As Kemp once told an interviewer: "You never heard of a quarterback in his life that goes into a huddle and says, does anybody have a play?" Football teaches resiliency, too. Eddie Mahe, a Republican political consultant, pointed out: "When you get pounded into the turf, you have to get up off your butt and get on with it. That's not bad training for this business."

During his years with the Chargers, Kemp fell under the influence of two men who helped form his political view of the world. One was Herbert G. Klein, editor of *The San Diego Union* and an insider in California Republican circles. Klein saw the young quarterback as a promising political property, and during the off-season, he had Kemp work for the paper, writing articles and absorbing tenets of the conservative creed.

A very different mentor was Sid Gillman, the coach of the Chargers, a liberal who belonged to the National Urban League. The team was integrated, and when it played in the South, Gillman never let his players use segregated facilities. Unlike many conservatives, Kemp is a strong advocate of civil rights and Federal help for minorities, and his position stems partly from his football experiences. "Jack," commented Newt Gingrich, "literally showered with guys that most Republicans never meet."

In 1962, a crushed knuckle on his throwing hand put Kemp out for the season, and when the Chargers failed to protect their rights to the quarterback, the Buffalo Bills snatched him away for the token price of $100. Kemp kept up his ties to California, and during the off-season in 1967, he even served a brief apprenticeship in the office of the new Governor, Ronald Reagan. But it was Buffalo that really advanced his political education.

Kemp found himself living and playing in a city dominated by blue-collar trade unionists with Democratic roots who worried about jobs and paychecks in a town in which the basic industries were collapsing around them. "That was a real blessing for me," he recalled as the flight neared Washington. "That disabused me very early about ideology winning campaigns. Those guys wanted answers, they wanted problems solved."

Kemp helped organize the first union of American Football League players in 1965. As president, he negotiated a pension plan with league owners, an exercise that honed his political skills. By 1968, the Republican organization in Buffalo was asking him to run for Congress, and by 1970 — with his arm fading — Kemp was ready to accept.

The old quarterback sneaked in with 52 percent of the vote, and he came to Washington as a freshman Congressman with a lot to learn about public policy. But he began reading widely, mainly in economics, and one bit of history intrigued him: The tax cut enacted during the Kennedy administration had engendered a strong recovery. Then *The Wall Street Journal* ran a piece by Jude Wanniski, one of its editorial writers, outlining the theories of Robert Mundell, a Canadian economist. Mundell made the case for "supply-side economics," the concept that tax cuts lead to economic expansion and an inevitable increase in tax revenues.

Soon Kemp made contact with Wanniski and other followers of the supply-side faith, particularly Irving Kristol, the editor of *The Public Interest*. During many months of talk, often far into the night at the Kemps' house in suburban Maryland, the supply-siders refined their thoughts into the Kemp-Roth tax-reduction bill.

"It was a radical idea," says Charlie Black, a political consultant who worked for the Republican National Committee at the time, "but politically, it had great value. The Republican Party since Hoover had been viewed as the party of the rich and 'Big Business.' After Watergate, the corruption image was added into it. Of the first 10 things people thought about Republicans, eight or nine were negative. It didn't take a genius to see the way to shake our terrible image was to take Jack Kemp's bill, his rhetoric, and spread it to the party's candidates. For the first time in years, Republican candidates were out there running for something, not just against something."

During the late 1970s, Ronald Reagan became enamored of supply-side ideas and espoused them during his campaign for the Republican nomination, but the Congressman's supporters were suspicious of Reagan's sincerity and urged Kemp to make the run himself. As Jude Wanniski tells the story, Kemp met Reagan for lunch during the summer of 1979 and spent hours grilling the candidate about his commitment to supply-side economics. Kemp's wife was along and, according to Wanniski, was "mortified" at her husband's behavior. But finally an agreement was reached: Reagan would support the Kemp-Roth tax cut.

During his first year in office, President Reagan kept his promise and eventually Kemp-Roth was passed, but the New Yorker shunned the tedious work of legislative deliberation. In fact, when the president agreed to a compromise bill that cut rates by only 25 percent rather than the 30 percent cut included in the original measure, Kemp stormed down to the White House and publicly criticized the president.

Kemp has never been very interested in the backroom maneuvering that gets things done on Capitol Hill. Only recently has he begun to play more of an inside game, and insist that he wants to be known as a "good legislator." His first real effort took place after the 1980 elections, when he became the ranking Republican on the Appropriations subcommittee handling foreign aid. When the foreign-aid bill came up, he spent days on the floor, carefully following the debate and helping to shape the final product. He also spent a lot of time in the Republican cloakroom, pressuring his conservative colleagues to swallow their ideological concerns. Representative Trent Lott of Mississippi, for example, said that the only reason he backed the bill was Kemp's "persistence and persuasion." Lott, the Republican whip, added: "In the last two years, Jack has showed that he was not just someone flying around the country making speeches."

He still does his share of flying around, though, and he can afford to. His seat is safe, helped by redistricting that cut out some heavily Democratic neighborhoods and spliced in some rural Republican territory. As a result, Kemp admits, he has not paid much attention to the home front. And though he stays on top of issues that affect the district, he is basically a national political figure who happens to represent upstate New York.

In that national role he is constantly on the go, building up his political contacts and capital. Not long ago, for instance, he flew to Texas at the behest of Steve Bartlett, a young Republican Congressman, to take part in a luncheon program at the Dallas Assembly, a high-powered civic association. He has made more than 100 such out-of-town appearances in the last two years, and now he can add Bartlett's IOU to the stack.

Kemp was dressed for the trip in his standard uniform: glistening white shirt, somber dark suit, gold collar pin, preppy striped tie. The trim figure is slightly padded at the waist now and the thick neck is creased with wrinkles; his immaculate swirl of sandy hair is threaded with gray. But as he waited to board the plane, fellow passengers could not keep their eyes off him. Kemp took it all in stride. As Ed Rollins notes, Kemp, like Ronald Reagan, has always been a star, has always had people looking at him. "That's what separates them from the rest of us earthlings," Rollins says.

At the airport in Texas, a young man who had helped organize the luncheon was waiting with a car. As the car passed Texas Stadium, the Congressman was telling a story that conveys the intensity that smolders inside this man. When his finger was injured while with the San Diego Chargers, he was told it would never be flexible again. So the quarterback asked the doctors to mold the cast while he gripped a football. That way, the finger would heal at the same angle as the ball. Kemp held up his hands for inspection, and the light caught two massive rings Kemp always wears.

The day before, he had been asked about them after a speech in Washington. One, he replied, was for the American Football League Championship in 1965, when he played with the Buffalo Bills; the other marked him as a member of the Bills' Hall of Fame. Looking straight at the questioner, the old quarterback said somberly, "There's a lot of blood in those babies."

On the way into Dallas from the airport, the driver described the format for the luncheon program, a debate between Kemp and Representative Richard A. Gephardt, a Missouri Democrat who has also sponsored a tax-reform bill. Kemp would speak first, the driver said innocently, since he had won the toss of the coin. Kemp flared up like a gas jet and hissed at the driver: "I thought winning the coin toss meant you get to choose whether you go first or not." For several more minutes he chewed on the issue, and finally snapped, "I suppose you'll decide who won the debate, too."

The luncheon was held in the Anatole, the glossy hotel where President Reagan stayed during the Republican convention, and the debate was vintage Kemp. He condemned the traditional Republican Party as following a "root-canal view" of economics that stressed austerity, not opportunity. "The tax system," he said to loud applause from the well-heeled and well-fed audience, "should not be aimed at making the rich poor, but aimed at making the poor rich."

To many Democrats, this sort of talk makes Kemp the Dr. Feelgood of American politics. Gephardt, a rusty-haired fellow with an even temper, was moved to fury. He turned on Kemp and snapped: "Nobody wants to talk about sacrifice. It is a bleak message. But the world doesn't work that way. There is no free lunch." Kemp was blithely unperturbed. "Some people have called my ideas simplistic," he retorted. "So be it."

Afterward, Kay Hutchison, a local Republican activist, explained Kemp's appeal this way: "The Republican Party is getting stronger by the minute here, and Kemp is considered very effective. He's been here quite a bit, so people know him. He's a personality, no doubt about that. And he's done a lot of substantive things. He's very good at keeping his name in the forefront."

Over the next six months, Jack Kemp's name is sure to stay in the forefront as Congress struggles with taxes and the budget. Out of his concern that Bob Dole, the new Republican leader in the Senate and a likely presidential contender in 1988, is placing too much emphasis on deficit reduction and not enough on pro-growth policies, Kemp has developed a two-part strategy. One is an outside move: get the president and the White House staff on your side and then convince them to use their political leverage on Congress. Last month, for instance, Kemp joined a group of like-minded House Republican leaders and met at the White House with James A. Baker, 3d, the chief of staff who has been designated as the new Treasury Secretary. The Republicans left, they say, with a commitment from Baker that, whenever budget cuts were discussed at the White House, tax simplification would be on the agenda as well.

The other element in Kemp's plan is a more traditional "inside" strategy. The man who denounced all compromise on Kemp-Roth four years ago is now welcoming suggestions, particularly from Democrats. The original enterprise zone bill, for instance, co-sponsored with Robert Garcia, Bronx Democrat, called for 75 districts around the country. Representative Charles B. Rangel, a Harlem Democrat who sits on the Ways and Means Committee, wanted three times that number as a way of boosting the bill's appeal. Recently, when Kemp was addressing a largely black audience in Washington, he proudly announced that he had accepted the amendment of his good friend, Charlie Rangel.

Compromise is also Kemp's approach to his tax-simplification bill, co-written by Senator Robert W. Kasten, Jr. of Wisconsin. His version would eliminate most deductions, tax credits and exemptions; all income would then be taxed at a flat rate of 25 percent, as opposed to the current schedule, which goes up to 50 percent. But Kemp lavishes praise on the two alternative proposals, one produced by Treasury Secretary Donald T. Regan before he was tapped to become White House chief of staff, the other by Representative Gephardt and Senator Bill Bradley, a New Jersey Democrat.

At a press conference several weeks ago called by House Republican leaders, Kemp stressed the need to cooperate with these Democrats and "build some kind of bridge across the aisle" on economic policy. His fellow Republicans, who were in a more combative and partisan mood, practically had to wrestle the microphone away from him. But Kemp says flatly that tax simplification "ain't gonna fly" in this Congress unless a plan is developed that has the support of both parties and the president.

Kemp and his ideas are not always popular in Congress. Much of the Republican leadership wants to put tax simplification on a back burner while they deal with the deficit, and they are impatient with Kemp's insistence that an expanding economy will erase the budget shortfall. Senator Alan K. Simpson of Wyoming, the new Republican whip, summed up the orthodox Republican view when he said: "No slot machine on earth pays off like that."

The new generation of young conservatives in the House, who have bedeviled the Democratic leadership over the last year, see Kemp as their "spiritual godfather," according to Representative Gingrich. But Kemp disagrees with their guiding premise, that confrontation with the Democrats is always the best policy. He shares such basic New Right positions as opposing abortion and favoring school prayer, but he has never taken a lead on these measures, and warns Republican candidates that they can narrow their political appeal by focusing on such "social issues."

Kemp's most natural allies on Capitol Hill these days are younger Democrats like Gephardt and Bradley. Both men say that the Republicans were politically astute to adopt the Kempian emphasis on economic growth, and that they would like to see the Democrats ride the same issue.

As these legislative battles develop, so will the political maneuvering for 1988. Kemp discussed his prospects one day in his Capitol Hill office, a room dominated by pictures of his wife and four irrepressibly photogenic children, ranging in age from 13 to 25. The oldest child, Jeff, is a quarterback for the Los Angeles Rams.

Will Jack Kemp run for the presidency? The minority view, based on his past cautiousness, is that he will shrink from the challenge. "I do not lust after the presidency," he will say, emphasizing the need to have something "burning in your belly." Does he have that fire? "I don't know," he says.

But most analysts do not give much weight to such obligatory coyness. The dominant view is that Kemp wants to be president, and that he will come under fierce pressure from his supporters to make the race. Meanwhile, the Congressman is certainly acting like a candidate. His own political action committee, the Campaign for Prosperity, raised and donated more than $200,000 in cash to Republican candidates for the 1984 elections. Another $50,000 was used to finance Kemp's travels around the country, where he is in demand more than any other Republican except Ronald Reagan and Gerald Ford. Among the Congressman's major contributors are the likes of George Champion, former chairman of Chase Manhattan Bank; Tom Landry, the coach of the Dallas Cowboys, and Herbert H. Dow, who sits on the board of the family chemical company. The list also includes Richard J. Fox, chairman of the Republican Jewish Coalition. Kemp's ardent support of Israel over the years has won him wide backing in the Jewish community.

But election laws strictly limit the size of individual contributions, making a wide base of support essential. Kemp's PAC has assembled a list of 50,000 proven supporters, and monthly fund-raising appeals to those donors are expected to begin shortly. For now, the proceeds will be funneled to other Republicans, but a quick change in the computer code, and that list becomes the basis of a Kemp-for-President campaign.

Kemp is also beefing up his staff with people who are not particularly interested in running a Congressional campaign in upstate New York. John P. Maxwell, a party official from Texas, joins the staff next month, and he just happens to have experience running Senate campaigns in Iowa — site of the first presidential caucuses. John Buckley, a nephew of William F. Buckley, Jr. and former Senator James L. Buckley, is Kemp's new press secretary; he was deputy press secretary for the 1984 Reagan-Bush campaign.

If Jack Kemp runs for the GOP nomination, can he win it? The conventional wisdom in Republican ranks is that George Bush's unswerving loyalty to the president has earned him the support of many Reaganites, and the position of front runner. But as John Sears, a veteran Republican strategist, noted, any vice president "is obliged to be the party's greatest loyalist." In Sears's view, Bush will have a "terrible problem" establishing himself as an independent figure apart from President Reagan.

Bob Dole, another potential rival, has made a strong start as the new majority leader of the Senate, but he is clearly gambling his future on the ability of Congressional Republicans to reduce the deficit and insure economic prosperity. Dole's predecessor as majority leader, Howard H. Baker, Jr., has quit the Senate altogether so he can devote full time to making money and running for president, but he has not yet been able to inspire any major political support for a run.

Ed Rollins, the former Reagan-Bush strategist, sums up a widely held view in Republican ranks when he says, "I think the potential is certainly there for Kemp to come down as the alternative to Bush."

For one thing, Kemp starts with an unusually broad geographical base: California, where he grew up; New York, where he now lives, and the so-called Southern Rim, where an emerging Republican Party responds to him eagerly. He also has strong ties to the party's right-wing activists. "Kemp," says Lee Atwater, Rollins's deputy on the Reagan-Bush campaign, "has a better chance to plug into Reagan's philosophical base than any other candidate."

The key to Kemp's campaign could well be his ability to reach beyond the people who usually decide Republican nominations and bring in new participants. At this early stage, many analysts agree that among traditional Republicans, Bush probably has the edge; but if Kemp can expand the pool of primary voters, he has a chance to overtake the vice president.

Should Kemp ever get the nomination, Democratic strategists agree he would be a tough opponent in the general election. More than any other Republican, some fear, he could appeal to that crop of young, independent-minded voters who flocked to the Republican cause in 1980 and 1984 but have made no permanent commitment to the party, and are up for grabs in future elections.

According to Lee Atwater, Reagan's appeal to this group in the last election can be summed up in one word: "success." The president was a winner who promised voters that he would give them a chance at success in their own lives by lowering taxes and expanding economic opportunity. Kemp, too, is a winner, offering the same promise of change and progress. As Raymond Strother, a Democratic consultant who worked for Gary Hart, put it: "Kemp seems to have the right message at the right time. He conveys the idea that he's willing to change, to experiment, to break patterns and traditions. The country is looking for change, and Kemp represents the best the Republicans have to offer."

To some analysts, Kemp shares something else with Ronald Reagan: the ability to run against Washington. "Jack Kemp appeals to little people," says Rollins. "He appeals to an anti-Establishment group out there, and Baker and Dole and all the rest are perceived as being part of the Establishment."

In the view of Robert Squier, the Democratic campaign consultant, the nation is "floating out of the party era as we have known it," and entering an era in which "we have to worry more about personalities and messages than party identification." Television is the key to that new era, and Kemp is a made-for-TV candidate who can reach those independent voters without appealing either to partisan loyalty or political ideology. Says Squier: "Kemp has a high enough level of energy to make the tube light up when he's on."

Kemp has one other quality that might be more important than all the rest: He can tap into one of the basic myths of American life, the myth of the hero who has fought in distant lands and survived the trial by fire. For millions of Americans today, professional sports — particularly football — has become a kind of civilian equivalent of war.

On the wall of Jack Kemp's office hangs a photograph of a huge defensive lineman named Ernie Ladd looming over the young Kemp, about to crush him to the earth. "That reminds me," Kemp jokes, "that the bigger they are, the harder they fall — on you." But that photo says something else, as well: "I've been there. I've slain the dragon and lived to tell the tale."

For all his advantages, though, Jack Kemp has significant drawbacks as a candidate. He has faced only one tough race in his political life, the first one, and he has never run beyond the narrow confines of his district. No House member has run successfully for a presidential nomination in this century, and one reason is that Congressmen find it hard to compete for media attention. Kemp has conquered that problem, but he still must overcome the notion that House members lack the scope and experience, particularly in foreign affairs, to make good presidents.

While many political strategists admire Kemp's strengths, they hardly consider him invincible.

The Congressman admits to being thin-skinned and oversensitive. On the MacNeil/Lehrer show, he once blew up at a reporter and later had to apologize for his outburst. Kemp can often sound like a "Jackie One Note," a speaker who tells you more than you ever wanted to know about the arcane intricacies of economic and monetary policy. Only recently has he begun to take himself a bit less seriously. Now he can sometimes look at a photograph, for example, and crack, "There's me in a typical pose — with my mouth open."

Some who know Kemp have reservations about his intellectual range. Supporters say he studies hard and can learn a subject if briefed thoroughly, but he can seem quite uneasy and uncomfortable when faced with new or complex issues. During the debate in Dallas, Gephardt departed from economics and closed with an emotional discussion of the need to build better relations with the Russians. Later, walking out of the hotel, Kemp admitted that he felt uneasy responding to the Democrat's tactic. "I don't have any training in dialectics," he said, "and no one has ever asked me to do anything like this before."

Some who are familiar with Kemp say that the old quarterback is too used to calling his own plays all the time, that though he is hiring new aides, he might not listen to them. "He just tends to believe he is capable of anything," said a seasoned Republican official. "He doesn't think he needs a lot of advice and counsel in getting something done. He has the strength of his own convictions — and that's good — but I'm not sure how capable Jack is of listening."

Kemp replies that he has been listening, and learning, since he came to Washington 14 years ago. "I survived," he said, "and I think I fooled a lot of people in this town. They didn't think that there was much staying power to Jack Kemp, that I really didn't have much below the surface, that I couldn't hold my own in the tough battles. But I think there is staying power to Jack Kemp, frankly."

Whether he has enough staying power for the exhausting grind of a presidential campaign remains to be seen. But a man who has been wildly cheered, and unmercifully booed, by 50,000 football fans on a Sunday afternoon in Buffalo knows something about the vicissitudes of life. And the pundits who underestimated Ronald Reagan all those years could be getting ready to make the same mistake about Jack Kemp.

CANDIDATES SEEKING THEIR party's presidential nomination must campaign at the grassroots where the party faithful in primaries or caucuses choose the vast majority of national-convention delegates. For years the most important early testing ground for candidates was the New Hampshire primary — the first in the nation — which the national media turned into a political event of great symbolic significance by proclaiming the winners of the Democratic and Republican primaries to be their party's front runners. Jimmy Carter's 1976 campaign for the Democratic party presidential nomination pushed the Iowa caucuses into the political limelight with the New Hampshire primary. Carter's concerted and successful effort to woo rank-and-file Iowa Democrats drew the attention of a national media that was fascinated with what it viewed as the "quixotic" presidential campaign of the relatively unknown former Georgia governor.

Carter's victories in New Hampshire, as well as in Iowa, gave him needed political credibility. Suddenly front-page stories in the New York Times and other major newspapers, as well as on television network news, were not only taking him seriously but changing his status from dark-horse to front-runner. Since 1976, dark-horse presidential aspirants in particular have looked equally to the Iowa caucuses and the New Hampshire primary to boost their credibility and give them national recognition.

The Iowa caucuses continue to be important in the 1988 presidential race, which is illustrated in the following account of Jack Kemp's and Richard Gephardt's early campaigning in this corn-belt state.

4

Paul Taylor

JACK KEMP AND RICHARD GEPHARDT: IMAGE-BUILDING IN IOWA

If the fellow who's going be elected president in 1988 has a shock of hair slung low over his forehead; if he's a trucker's son; if he chairs his party's caucus in the House of Representatives and was the coauthor of a major flat tax proposal; and if his strategy for becoming the first sitting House member ever to capture the White House involves outhustling all the name brands — well, by golly, he passed through here just the other day.

His name is Representative Jack Kemp — and his name is Representative Richard A. Gephardt.

Both of these look-alikes have been dashing around the country — a minimum of three weekends out of four — laying the groundwork for a presidential campaign that won't formally begin for another two years. Kemp, a New York Republican, touched down in 24 states in 1985; Gephardt, a Democrat from Missouri, in 30.

Recently, on Kemp's seventh visit to Iowa since the last presidential election and Gephardt's sixth, they found themselves on the same stage here, debating national economic policy before an underwhelmed audience of business and political leaders.

Their speeches made a point that their pedigrees, ambition and time-tables obscure: These two eager beavers from the House could hardly be more different.

Kemp, 50, the better known of the two, gave his familiar pitch for lower interest rates and a dollar as good as gold. He told the group that the economy can "grow out from underneath the budget deficit" as long as Congress doesn't "panic and resort to a tax increase." In a short speech, he quoted Emile Zola, GWF Hegel, Thomas Hobbes and Will Durant — a trademark display of erudition that some critics take to be the sign of an ex-jock's lingering intellectual insecurity.

He spoke rapidly, used a lot of body English, darted from one subject to another ("Someone needs to tell him not to try to preach the entire gospel in one sermon," remarked Arthur Davis, Iowa Democratic chairman) and was relentlessly upbeat, telling his listeners that "the glass is half full, not half empty." He came across as a man who knows.

Gephardt, 45, came across as a man who isn't sure. He opened by ripping Republicans as a bloodless horde of antigovernment social Darwinists who believe that "if you lose your job, home, or farm, that's your problem. You can always pack up and move to the Sun Belt."

But when he got to setting forth his own party's vision of government, he grew vague and tentative, resorting to words such as "catalyst" and "partnership," and sounding very much like the Eagle scout he used to be. "The team that won [the Super Bowl] was the team that had the best cooperation," he said at one point, an observation that seems unlikely to win converts in any audience that does not regularly watch Sesame Street.

"I don't think anybody is going to remember what either of them had to say," John Chrystal, president of Banker's Trust, one of the state's largest banks, said afterward. "It was disappointing."

It's probably a mistake to make too much of this tepid reception. Iowa is still in deep recession, and visiting politicians who don't deal specifically with the economic issues (and the two were not asked to) aren't likely to win many plaudits.

Yet the response also suggests that all the road work Kemp and Gephardt can get in between now and 1988 will be well-spent. John

Maxwell, an Iowan who heads Kemp's political action committee, Campaign for Prosperity, noted that his boss "likes to reach out and grab a crowd," and that sometimes he has difficulty with "unemotional" audiences. Kemp's dynamism and exuberance make him a big hit on the conservative circuit; his challenge over the next two years will be to find a style that goes over well when he isn't preaching to the choir.

Gephardt's problem is different: He is a man with no dogma, but also no sharply defined message. He isn't bashful about admitting it, either. "I'm not there yet," he says. "I need to spend more time at it. Keep traveling around, thinking, talking, listening, reading."

His earnest, boy-next-door personality and his strawberry-blond good looks make Gephardt an instantly likable candidate. And if his message is not honed, his method is. His strategy for 1988 is a carbon copy of Jimmy Carter's of 1976: Outhustle everyone in Iowa, make the big splash out of obscurity in the early caucus there, then move to the head of the Democratic field with some wins in the South.

A year ago, Gephardt helped form the Democratic Leadership Council, a sort of safe house for moderates from the South and West (he's from St. Louis) who don't want to be too closely identified with the Democratic National Committee. It has been a vehicle for speechmaking in the South and around the country, and for meeting the sort of fund-raisers who will come in handy in a presidential campaign.

Around the same time, he also formed his political action committee, the Effective Government Committee, which has seven professional staffers — of whom five have extensive experience in Iowa. The director, Bill Romjue, ran the Iowa effort for Carter in 1980 and for Senator Gary Hart during the early stages of the Colorado Democrat's 1984 campaign.

Local talent makes a difference. Gephardt's itinerary on his recent trip to Iowa ought to be enshrined in a syllabus of Political Scheduling 101. Day One began with breakfast with Chrystal, the banker; then a meeting with Lieutenant Governor Bob Anderson and the statehouse Democratic leaders; then an informal lunch at the statehouse to brief Democratic legislators on Gramm-Rudman-Hollings; then the speech at Drake University to the business and political audience; then private meetings with a few county chairmen; then a stop at a weekly state AFL-CIO meeting; then dinner with Jim Gannon and David Yepsen, editor and political writer, respectively, of the *Des Moines Register*, the state's most influential newspaper.

Day Two began with a 7:30 A.M. stop at the hospital bed of Joe Shanahan, a young political operative who had worked on local campaigns in Des Moines and whom Gephardt had never met. Then he drove to Iowa State University in Ames for a three-hour briefing from a half-dozen professors on the farm economy. Next came lunch at a local deli in Ames with a dozen Story County activists; then a flight east.

At this early stage, Gephardt is shooting not for endorsements, but good will. "We're human, we love to be courted," says Davis. "The personal touch now will definitely make a difference later on."

RONALD REAGAN'S VICTORY seemed assured by election eve, 1980. A Massachusetts bartender told a questioner who was conducting his own straw poll that he was going to vote Republican for the first time in his life. That, by itself, was an almost certain sign of a Reagan victory. More sophisticated pollsters, including Patrick Caddell in the Carter camp, knew as well that the die was already cast, that Carter would lose.

Reagan's victory was explained in many ways. Some, especially liberal Democrats, said that it was a vote against Carter. They confidently predicted that the Reagan phenomenon would be short lived, that Democrats would gain in both the House and the Senate in the 1982 elections, and that the party could once again win the White House in 1984.

Reagan's mastery of the media was more widely believed to have been the cause of his success. He had been an actor, after all, and knew how to appeal on television to popular emotions. His image, more than his views on major issues of public policy, was given credit for his victory. During the 1980 presidential campaign Garry Wills wrote that Reagan was the man on the white horse who would save the nation from its past foibles. Wills stressed Reagan's image and style. He was, suggested Wills, "the first serious counter-authority [to government] with an air of authority; the charismatic leader without a vision, just a role."[1] Reagan, concluded Wills,

was "both Henry Aldrich and Grandpa Walton, our remembered and our present selves, our fantasy of afternoons with popcorn and the 'real' world of TV politics. Where so little is stable, the emptiness at the center looks eternal. Reagan is the calm eye of history's hurricane; and we hope, by moving with it, never to slip toward the edges into chaos."[2]

While most commentators concentrated upon Reagan's media skills and image to explain his victory, journalist Jeff Greenfield, a TV commentator himself, concluded that Reagan won by following the more traditional rules of politics. He had a superb political organization, and his program offered a clear and apparently popular choice for the electorate.[3]

The Greenfield thesis about Reagan echoed the views of the late political scientist V. O. Key, Jr., who wrote:

Voters are not fools. To be sure, many individual voters act in odd ways indeed; yet in the large, the electorate behaves about as rationally and responsibly as we should expect, given the clarity of the alternatives presented to it and the character of the information available to it. In American presidential campaigns of recent decades the portrait of the American electorate that develops from the data is not one of an electorate straitjacketed by social determinants or moved by subconscious urges triggered by devilishly skillful propagandists. It is rather one of

---

[1] Garry Wills, "Ron and Destiny: Where Will He Lead Us, This Embodiment of Our Everyday Experience?" *Esquire*, August 1980, p. 37.

[2] Ibid.

[3] Jeff Greenfield, *The Real Campaign* (New York: Summit Books, 1982).

an electorate moved by concern about central and relevant questions of public policy, of governmental performance, and of executive personality.[4]

Whether voters chose Reagan because of his style, program, or a combination of both, remained conjecture during the first two years of his administration. There was no doubt, however, that Reagan had a program that he intended to carry out. His clarion call to the Conservative Political Action Conference a year after he had been in office reveals his determination: "Fellow citizens, fellow conservatives, our time is now. Our moment has arrived. We stand together shoulder to shoulder in the thickest of the fight."[5] The president had already achieved remarkable success in reducing taxes and government expenditures, but to change the face of government in the way that he wanted far more needed to be done.

Reagan's actions as president, particularly his direct confrontation of the Washington political establishment, which he carefully courted but whose powers he wanted to diminish, surprised political pundits. Reagan apparently meant what he said during his campaign, which made him a political novelty. The following selection, by a journalist who has closely followed Reagan's political career since its inception, depicts his character and style and examines the underlying forces that have shaped him.

5 Lou Cannon
RONALD REAGAN: A POLITICAL PERSPECTIVE

He seemed to many, from beginning to end, a most unlikely leader of the nation. As the United States of America entered the complex, computer age of the 1980s, Ronald Wilson Reagan reached backward and spoke to the future in the accents of the past. His suits were as out of date as his metaphors, most of which derived from the Great Depression or World War II. He quoted freely from the Founding Fathers and from his early hero, Franklin Delano Roosevelt. He viewed Soviet expansionism much as Roosevelt had viewed Nazi aggression. When others protested that he saw the world in stark and simple terms, Reagan would say: "For many years, you and I have been shushed like children and told there are no simple answers to complex problems that are beyond our comprehension. Well, the truth is there *are* simple answers — just not easy ones."

[4]V. O. Key, Jr., *The Responsible Electorate* (Cambridge, Mass.: The Belknap Press of Harvard University Press, 1966), pp. 7–8.

[5]*National Journal*, May 2, 1981, p. 779.

From *Washington Post* Staff Members, *The Pursuit of the Presidency*, ed. by Richard Harwood. © The Washington Post, 1980. Reprinted by permission.

By the historical standards of the American presidency, Reagan seemed an even more unlikely leader. Though he was vigorous and athletic, he was sixty-nine years old and would be seventy within a month of taking the presidential oath of office. The age showed in the dewlapped wrinkles of his neck. It showed in the Reagan campaign schedules, which were generously endowed with "staff time" that was the euphemistic reference to Reagan's afternoon nap. And Reagan in other ways seemed singularly unprepared for the office which he and others have ritualistically referred to as "the most important in the free world."

He had not held public office in six years. He had no foreign policy experience. He had never worked in Washington. He was a divorced man espousing the values of the family, a wartime stateside noncombatant advocating military preparedness, a fiscal conservative who as governor of California had sponsored the largest tax increases in the state's history.

But despite all this and the majority party and the White House incumbency against him, Reagan was a formidable candidate with an appeal that reached beyond his natural, conservative constituency. He was larger than the sum of his parts. Some said this was because he was a superb television performer whose skills were honed by years of professional experience. Others said he was a lucky politician (as some had said of Jimmy Carter), with the good fortune to face overrated opponents at the time they were most vulnerable. But there was another reason, and it was more important than the others. It was that whatever Reagan lacked in complexity or youth or consistency, he made up for in an unremitting vision of America. The vision was the thing. It was a vision frozen in time, which made it more powerful than transitory visions. Reagan believed in it, which made it even more powerful. A close personal aide, Michael K. Deaver, said this about Reagan's belief: "He's resolved something, his being or what he is, a long time ago. He seems to know what is right."

And whether Reagan did, in fact, know what was right, his vision of America was what made this aging, out-of-date exactor credible to other Americans. Reporters and Reagan aides would smile at one another and head for the press buses when Reagan approached his standard tear-jerker ending of the basic speech he used in early 1980. They would laugh outright when Reagan, for the thousandth time, quoted John Winthrop aboard "the tiny Arabella" in 1630 as telling his followers that they should be "as a city on a hill."

"The eyes of all mankind are still upon us," Reagan would conclude. "Our party came into being more than one hundred years ago, born of a great crisis at that time. We led this nation through that crisis. We are being called upon again. Let us keep our rendezvous with destiny, let us build a shining city upon a hill."

This was part of Reagan's vision, and the audience did not laugh at it. Most of the people who heard the speech applauded. A few of them cried. And they came back for the equally simplistic and more materialistic versions of the vision: "At the heart of our message should be five simple familiar words. No big economic theories. No sermons on political philosophy. Just five short words: family, work, neighborhood, freedom, peace."

Historically, Reagan's vision was rooted in small-town Midwestern America of the early twentieth century — then the real and symbolic heartland of the nation. His values were shaped in a day when most Americans lived not in the great, cluttered urban landscapes of our time but in towns and small cities surrounding a more pastoral land. When he was trying out self-characterizations early in the 1980 campaign, Reagan briefly referred to himself as a "Main Street Republican," a phrase intended to show that he was not a boardroom candidate like John Connally or an Ivy Leaguer like George Bush. The phrase, quietly discarded after the primaries because Reagan's advisers thought it made the candidate seem partisan and out of date, was an appropriate description of Reagan. Like all persons, he is a product of his time and region, his experience and his culture. For Reagan it was small-town Illinois, the quintessential Main Street celebrated in Middle America and satirized by Sinclair Lewis's famous novel of the same name. "Main Street is the climax of civilization," Lewis wrote in the preface to his novel, which appeared in 1920 when Reagan was nine years old. Lewis meant these words sardonically but Reagan would accept them as literal truth. In his autobiography, *Where's The Rest of Me?*, Reagan describes his childhood as "a rare Huck Finn-Tom Sawyer idyll."

"Reagan was shaped by the small towns of the Midwest, and that explains in large part the simple moral and conservative approach he brought to public life," wrote early biographer Bill Boyarsky in *The Rise of Ronald Reagan*. "Where Lewis satirized the Midwest communities, Reagan glorifies them. He enthusiastically accepts the values that Lewis criticized. As a result, he is deeply respectful of business; determinedly conservative; mistrusting of change; unintellectual and slightly suspicious of higher education . . . convinced that, as his father said, 'All men were created equal and man's own ambition determines what happens to him the rest of his life.' "

Reagan's father, John Reagan, known as Jack, was a gregarious, nomadic, hard-drinking Irish-American whose own life seems to have fallen far short of his ambition. He was a Catholic in a Protestant land and in Reagan's childhood a fierce opponent of the Ku Klux Klan, which was at the time a national force in American politics. In his autobiography, Reagan related how his father, then a traveling salesman, was told by a small-town hotel clerk that he would appreciate the accommodations because Jews weren't permitted there. "I'm a Catholic," Reagan quotes his father as saying, "and if it's come to the point where you won't take Jews, you won't take me, either." Jack Reagan then stalked out, spent a cold winter night in his car and became seriously ill.

At the time his second son Ronald was born, Jack was working as a clerk in the Pitney General Store in Tampico. Jack's ambition was to own his own store, a goal briefly realized but quickly crushed by the Depression. Ronald Reagan still seems troubled by what happened to his father. When he announced his presidential candidacy on November 13, 1979, Reagan repeated an oft-told story of Christmas Eve in 1931 when Reagan and his older brother Neil were home from college.

Their father received a special delivery letter he hoped would be a bonus. It was instead a "blue slip" telling him that he had been fired.

Ronald Reagan was born in a five-room flat above the Pitney General Store on February 6, 1911. For the first nine years of his life he lived in a procession of Illinois cities and towns: Chicago, Galesburg, Monmouth, Tampico again, and finally Dixon, the place Reagan still calls his hometown and where he lived until he was twenty-one. His mother, and the anchor of the Reagan family, was Nelle Wilson Reagan. She was a do-gooder, a lifelong member of the Christian Church who practiced what she preached. Reagan and his older brother remember many instances of her finding food or jobs for needy persons. Sometimes the Reagan home became — in a day when the phrase was unknown — a halfway house for released convicts.

Reagan was a prodigy. Born with a remarkable memory, he learned to read at an early age and dazzled his mother, who encouraged him to read newspapers aloud to her friends. Reagan recalls reading an account of the Preparedness Day bombing in San Francisco on July 22, 1916, when he was five years old.

There were other ways in which the Reagan home was avant-garde for Dixon. The Reagan boys called their parents by their first names and they called the boys by their nicknames — "Dutch" for Ronald and "Moon" for Neil. The Reagans were the town Democrats in a place and time devotedly Republican. Both Jack and Nelle participated in amateur theatricals, which stimulated the imagination of their children and which made both of them talk about an acting career.

But there also was the dark side of Jack Reagan's alcoholism. Even the relentlessly cheerful Reagan autobiography, written in 1965 with one eye to his coming political career, cannot disguise Reagan's feelings about his father's drinking. "I was eleven years old the first time I came home to find my father flat on his back on the front porch and no one there to lend a hand but me," Reagan writes. "He was drunk, dead to the world. I bent over him, smelling the sharp odor of whiskey from the speakeasy. I got a fistful of his overcoat. Opening the door, I managed to drag him inside and get him to bed. In a few days, he was the bluff, hearty man I knew and loved and will always remember."

Children are stronger than we expect them to be, and there is no evidence that Jack Reagan's alcoholism cast any permanent blight on the lives of his sons. Ronald Reagan would not drink at all for many years, and he was repelled by the Hollywood cocktail circuit. But by all accounts, including his own, he grew up to be a resolute, cheerful young man, hardworking and unintellectual, interested in football and girls and theatricals. Athletic and well built, Reagan enjoyed the role of local lifeguard, and the varying numbers of persons he saved from drowning became an obligatory part of his political biography. Most of all, he enjoyed talking. He had a nonstop gift of gab that had been encouraged by his mother's showing off of his precocious reading ability. As a freshman at tiny Eureka College, Reagan's fiery speechmaking made him the leader of a student strike (over Depression-cancelled classes that would have prevented some students from graduating), which cost the college president his job. He developed a consuming interest, which has never left him, in the medium of radio, which Franklin Roosevelt was then using to carry the gospel of the New Deal to the countryside. At Eureka, Reagan would listen for hours to sports broadcasts, sometimes interspersed with Roosevelt's "fireside chats." Thirty-five years later, as governor of California, Reagan would use the fireside chats as his model for broadcast and televised reports to the people on the public issues of the day.

The Depression and Hollywood stand with Main Street as the shaping symbols in the life of Ronald Reagan. Reagan still considers the Depression as the single most important influence upon him. The Depression cost his father a partnership in a Dixon shoe store. It sent his mother to work in a dress shop for fourteen dollars a week. Reagan, then working his way through Eureka, sent fifty dollars a week home so that his parents could continue to get credit at the local grocery store. But there were many others in as difficult a predicament, or worse. Often, in his days as governor, when Reagan was asked whether he had been poor as a child, he replied with the bromide that "we were poor but we didn't think of ourselves as poor." Sometimes he used the line when he was talking about limiting welfare, the way out for the modern poor. As a historical reference, however, Reagan's statement is an accurate one. What had happened to the Reagans had happened to America.

In his senior year at Eureka, Reagan won an acting award for his role in *Aria de Campo*, an antiwar play by Edna St. Vincent Millay, and he had thoughts of an acting career. But he had no job and he returned to Dixon, uncertain of his future and thinking of radio as an entry into show business. Reagan applied for work at several Chicago radio stations and was turned down. Then, in the fall of 1932, came a chance to broadcast University of Iowa football games for WHO, the NBC affiliate in Des Moines. Reagan had been a starting guard at Eureka, and he loved football. From his first broadcast, he gave a tense and evocative account of what was going on on the field of play below. When baseball season began, Reagan's proclivity for nonstop talking plunged him into the since-lost art of recreating baseball games from the laconic summaries of the action furnished by Western Union telegraph. At a time when everyone listened to radio, Dutch Reagan became a sportscasting star.

He used radio as his springboard to Hollywood. In 1937 he accompanied the Chicago Cubs to Catalina Island off the Southern California coast for spring training, and a friend arranged a screen test for him at Warner Brothers. Reagan passed easily and Hollywood proved even more suitable for Reagan's talents than had radio. Starting out on low-budget pictures, where his ability to quickly memorize scripts proved an enormous asset, Reagan advanced to become "the Errol Flynn of the B's." He made thirty-one movies in five years, progressing from his $200-a-week starting salary to the princely figure of $1,650 a week in 1941. Popular and invariably cast as a good guy, Reagan had mastered his craft and seemed to be rising to the pinnacle of stardom. Though burdened with "B" pictures, he won critical acclaim for performances in *Brother Rat* (where Eddie Albert made his debut and where Reagan met his first wife, Jane Wyman), in *Knute Rockne* (where Reagan plays the doomed Notre Dame football player George Gipp and Pat O'Brien plays Rockne), in *Dark Victory* (with Humphrey Bogart) and, especially in *King's Row*, where the cast included Claude Rains, Robert Cummings, and Charles Coburn.

King's Row, the story of a small Southern town more malevolent than Dixon, was Reagan's best picture. He portrayed Drake McHugh, a playboy whose legs are amputated by sadistic surgeon Coburn as revenge for the seduction of his daughter. "Where's the rest of me?" yells McHugh, coming to without his legs and uttering the future title of Reagan's autobiography. *Commonweal* praised Reagan for a "splendid performance," and other reviews were uniformly good. Reagan liked the film too, and in the tradition of ego-laden Hollywood would often show it to house guests after dinner. After Jane Wyman divorced him, she was quoted as saying, "I just couldn't stand to watch that damn *King's Row* one more time."

Reagan never quite fulfilled the acting promise of this period. His career, like so many others, was interrupted by World War II, most of which Reagan spent in Hollywood making training films with the First Motion Picture Unit of the Army Air Corps. Reagan's career couldn't hit its stride after the war, when newer, younger stars were coming along and Hollywood was fighting its own multifront war with television, labor unrest, foreign films, and domestic investigating committees. At the beginning of the war, Reagan had lost out to Humphrey Bogart for a role in a picture that was retitled *Casablanca*. When the war was over he lost his chance to play in another film classic which also starred Bogart,

The Treasure of the Sierra Madre. Reagan's choice of films, when he had a choice, had never been exceptional and by now his luck was running bad. Given a role in the movie version of the John Van Druten play, *The Voice of the Turtle,* Reagan objected to playing with a new leading lady and asked for June Allyson instead. The actress he objected to was the richly talented Eleanor Parker, subsequently to be nominated for four Oscars. "It took me only one scene with Eleanor to realize that I'd be lucky if I could stay even," Reagan acknowledges in his autobiography.

Reagan's marriage was on the skids along with his movie career. The low point of the career came in 1951, when Reagan played opposite a chimpanzee in *Bedtime for Bonzo.* His marriage had come to an end three years earlier, during Wyman's filming of *Johnny Belinda,* for which she won an Academy Award. Reagan quipped to a gossip columnist that *Johnny Belinda* should be named as correspondent in the divorce action. If Miss Wyman's testimony in the divorce action is to be believed, a better choice would be the Screen Actor's Guild, which increasingly was taking more and more of her husband's time. The picture she painted, both in court and outside of it, was of a bored wife who no longer shared her husband's interests.

Exit Ronald Reagan actor. Enter Reagan, labor negotiator, public spokesman, and future politician. By the early 1950s, although he was still appearing in occasional films, Reagan had in effect established a new career. As leader of the Screen Actors Guild and six times its president, Reagan had become fully embroiled in the economic and cultural issues which shook Hollywood after the war.

If Main Street represented the climax of American civilization in the 1920s, Hollywood was in this postwar era the undisputed capital of American mass culture. Everything that affected Hollywood was a page one story in Peoria — or in Dixon, where the preferred reading matter was the *Chicago Tribune.* These stories included sensational accusations that the movie industry was honeycombed with Communists, disclosures that a key union was operated by gangsters, the emergence of both television and foreign films as a major competitor and taxation-induced "runaway" of U.S. films to foreign countries. Reagan was in the midst of these battles. During the Red-hunting days, which Hollywood now remembers with embarrassment and some shame, Reagan opposed Communists but also disputed the basic thesis of the House Committee on Un-American Activities in these words: "I do not believe the Communists have ever at any time been able to use the motion picture screen as a sounding board for their philosophy or ideology." At the time of the Congressional investigations, his stand fully pleased neither side. But he emerged from that period as an effective and adroit political leader who had kept his union intact.

Reagan's personal life and political views were now changing. He had described himself as a "near hopeless hemophiliac liberal." But in 1952, four years after his divorce from Wyman, Ronald Reagan married Nancy Davis, adopted daughter of a conservative and wealthy Chicago surgeon Loyal Davis. In 1954, he became the host for "General Electric Theater," a new half-hour television series, with a salary of $125,000 a year and generous expenses. The GE contract, which might be said to have launched Reagan's political career, gave him an opportunity to be seen each week on television and to talk to GE employees all over the country.

While some old Hollywood friends ascribe Reagan's increasing conservatism of this time to Nancy or her father, it is probable that General Electric, and Reagan's growing prosperity, had much to do with Reagan's changing political views.

At the outset, Reagan's message in his speeches to GE employees was patriotic, anti-Communist, pro-Hollywood. Reacting to the general nature of his talk, GE Board Chairman Ralph Cordiner suggested to Reagan that "you work out a philosophy for yourself." Increasingly, that philosophy became probusiness, antigovernment conservatism. It was a philosophy more congenial to the Republican party than to the Democrats, at least in California. But Reagan, like many Americans, found it easier to embrace Republican principles than to abandon the political faith of his family. As a Democrat, Reagan had supported Helen Gahagan Douglas in her U.S. Senate race against Richard Nixon in 1950. By 1952, he was a Democrat for Eisenhower. When Nixon ran for president in 1960, Reagan was still a Democrat but this time supporting Nixon. Two years later, when Reagan was speaking for Nixon during his unsuccessful campaign for governor of California, a woman in the audience asked him if he were a registered Republican. Reagan said he wasn't, but indicated his willingness to join the GOP. The woman, a volunteer registrar, marched down the aisle and signed him up as a Republican on the spot.

By this time, Reagan had become a partisan politician almost without recognizing it. He was becoming an embarrassment to General Electric, which did much business with the government Reagan was consistently denouncing. When Reagan used the Tennessee Valley Authority, a major customer of GE, as an example of government waste, the company asked him to delete the reference. Reagan complied, but there were those at General Electric who now wanted to be rid of Reagan altogether. In 1962, GE suggested that Reagan limit his speeches to touting the company's products. By then, "General Electric Theater" also was in trouble, facing competition from "Bonanza," a show which became one of Reagan's favorites. When Reagan balked at the limitations GE wanted to place on him, the company abruptly cancelled "GE

Theater." Reagan never knew whether it was his speeches or "Bonanza" which hurt him most.

However, Reagan was now prepared for a political career. He had shaken hands with 250,000 GE employees during his eight years as company spokesman and made speeches from one end of the country to the other. He had a philosophy, name recognition, and a winning smile. He also had money, and owned valuable ranch land in the Malibu hills. Increasingly active in Republican politics, Reagan in 1964 was named California chairman of the Barry Goldwater presidential campaign. The leaders of that floundering effort, short on money and party unity, decided to put Reagan on national television. The result, wrote David S. Broder after that campaign, was "the most successful national political debut since William Jennings Bryan electrified the 1896 Democratic convention with his 'Cross of Gold' speech."

Reagan's emotional speech on the night of October 27, 1964, stirred millions of Americans, but it was familiar to those who had heard him on the GE circuit. Basically, it was the same speech he had given for eight years and would give for another sixteen until it grudgingly gave way to new material in the 1980 campaign. There was the celebration of economic individualism: "We need true tax reform that will at least make a start toward restoring for our children the American dream that wealth is denied to no one." And, there were statistics: "The Defense Department runs 269 supermarkets. They do a gross business of $730 million a year and lose $150 million." And, there was democratic idealism: "This idea that government was beholden to the people, that it had no other source of power except the sovereign people, is still the newest, most unique idea in the long history of man's relation to man." And, finally, inevitably, there was the influence of Franklin Roosevelt, who first discovered an American "rendezvous with destiny" while accepting the Democratic renomination for president in 1936. Americans have been holding clandestine meetings with destiny ever since, this one from the perforation of the Reagan speech for Goldwater: "You and I have a rendezvous with destiny. We can preserve for our children this the last best hope of man on earth or we can sentence them to take the first step into a thousand years of darkness. If we fail, at least let our children, and our children's children, say of us we justified our brief moment here. We did all that could be done."

Although Reagan didn't know it then — and though he resisted the idea for nearly a year and a half — this speech stands as his opening address in the campaign for the California governorship in 1966. It raised nearly $1 million for the Republican party and its candidates. And it caused wealthy Republican contributors in California, such as auto dealer Holmes Tuttle, industrialist Henry Salvatori, and the late A. C. (Cy) Rubel, chairman of the board of Union Oil Company, to consider

Reagan the best hope to wrest the governorship of the nation's most populous state from the Democrats. When an exploratory committee run by his millionaire GOP backers, "The Friends of Ronald Reagan," raised both money and enthusiasm, Reagan agreed to make the race. The rest, as they say, is history.

Reagan's eight years as governor of California also are history — and there is general agreement among the historians that he was at least an adequate governor and perhaps a good one. State Treasurer Jesse Unruh, a Democratic legislative powerhouse at the time Reagan arrived in Sacramento and the man Reagan defeated to win his second term as governor, offered this balanced viewpoint to the *Los Angeles Times* in 1974: "As a governor, I think he has been better than most Democrats would concede and not nearly as good as most Republicans and conservatives might like to think." Bob Moretti, the Democratic speaker with whom Reagan negotiated his historic welfare bill in 1971, wound up liking and respecting his adversary. In the legislative hyperbole of the time Moretti (and Unruh, and most other Democrats) frequently described Reagan as a heartless, know-nothing foe of the poor, higher education, and racial minorities. But in retrospect, Moretti finds Reagan both a reasonable politician and a man of his word, saying of him: "His bark was worse than his bite."

Any serious evaluation of the Reagan governorship collides squarely with Reagan's own exalted view of his accomplishments. As Reagan told the story on the campaign trail in 1980, it was a golden age during the eight years he served as great helmsman of California's ship of state. "Every time we had a surplus, because I don't think government has a right to take one dollar more than government needs, we gave the surpluses back to the people in the form of tax rebates," Reagan would tell his approving audiences. "We gave back over eight years $5.7 billion to the people of California. We stopped the bureaucracy dead in its tracks, the same way I would like to stop it at the national level."

This account omits as much as it relates. What Reagan does not say is that these surpluses, in part, were a result of his own policies. He does not say that he sponsored what was then the largest tax increase in California state history and that state spending and taxes more than doubled during his tenure. Corporation, bank, sales, and personal income taxes all rose sharply during the Reagan years. The annual state budget increased from $4.6 billion to $10.2 billion and the operations portion of the budget, over which the governor has more control, increased from $2.2 billion to $3.5 billion. State taxes per $100 of personal income, a better measurement because it adjusts for population and price changes, went from $6.64 to $7.62.

But a case can be made that, despite these figures, Reagan succeeded in his basic goal of controlling the cost of government. "Reagan was not so much an underachiever as he was an overcommitter," says one-time legislative aide Judson Clark of the Sacramento consulting firm, California Research. "He did some important things, but not as much as he said he would do and not as much as he said he did." Among the things Reagan did do was slow the growth of the state work force, which had increased nearly 50 percent during the eight years of his Democratic predecessor, Edmund G. (Pat) Brown. There are different measurements of work force growth, but the generally accepted one shows a 7 percent increase during the Reagan years at a time when state work forces elsewhere were growing far more rapidly. Reagan cut by 40 percent a capital outlay budget which had increased 200 percent during the Brown years. And if the $4 billion which the state gave back in property tax relief is subtracted from Reagan's budgets, they roughly kept pace with inflation during his two administrations.

Had Reagan accomplished this result with the tax structure he inherited, the result would have been that low-income taxpayers would have shouldered most of the financial burden. The supreme irony of his governorship is that the burden was instead thrust in great part on the corporations and middle-class taxpayers which Reagan had been ritually defending in his speeches to conservative audiences. Under Reagan, in that first tax bill the levy on banks was boosted from 9.5 to 13 percent. The tax on corporations increased 61 percent — from a 5.5 to a 9 percent rate. This happened, in part, because of Reagan's ignorance of the way government actually worked. And it happened, also, because even in his ignorance he proved a masterful and intuitive politician.

This combination of ignorance and intuition worked reasonably well for Reagan as he struggled to understand the intricacies of government. At least it did on most issues. Where it failed him was on the emotional issue of abortion. In 1967, sponsors of liberal abortion legislation had chosen California as the testing ground on which to promote the nation's first liberal abortion law. California at the time, like a majority of other states, permitted abortions only to save the life of the mother. The liberalizing U.S. Supreme Court decision opening the abortion floodgates was yet to come, as was the counterrevolution of the pro-life movement. In those days the leading body of opposition was the Roman Catholic Church, which launched a letter-writing campaign that produced more mail than most legislators have ever seen. Reagan, as he puts it, had never thought much about the issue one way or the other. At one critical press conference, after the bill had advanced through key committees, Reagan showed almost total confusion about the measure's provisions, freely contradicting himself and describing as "loopholes" provisions which sponsors said were the major purpose of the bill. On one side, Reagan was lobbied for the bill by physicians including his father-in-law, Chicago surgeon Loyal Davis. On the other, the church brought its big guns to bear, and Francis Cardinal McIntyre called the governor and urged him to veto the legislation. Reagan finally signed the bill after the author had made some amendments which supposedly made abortions more difficult to obtain. The statistics of what happened after enactment tell another story. In 1967, there were 518 legal abortions in California hospitals. In 1978, the last year for which complete figures are available, there were 171,982 abortions. From 1967 through 1978 there were 1,230,359 abortions performed under the bill signed by Reagan, now the ardent champion of a U.S. constitutional amendment that would impose the restrictions on abortion that were on the books in California when he became governor.

Reagan did better on other issues. He conducted his office with integrity and his governmental appointments, many of them drawn from the business community, were of high quality. So were his judicial appointments, which usually followed the recommendations of the bar. Sometimes this produced a judiciary more independent than Reagan would have liked — as it did when Reagan-appointed Supreme Court Justice Donald Wright tipped the balance in striking down a Reagan-backed capital punishment law.

Occasionally, Reagan approved truly innovative programs, as in authorizing conjugal visits for prisoners with good behavior records. Reagan supported legislation increasing the length of sentences for criminals and more funding for state prisons. Originally, he slashed the funds for state mental hospitals. Then, he restored the funds and gave additional money to community health programs being pioneered in California. State expenditures for mental health doubled during the Reagan administration.

He entered office waging what some called a vendetta against the University of California, scene of a controversial and prophetic "free speech" demonstration. "Obey the rules or get out," thundered Reagan, as he called upon campus authorities to expel "undesirables." Under threat of budget cuts, Reagan tried to force the university to abandon its historic policy of "free tuition" and make students pay more of the costs of higher education. Reagan helped force out University of California administrator Clark Kerr, who had unwisely provoked a vote of confidence, and he did persuade the regents to accept tuition under another name. But the budget-cutting never materialized. Once Reagan had made his point, he was generous to the university. State spending for higher education rose 136 percent during the Reagan years compared to an overall state spending increase of 100 percent and an enrollment growth of 40 percent. Even educators who resented the antiintellectualism of Reagan's approach — he had once accused universities of "subsidizing intellectual curiosity" — praised the governor for the increased funding. There is disagreement to this day, however, on whether the verbal attacks on the university caused intangible damage which cost the university topflight faculty.

It was the performance of the Reagan administration on environmental issues which proved the greatest surprise. "A tree's a tree — how many do you need to look at," Reagan had said during his campaign for governor. Environmentalists viewed Reagan's election as the coming of the dark ages in a state which always has been in the forefront of the conservationist movement. Reagan fought this impression by choosing William Penn Mott, a nationally known park director, as director of state parks. He picked Norman (Ike) Livermore, a lumberman who also was a Sierra Club member, as director of resources. Together, Livermore and Mott compiled a generally enviable record for the Reagan administration — although it was notably pro-industry on smog control issues. A total of 145,000 acres, including forty-one miles of ocean frontage, were added to an already impressive state park system. Two underwater park preserves were set aside off the Pacific coast. A major bond issue for park development was proposed and the endangered middle fork of the Feather River was preserved.

What some think was Reagan's finest hour as governor came on the issue of the Dos Rios Dam, a proposed 730-foot structure on the middle fork of the Eel River, a steelhead-spawning stream that is one of California's few remaining wild rivers. The California water bureaucracy, then considered more powerful than the highway lobby, was enthusiastic about the Dos Rios high dam. When the Army Corps of Engineers joined forces to formally propose Dos Rios under the battlecry of water for populous Southern California, its approval was considered a foregone conclusion. Against an array of big battalions, which included wealthy Reagan contributors, were a few Reagan aides (including Livermore, State Finance Director Caspar W. Weinberger, and Reagan's present chief of staff Edwin Meese) and a few conservationists from Round Valley, which would have been flooded by the impounded waters of Dos Rios. Among these residents were descendants of Indian tribes which had been herded into the valley by army troops late in the nineteenth century. The Indians argued that Round Valley contained gravesites and valley land that was secured by treaty. It was their plea which proved decisive. "We've broken too damn many treaties," Reagan said in turning down the Dos Rios Dam. "We're not going to flood them (the Indians) out."

The major legislative achievement of Reagan's eight years in office was the 1971 Welfare Reform Act. It is one of many bills which looks good on its own and insufficient when matched against the Reagan rhetoric. "When I took office, California was the welfare capital of the nation," Reagan says on the stump. "Sixteen percent of all those receiving welfare in the country were in California. The caseload was increasing 40,000 a month. We turned that 40,000 a month increase into an 8,000 a month decrease. We returned to the taxpayers $2 billion and we increased grants to the truly needy by 43 percent." Most of these figures are exaggerations, or otherwise misleading. The average caseload increase for the two years prior to enactment of the welfare reform measure was 26,000 not 40,000. Reagan's bill did increase the grants for the poorest recipients — which had not been raised a penny during the supposedly liberal regime of Pat Brown — but half of this increase was mandated by federal litigation. The $2 billion which Reagan talks about is a legislative projection which made no allowance for the dropping birth rate or increasing employment in California at this time.

Still, the Welfare Reform Act was good legislation which could be defended as easily in New Deal terms as the ones Reagan used for his conservative audiences. The Urban Institute, a nonprofit Washington research group, called the legislation "a major policy success" in a report issued in 1980. Even taking into account the birth rate, and increasing employment, the institute said that the Reagan program had reduced the welfare rolls by 6 percent under what they otherwise would have been while increasing maximum grants. Frank Levy, the senior research associate who wrote the report, said there were "big symbolic differences in the rhetoric" between what Reagan and various liberals had proposed to improve the welfare system but that the substantive differences were far less than either side was likely to admit. The Reagan program, said Levy, was "reoriented toward fiscal control" but "on balance, more recipients appear to have been helped than hurt." By the time the legislation was passed, there were 1,608,000 persons on the welfare rolls — about one in every eleven Californians. In the next three years the total declined to 1,333,000 — significantly lower but still among the highest in the nation. The Urban Institute study found that the major feature of the control was a simple device requiring each recipient of a welfare check to mail a signed postcard each month certifying income and eligibility. In the face of this rudimentary requirement, welfare fraud seemed to melt away. On the other hand, Reagan's ballyhooed required-work program had little direct effect on the rolls, with only 9,600 persons assigned to jobs during a three-year period.

At ground level, Ronald Reagan is decent, likable, and homespun, used to being the center of attention but reserved to the point of occasional shyness. Unless aroused by some challenge, he is basically a passive person — reacting to Nancy, reacting to staff, reacting to autograph seekers and to questions that are put to him. He seems to like who he is, and the names other men have called him — "Dutch" and "the Gipper" and "the cowboy" — are names of affection and respect. He is considerate of other people. Many who have seen Reagan up close think he is literally considerate to a fault with aides, neither demanding enough of them nor reprimanding them when they do poor work. But he is sensible about some things that other men are not sensible about.

When Nancy Reagan was incensed by an anti-Reagan editorial campaign in the *Sacramento Bee*, Governor Reagan acceded to her request and cancelled the subscription at home. Then he took the paper at the office, confiding that it was a way to have the *Bee* (which he regularly read) and keep Nancy happy at the same time.

Reagan has a genuine sense of humor. When students pressed around his limousine during a college demonstration and yelled, "We are the future," Reagan scrawled a reply on a piece of paper and held it up to the window. "I'll sell my bonds," it said. And when a wire-service reporter of long acquaintance brought him a reissued promotion picture from *Bedtime for Bonzo* showing Reagan and the chimpanzee in bed together, Reagan autographed it with the words, "I'm the one with the watch."

Reagan comes from a milieu where reaction is required. An actor must be prepared, but he awaits the call of others before he can come onto the stage. And the working hours are different, or at least they were in Reagan's day. The phrase "9 to 5 governor" is accurate in a sort of rough-hewn way, but it is not a complete description of Reagan's working habits. As an actor, Reagan might work with great concentration on a film for six weeks or two months and then have a long period of inactivity. He is capable of bursts of very intensive campaigning, as anyone who saw him in New Hampshire in 1980 can attest. But he does not function well working long and hard over an extended period, and he does not want to work that way. "Show me an executive that works long overtime hours and I'll show you a bad executive," Reagan once said. What's more, he really believes this.

Reagan's nature and working habits combine to make him a delegator of authority. Edwin Meese, who served Reagan as chief of staff in Sacramento and then again in the 1980 presidential campaign, once remarked that Reagan was a near-perfect delegator because he gave a grant of authority that was clearly defined. "If you operated within the limits of what he wanted to accomplish, he wouldn't second-guess you," Meese said. "And he was decisive when you brought something to him."

Even those who concede that Reagan delegates well and decides quickly have questions about his basic intelligence. Reagan is, as they say, no rocket scientist. Many find him lacking in imagination. But Reagan consistently has confounded those who have underestimated him. There is a kind of small-town common sense about him that serves him well and shows in moments when it is least expected. And more than most people would suspect, Reagan has an appreciation of his own limitations. "I think any adult man knows his shortcomings and knows his strengths," Reagan has said. "I've never claimed to be the originator of every idea we had in Sacramento, but I do think I have the ability to recognize good ideas. I do think, also, that I set the tone and direction in which we wanted to go. We were fortunate enough in surrounding ourselves with people who shared our beliefs and whose talent was turned in the direction of implementing them." These are not the words of a stupid man. But Reagan's intelligence is functional rather than reflective. He is best under pressure — as at the Nashua debate and again on August 9 in the South Bronx where Reagan turned a disastrously advanced event into a triumph by telling a woman who was screaming at him: "I can't do a damn thing for you if I'm not elected."

Reagan's most unnerving quality is his proclivity for giving verbatim memorized responses he has used repeatedly as if he were saying them for the first time. It is like punching the button of a tape recorder and hearing the coded message, complete with sincere gestures and that "aw shucks" smile. Partly, this may be a learned defense mechanism which permits Reagan to talk safely to reporters and supporters on the campaign trail. But he has done this with friends in private conversations, too, and it leaves some of them wondering whether he has an original thought in his head. Others, more charitably, regard the mind-taped messages as a natural consequence of Reagan's combined acting and speaking career and say he gives memorized answers without realizing that he is doing it.

Perhaps Reagan has simply made too many speeches. There is much to recommend the observation of old foe Hale Champion (Pat Brown's last finance director) that Reagan is "the Reader's Digest of politics." At least well into the 1980 campaign, *Reader's Digest* was certainly Reagan's favorite reading material. "In both cases," wrote Champion in the *Washington Post*, "their statistics and illustrations have a folklore character. They are, if I may use a nonword, factitious. The figures aren't very good, they often don't prove anything and sometimes they are barely tangential to the issue at hand. But they sound great, and they seem to strengthen the message by making it seem more real, even more concrete." These dubious statistics also enable Reagan, in public or private, to tell his audiences what they want to hear. And this desire to please, more than anything else, has been the source of Reagan's trouble in presidential campaigns. Reagan is almost never embarrassed in direct confrontation, where both the physical and the mental juices are flowing. But before a friendly audience he is likely to say almost anything — once calling for a "bloodbath" if necessary to quell student demonstrations, and, in this year's election campaign blandly referring to the Vietnam war as "a noble cause" before a veterans' convention and then four days later questioning the theory of evolution before an audience of fundamentalist ministers.

Reagan's nature and way of doing business make him a natural target for anyone on his staff or in his constituency who wants to foist off a pet proposal on him. Reagan is considerate of others and he wants people to bring ideas to him. While he is pragmatic enough to know that he can't accomplish everything contained in his rhetoric, he nonetheless has real goals and fundamental beliefs.

Watching Reagan struggling to find himself after Noble Cause and Evolution and Taiwan, it occurred to me that he may be more complicated than we have made him out to be. Most of us are. I have been covering Reagan, on and off, since his first campaign for office fourteen years ago, have covered him in office, and have written a book about him. I have seen him on bad days and good, in triumph and defeat. He seems to me a good, if limited, man who has demonstrated that it is possible to govern constructively from a conservative ideological base. And yet there is something about Reagan which remains hidden, never glimpsed in those predictable airplane interviews or in the dreary accounts of how Reagan would use the experience he gained in Sacramento to remake Washington. The something shows occasionally in those "vision of America" endings which drive reporters to the press buses. But it shows even more on those rare occasions when Reagan admits visitors to Rancho del Cielo, the remote fog-shrouded ranch north of Santa Barbara which he has chosen as a haven for himself and his wife Nancy. Watching him tell proudly of how he laid the floors and rebuilt the roof of his understated ranch house and put in the fence around it, watching him saddling horses for the obligatory media ride down the old Western trail, watching him look at Nancy to see if she approved of what he was doing and saying, I thought of the passage in *Death of a Salesman* where the son tells about the porch his father built and says that there is more of Willy Loman in that porch than in all the sales he ever made. I wondered if this were also true of Reagan. He had grown up in Main Street America in the first third of this century believing as his father had told him that the only limits on what he could accomplish were those imposed by his ambition. It is a conceit of our system that anyone can be president and Reagan had taken this idea — this fundamental democratic notion which is close to the wellsprings of our national existence — quite literally. He had become a popular sportscaster, a well-known actor, the leader of his labor union, and twice the governor of the nation's most populous state. Now he was the Republican nominee for president. Because of what he had done, Reagan was Everyman. And because this is America, and it is what America expects of its Everymans, Reagan had not been ruined by this, at least not that I could see. He still liked working with his hands, and he liked to ride. He still hammed it up for his friends, as he must have done in Dixon, and he still needed and desired the public and private approval of those closest to him. But he was not riding off into the sunset, at least not this day. The sun was behind him as he rode down into the television cameras. Ronald Reagan was about to put the democratic ideal to one of its sternest tests. And he had every confidence that he could do it.

THE PRECEDING SELECTIONS have illustrated that increasingly at the national level candidates and their followers give an individualistic cast to party organization. Each candidate has his or her own organization that exists within the broader party. Neither national party committees nor leaders can determine who will run under their party labels.

Political parties have been stronger in the past, especially at local levels. Occupying an important place in party history is the urban party machine, the paradigm of which was the Daley machine in Chicago.

The following selection describes the kinds of people and personalities that controlled the political machine in Chicago, from its powerful leader, Mayor Richard J. Daley, to the men who helped to keep him in office, including precinct workers and captains and city bureaucrats appointed by the mayor to serve the party. Chicago politics clearly revealed a cult of personality in operation. The organization, operations, and policies of the Democratic party in Chicago were a perfect reflection of the personality of Mayor Richard J. Daley.

Mike Royko
THE BOSS

KUNSTLER: Mayor Daley, do you hold a position in the Cook County Democratic Committee?

WITNESS: I surely do, and I am very proud of it. I am the leader of my party.

KUNSTLER: What was that?

WITNESS: I surely do, and I am very proud of it. I am the leader of the Democratic party in Cook County.

KUNSTLER: Your honor, I would like to strike from that answer anything about being very proud of it. I only asked whether he had a position in the Cook County Democratic party.

HOFFMAN: I will let the words "I surely do" stand. The words after those may go out and the jury may disregard the expression of the witness that he is very proud of his position.

The Hawk got his nickname because in his younger days he was the outside lookout man at a bookie joint. Then his eyes got weak, and he had to wear thick glasses, so he entered politics as a precinct worker.

He was a hustling precinct worker and brought out the vote, so he was rewarded with a patronage job. The Hawk, who had always loved

From *Boss: Richard J. Daley of Chicago* by Mike Royko. Copyright © 1971 by Mike Royko. Reprinted by permission of the publisher, E. P. Dutton, a division of New American Library.

uniforms but had never worn one, asked his ward committeeman if he could become a member of the county sheriff's police department. They gave him a uniform, badge, and gun, and declared him to be a policeman.

But the Hawk was afraid of firearms, so he asked if he could have a job that didn't require carrying a loaded gun. They put him inside the County Building, supervising the man who operated the freight elevator. He liked the job and did such a good job supervising the man who operated the freight elevator that the Hawk was promoted to sergeant.

When a Republican won the sheriff's office, the Hawk was out of work for one day before he turned up in the office of the county treasurer, wearing the uniform of a treasurer's guard. His new job was to sit at a table near the main entrance, beneath the big sign that said "County Treasurer," and when people came in and asked if they were in the county treasurer's office, the Hawk said that indeed they were. It was a good job, and he did it well, but it wasn't what he wanted because he really wasn't a policeman. Finally his committeeman arranged for him to become a member of the secretary of state's special force of highway inspectors, and he got to wear a uniform that had three colors and gold braid.

The Hawk is a tiny piece of the Machine. He is not necessarily a typical patronage worker, but he is not unusual. With about twenty-five thousand people owing their government job to political activity or influence, nothing is typical or unusual.

The Hawk keeps his job by getting out the Democratic vote in his precinct, paying monthly dues to the ward's coffers, buying and pushing tickets to his ward boss's golf outing and $25-a-plate dinners. His reward is a job that isn't difficult, hours that aren't demanding, and as long as he brings out the vote and the party keeps winning elections, he will remain employed. If he doesn't stay in the job he has, they will find something else for him.

Some precinct captains have had more jobs than they can remember. Take Sam, who worked his first precinct forty-five years ago on the West Side.

"My first job was as a clerk over at the election board. In those days to succeed in politics you sometimes had to bash in a few heads. The Republicans in another ward heard about me and they brought me into one of their precincts where they were having trouble. I was brought in as a heavy, and I took care of the problem, so they got me a job in the state Department of Labor. The job was . . . uh . . . to tell the truth, I didn't do anything. I was a payroller. Then later I went to another ward as a Democratic precinct captain, where they were having a tough election. I did my job and I moved over to a job as a state policeman. Then later I was a city gas meter inspector, and a pipe fitter where they had to get me a union card, and an investigator for the attorney general, and when I retired I was an inspector in the Department of Weights and Measures."

The Hawk and Sam, as precinct captains, are basic parts of the Machine. There are some thirty-five hundred precincts in Chicago, and every one of them has a Democratic captain and most captains have assistant captains. They all have, or can have, jobs in government. The better the captain, the better the job. Many make upwards of fifteen thousand dollars a year as supervisors, inspectors, or minor department heads.

They aren't the lowest ranking members of the Machine. Below them are the people who swing mops in the public buildings, dump bedpans in the County Hospital, dig ditches, and perform other menial work. They don't work precincts regularly, although they help out at election time, but they do have to vote themselves and make sure their families vote, buy the usual tickets to political dinners and in many wards, contribute about 2 percent of their salaries to the ward organization.

Above the precinct captain is that lordly figure the ward committeeman, known in local parlance as "the clout," "the Chinaman," "the guy," and "our beloved leader."

Vito Marzullo is a ward committeeman and an alderman. He was born in Italy and has an elementary school education, but for years when he arrived at political functions, a judge walked a few steps behind him, moving ahead when there was a door to be opened. Marzullo had put him on the bench. His ward, on the near Southwest Side, is a pleasant stew of working class Italians, Poles, Mexicans, and blacks. A short, erect, tough, and likable man, he has had a Republican opponent only once in four elections to the City Council. Marzullo has about four hundred patronage jobs given to him by the Democratic Central Committee to fill. He has more jobs than some ward bosses because he has a stronger ward, with an average turnout of something like 14,500 Democrats to 1,200 Republicans. But he has fewer jobs than some other wards that are even stronger. Marzullo can tick off the jobs he fills:

"I got an assistant state's attorney, and I got an assistant attorney general, I got an electrical inspector at twelve thousand dollars a year, and I got street inspectors and surveyors, and a county highway inspector. I got an administrative assistant to the zoning board and some people in the secretary of state's office. I got fifty-nine precinct captains and they all got assistants, and they all got good jobs. The lawyers I got in jobs don't have to work precincts, but they have to come to my ward office and give free legal advice to the people in the ward."

Service and favors, the staples of the precinct captain and his ward boss. The service may be nothing more than the ordinary municipal functions the citizen is paying taxes for. But there is always the feeling that they could slip if the precinct captain wants them to, that the garbage pickup might not be as good, that the dead tree might not be cut down.

Service and favors. In earlier days, the captain could do much more. The immigrant family looked to him as more than a link with a new and strange government: He was the government. He could tell them how to fill out their papers, how to pay their taxes, how to get a license. He was the welfare agency, with a basket of food and some coal when things got tough, an entree to the crowded charity hospital. He could take care of it when one of the kids got in trouble with the police. Social welfare agencies and better times took away many of his functions, but later there were still the traffic tickets to fix, the real estate tax assessments he might lower. When a downtown office didn't provide service, he was a direct link to government, somebody to cut through the bureaucracy.

In poor parts of the city, he has the added role of a threat. Don't vote, and you might lose your public housing apartment. Don't vote, and you might be cut off welfare. Don't vote, and you might have building inspectors poking around the house.

In the affluent areas, he is, sometimes, merely an errand boy, dropping off a tax bill on the way downtown, buying a vehicle sticker at City Hall, making sure that the streets are cleaned regularly, sounding out public opinion.

The payoff is on election day, when the votes are counted. If he produced, he is safe until the next election. If he didn't, that's it. "He has to go," Marzullo says. "If a company has a man who can't deliver, who can't sell the product, wouldn't he put somebody else in who can?"

Nobody except Chairman Daley knows precisely how many jobs the Machine controls. Some patronage jobs require special skills, so the jobholder doesn't have to do political work. Some are under civil service. And when the Republicans occasionally win a county office, the jobs change hands. There were more patronage jobs under the old Kelly-Nash Machine of the thirties and forties, but civil service reform efforts hurt the Machine. Some of the damage has been undone by Daley, however, who let civil service jobs slip back into patronage by giving tests infrequently or making them so difficult that few can pass, thus making it necessary to hire "temporary" employees, who stay "temporary" for the rest of their lives. Even civil service employees are subject to political pressures in the form of unwanted transfers, withheld promotions.

On certain special occasions, it is possible to see much of the Machine's patronage army assembled and marching. The annual St. Patrick's Day parade down State Street, with Daley leading the way, is a display of might that knots the stomachs of Republicans. An even more remarkable display of patronage power is seen at the State Fair, when on "Democrat Day" thousands of city workers are loaded into buses, trains, and cars which converge on the fairgrounds outside Springfield. The highlight of the fair is when Daley proudly hoofs down the middle of the grounds' dusty racetrack in ninety-degree heat with thousands of his sweating but devoted workers tramping behind him, wearing old-fashioned straw hats and derbies. The Illinois attorney general's staff of lawyers once thrilled the rustics with a crack manual of arms performance, using Daley placards instead of rifles.

Another reason the size of the patronage army is impossible to measure is that it extends beyond the twenty to twenty-five thousand government jobs. The Machine has jobs at racetracks, public utilities, private industry, and the Chicago Transit Authority, which is the bus and subway system, and will help arrange easy union cards.

Out of the ranks of the patronage workers rise the Marzullos, fifty ward committeemen who, with thirty suburban township committeemen, sit as the Central Committee. For them the reward is more than a comfortable payroll job. If they don't prosper, it is because they are ignoring the advice of their Tammany cousin George Washington Plunkett, who said, "I seen my opportunities and I took 'em." Chicago's ward bosses take 'em, too.

Most of them hold an elective office. Many of the Daley aldermen are ward bosses. Several are county commissioners. Others hold office as county clerk, assessor, or recorder of deeds and a few are congressmen and state legislators. Those who don't hold office are given top jobs running city departments, whether they know anything about the work or not. A ward boss who was given a $28,000-a-year job as head of the city's huge sewer system was asked what his experience was. "About twenty years ago I was a house drain inspector." "Did you ever work in the sewers?" "No, but many a time I lifted a lid to see if they were flowing." "Do you have an engineering background?" "Sort of. I took some independent courses at a school I forget the name of, and in 1932 I was a plumber's helper." His background was adequate: his ward usually carries by fifteen thousand to three thousand votes.

The elective offices and jobs provide the status, identity, and retinue of coat holders and door openers, but financially only the household money. About a third of them are lawyers, and the clients leap at them. Most of the judges came up through the Machine; many are former ward bosses themselves. This doesn't mean cases are always rigged, but one cannot underestimate the power of sentimentality. The political lawyers are greatly in demand for zoning disputes, big real estate ventures, and anything else that brings a company into contact with city agencies. When a New York corporation decided to bid for a lucrative Chicago cable TV franchise, they promptly tried to retain the former head of the city's legal department to represent them.

Those who don't have the advantage of a law degree turn to the old reliable, insurance. To be a success in the insurance field, a ward boss needs only two things: an office with his name on it and somebody in the office who knows how to write policies. All stores and businesses need insurance. Why not force the premium on the friendly ward boss? As Marzullo says, everybody needs favors.

One of the most successful political insurance firms is operated by party ancient Joe Gill. Gill gets a big slice of the city's insurance on public properties, like the Civic Center and O'Hare Airport. There are no negotiations or competitive bidding. The policies are given to him because he is Joe Gill. How many votes does Prudential Life deliver? The city's premiums are about $500,000 a year, giving Gill's firm a yearly profit of as much as $100,000.

Another firm, founded by the late Al Horan, and later operated by his heirs and County Assessor P. J. Cullerton gets $100,000 a year in premiums from the city's park district. Since Cullerton is the man who sets the taxable value of all property in Cook County, it is likely that some big property owners would feel more secure being protected by his insurance.

When the city's sprawling lakefront convention hall was built, the insurance business was tossed at the insurance firm founded by George Dunne, a ward boss and County Board president.

Another old-line firm is operated by John D'Arco, the crime syndicate's man in the Central Committee. He represents the First Ward, which includes the Loop, a gold mine of insurable property. D'Arco has never bothered to deny that he is a political appendage of the Mafia, probably because he knows that nobody would believe him. A denial would sound strained in light of his bad habit of being seen with Mafia bosses in public. Besides, the First Ward was controlled by the Mafia long before D'Arco became alderman and ward committeeman.

D'Arco's presence in the Central Committee has sometimes been an embarrassment to Chairman Daley. Despite D'Arco's understandable efforts to be discreet, he can't avoid personal publicity because the FBI is always following the people with whom he associates. When D'Arco announced that he was leaving the City Council because of poor health, while remaining ward committeeman, the FBI leaked the fact that Mafia chief Sam Giancana had ordered him out of the council in a pique over something or other. Giancana could do that, because it is his ward; D'Arco only watches it for him. One of Giancana's relatives has turned up as an aide to a First Ward congressman. Another Giancana relative was elected to the state senate. At Daley's urging, the First Ward organization made an effort to improve its image by running a young banker for alderman. But the banker finally resigned from the council, saying that being the First Ward's alderman was ruining his reputation.

When he is asked about the First Ward, Daley retreats to the democratic position that the people elect D'Arco and their other representatives, and who is he to argue with the people? He has the authority, as party chairman, to strip the First Ward, or any ward, of its patronage, and there are times when he surely must want to do so. Raids on Syndicate gambling houses sometimes turn up city workers, usually sponsored by the First Ward organization. While he has the authority to take away the jobs, it would cause delight in the press and put him in the position of confirming the Mafia's participation in the Machine. He prefers to suffer quietly through the periodic flaps.

The question is often raised whether he actually has the power, in addition to the authority, to politically disable the Mafia. It has been in city government longer than he has, and has graduated its political lackeys to judgeships, the various legislative bodies, and positions throughout government. While it no longer is the controlling force it was in Thompson's administration, or as arrogantly obvious as it was under Kelly-Nash, it remains a part of the Machine, and so long as it doesn't challenge him but is satisfied with its limited share, Daley can live with it, just as he lives with the rascals in Springfield.

Ward bosses are men of ambition, so when they aren't busy with politics or their outside professions, they are on the alert for "deals." At any given moment, a group of them, and their followers, are either planning a deal, hatching a deal, or looking for a deal.

Assessor Cullerton and a circle of his friends have gone in for buying up stretches of exurban land for golf courses, resorts, and the like. Others hold interests in racetracks, which depend on political goodwill for additional racing dates.

The city's dramatic physical redevelopment has been a boon to the political world as well as the private investors. There are so many deals involving ranking members of the Machine that it has been suggested that the city slogan be changed from *Urbs in Horto*, which means "City in a Garden," to *Ubi Est Mea*, which means "Where's mine?"

From where Daley sits, alone atop the Machine, he sees all the parts, and his job is to keep them functioning properly. One part that has been brought into perfect synchronization is organized labor — perhaps the single biggest factor in the unique survival of the big city organization in Chicago. Labor provides Daley with his strongest personal support and contributes great sums to his campaigns. Daley's roots are deep in organized labor. His father was an organizer of his sheet-metal workers' local, and Bridgeport was always a union neighborhood. With politics and the priesthood, union activity was one of the more heavily traveled roads to success. Daley grew up with Steve Bailey, who became head of the Plumbers' Union, and as Daley developed politically, Bailey brought him into contact with other labor leaders.

Thousands of trade union men are employed by local government. Unlike the federal government and many other cities, Chicago always pays the top construction rate, rather than the lower maintenance scale, although most of the work is maintenance. Daley's massive public works projects, gilded with overtime pay in his rush to cut ribbons before elections, are another major source of union jobs.

His policy is that a labor leader be appointed to every policymaking city board or committee. In recent years, it has worked out this way: The head of the Janitors' Union was on the police board, the park board, the Public Buildings Commission, and several others. The head of the Plumbers' Union was on the Board of Health and ran the St. Patrick's Day parade. The head of the Electricians' Union was vice-president of the Board of Education. The Clothing Workers' Union had a man on the library board. The Municipal Employees' Union boss was on the Chicago Housing Authority, which runs the city's public housing projects. The head of the Chicago Federation of Labor and somebody from the Teamsters' Union were helping run the poverty program. And the sons of union officials find the door to City Hall open if they decide on a career in politics.

The third major part of the Machine is money. Once again, only Daley knows how much it has and how it is spent. As party chairman, he controls its treasury. The spending is lavish. Even when running against a listless nobody, Daley may spend a million dollars. The amount used for "precinct money," which is handed out to the precinct captains and used in any way that helps bring out the Democratic vote, can exceed the entire Republican campaign outlay. This can mean paying out a couple of dollars or a couple of chickens to voters in poor neighborhoods, or bottles of cheap wine in the Skid Row areas. Republicans claim that the Democrats will spend as much as $300,000 in precinct money alone for a city election. To retain a crucial office, such as that of county assessor, hundreds of thousands have been spent on billboard advertising alone. Add to that the TV and radio saturation, and the spending for local campaigning exceeds by far the cost-per-vote level of national campaigning.

The money comes from countless sources. From the patronage army, it goes into the ward offices as dues, and part of it is turned over to party headquarters. Every ward leader throws his annual $25-a-head golf days, corned beef dinners, and picnics. The ticket books are thrust at the patronage workers and they either sell them or, as they say, "eat them," bearing the cost themselves.

There are "ward books," with page after page of advertising, sold by precinct workers to local businesses and other favor-seekers. Alderman Marzullo puts out a 350-page ad book every year, at one hundred dollars a page. There are no blank pages in his book. The ward organizations keep what they need to function, and the rest is funneled to party headquarters.

Contractors may be the biggest of all contributors. Daley's public works program has poured billions into their pockets, and they in turn have given millions back to the party in contributions. Much of it comes from contractors who are favored, despite the seemingly fair system of competitive bidding. In some fields, only a handful of contractors ever bid, and they manage to arrange things so that at the end of the year each has received about the same amount of work and the same profit. A contractor who is not part of this "brotherhood" refrains from bidding on governmental work. If he tries to push his way in by submitting a reasonable bid, which would assure him of being the successful low bidder, he may suddenly find that the unions are unable to supply him with the workers he needs.

Even Republican businessmen contribute money to the Machine, more than they give to Republican candidates. Republicans can't do anything for them, but Daley can.

The Machine's vast resources have made it nearly impossible for Republicans to offer more than a fluttering fight in city elections. Daley, to flaunt his strength and to keep his organization in trim, will crank out four hundred thousand primary votes for himself running unopposed. His opponent will be lucky to get seventy thousand Republicans interested enough to cast a primary vote.

Unlike New York, Los Angeles, and other major cities, Chicago has no independent parties or candidates jumping in to threaten, or at least pull votes away from the leaders. It is no accident. Illinois election laws are stacked against an independent's ever getting his name on a voting machine.

In New York, a regular party candidate needs five thousand signatures on his nominating petitions, and an independent must have seventy-five hundred. With any kind of volunteer organization, an independent can get the names, which is why New York will have half a dozen candidates for mayor.

The requirements are even less demanding in Los Angeles, where a candidate needs a seven-hundred-dollar filing fee and petitions bearing five hundred names. Los Angeles voters have a dozen or so candidates from which to choose.

But Chicago has never, in this century, had more than two candidates for the office of mayor. The state legislature took care of the threat from troublesome independents years ago.

When Daley files his nominating petitions, he needs about thirty-nine hundred names, a figure based on one-half of one percent of his party's vote in the previous election. Daley usually gets so many names that the petitions have to be brought in by truck. Using the same formula his Republican opponent needs about twenty-five hundred signatures, which isn't difficult, even for a Chicago Republican.

But an independent would have to bring in about sixty to seventy thousand signatures. He needs 5 percent of the previous total vote cast. And not just anybody's signature: only legally defined independents, those who have not voted in the recent partisan primaries.

That's why there are only two candidates for mayor and the other offices in Chicago — a Republican and a Democrat. And sometimes there aren't even that many, Mayor Kelly having once handpicked his Republican opponent.

The only alternative for an independent is to run as a write-in candidate, a waste of time.

It has never happened, but if an independent somehow managed to build an organization big and enthusiastic enough to find seventy thousand independent voters who would sign his petition, he would probably need an extra thirty thousand signatures to be sure of getting past the Chicago Election Board, which runs the city's elections and rules on the validity of nominating petitions. Names can be ruled invalid for anything short of failing to dot an "i." An illiterate's "X" might be acceptable on a Machine candidate's petition, but the Election Board is meticulous about those of anybody else.

The board used to be run by a frank old rogue, Sidney Holzman, who summed up its attitude toward the aspirations of independents, Republicans, and other foreigners:

"We throw their petitions up to the ceiling, and those that stick are good."

Despite all these safeguards and its lopsided superiority over local opposition, the Machine never fails to run scared. For this reason, or maybe out of habit, it never misses a chance to steal a certain number of votes and trample all over the voting laws. Most of it goes on in the wards where the voters are lower middle class, black, poor white, or on the bottle. To assure party loyalty, the precinct captains merely accompany the voter into the voting machine. They aren't supposed to be sticking their heads in, but that's the only way they can be sure the person votes Democratic. They get away with it because the election judges, who are citizens hired to supervise each polling place, don't protest. The Democratic election judges don't mind, and the Republican election judges are probably Democrats. The Republicans assign poll watchers to combat fraud but they never have enough people to cover all of the precincts. If they prevented the common practices, imaginative precinct captains would merely turn to others. In some wards, politically obligated doctors sign stacks of blank affidavits, attesting to the illness of people they have never seen, thus permitting the precinct captain to vote the people in their homes as absentee voters for reasons of illness. And several investigations have established that death does not always keep a person's vote from being cast.

The aforementioned Holzman was always philosophical about vote fraud, conceding that it occurred, and even saying that "a good precinct captain will always find a way to steal votes," but asserting: "In city elections, we don't have to steal to win. And in statewide elections, the Republicans are stealing so much downstate, that all we do is balance it out."

Out of this vast amalgam of patronage, money, special interests, restrictive election laws, and organizational discipline emerge a handful of candidates, and they are what it is supposed to be all about.

Most of them come up through the system, as Daley did, beginning as doorbell ringers, working in the jobs their sponsors got for them, pushing the ward book, buying the tickets, doing the favors, holding the coats, opening the doors, putting in the fix, and inching their way up the organizational ladder, waiting for somebody to die and the chance to go to the legislature, into the City Council, and maybe someday something even bigger.

As hard as a party member may try, and as bright and presentable as he may be, he probably won't make it if he isn't from a strong ward with an influential ward boss. A loyal, hard-working City Hall lawyer can become a judge, if his ward brings in the vote and his sponsor pushes him, while in another ward, where the Republicans dominate and the ward boss just hangs on, the City Hall lawyer can only dream of his black robe.

Judge Wexler, Daley's night school classmate, lived with this problem. Wexler had worked feverishly as the city's chief prosecutor of slum cases, dragging landlords into court, reaping publicity for the mayor's administration, while deftly avoiding the toes of slum landlords who had political connections. For years he trotted into Daley's office with his news clippings. But when slate-making time came around, other people got to be judges.

"My ward committeeman was so weak, he couldn't do anything. I used to ask him for a letter to the Central Committee sponsoring me for a judgeship. You have to have a sponsoring letter. And he'd say: 'A letter for you? I want to be a judge myself, and I'm not getting anywhere.' I would have never made it if it hadn't been for Daley and knowing him from night school. He did it for me personally."

Wexler was fortunate. For the others with ambitions, it is either a strong committeeman and advancement, or an obscure job with nothing to put in the scrap book.

Only one other shortcut exists, and it is part of the system of the Machine: nepotism. A Chicago Rip Van Winkle could awaken to the political news columns and, reading the names, think that time had stood still.

There was Otto Kerner, Cermak's confidante and a federal judge, and he begat Otto Kerner, governor, federal judge, and husband of Cermak's daughter; John Clark, ward boss and assessor, begat William Clark, attorney general and 1968 U.S. Senate candidate; Adlai Stevenson, governor and presidential candidate, begat Adlai Stevenson, U.S. senator; Dan Ryan, ward boss and county board president, begat Dan Ryan, ward boss and county board president; Edward Dunne, mayor, begat Robert Jerome Dunne, judge; John J. Touhy, ward boss and holder of many offices, begat John M. Touhy, Illinois House Speaker; Joe Rostenkowski, ward boss, begat Daniel Rostenkowski, congressman; Arthur Elrod, ward boss and county commissioner, begat Richard Elrod, sheriff; John Toman, ward boss and sheriff, begat Andrew Toman, county coroner; Thomas Keane, ward boss and alderman, begat Thomas Keane, ward boss and alderman; Joe Burke, ward boss and alderman, begat Edward Burke, ward boss and alderman; Paul Sheridan, ward boss and alderman, begat Paul Sheridan, alderman; Theodore Swinarski, ward boss, begat Donald Swinarski, alderman; David Hartigan, alderman, begat Neil Hartigan, ward boss and chief park district attorney; Louis Garippo, ward boss, begat Louis Garippo, judge; Michael Igoe, federal judge, begat Michael Igoe, county board secretary; Daniel McNamara, union leader, begat Daniel McNamara, judge; Thomas Murray, union leader and school board member, begat James Murray, congressman and alderman; Peter Shannon, businessman and friend of Daley, begat Dan Shannon, Park District president; Morgan Murphy, Sr., business executive and friend of Daley, begat Morgan Murphy, Jr., congressman; William Downes, real estate expert and friend of Daley, begat a daughter, who married a young man named David Stahl, who became deputy mayor; James Conlisk, police captain and City Hall favorite, begat James Conlisk, police superintendent; Daniel Coman, ward boss and city forestry chief, begat Daniel Coman, head of the state's attorney's civil division.

They are their brothers' keepers, too.

Alderman Keane keeps his brother on the powerful board of real estate tax appeals; Assessor Cullerton keeps his brother in the city council and his brother-in-law as his chief deputy assessor; Alderman Harry Sain kept his brother as city jail warden when sheriff; and County

Board President Dunne Keeps his brother as boss of O'Hare and Midway airports, and Congressman John Kluczynski keeps his brother on the state Supreme Court.

Nobody in the Machine is more family conscious than Chairman Daley. Cousin John Daley became a ward committeeman and served several terms in the state legislature, where his remarkable resemblance to the mayor sometimes unnerved his associates. Uncle Martin Daley had a well-paying job in county government that he did so skillfully he seldom had to leave his home. Cousin Richard Curry heads the city's legal department. Daley's four sons are just finishing law school, so their public careers have not yet been launched, but the eldest, Richard, at twenty-seven, was a candidate for delegate from his district to the state constitutional convention. He piled up the biggest vote in the state. The people in Bridgeport recognize talent. And the sons have been judge's clerks while going through school. When one of the mayor's daughters married, Daley promptly found a city executive job for the father of his new son-in-law.

Daley didn't come from a big family but he married into one, and so Eleanor Guilfoyle's parents might well have said that they did not lose a daughter, they gained an employment agency. Mrs. Daley's nephew has been in several key jobs. Her sister's husband became a police captain. A brother is an engineer in the school system. Stories about the number of Guilfoyles, and cousins and in-laws of Guilfoyles, in the patronage army have taken on legendary tones.

There are exceptions to the rules of party apprenticeship and nepotism. A few independent Democrats have been dogged enough to defeat weak Machine candidates in primaries for alderman, or, as happened once in the Daley years, for a seat in Congress. But it is never easy, and the strain leaves most independents so exhausted that most of them eventually embrace the Machine, at least gently, to avoid recurring primary struggles.

In theory, anybody can walk right into party headquarters at slate-making time, go before the ward bosses who make up the committee, and present themselves as prospective candidates. One political hanger-on, a disc jockey, even caught them in a mirthful mood, and when he actually got down on his knees and begged, they let him run for a minor office. But even the slate makers do not kid themselves into thinking they are deciding who the candidates will be. They listen to the applicants, push their favorites, the men from their wards, and wait for Chairman Daley to make up his mind. Some of the men on the slate-making committee have been surprised to find that they themselves were slated to run for offices they hadn't even sought. It is a one-man show, and they know it. This vignette illustrates it:

In 1968, slate makers were putting together their county ticket. They listened to the applicants, talked it over, then Daley and a couple of the party ancients came out of another room with the list.

Daley had decided that the strongest candidate for the crucial office of state's attorney, the county's prosecutor, would be Edward Hanrahan, a former federal prosecutor. It is a "must" office because a Republican would use it to investigate City Hall. Hanrahan was the strongest candidate because his Republican opponent also had an Irish name.

But slating Hanrahan required that the incumbent, John Stamos, who had been appointed to fill a vacancy, be shifted to something else. Stamos, a diligent and skilled young prosecutor, was Greek; Greeks were a small voting bloc, and Stamos was just professional and aloof enough to make some party elders nervous. Daley had decided to let Stamos run for the office of Illinois attorney general, which has prestige but less power and challenge. That completed the ticket.

Their decision made for them, the slate makers filed out of the conference room to go downstairs and meet the news media. As they came out, one of them saw Stamos and said, "Congratulations, John, you're going for attorney general."

"Bullshit," Stamos said, adding, "I won't go for it." Daley reasoned, but Stamos repeated, "Bullshit." And left the hotel.

While the slate makers stood around looking confused, Daley told a secretary to call Frank Lorenz, an obeident party regular who was between elective offices. She got him on the phone and Daley said, "Come on over, Frank, you're the candidate for attorney general."

One of the slate makers later said: "If Lorenz had stepped out to take a piss, he would have missed out, and the next guy Daley thought of would have got it, if he answered his phone. That's the way things are run sometimes, and everybody says we're so goddamn well organized."

A minute or two later, it was all resolved. Normally, Stamos would have been punished. But for party unity and to avoid alienating big Greek financial contributors, he was elevated to the state appellate court.

"You never know what in the hell is going to happen in there," a ward boss said. "He moves us around like a bunch of chess pieces. He knows why he's doing it because he's like a Russian with a ten-year plan, but we never know. I think his idea is to slate people who aren't going to try to rival him or add to someone else's strength. Look at how Cullerton got to be assessor. First he was a nothing alderman. He was a real nothing. But Daley put him in as finance chairman so he could have somebody who wouldn't get out of line. Then he put him in as assessor. Keane wanted assessor for his brother George. George would have loved it. Funny how people love to be assessor, haw! But Daley wasn't about to give Tom Keane the assessor's office, so he looked around and there was faithful Parky Cullerton.

"When he had to pick a chief judge, who were the logical guys? Neil Harrington, but he couldn't give it to Neil because he used to be part of the old South Side faction, and Daley wouldn't trust him. Harold Ward? He is independent, he might tell Daley to go screw himself or something.

"So he gave it to John Boyle, because he knew he'd have Boyle's complete loyalty. Why? Because Boyle had that scandal when he was state's attorney years ago and after that he couldn't get elected dog-catcher. He was a whipped dog, so he was perfect for Daley.

"And there's this thing he has with old people. Jesus, we've reslated people who were so senile they didn't even know what office they were running for. When it gets to that point, you know it has got to be something more than him being soft-hearted. There were some we could have just told them they were being reslated, and they would never have known the difference. He does it because then he doesn't have to worry about them. They'll sit there on the county board or wherever they are and do just what they're told.

"It's one-man rule, absolutely. It used to be that if Kelly got mad at you, there were seven or eight guys you could go to and get it squared. The same thing with Nash, and when Arvey was chairman. But there's only one Daley. You're dead if he doesn't like you. There's no point in going to someone to try to get it squared because they can't, and they won't even try because they're afraid it'll get him mad at them. He's a friend of mine, but he can be a mean prick."

Just how mean, and how subtle, was discovered by Arnold Maremont, a millionaire industrialist and art collector who decided he wanted to go into politics and to start at the top.

Daley does not dislike millionaires. He lets them contribute to the party, serve on advisory boards, take on time-consuming appointments, and help elect Machine Democrats to office.

Maremont had done it all. He contributed money, worked in Governor Kerner's campaign, led a campaign to pass a $150,000,000 bond issue that revitalized the state's mental health program, and pitched in on numerous liberal causes and mental health and welfare programs.

His dream was to be a U.S. senator, and in early 1961 he went to Daley's office and told him that he'd like to run against Senator Everett Dirksen. He made it clear that he wanted to do it properly and not jump into the primary as a maverick. The party's blessing was what he was after.

Daley showed interest, but said he had certain reservations: mainly he wasn't sure if downstate county chairmen would support a Jew. He suggested that Maremont tour the state, talk to the county chairmen, and he indicated strongly that if Maremont made a good showing, he'd be Daley's man.

Maremont pushed aside his business and civic work and spent most of the early summer barnstorming through Illinois. A spunky, brash man, he'd walk into a bar in a tiny southern Illinois town — grits and gravy country — and announce: "My name's Arnold Maremont. I want to run for the Senate and I'm a Jew." People seemed to like him, as he wolfed down chicken and peas dinners at the county meetings, charming little old ladies, and picking up support from the chairmen.

All the while, he sent back regular reports to Daley: They will go for a Jew! Elated, he headed back to Chicago, ready to give Daley his final report and the good news. He got back to town just in time to pick up that day's papers and read that Daley had, indeed, decided to slate a Jewish senatorial candidate: Congressman Sidney Yates, a party regular.

That ended Maremont's political ambitions. Furious, he was convinced that Daley had merely used him to conduct a free one-man survey of downstate Illinois. He wouldn't have even tried had he ever heard Daley explain why he is so dedicated a party man: "The party permits ordinary people to get ahead. Without the party, I couldn't be mayor. The rich guys can get elected on their money, but somebody like me, an ordinary person, needs the party. Without the party, only the rich would be elected to office."

If Daley's one-man rule bothers the men who sit on the Central Committee, they are careful to keep it to themselves. The meetings take on the mood of a religious service, with the committeemen chanting their praise of his leadership. "It has been . . . my pleasure and honor . . . to give him my advice. . . . The greatest mayor . . . in the country . . . the world . . . the history of the world . . ."

Only once in recent years has anybody stood up and talked back, and he was one of the suburban committeemen, generally referred to around party headquarters as "a bunch of meatheads."

The suburban committeeman, Lynn Williams, a wealthy manufacturer and probably the most liberal member of the Central Committee, had been angered by Daley's attacks on liberals after the 1968 Democratic convention. Daley had been making speeches lambasting pseudoliberals, liberal-intellectuals, suburban liberals, suburban liberal-intellectuals, and pseudoliberal-intellectual suburbanites. He had been shouting: "Who in the hell do those people think they are? Who are they to tell us how to run our party?"

Williams, a strong supporter of young Adlai Stevenson, who had angered Daley with an attack on "feudal" politics, stood up, finally, at a Central Committee meeting and delivered a scathing rebuttal to Daley, saying that without liberal participation the party would be nothing but a skeleton, its only goal, power.

As he talked, the committeemen's heads swiveled as if they were watching a tennis game, wonder and fear on their faces. They had never heard such talk, and wondered what Chairman Daley would do. Strike him with lightning. Throw the bum out?

When Williams finished, Daley, in a surprisingly soft voice, said, "I've always been a liberal myself."

Other committeemen joined in his defense, recalling countless liberal acts by Daley. One man shouted at Williams, "Perhaps you didn't know, but this happens to be a very liberal outfit."

The shock of the committeemen at the sound of somebody criticizing Daley didn't surprise Williams. He has said: "Most of them are mediocrities at best, and not very intelligent. The more successful demonstrate cunning. Most are in need of slavery — their own — and they want to follow a strong leader."

In March 1970, the committeemen met for the purpose of reelecting Daley chairman. Alderman Keane nominated him and eighteen other committeemen made lengthy speeches seconding the nomination. One of them recited, "R, you're rare; I, you're important; C, you're courageous; H, you're heavenly; A, you're able; R, you're renowned; D, you're Democratic; J, is for your being a joy to know; D, you're diligent; A, you're adorable; L, you're loyal; E, you're energetic; and Y, you're youthful."

Once again Lynn Williams stood, but not to criticize. He, too, joined in the praise and made one of the seconding speeches. Daley had since slated young Adlai Stevenson III, whom Williams had supported, for the U.S. Senate. Daley and Williams even exchanged handshakes. In a way, Williams seemed to emphasize his own point about the committee's need to follow a strong leader.

PRESSURE GROUPS AND LOBBYISTS

Chapter Two

Since the publication of David Truman's classic, *The Governmental Process,* in 1951, many political scientists have become enamored of the "group theory" of politics.[1] Although the origins of group theory date back at least as far as John C. Calhoun, who stated its premises and implications in his posthumously published work, *A Disquisition on Government,* in 1853, real acceptance of the group theory did not come until the twentieth century. There are two essential premises of group theory: (1) individuals function in the political process only through groups; (2) the interaction of political interest groups produces the national interest. Today, group theory is not as widely accepted as it once was. Theodore Lowi, in particular, has led an attack on the group theorists' second assumption.[2] But the idea that politics is essentially a group process, rather than an individual process remains largely unchallenged. The extreme expression of this view treats groups anthropomorphically, that is, as if they are persons. But groups are not mystical entities that can exist apart from the individuals who act as their leaders and members, or from the important intermediaries, such as the Washington lawyers, between pressure groups and government.

Individual character, personality, and style affect the ways in which pressure groups interact with government. The selections in this chapter have been chosen to demonstrate the personal dimension of the group process.

[1]David B. Truman, *The Governmental Process* (New York: Alfred A. Knopf, 1951).
[2]Theodore J. Lowi, *The End of Liberalism,* 2nd ed. (New York: W.W. Norton, 1979).

THE PRACTICE OF LOBBYING IS as old as government itself. Lobbying styles and techniques have changed over the years in response to different political environments. The crasser forms of influence-peddling in the nineteenth century, which often included outright bribery of state and national legislators, have given way to subtler techniques. A vast lobbying corps continues to roam the capital's corridors of power, seeking to influence legislators and other government officials. But laws as well as social and political customs circumscribe, at least to some degree, their freedom to act. They certainly cannot, for example, do what railroad tycoon Jay Gould did in attempting to influence the Albany legislature in his competition with railroad magnate Cornelius Vanderbilt in the late nineteenth century. Gould arrived in the state's capital with a valise stuffed with $500,000 in greenbacks with the obvious intention of bribing the lawmakers. His behavior, in the words of one of the times chroniclers, had "the most frenzying and overstimulating effect . . . which would take many years of disciplined machine leadership to eliminate."[1]

While modern-day lobbying may be less crude than in the past, the Washington lobbying corps has expanded in numbers and power. Many individuals have turned positions of public trust into private gain as former Congressman, staffers, and administration officials become high-paid lobbyists. The following depiction of lobbying in the 1980s highlights the personalities, styles, and techniques that are involved. Also discussed is the perennial question of what, if any, limits should be placed upon lobbying.

7 Evan Thomas
INFLUENCE PEDDLING IN WASHINGTON

The hallway is known as "Gucci Gulch," after the expensive Italian shoes they wear. At tax-writing time, the Washington lobbyists line up by the hundreds in the corridor outside the House Ways and Means Committee room, ever vigilant against the attempts of lawmakers to close their prized loopholes. Over near the House and Senate chambers, Congressmen must run a gauntlet of lobbyists who sometimes express their views on legislation by pointing their thumbs up or down. Not long ago, Senator John Danforth, chairman of the Senate Commerce Committee, could be seen on the Capitol steps trying to wrench his hand from the grip of a lobbyist for the textile industry seeking new

[1]Quoted in Edgar Lane, *Lobbying and the Law*, (Berkeley and Los Angeles: University of California Press, 1964), p. 24.

protectionist legislation. Though Danforth himself wants help for the shoe, auto, and agricultural industries in his native Missouri, the Senator — an ordained Episcopal minister — rolled his eyes heavenward and mumbled, "Save me from these people."

There have been lobbyists in Washington for as long as there have been lobbies. But never before have they been so numerous or quite so brazen. What used to be, back in the days of Bobby Baker, a somewhat shady and disreputable trade has burst into the open with a determined show of respectability. Tempted by the staggering fees lobbyists can command, lawmakers and their aides are quitting in droves to cash in on their connections. For many, public service has become a mere internship for a lucrative career as a hired gun for special interests.

With so many lobbyists pulling strings, they may sometimes seem to cancel one another out. But at the very least, they have the power to obstruct, and their overall effect can be corrosive. At times the halls of power are so glutted with special pleaders that government itself seems to be gagging. As Congress and the administration begin working this month to apportion the deepest spending cuts in America's history and to sort out the most far-reaching reform of the tax laws since World War II, the interests of the common citizen seem to stand no chance against the onslaught of lobbyists. Indeed, the tax bill that emerged from the House already bears their distinctive Gucci prints, and the budget is still filled with programs they have been able to protect.

Of course, the common citizen often benefits from various "special interest" breaks (for example, a deduction for home mortgages or state and local taxes). One man's loophole is another man's socially useful allowance, and one's man's lobbyist is another man's righteous advocate. Nonetheless, the voices most likely to be heard are often the ones that can afford the best-connected access brokers.

As the legislative year cranks up, the whine of special pleaders resonates thoughout the Capitol:

In the Senate Finance Committee, heavy industries like steel and autos, led by Veteran Lobbyist Charles Walker, are working to restore tax breaks for investment in new equipment that were whittled down last fall by the House Ways and Means Committee.

In the House and Senate Armed Services Committees, lobbyists for weapons manufacturers are fanning out to make sure that lawmakers do not trim their pet projects from the defense budget.

In the Senate Commerce Committee, business lobbyists are pressing for legislation to limit liability for defective products. They face fierce opposition from consumer groups and personal-injury lawyers.

Throughout the House and Senate, lobbyists for interests ranging from commercial-waterway users to child-nutrition advocates are laboring to spare their favorite federal subsidies from the exigencies of deficit reduction.

A superlobbyist like Robert Gray, a former minor official in the Eisenhower administration who parlayed his promotional genius and friendship with the Reagans into a $20 million-a-year PR and lobbying outfit, is in the papers more than most congressional committee chairmen. He would have his clients believe that he is at least as powerful. "In the old days, lobbyists never got any publicity," says Veteran Lobbyist Maurice Rosenblatt, who has prowled the halls of Congress for several decades. "Congressmen didn't want to be seen with notorious bagmen. But now, he shrugs, "the so-called best lobbyists get the most publicity."

Influence peddling, says Jack Valenti, head of the Motion Picture Association and no mean practitioner of the craft, "is the biggest growth industry around." The number of registered domestic lobbyists has more than doubled since 1976, from 3,420 to 8,800. That figure is understated, however, since reporting requirements under a toothless 1946 law are notoriously lax. Most experts put the influence-peddling population at about 20,000 — or more than 30 for every member of Congress. Registered lobbyists reported expenditures of $50 million last year, twice as much as a decade ago, but the true figure is estimated at upwards of $1.5 billion, including campaign contributions.

What does the money buy? "Everybody needs a Washington representative to protect their hindsides, even foreign governments," says Senator Paul Laxalt. "So the constituency for these people is the entire free-world economy." Joseph Canzeri, a former Reagan aide who calls himself a Washington "facilitator," notes, "It's a competitive business. There are a lot of wolves out there. But there are a lot of caribou in government too."

In the amoral revolving-door world of Washington, it has become just as respectable to lobby as to be lobbied. Ronald Reagan may have come to Washington to pare down the size of the Federal Government, but many of his former top aides have quit to profit off Big Government as influence peddlers. None has been more successful more swiftly than Reagan's former deputy chief of staff Michael Deaver, who may multiply his White House income sixfold in his first year out of government by offering the nebulous blend of access, influence and advice that has become so valued in Washington. Other Reaganauts now prowling Gucci Gulch include ex-Congressional Liaison Kenneth Duberstein and two former White House political directors, Lyn Nofziger and Ed Rollins. "I spent a lot of years doing things for love. Now I'm going to do things for money," Rollins told the *Washington Post* after he left the White House. By representing clients like the Teamsters Union, Rollins, who never earned more than $75,000 a year in government, boasts that he can earn ten times as much.

Former administration officials are often paid millions of dollars by special interests to oppose policies they once ardently promoted. This is particularly true in the area of foreign trade, as documented by the *Washington Post* a week ago. For example, Reagan has ordered an investigation into the unfair trade practices of South Korea. That country will pay former Reagan aide Deaver $1.2 million over three years to "protect, manage and expand trade and economic interests" of the nation's industry. Deaver refuses to say exactly what he will do to earn his fee, but he has hired Doral Cooper, a former deputy trade representative in the Reagan administration, as a lobbyist for his firm. Japanese semiconductor and machine-tool firms are also charged by the administration with engaging in unfair trade practices. They have hired Stanton Anderson, who had served as director of economic affairs for the administration's 1980 transition team.

Foreign governments are particularly eager to retain savvy Washington insiders to guide them through the bureaucratic and congressional maze, and polish their sometimes unsavory images in the U.S. The Marcos government in the Philippines has retained the well-connected lobbying firm of Black, Manafort & Stone for a reported fee of $900,000. Another Black, Manafort client is Angolan rebel Jonas Savimbi. Not to be outdone, the Marxist regime of Angola hired Bob Gray's firm to front for it in Washington. Two years ago, Gray told *Time* that he checks with his "good friend," CIA Director William Casey, before taking on clients who might be inimical to U.S. interests. It is unclear just what Casey could have said this time, since the CIA is currently funneling $15 million in covert aid to Savimbi to help his rebellion against the Angolan regime. Last week outraged Savimbi backers chained themselves to a railing in Gray's posh offices in Georgetown and had to be forcibly removed by local police.

Lobbyists call themselves lawyers, government-affairs specialists, public relations consultants, sometimes even lobbyists. They offer a wide array of increasingly sophisticated services, from drafting legislation to creating slick advertisements and direct-mail campaigns. But what enables the big-time influence peddlers to demand upwards of $400 an hour is their connections. "I'll tell you what we're selling," says Lobbyist Frank Mankiewicz. "The returned phone call."

Old-time fixers such as Tommy "the Cork" Corcoran and Clark Clifford were not merely practiced lawyers but had some genuine legislative expertise to offer. Lately, however, Washington has seen the rise of a new breed of influence peddler, whose real value is measured by his friends in high places — particularly in the White House. Clifford prospered no matter who was in office; after the Reagans go home to

California, it is hard to believe that Deaver or Gray will remain quite such hot commodities.

There is, and has long been, a strong whiff of scam about the influence-peddling business. Its practitioners like to imply that they have more clout than they truly do. In the post-Watergate era, power has been fractionated on Capitol Hill. Where a few powerful committee chairmen once held sway, Congress has become a loose federation of 535 little fiefdoms. This has made a lobbyist's job more difficult, but it hardly means that Congress has been liberated from the thrall of special interests. Well-intentioned congressional reform has been subverted over the years by the proliferation of lobbyists and the spiraling cost of election campaigns, two trends that go together like a hand and a pocket. The result has often been institutional paralysis. The very fact that Congress and the White House felt compelled to enact the Gramm-Rudman measure, requiring automatic spending cuts, is a monument to the inability of weak-willed legislators to say no to the lobbyists who buzz around them.

President Reagan has tried to sell his tax-reform bill as the supreme test of the public interest vs. the special interests. In pitching his campaign to the public, he has accused special interests of "swarming like ants through every nook and cranny of Congress," overlooking, perhaps, that many of the most prominent ants are his former aides. Few lobbyists, however, seem especially offended by his rhetoric, and certainly their livelihoods are not threatened. Indeed, many lobbyists candidly admit that true tax reform would actually mean more business for them, since they would have a fresh slate upon which to write new loopholes.

The way lobbyists have feasted on the President's tax-reform bill illustrates why the bill is known in the law firms and lobbying shops of K Street as the "Lobbyists' Full Employment Act." The 408-page proposal first drafted by the Treasury Department 16 months ago, known as Treasury I, was called a model of simplicity and fairness. It would have swept the tax code virtually clean of loopholes for the few in order to cut tax rates sharply for the many. But the 1,363-page tax bill sent by the House to the Senate last December is so riddled with exemptions and exceptions that the goal of fairness was seriously compromised, and simplicity abandoned altogether.

The lobbyists wasted no time biting into Treasury I. Insurance executives calculated that such loophole closings as taxing employer-paid life insurance and other fringe benefits would cost the industry about $100 billion over five years. Led by Richard Schweiker, who was President Reagan's Secretary of Health and Human Services before becoming head of the American Council of Life Insurance, the industry launched a

$5 million lobbying campaign that can only be described as state of the art.

Even before Treasury had finished drafting its original plan, the insurers were showing 30-second spots on TV that depicted a bird nibbling away at a loaf of bread labeled "employee benefits." An actress in the role of frightened housewife exclaimed, "We shouldn't have to pay taxes for protecting our family!" Life insurance agents around the country were revved up by a twelve-minute film entitled *The Worst Little Horror Story in Taxes*. In the film, Senate Finance Chairman Robert Packwood, a strong advocate of preserving tax breaks for fringe benefits, was shown urging the public to write their Congressmen. The insurers also mounted a direct-mail campaign that inundated Congress last year with 7 million preprinted, postage-paid cards. The campaign was successful: by the time the bill passed the House of Representatives last December, the insurance lobby figured that it had managed to restore about $80 billion of the $100 billion in tax breaks cut out by Treasury I. The insurers hope to win back most of the rest when the bill is reported out by the Senate Finance Committee this spring.

Threats to close a single loophole can bring scores of lobbyists rallying round. The original Treasury proposal sought to eliminate Section 936 of the U.S. Tax Code, which gives tax breaks worth some $600 million to companies that invest in Puerto Rico. Treasury Department officials conceded that the tax break helped create jobs by luring business to the island, but figured that each new job was costing the U.S. Treasury about $22,000. To defend Section 936, a coalition of some 75 U.S. companies with factories on the island formed a million-dollar "Puerto Rico–U.S.A. Foundation" and hired more than a dozen lobbyists, including Deaver. Last fall Section 936 advocates flew some 50 Congressmen and staffers to Puerto Rico on fact-finding trips.

Deaver, meanwhile, coordinated a lobbying campaign aimed at National Security staffers and officials in the State, Commerce, and Defense Departments. The strategy was to cast Section 936 as a way to revive the President's moribund Caribbean Basin Initiative and erect a bulwark against Communism in the region. Some two dozen companies with plants in Puerto Rico promised that if Section 936 was retained, they would reinvest their profits in new factories on other Caribbean islands. During a tense moment in the negotiations with the administration, Deaver even managed to place a ground-to-air call to Air Force One as it flew to the Geneva Summit last November. He wanted to alert Secretary of State George Shultz to stand fast against the maneuverings of tax reformers at the Treasury. Not surprisingly, the Treasury gnomes were overwhelmed. Later that month the administration committed itself to preserving Section 936.

The fabled "three-martini lunch," threatened by the Treasury Department's proposal to end tax deductions for business entertainment, was preserved as at least a two-martini lunch after heavy lobbying by the hotel and restaurant industry. In the House-passed bill, 80 percent of the cost of a business lunch can still be deducted. The oil-and-gas lobby managed to restore over half the tax breaks for well drilling removed by the original Treasury bill. Lawyers, doctors, and accountants won an exemption from more stringent new accounting rules. The lobbying by lawyers was a bit crude: Congressmen received letters that were supposedly written by partners of different law firms but were all signed by the same hand. No matter. Though congressional etiquette demands that each constituent's letter be answered personally, "We just let our word processors talk to their word processors," shrugged a congressional staffer.

The real deal making was done over so-called transition rules, which postpone or eliminate new taxes for certain individual businesses. The House-passed bill is studded with some 200 transition rules, which have been written to protect pet projects in a Congressman's district or large industries with particular clout on the Hill. Drafted behind closed doors, these rules are written in language designed to make it difficult to identify the real beneficiaries. One transition rule, for instance, waives the cutbacks on investment tax credits and depreciation for the fiber-optic networks of telecommunications companies that have committed a certain number of dollars for construction by a certain date. It turns out that just two companies profit from the exemption: AT&T and United Telecom.

Not every lobbyist made out in the wheeling and dealing, by any means. Some were a little too greedy. The banking lobby pushed an amendment that would actually *increase* its tax breaks for bad-debt reserves. The lobbyists figured that they were just making an opening bid; their real aim was to protect existing tax breaks. To their surprise, however, the amendment passed in the confusion of an early Ways and Means Committee drafting session. When jubilant banking lobbyists began shouting "We won! We won!" outside the hearing room, some Congressmen became angry. Giving more tax breaks to the already well-sheltered banking industry was no way to sell voters on tax reform. The amendment was repealed.

Despite the predations of lobbyists, a tax-reform bill may be signed into law this year. But it must first survive the Senate, and already the advocates are queuing up to be heard. "I wish there were a secret elevator into the committee room," laments Senator David Pryor of Arkansas, a member of the Finance Committee. "Whenever I go there to vote, I try to walk fast and be reading something."

Some Congressmen may try to avoid lobbyists, but many have come to depend on them. "God love 'em," quips Vermont Senator Patrick Leahy. "Without them we would have to decide how to vote on our own." Sarcasm aside, lobbyists do serve a useful purpose by showing busy legislators the virtues and pitfalls of complex legislation. "There's a need here," says Anne Wexler, a former Carter administration aide turned lobbyist. "Government officials are not comfortable making these complicated decisions by themselves." Says Lobbyist Van Boyette, a former aide to Senator Russell Long of Louisiana: "We're a two-way street. Congress often legislates on issues without realizing that the marketplace has changed. We tell Congress what business is up to, and the other way around."

Lobbyists and government officials alike are quick to point out that lobbying is cleaner than in earlier eras, when railroad barons bought Senators as if they were so much rolling stock. "It's an open process now," says Jack Albertine, president of the American Business Conference, a trade association of medium-size, high-growth companies. "All sides are represented, the contributions are reported, and the trade-offs are known to everybody. In the old days you never knew who got what until a waterway project suddenly appeared in someone's district."

In some ways the growth of interest groups is healthy. Capitol Hill at times seems like a huge First Amendment jamboree, where Americans of all persuasions clamor to be heard. Movie stars plead on behalf of disease prevention, Catholic clerics inveigh against abortion, farmers in overalls ask for extended credit, and Wall Street financiers extol the virtues of lower capital-gains taxes. No single group dominates. When the steel, auto, and rubber industries saw the Reagan administration as an opening to weaken the Clean Air and Clean Water acts, the "Green Lobby," a coalition of environmental groups, was able to stop them.

But not every voter has a lobby in Washington. "Sometimes I think the only people not represented up here are the middle class," says Democratic Congressman Barney Frank of Massachusetts. "The average folks — that's what bothers me." Of course, that is not entirely true; many ordinary citizens are represented by such lobbies as the National Association of Retired Persons and Common Cause.

Lobbyists cannot afford to rely solely on well-reasoned arguments and sober facts and figures to make their case. In the scramble to win a hearing, they have developed all manner of stratagems designed to ingratiate themselves and collect IOUs.

Helping Congressmen get re-elected is an increasingly popular device. Veteran Washington Lobbyist Thomas Hale Boggs, Jr. is on no fewer than 50 "steering committees" set up to raise money for congressional election campaigns. By night, "Good Ole Boy" Boggs can be found shmoozing at Capitol Hill fund raisers, where lobbyists drop off envelopes containing checks from Political Action Committees at the door before digging into the hors d'oeuvres. By day, Boggs lobbies Congressmen, often the same ones for whom he has raised money the night before. Lately high-power political consulting firms such as Black, Manafort & Stone have taken not only to raising money for candidates but actually to running their campaigns: planning strategy, buying media, and polling. These firms get paid by the candidates for electioneering services, and then paid by private clients to lobby the Congressmen they have helped elect. In the trade this cozy arrangement is known as "double dipping."

Special-interest giving to federal candidates has shot up eightfold since 1974, from $12.5 million to more than $100 million by the 1984 election. Nonetheless, PACs can give no more than $5,000 to a single campaign, and all contributions are publicly filed with the Federal Election Commission. "Elections are so expensive that the idea of a PAC's having inordinate influence is ridiculous," says Boggs.

Some Congressmen are not so sure. "Somewhere there may be a race of humans who will take $1,000 from perfect strangers and be unaffected by it," dryly notes Congressman Frank. Says Congressman Leon Panetta of California: "There's a danger that we're putting ourselves on the auction block every election. It's now tough to hear the voices of the citizens in your district. Sometimes the only things you can hear are the loud voices in three-piece suits carrying a PAC check."

Even the most reputable influence peddlers use their political connections to build leverage. As director of the 1984 GOP Convention, Lobbyist William Timmons, a quietly genial man who represents such blue-chippers as Boeing, Chrysler, ABC, and Anheuser-Busch, controlled access to the podium. GOP Senators lobbied *him* for prime-time appearances. A *Wall Street Journal* reporter described Senator Pete Domenici of New Mexico, who was running for re-election in the fall of 1984, thanking Timmons a bit too effusively for allotting time for him to address the convention. "You told me you'd give me a shot," gushed Domenici. "So I appreciate it, brother."

Family ties help open doors. Tommy Boggs' mother, Lindy, is a Congresswoman from Louisiana; his father, the late Hale Boggs, was House majority leader. Other congressional progeny who as lobbyists have traded on their names for various interests: Speaker Tip O'Neill's son Kip (sugar, beer, cruise ships); Senate Majority Leader Robert Dole's daughter Robin (Century 21 real estate); Senator Paul Laxalt's daughter Michelle (oil, Wall Street, Hollywood); and House Appropriations Committee Chairman Jamie Whitten's son Jamie Jr. (steel, barges, cork).

Then there is so-called soft-core (as opposed to hard-core) lobbying.

Since the real business of Washington is often conducted by night, a whole cottage industry has grown up around the party-giving business. Michael Deaver's wife, Carolyn, is one of half a dozen Washington hostesses who can be hired to set up power parties, which bring top government officials together with private businessmen. "Facilitator" Canzeri puts on charitable events to burnish corporate images, like a celebrity tennis tournament that drew scores of Washington lobbyists and netted $450,000 for Nancy Reagan's antidrug campaign. Lobbyists, not surprisingly, work hard not just at re-electing Congressmen but also at befriending them. Congressman Tony Coelho of California describes the methods of William Cable, a former Carter administration aide who lobbies for Timmons & Co. "Three out of four times," says Coelho, "he talks to you not about lobbying, but about sports, or tennis — I play a lot of tennis with him — or your family. He's a friend, a sincere friend." Congressman Thomas Luken of Ohio is so chummy with lobbyists that he has been known to wave at them from the dais at committee hearings.

Congressmen often find themselves being lobbied by their former colleagues. More than 200 ex-Congressmen have stayed on in the capital to represent interest groups, sometimes lobbying on the same legislation they helped draft while serving in office. Former Congressmen are free to go onto the floor of Congress and into the cloakrooms, though they are not supposed to lobby there. "Well, they don't call it lobbying," shrugs Senator Pryor. "They call it visiting. But you know exactly what they're there for."

Congressional staffers also cash in by selling their expertise and connections. Indeed, members of the House Ways and Means Committee were concerned that the president's tax-reform bill would provoke an exodus of staffers into the lobbying ranks. Their fears were not unfounded: the committee's chief counsel, John Salmon, quit to work as a lobbyist for the law firm of Dewey, Ballantine; James Healey, former aide to Committee Chairman Dan Rostenkowski, quit to join Black, Manafort.

As Congressmen became more independent of committee chairmen and party chieftains, they have tended to listen more to the folks back home. Predictably, however, lobbyists have skillfully found ways to manipulate so-called grass-roots support. Direct-mail outfits, armed with computer banks that are stocked with targeting groups, can create "instant constituencies" for special-interest bills. To repeal a 1982 provision requiring tax withholding on dividends and interest, the small banks and thrifts hired a mass-mailing firm to launch a letter-writing campaign that flooded congressional offices with some 22 million pieces of mail. The bankers' scare tactics were dubious — they managed to convince their depositors that the withholding provision was a tax hike, when in fact it was set up merely to make people pay taxes that they legally owed. But the onslaught worked. Over the objections of President Reagan and most of the congressional leadership, Congress voted overwhelmingly in 1983 to repeal withholding.

Onetime liberal activists who learned grass-roots organizing for such causes as opposition to the Viet Nam War now employ these same techniques on behalf of business clients. Robert Beckel, Walter Mondale's campaign manager in 1984, has set up an organization with the grandiose title of the Alliance to Save the Ocean. Its aim is to stop the burning of toxic wastes at sea. Beckel's fee is being paid by Rollins Environmental Services, a waste-disposal company that burns toxic waste on land.

Grass-roots organizations sometimes collide. Lobbyist Jack Albertine recently established the Coalition to Encourage Privatization. Its public policy purpose: to enable private enterprise to run services now performed by the government. Its more immediate goal: to persuade Congress to sell Conrail to the Norfolk Southern railroad. In the meantime, Anne Wexler has been building the Coalition for a Competitive Conrail, a farm-dominated group pushing for Morgan Guaranty as the prospective purchaser.

Booze, broads, and bribes — what nineteenth-century congressional correspondent Edward Winslow Martin called "the levers of lust" — are no longer the tools of the trade. This is not to say, however, that lobbyists have stopped wining and dining Congressmen and their staffs. Public records indicate that Ways and Means Chairman Rostenkowski spends about as much time playing golf as the guest of lobbyists at posh resorts as he does holding hearings in Washington.

Though it has become more difficult to slip a special-interest bill through Congress in the dead of night, it is not impossible. In 1981, when a group of commodity traders began lobbying for a tax loophole worth $300 million, then Senate Finance Chairman Dole poked fun at the commodity traders on the Senate floor. "They are great contributors. They haven't missed a fund raiser. If you do not pay any taxes, you can afford to go to all the fund raisers." But then commodity PACs and individual traders increased their contributions to Dole's own political action committee from $11,000 in 1981–82 to $70,500 in 1983–84. Dole, engaged in a campaign to become Senate majority leader, badly needed the money (his PAC contributed some $300,000 to 47 of the Senate's 53 Republicans). In a late-night tax-writing session in the summer of 1984, Dole quietly dropped his opposition to the tax break for the commodity traders, and it became law.

Such victories inspire other loophole-seeking businessmen to hire guides through the congressional maze, at any price. There is no shortage of hungry lobbyists ready to relieve them of their money. "You get hustlers in Washington who get hooked up with hustlers outside of Washington, and the money moves very quickly," says Peter Teeley, former press aide to Vice President George Bush and now a Washington PR man. "Some people are getting ripped off." Says Senator Pryor: "Businessmen are very, very naive. It's amazing what they pay these lobbyists. The businessmen panic. They really don't understand Washington."

As one of the most successful lobbyists in town, Bob Gray naturally has his detractors, and they accuse him of overselling businessmen on his ability to solve all their Washington problems with a few phone calls. "Gray is so overrated it's unbelievable," says one U.S. Senator. "He makes a big splash at parties, but his clients aren't getting a lot for their money." Gray insists that he never promises more than he can deliver. But his own clients sometimes grumble that, for a fat fee, they get little more than a handshake from a Cabinet member at a cocktail party.

When the big lobbying guns line up on opposite sides of an issue, they tend to cancel each other out. Threatened with a takeover by Mobil Oil in 1981, Marathon Oil hired Tommy Boggs' firm to push a congressional bill that would block the merger. The firm managed to get the bill through the House by using a little-known procedural rule at a late-night session. In the Senate, however, Mobil — represented by former Carter aide Stuart Eizenstat — was able to stop the bill when Senator Howell Heflin of Alabama blocked consideration on the Senate floor. Heflin is a friend of Mobil Chairman Rawleigh Warner.

"We're getting to the point of lobbylock now," says Lobbyist Carl Nordberg. "There are so many lobbyists here pushing and pulling in so many different directions that, at times, nothing seems to go anywhere." The most pernicious effect of the influence-peddling game may simply be that it consumes so much of a Congressman's working day. Every time a Congressmen takes a PAC check, he is obliged at least to grant the contributor an audience. The IOUs mount up. "Time management is a serious problem," says Frank. "I find myself screening out people who just want to bill their clients for talking to a Congressman." The lobbyists are not unmindful of congressional impatience. Lobbyist Dan Dutko, for instance, has a "five-second rule" — all background documents must be simple enough to be absorbed by a Congressman at the rate of five seconds per page. It is no wonder that Congress rarely takes the time to debate such crucial national security questions as whether the U.S. really needs to build a 600-ship Navy, as the Reagan administration contends; most Congressmen are too preoccupied listening to lobbyists for defense contractors telling them how many jobs building new ships will create back in the district.

In theory at least, there is a partial cure to the growing power of the influence-peddling pack: further limits on campaign expenditures and public financing of elections. But Congress is not likely to vote for these reforms any time soon, in large part because as incumbents they can almost always raise more money than challengers can. Certainly, most Congressmen have become wearily resigned to living with lobbyists. They are sources of money, political savvy, even friendship. In the jaded culture of Washington, influence peddlers are more envied than disdained. Indeed, to lawmakers on the Hill and policymakers throughout the Executive Branch, the feeling increasingly seems to be: well, if you can't beat 'em, join 'em.

Cashing In on Top Connections

After former White House Deputy Chief of Staff Michael Deaver quit last May to become a "public affairs consultant," he drove about town for a while in a dark blue Dodge, very much like the limousines that transport top Executive Branch officials. The car served to get Deaver where he was going in more ways than one: in status-conscious Washington, it was a not-so-subtle reminder of his White House connections. Now Deaver has given up the status symbol of public power for one of private wealth. These days he rides in a chauffeur-driven Jaguar XJ6 equipped with a car phone that keeps him plugged in to some of the highest offices in the land.

The onetime California PR man who followed Ronald Reagan to Washington five years ago has cashed in. As a White House official, he had to moonlight by writing a diet book, while his wife Carolyn, went to work for a PR outfit, throwing parties on behalf of private clients. But now a dozen corporations and foreign countries, including CBS, TWA, South Korea, Singapore, and Canada, pay him annual retainers that are, he says, "in the six figures." This year he should take home around $400,000 — at the White House, his top salary was $70,200.

What makes Deaver so valuable? "There's no question I've got as good access as anybody in town," says Deaver, as he reclines on a couch in his tastefully appointed office overlooking the Lincoln Memorial. Alone among departing White House aides, Deaver was permitted to keep his White House pass. He also still chats regularly on the phone with Nancy Reagan. But Deaver insists that he never discusses his clients' problems with the First Lady or the president. Actually, Deaver says, he does not do much lobbying. Nor does he do any public relations work, or legislative drafting, or direct mail, or polling, or any of the sorts of services performed by most high-powered influence shops. So what exactly does he do?

"Strategic planning," he says somewhat airily. His clients tell him "where they want to be vis-à-vis Washington in three to five years, and I help them develop a plan to get there." In fact, although Deaver is a relative newcomer to Washington, it is hard to think of a lobbyist who has a better sense of how the Reagan administration works or who has more clout among the Reaganauts. And in a city where perception is often reality, Deaver is known as a master imagemaker who kept Reagan's profile high and bright. It is not hard to see why the government of South Korea, under fire for unfair trade practices abroad and repression of political dissidents at home, would want to hire him, even at Deaver's asking price of $1.2 million for a three-year contract. "There's a new breed in Washington," says Canadian Ambassador Allan Gotlieb. "Consultants about consultants." Canada hired Deaver — at $105,000 a year — for "his unique knowledge of how this government works from the inside," says Gotlieb.

There are some who think that Canada got more than gossip and advice from Deaver. Though the former deputy chief of staff was rarely involved in policy details at the White House, the *Washington Post* reports that before he left, he showed surprising interest in the debate over acid rain. It was Deaver who is believed to have persuaded Reagan to accede to the request of the Canadian government for a special commission to investigate the problem and make recommendations. The commission's report, issued in January, called for much stronger measures to reduce acid rain than the administration had previously sought.

Canada was one of the first clients signed up by Deaver. Acting on complaints from Democratic Congressman John Dingell of MIchigan, the General Accounting Office is now investigating Deaver's role for possible conflict of interest. The public official turned private sage dismisses the charges, noting that while he played a role in creating the acid-rain commission, he had nothing to do with its report. "What I did at the White House was part of my public responsibilities. If I'd gone back there after leaving and tried to influence the acid-rain study, that would be a different story. But I really can't understand what the conflict is."

Under the Ethics in Government Act, Deaver is legally barred from discussing private business matters with anyone in the White House for a period of one year after leaving office. "I can't ask the president or anyone in the White House for anything now," he shrugs. Then, brightening, he adds, "I can, starting in May, though."

The Slickest Shop in Town

A lobbyist can perform no greater favor for a lawmaker than to help get him elected. It is the ultimate political IOU, and it can be cashed in again and again. No other firm holds more of this precious currency than the Washington shop known as Black, Manafort.

Legally, there are two firms. Black, Manafort, Stone & Kelly, a lobbying operation, represents Bethlehem Steel, the Tobacco Institute, Herba-life, Angolan "Freedom Fighter" Jonas Savimbi, and the governments of the Bahamas and the Philippines. Black, Manafort, Stone & Atwater, a political-consulting firm, has helped elect such powerful Republican politicians as Senator Phil Gramm of Texas and Senate Agriculture Committee Chairman Jesse Helms.

The political credentials of the partners are imposing. Charles Black, 38, was a top aide to Senator Robert Dole and the senior strategist for President Reagan's re-election campaign in 1984. Paul Manafort, 36, was the political director of the 1984 GOP national convention. Roger Stone, 33, was the Eastern regional campaign director for Reagan in 1984 and is now one of Congressman Jack Kemp's chief political advisers. Peter Kelly, 48, was finance chairman of the Democratic National Committee from 1981 to 1985. Lee Atwater, 34, was Reagan's deputy campaign manager in 1984 and is now Vice President George Bush's chief political adviser. Alone among the firm's partners, Atwater sticks to advising electoral candidates and does not lobby.

The partners of Black, Manafort say that the lobbying and political-consulting functions are kept separate. "It's like a grocery store and a hardware store," insists Black. "You can't buy eggs at a hardware store and you can't buy tires at the grocery." Yet these are but fine distinctions in Washington, where the firm is considered one of the most ambidextrous in the business, the ultimate supermarket of influence peddling. "You are someone's political adviser, then you sell yourself to a corporation by saying you have a special relationship with Congress," says Democratic Media Consultant Robert Squier, who does no lobbying himself. Is it proper to get a politician elected, then turn around and lobby him? "It's a gray area," sidesteps Squier. Charges Fred Wertheimer, president of the public-interest lobbying group Common Cause: "It's institutionalized conflict of interest."

It certainly is good for business. The partners charge six-figure fees to lobby and six-figure fees to manage election campaigns. As a result, they take home six-figure salaries. (Their stated aim is to make $450,000 apiece each year; they are assumed to have achieved it last year.) They unabashedly peddle their access to the Reagan administration. The firm's proposal soliciting the Bahamas as a client, for instance, touted the "personal relationships between State Department officials and Black, Manafort & Stone" that could be "utilized to upgrade a backchannel relationship in the economic and foreign policy spheres."

When Savimbi came to Washington last month to seek support for his guerrilla organization, UNITA, in its struggle against the Marxist regime in Angola, he hired Black, Manafort. What the firm achieved was quickly dubbed "Savimbi chic." Doors swung open all over town for the guerrilla leader, who was dapperly attired in a Nehru suit and ferried about in a stretch limousine. Dole had shown only general interest in Savimbi's cause until Black, the Senate majority leader's former aide, approached him on his client's behalf. Dole promptly introduced a congressional resolution backing UNITA's insurgency and sent a letter to the State Department urging that the U.S. supply it with heavy arms. The firm's fee for such services was reportedly $600,000.

The Black, Manafort partners have woven such an intricate web of connections that the strands become entangled at times. Lobbyist Kelly served as finance chairman of the National Democratic Institute, a public-interest organization established by Congress to promote democracy in underdeveloped countries. The institute recently sent observers to try to ensure a fair election in the Philippines. Yet Kelly's firm, for a reported $900,000 fee, represents Philippine President Ferdinand Marcos, who stands accused of having stolen the vote. Manafort for one sees no conflict. He points out that the firm urged Marcos to try to make the elections more credible to American observers. "What we've tried to do is make it more of a Chicago-style election and not Mexico's," he explained.

As a political firm, Black, Manafort represents Democrats and Republicans alike — and sometimes candidates running for the same seat. Kelly, for instance, is doing some fund raising for Democratic Senate candidates John Breaux in Louisiana, Bob Graham in Florida and Patrick Leahy in Vermont. Atwater and Black are consultants for the Republican opponents in these contests. In the race for the 1988 Republican presidential nomination, Atwater advises Bush, while Stone advises Kemp. Stone and Atwater's offices are right across the hall from each other, prompting one congressional aide to ask facetiously, "Why have primaries for the nomination? Why not have the candidates go over to Black, Manafort & Stone and argue it out?"

Stone and Atwater present a contrast in styles. Stone, who practices the hardball politics he first learned as an aide to convicted Watergate co-conspirator Charles Colson, fancies $400 suits and lawn parties. With his heavy-lidded eyes and frosty demeanor, he openly derides Atwater's client, Vice President Bush, as a "weenie." Atwater, an impish "good ole boy" from South Carolina, wears jeans and twangs an electric guitar. Both, however, drive Mercedes.

For all its diverse interests, the firm remains "loyal to the president," says Black. "We would never lobby against Star Wars, for example." The firm has nonetheless attacked the president's tax-reform bill on behalf of corporate clients seeking to preserve their loopholes, and it did not hesitate to lobby for quotas on shoe imports on behalf of the Footwear Industries of America, even though Reagan strongly opposed the bill as protectionist. And at times the firm does show some selectivity. A few years back, it turned down Libya's Muammar Qaddafi as a client.

POLITICAL ACTION COMMIT-
tees (PACs) are arms of interest
groups that receive voluntary
contributions from group members and
in turn give money, within the limits
allowed by the campaign finance laws,
to political candidates. The law permits
PACs to contribute a total of $10,000 to
a political candidate, $5,000 each for
the primary and general election campaigns. There are no limits upon *indirect*
PAC expenditures in behalf of political
candidates.

PACs are a perfectly legitimate, indeed legally sanctioned, part of the political process. The campaign finance
laws of the 1970s which Congress
passed to reduce the influence of interest
group money in congressional and presidential elections, allowed and even encouraged groups to create PACs while
restricting the political contributions
they could make. Interest groups of all
kinds, taking their cue from Congress
itself, began to create PACs in the mid-
1970s to collect money and channel it to
congressional candidates and, in the
pre-convention stage, presidential aspirants. Because presidential elections are
federally financed, the influence of PAC
money is mostly felt in congressional
elections.

The pros and cons of PACs have been
hotly debated. Supporters argue that
they are nothing more than an extension
of a legitimate and healthy interest group
process. The tight restriction on contributions to political candidates limit the
influence of PAC money. While single
contributions are small, PAC contributions collectively help to finance congressional campaigns in an era of increased costs that would otherwise place
severe financial burdens on candidates.

Critics charge that PAC money cor-
rupts the political process by giving dis-
proportionate weight in Congress to
special interests. The public interest
group Common Cause has declared a
"War on PACs," charging that Congress
has become a special-interest outpost.
Particularly sinister in the view of Common Cause leaders is the fact that PAC
donations are made mostly to congressional incumbents, strengthening
the political and special-interest status
quo. As a result, Common Cause argues,
Congress becomes an entrenched political institution, unresponsive to the people and the public interest.

The following selection describes the
interplay between congressional candidates — incumbents and challengers
alike, and PAC managers whose influence over campaign financing is
steadily increasing.

8

Tom Watson
PAC PILGRIMAGE BECOMES
CANDIDATES' RITUAL

Though congressional candidates talk passionately about someday coming to Washington, many of them are already spending a lot time here stalking one of the capital's corridors of power — Political Action Committees (PACs).

For months now, congressional contenders from across the country have been trooping to Washington in search of PAC contributions they hope will help pave the way to victory.

This pilgrimage has become an integral part of running for Congress in recent years, as challengers and open-seat contenders have come to view PACs as vital to their political welfare.

Consultants and professional fund-raisers have helped promote the pilgrimage by peddling opportunities for access to the PAC community. They are finding an increasing number of candidates eager for their services.

Candidates make their journeys in the face of daunting odds. According to a Federal Election Commission study released last May, incumbents sopped up 72 percent of all PAC contributions made during the 1983–84 election cycle. Challengers to incumbents attracted only 16 percent of all PAC money, while candidates for open seats netted 11 percent. Most PACs have been showing decidedly pro-incumbent tendencies for many years (Figure 1).

What little money political action committees do invest in non-incumbents often is funneled to a small coterie of top-flight contenders who are strongly favored to win. PAC managers who amass a poor won-lost record know that they will be required to account for their defeats by a hostile board of directors. As a result, they are extremely wary of taking risks.

Beating Down the Doors

But if candidates realize the problems they face in trying to tap the Washington PAC community, one would not know it from the way they behave. The number of candidates making the Washington pilgrimage seems to be growing with each election cycle, as they eagerly compete for a slice of the PAC pie.

"Nearly everybody comes through here," says Bernadette Budde, political strategist for the Business-Industry Political Action Committee (BIPAC), one of the country's most influential corporate PACs. "Some-

From *Congressional Quarterly Weekly Report,* Vol. 44, No. 12, pp. 655–659 (March 22, 1986). Reprinted by permission.

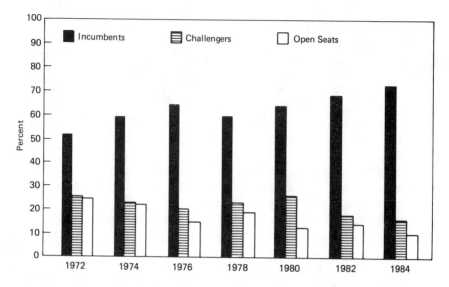

Figure 1. PAC contributions to congressional candidates. *Sources:* Federal Election Commission, Common Cause.

times even after I've told them that we have consistently supported the incumbent, they still want to come by."

Tom Baker, vice president for political affairs for the National Association of Home Builders (NAHB), concurs. "Frankly," Baker says, "it's hard to keep most of them out of town."

Candidates not only are showing up in Washington in increasing numbers; they are showing up earlier and earlier with each passing campaign. Far from being a biennial event, the Washington pilgrimage often begins immediately after Election Day for a contest two years down the road.

"We started seeing 1986 candidates in 1984." said one analyst for a health association PAC. "We view it as a two-year process. . . . It's a fulltime job."

"There's a parade that starts in September of the off-year," echoes Al Jackson, political director for the liberal-minded National Committee for an Effective Congress (NCEC). "It can be a revolving door some days."

Washington is not the only place to which candidates travel in search of PAC money. Houston and Los Angeles are prominent among the other cities that are emerging as important PAC centers. But Washington still is regarded as the symbolic and financial capital of the PAC world.

"There are PACs in other places," said Baker of the NAHB, whose Build PAC gave more money to federal candidates than all but two other political action committees during the 1983–84 cycle. "But Washington . . . is the mecca. This is the mother lode."

"I recognize that I'm going to have to have financial help from Washington," says Indiana state Senator Jim Jontz, the likely Democratic nominee for retiring GOP Representative Elwood Hillis' House seat. "I'm committed to spending time seeking it. . . . It's a part of the process I have to pursue."

Value of the Visits

While it is clear that a desire to collect campaign cash is the major reason candidates come to Washington to visit PACs, there are other potential benefits from such journeys that may not be as apparent. The PAC pilgrimage affords candidates an opportunity to test their political appeal before a critical, seasoned audience. It also gives them valuable practice at trying to raise funds — practice that could pay off when they return home.

Some candidates feel that a trip to Washington can help them convince PAC managers they are serious about their race.

"I think making the trip shows that your're really . . . committed to your campaign," says Minnesota state Senator Collin C. Peterson, a Democrat who has decided to challenge Republican Representative Arlan Stangeland again after losing his initial bid in 1984. "If you don't go to Washington . . . it sends a negative signal. They expect you to make the trip."

Candidates also may gain an intangible sense of purpose and excitement from visiting the capital that fires their imaginations — and their campaigns.

"There may be some deep psychological reasons why a candidate has to come to Washington to feel that he is a real candidate." say BIPAC's Budde. "They may have been told by people who have been elected . . . 'Once you come and see the Capitol at night, and see your party heroes in action on the floor, you may never feel the same again.' They may need the charge that they get out of being here. The search for dollars may be secondary."

Weeding Out the Dogs

PAC managers, too, can benefit from the pilgrimage. It often provides the only chance they get to develop a firsthand feel for contenders they have known only through press clippings, poll numbers and other analysts' remarks.

"I think a lot of people in this business are like me," said David Michael Staton, a former House Republican from West Virginia (1981–83) who now heads the political-action programs for the U.S. Chamber of Commerce. "They like to look and see and evaluate candidates from firsthand. The guy may have great numbers, but he may be a nerd."

By meeting personally with a particular candidate, PAC managers say, they stand a better chance of keeping track of that contender's campaign. With a field of hundreds of candidates for federal office, that is no easy task.

"If you're a challenger, you've got to come — and more than once," says the NCEC's Jackson. "You've got to come and make sure that everyone sees your name and your face a lot . . . so that we remember who you are. There are too many races, too many candidates for us to keep track of it unless you keep your name in front of us."

"They get the challengers mixed up," echoes GOP consultant Terry Cooper, who also has worked as director of a corporate PAC. "They're going to forget whether that neat story they heard was about you in Oregon or about somebody who is running against somebody with a similar name in Missouri."

Secrets to Success

A variety of factors determine whether candidates succeed when they solicit funds from the Washington PAC community, but a surprising number of those factors are already decided before candidates arrive in town.

At a fundamental level, candidates strengthen their case if they are committed to waging a campaign before they come looking for money. A potentially strong contender arguably should face no penalty for visiting a PAC director in the course of deciding whether to run. But in practice, it often does not work out that way.

"We see some candidates who aren't even candidates," laments Budde, expressing irritation at being used as a sounding board for a prospective campaign. "I don't understand why they come to me to get my opinion about whether they should run. At the very least, they should have decided and announced. We don't like making decisions based on shadows and phantoms."

Many challengers also misuse time and resources trying to get money from PACs that have a strong record of support for the incumbents the contenders hope to unseat.

"There's no point in bringing a guy up here against an incumbent with a 90 percent voting record on our issues, the kind of guy we've mixed with," warns the NAHB's Baker. "Those records are all available. . . . That's something someone could find out in advance and save the guy a trip."

"It's not only a bad use of time," Baker continues, "it's also not good for a candidate's morale. . . . I've had guys who go through the drill with me and then ask how to get to the next association . . . where I know they're going to get exactly the same thing. My God, by the end of the day this guy is going to be totally depressed."

Primaries: Peril or Promise?

Many PAC managers also have a tendency to avoid candidates who are involved in crowded or difficult primaries. Most PACs are leery of being on the losing side of an intraparty battle, so they steer clear of primaries until one candidate emerges as the likely nominee.

Freshman Republican Representative John G. Rowland of Connecticut learned that lesson in a painful way during his 1984 challenge to Democratic Representative William R. Ratchford. "When I went down to Washington, I didn't have the nomination yet," Rowland recalls. "I had 25 appointments, a poll under my arm, but no nomination. I got zero out of those visits. It was a total waste of time and money."

There is, however, an important exception to that rule. Directors of ideologically oriented PACs are much more likely than their corporate or labor colleagues to enter a primary if they find a candidate who is a clear philosophical ally.

"We use two criteria," says Jackson of the liberal NCEC. "One is that there is a clear philosophical difference between the two candidates involved. That involves both primaries and generals. The second criteria is that the race is marginal and winnable."

That policy also applies to ideological PACs on the conservative side. Jim Ellis, who until late last year worked as assistant director of the Free Congress PAC (affiliated with the Committee for the Survival of a Free Congress), said his organization also was willing to foray into a primary for an ideologically compatible candidate because "philosophical commitment for us is No. 1."

Naive Need Not Apply

Perhaps the most decisive event in a candidate's PAC pilgrimage takes place behind the PAC manager's door. There a congressional hopeful faces the same kind of pressure to make a favorable impression that is felt by an anxious applicant interviewing with a potential employer.

"You've got to know what you're talking about, and you've got to come across well . . . the simplest things you'd think a candidate would know to have," says Denis Calabrese, vice president of Southern Political Consulting, a Texas-based Republican firm. "But an amazing number of candidates walk into their first PAC meeting without having their act down."

A good performance at that meeting can help a candidate establish credibility and spread interest in his campaign throughout the PAC community. A bad showing can effectively shut a candidate out of PAC money.

"They have to convince the PAC money that they are viable," says Gary Nordlinger, head of a consulting firm that caters to a Democratic clientele. "Most of them lose it right there."

Adds Calabrese, "You've got to say, 'I'm politically sophisticated and I'm not charging at windmills here.' You've got to be able to go in there and talk about streets and counties. You can buy yourself so many points if you're not naive."

"Just the Facts, Mister"

PAC managers also agree that political naiveté on the part of the candidates is a recurrent problem that damages their chances of establishing credibility. Too often contenders cite broad partisan trends and offer shallow political complaints in lieu of a developed case for their candidacy.

"If you come in and say, 'I could beat Teddy Kennedy because he has not voted the way the people of Massachusetts think,' . . . I'm going to say I'm interested in seeing this happen, but how will it take place?" says the Chamber's Staton. "You're going to have to come up with some pretty concrete evidence to back up what you've got to say, or no one is going to pay much attention to your campaign."

"But if you come in with the right information . . .," Staton continues, "about how you're going to win this race, how you're going to take the resources, what you're going to do in fund raising, what's your campaign plan. . . . If you spell out what you're going to do, then you're going to impress a lot of people."

PAC managers say a candidate can build credibility by presenting poll results, a realistic budget, an assessment of an opponent's vulnerabilities, and names of prominent political and financial supporters back home.

Keep Those Cards and Letters Coming

A successful PAC pilgrimage seldom ends with a single visit. By supplying a steady barrage of updated poll results, press releases and newspaper clippings, a candidate can keep the PAC community abreast of his progress and reinforce PAC interest in the campaign. PAC fund raising has become, as one consultant put it, "almost a constant public relations job."

Michigan Republican Representative Bill Schuette demonstrated his understanding of that law of PAC politics in his successful 1984 challenge to three-term Democrat Donald J. Albosta.

"The key thing is follow-up," Schuette reflects. "I would do a personal follow-up: letters, notes, newsletters, and press clips to let them know that you have something ongoing. In that respect, it's no different than when you're going after votes. I would go back to individuals time and time again, saying, 'I need your support.' Sometimes, approaching the PAC community is a similar process."

GOP consultant Cooper also sees similarities between the campaign a candidate undertakes for PAC money and the one he wages for votes back home. "You've got to keep hitting the PACs with material that establishes an identity. Nobody thinks of [the need to establish] name identification in the PAC community. But there is such a thing as name ID in the PAC community. You've really got to get it."

Great Expectations

Those who counsel candidates about PAC fund raising often urge them to temper their expectations about what their PAC pilgrimage will bring. Challengers and open-seat contenders who think a PAC visit pays big monetary dividends up front are in for a big shock.

"Candidates arrive here thinking that they're going to get $1 million just because they're wonderful, special, and running," says Nordlinger, who advises Democratic campaigns. "They are running to be 1/435th of one-half of one-third of the U.S. government. Yet somehow they think that they're a man of destiny at the moment of destiny and that the coffers will open and millions will roll into their war chest. . . . There's kind of a rude awakening."

Some candidates apparently are unaware of the pro-incumbent bias most PACs maintain; others misunderstand the limits governing the legal amount a PAC can contribute. Under the Federal Election Campaign Act, PACs can give $5,000 to a candidate in any primary, runoff, or general election.

Still others fail to make a distinction between the different kinds of aid offered a candidate by different kinds of political committees. Most corporate and labor PACs make financial contributions as well as so-called "in-kind" contributions — assistance of an organizational or technical nature.

For the ideological PACs, however, in-kind contributions usually are the rule. "We very rarely do any financial contributing," said Ellis of the conservative Free Congress PAC. "We might pay for a staff member on a candidate's staff to run the organization. . . . If they have a specific action, we might give cash for that. But the field man would make sure it goes for a specific project — manning phone banks, paying to install phones, that type of thing."

Jackson of the liberal NCEC buttresses that point. "NCEC doesn't just give cash," he says. "In fact, we'd rather not give money away. We do services better than we do money."

Heard It Through the Grapevine

If candidates often overestimate the amount of money they will receive from their Washington forays, they often underestimate how much their requests for money are influenced by communication within the PAC community. The conversation between one PAC director and another about a candidate may be crucial to that candidate's chances of receiving PAC support.

Pennsylvania Democrat Joe Hoeffel, who is seeking to avenge his 1984 loss to GOP Representative Lawrence Coughlin, has learned that the Washington PAC community acts as a network. "I was advised," Hoeffel says, "that the PACs in Washington are . . . somewhat inbred. They talk to themselves."

By landing a PAC's endorsement, a candidate assures himself access to that PAC grapevine. Through regular meetings, "meet-and-greet" sessions with candidates and other informal contact, members of the Washington PAC community share their lists of contenders who are strong and incumbents who are in trouble.

"These lists are the key to all of this," says Jackson. "Nobody gives away without looking at somebody's list."

Some PAC directors urge candidates to use their endorsement as a way of courting other PAC support. "We ask you to carry [our endorsement] with you as entree," says Staton of the Chamber of Commerce. "Because if people have confidence in us as an organization and feel that we've done good work in analyzing your race, then you won't have to work as hard to convince them to . . . help you."

Support for a candidate also can spread through the PAC community via the national parties, which have become an increasingly vital link between PACs and campaigns. PAC managers of all stripes say both national party organizations generally provide good intelligence about challengers and open-seat candidates — as well as coaching contenders about how to win support from PACs.

The national parties' attitude toward a challenger often helps PAC managers decide whether or not to recommend committing support.

"You need to get the NRCC [National Republican Congressional Committee] to run around saying, 'This is a great race; this is a targeted race; we need this race,' " said Calabrese. "PACs don't say, 'OK, the NRCC has targeted this race, so we should support.' What they say is, 'That guy got the NRCC to target; therefore that guy convinced the NRCC of the same thing he convinced me of — that he's got his act together, that he's got a plan, that he's a viable contender.' "

Fund Raising in Reverse

Candidates who do not find themselves on PAC support lists should not abandon hope. An increasing number of contenders are taking advantage of a defensive strategy toward PACs.

Courting PACs that are unlikely to give to a challenger's campaign can prove profitable — if the challenger can convince the PAC to remain neutral or scale back support for the incumbent. Consultant Cooper calls this process "negative fund raising."

"In negative fund raising . . . you don't expect a nickel from anybody you send a communication to," says Cooper. "You're just trying to shut the opposition down."

"What you have to do is go out and be the salesman for the other side," Cooper continues. "Point out that, really, the incumbent is not a good bet — based on issues, winnability or otherwise."

GOP Representative Pat Swindall of Georgia, who won his suburban Atlanta House seat by ousting veteran Democrat Elliott H. Levitas in 1984, is quite familiar with negative fund raising.

Much of my objective in coming to Washington," Swindall said of his 1984 PAC trips, "was not so much to raise money, but to minimize the contributions PACs gave to my opponent. If you can't get their PAC dollars, at least minimize their impact on your race."

"You'd certainly rather have the cash," echoed Missouri Republican Carrie Francke, who hopes to reverse the outcome of her unsuccessful 1984 challenge to Democratic Representative Harold L. Volkmer. "But if you can make a presentation to a PAC and influence them so they think it's questionable who will win — and so stay out of it — you've benefited your campaign."

Democrats also play the negative fund-raising game. "You've still got to go around to the Republican-oriented PACs, if for no other reason than to neutralize them or to keep their contributions lower," said Nordlinger, whose firm is advising Jontz' bid for the open 5th District in Indiana.

No Place Like Home?

While there is little argument that the Washington pilgrimage has become an institution in congressional campaigns, not everyone agrees that this is a positive development. A significant number of PAC directors feel that many candidates place too much emphasis on Washington — when they should be tending to PACs' local constituencies back home.

BIPAC's Budde is a prominent member of that camp. "I firmly believe that a good candidate with the right support from the local business community never has to leave the district in order to raise PAC money."

She places special emphasis on local support. Budde says that BIPAC's decision to back a challenger is influenced heavily by the level of support that candidate enjoys among members of his district's corporate community. The trip to Washington, she says, takes a back seat.

"They all have it backwards," Budde says. "They think that they come to Washington first . . . then they go back home and do all the rest of the stuff. But the real action is back home. . . . We're a lot more interested in how it plays in Peoria than how does it play in Washington."

Budde cites Connecticut's Rowland as one 1984 challenger who played the PAC game correctly. Following a rocky first trip to Washington in early spring of the election year, Rowland decided to steer clear of the PAC community and concentrate on cultivating elements closer to home.

"In essence . . . I didn't go back down to Washington," says Rowland. "I just realized that all I needed was some good people. I didn't need a bunch of fancy consultants and fancy polls. What I needed to do was go to supermarkets and win votes."

Rowland's analysis may sound like wishful thinking to challengers facing the rigors of raising money against an entrenched incumbent. But his strategy of courting local business backing did help him attract BIPAC's attention.

Impressed with Rowland's support in the local business community, Budde says that BIPAC gave him a better-than-average campaign contribution in 1984 — even though she did not meet him until roughly a year after the election.

Not all of Budde's PAC colleagues share her militant attitude toward the Washington pilgrimage. But there is widespread agreement that by sowing seeds at home, a candidate vastly enhances his chances of reaping benefits from Washington PACs.

"You always have to struggle to convince candidates that they must raise . . . most of their money in their districts," said a political analyst working with a labor PAC. "They look at you like you're crazy. PACs are everything to them."

"I cannot envision a House race in which any of my clients — and they are all non-incumbents — is ever going to get more than 30 percent of his budget from PACs," said Cooper. "It would be folly for me to say, 'Focus on 30 percent and ignore the 70 percent.' "

WASHINGTON IS THE MAGnet city for political power seekers. It is the Super Bowl of politics, attracting players and spectators from every part of the nation and around the world. Playing the game of Washington politics is a constantly exciting and often rewarding experience.

The Washington political establishment is a closely knit fraternity. Congressmen, bureaucrats, and lobbyists not only know each other but also frequently strive for the same goals. All ambitious members of the political establishment seek to establish their reputations for power. On Capitol Hill, power translates into money for campaign chests, better prospects for reelection, and respect from colleagues. The bureaucrats with a reputation for power have a better chance of withstanding the frequently changing political winds. Lobbyists who can convince their clients that they have power can charge higher fees.

An effective lobbying style maintains the appearance of power. Who the lobbyist is, and what his or her connections may be, are an important part of that appearance. Former members of Congress and their aides often find that lobbying can be an extremely lucrative career, enabling them to stay in Washington and continue to play the game of politics. Former Congressman Dan Kuykendall (R., Tenn.) commented, "A former U.S. Congressman, no matter how capable, is worth more in Washington than any place else — considerably more. Even those members who go to law firms back home end up getting sent back to Washington."[1] The same could be said for former congressional staffers.

The following selection describes the style of a leading Washington lobbyist, Thomas Boggs, Jr., the son of a former congressman and an unsuccessful candidate for Congress himself. Over the years, Boggs has built a reputation for power that enabled him to rise from a $12,000-a-year associate to a $500,000-a-year partner in what has become one of Washington's largest law firms.

Albert R. Hunt
THE WASHINGTON POWER BROKERS

Patton, Boggs, and Blow, one of the capital's fastest-growing law firms, is known as a "full-service lobbying firm."

It represents a multitude of conservative clients ranging from the Business Roundtable to right-wing Guatemalan businessmen. Simultaneously, the firm's most celebrated partner, Thomas H. Boggs, Jr., is

[1]*Congressional Quarterly Weekly Report,* December 27, 1980, p. 3643.

raising campaign funds for some of the most liberal lawmakers in Congress. Over the past fifteen months, the firm has hired two top political operatives of the 1980 presidential campaign: One worked for Ted Kennedy and the other for Ronald Reagan.

"The Boggs firm," one Washington insider says, "looks more like a fusion government than a law firm."

Although some senior partners try to play down this wheeling-and-dealing image, it is these well-advertised political connections that keep clients coming in droves. "You don't hire Patton, Boggs, and Blow because of their legal expertise," says James Mooney, the executive director of the National Cable Television Association. "You hire them because they have good connections with a broad spectrum" of Congress. This reputation attracts such contradictory clients as General Motors Corp., Chrysler Corp., and the Automobile Import Dealers Association.

Although the firm has eighty-two lawyers here, it usually is known as the "Boggs firm." At age forty-one, Tommy Boggs, son of the late Democratic Majority Leader Hale Boggs and Democratic Representative Corrine (Lindy) Boggs of Louisiana, is one of the capital's most powerful lobbyists.

Mr. Boggs makes about $500,000 a year and recently increased his fee to $250 an hour from $225. He is widely credited with playing a major role in congressional approval of the Chrysler bailout bill a few years ago and always seems to be active in special-interest tax legislation, including the tax-leasing provision enacted last year.

There are thousands of lobbyists trying to influence policy in Washington ranging from the proverbial, single-issue "little old ladies in tennis shoes" to well-heeled corporate influence brokers. In addition to law firms, the most successful influence brokers these days include public-relations practitioners, registered agents for foreign governments, and corporate representatives.

Despite the Reagan administration's pledge to reduce regulation and the size of government, the political climate never has seemed better for many of these special-interest pleaders. While some regulatory activities, such as antitrust, may be drying up a bit at some law firms here, any decline is more than offset for many lobbying operations by increased activity in other areas, such as taxes and defense. Money, specifically campaign contributions, is the fuel that generates much of this lobbying prowess. "I won't even take a client now unless he's willing to set up a political action committee and participate in the [campaign donations] process," Robert McCandless, a lobbyist, says. Although Mr. Boggs and some others won't go that far publicly, a major asset clearly is their ability to funnel funds to politicians from clients and friends.

Tommy Boggs is widely seen as the prototype of the high-powered Washington lobbyist. The affable, moon-faced, and slightly paunchy Mr. Boggs is very bright, inordinately savvy, and genuinely engaging. He also is cunning, calculating, and seemingly devoid of any real moral compass, driven mainly by money and success.

In short, Tommy Boggs is a nonmalicious, Washington version of TV's J. R. Ewing.

Mr. Boggs uses more soft-sell sophistication than hard-line pressure, and he shows keen awareness of the political process, especially in the House. "Tommy combines an enormous sense of the way things work with an understanding of where power is and where money is in this town," says Representative Thomas Downey of New York, a liberal Democrat on the House Ways and Means Committee and a beneficiary of Mr. Boggs's fund-raising talents.

Mr. Boggs and his firm have their critics, too. "The Boggs firm, in representing legitimate special interests, contributes to the fragmentation of things," says David Cohen, a former president of Common Cause, the self-styled citizens' lobby. "But unlike the big, prestigious law firms of the past, there's no evidence they play much part in helping government put things back together." And Joan Claybrook, who oversees the Ralph Nader operations here, says: "Some attorneys or lobbyists have a reputation of trying to persuade their clients to do the right thing. Nobody ever says that about Tommy Boggs."

Mr. Boggs isn't comfortable talking about what he hopes to contribute to society or about his political philosophy. But criticism doesn't appear to affect the effervescent lobbyist very much. He says, with a big smile, "I really enjoy playing the game."

He certainly works hard for his clients. He is always prowling the corridors of Congress, talking with members and picking up political intelligence. Some weeks he goes to as many as ten political receptions. "I'll go to two a night if one is for a Ways and Means Committee guy and the other is for defense types," he says. But "it's useless to go to two Ways and Means things," he adds.

That constant motion and energy have honed keen instincts for what motivates politicians. A few years ago, he was helping Marathon Oil Co. fight a move to lower duties on some imported specialty steel that competed against a Marathon subsidiary. He first won over liberal Representative Charles Rangel, a Harlem Democrat, with the argument that some of the imports would come from apartheid South Africa. Then he won over a conservative, the late Representative William Ketchum, with the argument that the Marathon subsidiary was based in the congressman's California district. Mr. Boggs still delights in thinking about this left-right coalition.

And he seems omnipresent. When Jimmy Carter was president, a meeting to plot strategy for a "tax reform" bill was held at the White House. Suddenly, Tom Boggs walked into the session. "I almost fell out of my chair," recalls Robert Brandon, a veteran liberal lobbyist on tax measures. Then, Mr. Boggs, others speculate, was able both to talk about his access to the White House and also to advise business clients what the "enemy" was up to.

Mr. Boggs's reputation is probably exaggerated. He does lose sometimes. Last year, his lobbying on behalf of the cable-TV industry was a decided failure in the Senate. And some congressional aides contend that although he gets much of the credit for the Chrysler bailout measures and some tax breaks, most of the real work was done by others.

Nevertheless, as the belief grows that Tom Boggs can make things happen on Capitol Hill, clients come to the firm specifically for his services. William McGowan, the chairman of MCI Communications Corp., recently insisted that Mr. Boggs personally lobby on the company's behalf before MCI would retain the firm. MCI hired the Boggs firm, one communications expert says, not because of any expertise in that area but because "they wanted the biggest rainmaker they could get."

Money Crucial

It's hard to overestimate the importance of money to all this. Mr. Boggs started off with an advantage — he inherited his father's majority leader's campaign fund in 1973 and, with an eye to his own lobbying interests, doled out more than $60,000 over several elections. Now, he gives the maximum legal limit of $25,000 every two years.

More important, however, he funnels much larger amounts of money to strategically situated lawmakers. Six years ago, he advised the American Trial Lawyers Association to start a political action committee as part of its effort to beat federal no-fault insurance legislation. Now, Mr. Boggs and a representative of a Republican lobbyist, William Timmons, advise the lawyers every election on how to dish out some $500,000 from that PAC to congressional candidates.

Mr. Boggs persuaded Chrysler to give to such Democrats as Representative Tony Coelho, the Californian who now heads the House Democratic Campaign Committee. And he gets his clients to contribute regularly to various Democratic party functions. "Some of these clients are getting had," one Capitol Hill insider charges. "They're giving the money, but Tommy is getting the credit."

Network of Lobbyists

Mr. Boggs also has a network of other Washington lobbyists that he calls on. For example, in trying to raise money for Representative Fortney Stark, a liberal Californian on the House Ways and Means Committee, Mr. Boggs is seeking $250 each from a list of three dozen lobbyists. "I hit these guys, and I know they'll come back and hit me up," he notes.

He goes to great lengths to keep this network flowing. Shortly after Tosco Inc., the big oil-shale concern, received a $1.1 billion federal loan guarantee last year, its representatives started getting solicitations to Mr. Boggs's fund raisers and other political activities. A short while later, Patton, Boggs, and Blow started lobbying with Tosco to get its legal business.

When Mr. Boggs deals with a member of Congress legislatively, though, he is the consummate professional. "Tom Boggs never embarrasses me; he never pushes me to vote for something that would be impossible for me to support," Representative Rangel says. But other politicians acknowledge that Mr. Boggs's fund raising gives him special access, and some say they are inclined to give him the benefit of the doubt on some legislative matters.

Family Ties

Mr. Boggs has come a long way since he joined the law firm sixteen years ago. "When Tommy was first around, everybody thought he was just using his family connections," says his law partner, James O'Hara, who then was a Michigan congressman. After his father died in a 1972 plane crash, it was Tommy, on behalf of the family, who gave Tip O'Neill the green light to run for House Democratic majority leader. His mother succeeded his father in Congress. (This year, a sister, Barbara Sigmund, is running for Congress from New Jersey.)

Tommy Boggs himself ran unsuccessfully for a suburban Maryland House seat in 1970 but says electoral politics is out of his system: "I couldn't afford it." His senior partner, James Patton, thinks that the youthful super-lobbyist aspires to be chairman of a major corporation or secretary of defense someday.

Patton, Boggs, and Blow was started twenty years ago by Mr. Patton, a succsssful international lawyer with the city's most established law firm, Covington and Burling. He hired Tom Boggs, "for $10,000 or $12,000 a year," he recalls. The fifty-three-year-old Mr. Patton has directed the firm's enormous growth. A decade ago, the firm had a dozen lawyers; sometime this year, it expects to exceed one hundred attorneys.

Clients number anywhere from four hundred to five hundred, Mr. Patton says, though many are short-term customers. Steady, major clients range from the Mars candy company to Reader's Digest and Northwest Energy Corp. to the state of Louisiana. And yet Patton, Boggs, and Blow (Mr. Boggs became a partner in 1967) isn't considered, among lawyers at least, a top-flight legal firm. Last year, one of its partners left because he wanted to practice substantive tax law instead of always lobbying.

Areas of Expertise

This reputation may be a bit of a bum rap. The firm now has large sections for litigation, international law, administrative practices, and energy. Senior partners say more than 80 percent of their work doesn't involve lobbying.

Still, the political presence of Mr. Boggs and others is ever evident. It is hardly a secret, for instance, that the firm's foreign clients — including retainers of $100,000 a year from the government of Oman and $60,000 from Amigos del Pais, the Guatemalan business group — are based on political connections and not geopolitical expertise. Although the Guatemalan group's chief interest is to spruce up the image here of that country's military dictatorship, Mr. Boggs says he believes that the businessmen are a "moderating influence" and adds that for philosophical reasons his firm wouldn't represent the right-wing government itself.

In keeping with the recent trend in Washington, the firm's lobbying operations have a distinctly bipartisan coloration. The Democratic side is led by Mr. Boggs, former Congressman O'Hara, former Senator William Hathaway of Maine, and Ronald Brown, a former deputy chairman of the Democratic National Committee and a top adviser to Senator Edward M. Kennedy's 1980 presidential campaign.

The Republican Side

The Republican services are no slouches, either. They include Ernest Christian, a top tax official in the Nixon administration; Cliff Massa, a former high official at the National Association of Manufacturers; William Colley, a former American Medical Association lobbyist, and Frank Donatelli, who was hired after the 1980 elections, in which he ran the Midwestern-states campaign for Ronald Reagan.

"This political smorgasbord of lawyers," Mr. Patton argues, "gives our clients the whole spectrum of thinking in this town. . . . It can be very exciting and very stimulating."

It also can be very effective politically. For instance, Representative Barber Conable, the ranking Republican on the House Ways and Means Committee, says he has met Mr. Boggs only "once or twice, and I don't think he has ever been to my office." But asked about Mr. Boggs's partner, Mr. Christian, the New York lawmaker says, "Oh, Ernie is a fine fellow. I talk to him all the time."

Privately, Mr. Boggs also apparently believes that someone with Democratic connections can lobby more effectively for business interests than someone with GOP ties. "Republicans usually vote with you anyway" one corporate lobbyist says. "So Tommy knows he has most of them, and every time he gets a Democrat, particularly a liberal, that's icing on the cake."

Mr. Boggs also sees benefits from the firm's contradictory mix of clients. "With our client list we can build a minicoalition on almost any issue," he declares. A good example, he says, is the controversial tax leasing provision passed by Congress last year. During consideration of the bill, the firm's leverage on Capitol Hill was increased because the firm represented major retailers, which are potential buyers of tax-leasing plans, and Chrysler, a potential seller.

The firm admits that client interests aren't always the same. But it notes that it represents diverse customers on separate issues; Chrysler on the bailout and tax issues, GM on the Clean Air Act, and import-auto dealers on trade legislation. As for the appearance of conflict of interest in some fields, Timothy May, a senior partner, says: "I've wondered about some of this myself, but we've talked to the clients and they don't see it as a problem."

Neither does Mr. Boggs. He enjoys high-powered lobbying and thinks that in time it may bring respectability as well as money and power. "In recruiting, a few years ago, it was a real disadvantage to say you were a firm that lobbied; we hid it," he says. "But now, it's a recruiting asset. The kids love it. They call lobbying public-policy law."

THE REVEREND JERRY FALWELL seemed to burst upon the political scene in 1980 leading the disciplined, charging army of the Moral Majority to the polls to elect candidates who supported the fundamentalist Christian positions on a variety of issues. The evangelical community had been politically apathetic, but Falwell and other evangelists exhorted their flocks to join together to make their religious principles a beacon for political leaders at all levels of government. As the 1980 elections approached, Falwell told the four thousand worshipers who packed his Thomas Road Baptist Church in Lynchburg, Virginia, "The moralists in America have had enough. We are joining hands together for the changing, the rejuvenating of a nation."[1]

For Falwell, rejuvenating the nation required the injection of Christian morality, as he defined it, into public policy. The Moral Majority strongly opposed abortion, and supported voluntary prayers in public schools. Falwell and his movement also attacked the Equal Rights Amendment, homosexuality and gay rights, and pornography, all of which the fundamentalist leaders believe undermine the security, integrity, and central role of the family in society.

As a Southerner, Falwell was well acquainted with the civil rights movement of the 1960s, which had increased the political power of blacks by encouraging them to register and vote. Somewhat belatedly, Falwell took a leaf from the political notebook of Martin Luther King, Jr., and other civil rights leaders when he conducted massive voter registration campaigns among his followers, an estimated 21 million of the faithful.

Outside of his luxurious, church-supported white-columned mansion in Lynchburg, Falwell prefers three-piece polyester suits, but within the grounds of his estate he often works in a bathing suit beside his Olympic-sized pool. Adjacent to the pool is a recording studio where he tapes the "Old-Time Gospel Hour," his Sunday service, which is carried by 681 TV and radio stations.

The Moral Majority, like the New Right, represents a rising conservative tide in American politics. Both the presidential and congressional elections of 1980 appeared to reflect the strength of evangelicals and political conservatives. The Moral Majority joined the New Right in claiming credit for the election of Ronald Reagan and for the defeat of a number of liberal Democratic senators, including Frank Church of Idaho, George McGovern of South Dakota, John Culver of Iowa, and Birch Bayh of Indiana.

The following selection examines the world of Jerry Falwell and other evangelical leaders, describing how they have led the Moral Majority into political combat.

[1]*Newsweek*, September 15, 1980, p.28.

10

Allan J. Mayer
THE REVEREND JERRY FALWELL
AND THE TIDE OF BORN AGAIN

The Reverend Jerry Falwell fidgeted impatiently as he waited for a colleague to finish thanking the Lord for his bounty. Finally, the Wednesday evening prayer service almost at an end, Falwell strode to the pulpit to address the well-scrubbed congregation of 3,900 that filled the Thomas Road Baptist Church in Lynchburg, Virginia, a fortnight ago. "Senator [Mike] Gravel of [Alaska] was ousted last night," he told them. "He lost the primary. And that's the beginning." Before the year was out, Falwell intoned, a half dozen more liberal senators would fall: George McGovern of South Dakota and Frank Church of Idaho, John Culver of Iowa and Alan Cranston of California, Birch Bayh of Indiana and Gaylord Nelson of Wisconsin. "The moralists in America have had enough. [We] are joining hands together for the changing, the rejuvenating of a nation."

It was an unconventional litany, to be sure. But such overtly political preaching is an increasingly common — and, to many, worrisome — phenomenon in evangelical churches across the country. Over the last eighteen months a new and potent political force has been taking shape — a "New Christian Right," in the words of theologian Martin E. Marty. Led by religious-TV stars such as Falwell, whose "Old-Time Gospel Hour" reaches an estimated 18 million viewers each week, this movement is attempting to enlist the nation's 30 million to 65 million evangelical Christians in an unabashedly political crusade based on fundamentalist morality. Its ideological bent is distinctly conservative, embracing "pro-family" positions against abortion, the Equal Rights Amendment, and gay rights — but also extending to right-wing stands on such secular issues as the strategic arms limitation treaty (which it opposes) and the Kemp-Roth proposal to cut taxes by 30 percent (which it supports). The strategy is more electoral than Biblical. "We want to see more and more politicians in office who believe what we believe," says Charlotte, North Carolina, TV evangelist Jim Bakker.

To that end, politically oriented groups such as Falwell's Moral Majority and the California-based Christian Voice run massive voter-registration and education drives designed to turn traditionally apolitical elements of the evangelical community into a potent force at the polls. They are committed to partisan combat at every level — from campaigns for town council to the 1980 presidential race — throwing imposing organizational and financial resources behind candidates who share their born-again priorities. The movement's leaders maintain that their interest is in principle, not partisan personalities, and they insist that they have no intention of hitching their moral wagon to any secular star. But the main beneficiary of their activism, so far at least, has been the Republican party in general — and GOP presidential nominee Ronald Reagan in particular. "Christians gave Jimmy Carter his razor-thin margin of victory in 1976," says chief strategist Colonel Donner of Christian Voice. "We plan to reverse that in 1980."

Victories

Politics does not come naturally to the evangelical community, which has long held that the road to salvation lies in the Bible — not the ballot box. But many evangelicals have clearly become convinced that their fiercely held conservative values of God, country, and family are threatened by a rising tide of what they call "secular humanism" sweeping through government. "All across the country, Christians are registering to vote like never before," says Gainesville, Florida, minister Gene Keith, who successfully exhorted his flock to take over the local Democratic committee — and who is now a candidate for the state legislature. "We're running for everything from dogcatcher to senator."

And they are winning. In 1978 evangelical activists helped to unseat at least two liberal U.S. senators (Dick Clark of Iowa and Thomas McIntyre of New Hampshire) and elect one governor (Fob James of Alabama). Since then they have helped to block passage of the ERA in fifteen states, disrupt the White House Conference on the Family, impede the most recent Congressional effort at criminal-code reform and force both the Federal Communications Commission and the Internal Revenue Service to back down on challenges to religious organizations. This year their candidates have scored upset victories in primaries for the Senate and House in Alaska, Iowa, and Alabama — and though they lost the fight to keep George Bush off the Republican ticket, they did manage to shape large sections of the GOP platform.

The movement's rapid growth and early success worries not only its political opponents, but many mainstream theologians as well. "Its leaders are profoundly immature," says Richard John Neuhaus, a Lutheran pastor and member of the board of the influential *Worldview* magazine. "They don't really understand the ethical and philosophical traditions of democracy or how to bring about change in a pluralistic society." Even some evangelists themselves are uneasy about the new movement's often strident partisanship and its creative use of scripture to justify the most secular of political positions. "God isn't a right-winger or a left-winger," argues preacher Pat Robertson, president of the Christian Broadcasting Network and host of "The 700 Club," a popular daily religious program. "The evangelists stand in danger of being used and manipulated." In judging political performance on the basis of Biblically derived standards, others contend, the movement is in danger of crossing the constitutionally drawn line between church and state. "They are violating Article Six of the Constitution, which says there must not be any religious test for holding office," says Rabbi Marc Tanenbaum of the American Jewish Committee.

"Buzzards"

Predictably defensive, evangelical politicians charge that such criticisms are themselves political sour grapes from liberal opponents. "Nobody's ever accused the National Council of Churches of mixing religion and politics," Falwell says. "But when ol' Jerry gets into it, that's violating separation of church and state. The problem isn't violating anything. The problem is that we don't agree with those buzzards — and that we outnumber them." Perhaps — although there is a real question whether leaders like Falwell really do represent a huge and potentially monolithic political bloc. According to a new Gallup poll, evangelical Christians are as politically divided as most Americans (see Table 1). Though as a group they are somewhat more conservative than the nation as a whole, the majority of the registered voters among them nonetheless identify

Table 1. How far right?
Despite the conservative message of many evangelical political leaders, a new Gallup poll [found] President [Carter] ahead among born-again Christians registered to vote; they [were] not very far to the right except on abortion and prayer.

If the presidential elections were being held today, which candidate would you vote for?

	Carter	Reagan	Anderson
Evangelicals	52%	31%	6%
All voters	39%	38%	13%

Which category best describes your own political position?

	Left of center	Middle of the road	Right of center
Evangelicals	20%	31%	37%
All voters	22%	37%	31%

How they differ on issues:

	Evangelicals	All voters
Favor death penalty for persons convicted of murder	51%	52%
Favor government programs to deal with social problems	54%	53%
Favor increased spending for defense	78%	70%
Favor banning all abortions	41%	31%
Favor requiring prayer in public schools	81%	59%

themselves as Democrats, and they favor Jimmy Carter by a wide margin over Ronald Reagan. What's more, a majority (53 percent) support ERA, and only 41 percent favor the extreme position of banning abortion entirely.

Still, there is no mistaking the enormous potential of evangelical politics. The movement's basic raw material is the vast number of fundamentalist Americans who do not normally vote — Christian Voice's Donner estimates it as 25 million — and whose attitudes, as a result, are not reflected in Gallup's findings. So far this year, the movement claims to have registered some 2 million new voters from the ranks of the born again — and, says Falwell, the total should reach 4 million by Election Day. Even if those figures are inflated, born-again politics could well play a decisive role in this year's presidential race. "The significance of the fundamentalist vote is not numbers but geography," says Reagan campaign aide Roger Stone. Close elections, he notes, tend to be won or lost in the heartland states of Ohio, Illinois, and Michigan — all of which boast growing evangelical communities. "Some of the southern counties in Ohio are as fundamentalist as the Deep South," Stone says. "The return of the fundamentalist vote [to the GOP] will allow Reagan to carry Ohio and, conceivably, the country."

The movement's political gurus are prone to play down their immediate prospects. "Anybody who thinks this group is going to contribute to a political revolution this election is going to be disappointed," says Paul Weyrich, who runs a highly regarded "training school" in Washington for conservative candidates as well as a clearinghouse operation for thirty or so evangelical and secular pro-family groups. But as the strategists see it, the longer-term future is bright. "The basic problem, only now being overcome, is to get people involved," says Howard Phillips, organizer of a right-wing lobbying group called The Conservative Caucus. "Once that is done, this movement will be formidable."

The effort began in earnest less than three years ago, spurred in part by disappointment with the first born-again candidate, Jimmy Carter. "It was a tremendous letdown, if not a betrayal, to have Carter stumping for the ERA, for not stopping federally paid abortions, for advocating homosexual rights," says Donner. The original movers and shakers were mainly political pros, not preachers. The core group consisted of Phillips and Weyrich (who were old comrades-in-arms from the political wars), Robert Billings (a failed GOP Congressional candidate from Indiana who had attended Weyrich's candidate-training school) and Ed McAteer, a veteran marketing man for the Colgate-Palmolive Co. who had come to know hundreds of evangelical preachers around the country. In January of last year they persuaded Falwell to set up a political organization — which Weyrich suggested calling "Moral Majority" and which Billings was assigned to direct. Falwell's backing was crucial; the financial and logistical resources that he commanded were immense.

Allies

There were other allies as well. McAteer had set up a nonpartisan, interdenominational group called the Religious Roundtable. It had just fifty-six members, but among them were most of the major television preachers as an impressive list of New Right politicians. Funded mainly by what McAteer describes as "some gifts from businessmen," it sponsored rallies, seminars, and training sessions aimed at increasing the political sophistication of evangelists. Meanwhile, Weyrich had begun holding informal get-togethers for evangelical and pro-family activists every other Thursday in his Washington offices on Library Court, behind the Library of Congress. The Library Court group, as it came to be known, now coordinates strategy for the entire movement.

Another politically potent evangelical group had arisen on the West Coast. Called Christian Voice, it sidestepped IRS strictures on political lobbying by setting up a political action committee (PAC) called the Christian Voice Moral Government Fund. Unlike the other born-again political organizations, Christian Voice has no compunctions about endorsing specific candidates for office. "We make judgments based on principles," says Gary Jarmin, executive director of the Moral Government Fund. "When you go into a voting booth, you pull a lever for a name, not a principle." Last February it set up another group — called Christians for Reagan.

Agenda

Working together in an informal but very real alliance, these organizations are trying to mobilize a conservative evangelical electorate. The concerns of born-again politics are defined by Falwell's "agenda for the '80s" — a pro-family, pro-life, pro-morality platform that, in a triumph of political packaging, turns out to be considerably more "anti" than "pro." Among other things, Moral Majority — and its evangelical allies — are against abortion, ERA, gay rights, sex education, drugs, pornography, SALT II, the Department of Education, and defense cuts. They are for free enterprise, a balanced budget, voluntary prayer in the public schools, and a secure Israel.

Using Falwell as its main drawing card, Moral Majority has been holding rallies around the country to spread the word and develop a truly national base. The work is already beginning to pay dividends as a cadre of budding evangelical politicos takes root. Reverend Keith of Gainesville, Florida, is typical — a total neophyte when Moral Majority suggested he attend the weeklong "Campaign Training Conference" run by Weyrich in Washington last November. When he returned to his pulpit at the Southside Baptist Church he persuaded his congregation to run for seats on the local county Democratic committee. Ultimately, they swept forty-two of the fifty-three seats they went after.

Falwell says he is not "candidate oriented." Still, he has managed to lend a hand in several campaigns. At a recent Moral Majority rally in Des Moines, for example, he made a point of praising Senate candidate Representative Charles Grassley as a "dear friend of ours and a fine Christian." And in Birmingham, Alabama, a fortnight ago, Falwell noted pointedly that Moral Majority's local bête noire, Representative John Buchanan, had "unfortunately" voted to extend the time limit for passage of the ERA. Buchanan lost in last week's GOP primary.

Falwell's political sermonizing doesn't always work out so well. Several months ago he told a Moral Majority rally in Alaska a completely fabricated story about an actual meeting he and other evangelists had with President Carter in the White House last February. According to Falwell's first account, he had boldly asked the president why he had "known practicing homosexuals" on his staff — to which Carter supposedly replied that it was because he considered himself "President of all the American people." When the story got back to the White House, angry Carter aides released a transcript of the meeting — which showed that there never had been any such exchange. "I shouldn't have said it," Falwell conceded recently. "Obviously it was a reckless statement."

Questions

Such gaffes don't really worry him. "There are only two things a preacher just can't afford to be accused of," he says. "One of them is sexual impropriety . . . the other is messing with the church funds." Falwell's reputation as a family man is impeccable. But the Securities and Exchange Commission once raised questions about his ministry's finances (see box) — and there are indications that Moral Majority, ostensibly independent, has received favored treatment from Falwell's lucrative religious enterprises Although contributions have been flowing into Moral Majority lately at the rate of $400,000 a month, the organization has been strapped for cash all year. It has been consistently bailed out by the "Old-Time Gospel Hour," which has allowed Moral Majority to run up debts to it for months — apparently free of any interest charges.

By far the most controversial of the evangelical political groups is the unabashedly partisan Christian Voice. Earlier this year it raised hackles by rating all the members of Congress on how they voted on what it described as "fourteen key moral issues" — ranging from prayer in the schools to the security of Taiwan. On the basis of the ratings, it issued a "hit list" of thirty-six senators and congressmen, each of whom it accused of having a poor "moral voting record." Though lobbying groups do this sort of thing all the time, Christian Voice's ratings drew heavy fire. For one thing, four ordained clergymen in Congress received among the lowest marks — while Representative Richard Kelly, one of the Abscam bribery defendants, was given a perfect, 100 percent rating. For another, the group's equation of Christian morality with political conservatism outraged preachers and pols alike. Even Senator Jesse Helms, the influential conservative who agrees wholeheartedly with Christian Voice's politics, found the rating system questionable. "I could never take the position that anyone who disagreed with me was less a Christian," he says. "Hubert Humphrey and I didn't agree 90 percent of the time. Does that mean he was more immoral?"

Flood

Unfazed by the criticism, Christian Voice is now gearing up for a massive effort in behalf of Ronald Reagan, including plans to flood the Midwest and the South with 5 million pieces of pro-Reagan literature between now and the election. "The South is reputed to be Jimmy Carter's base," says strategist Donner, "but remember, it's the Bible belt. Our message that Ronald Reagan is *the* Christian candidate of 1980 may sufficiently weaken Carter in the one solid base he still has."

The Reagan campaign takes such analyses seriously, and has been assiduously wooing the evangelicals all year — in the process, hiring Billings away from Moral Majority to become Reagan's liaison with the born-again community. The courtship began in earnest at the GOP convention, to which both Falwell and his Liberty Baptist College choir were invited. Perhaps more important, Falwell and his fellow evangelical politicians got a good crack at shaping the Republican platform.

"Out of the Closet"

Reagan further solidified his hold on the evangelical pols by being the only major presidential candidate to appear at the Religious Roundtable's National Affairs Briefing, a revival meeting cum political rally held in Dallas three weeks ago. More than 15,000 of the faithful turned out for two days of speechmaking and organizing. "It's time for God's people to come out of the closet and the churches — and change America," thundered James Robison, the fire-and-brimstone Ft. Worth evangelist whose weekly TV show is syndicated to 100 stations. Said Reagan: "I know you can't endorse *me*. But . . . I want you to know that I endorse *you*."

Not everyone there shared Reagan's enthusiasm. Preacher Pat Robertson, for one, argues that "active partisan politics" is the wrong path for true evangelicals. "There's a better way," he says: "Fasting and praying . . . appealing, in essence, to a higher power." That feeling is shared by many in the evangelical community who are uneasy over the fact that, as the Reverend Jimmy Allen of Ft. Worth puts it, what is supposed to be "a nonpartisan movement for Jesus . . . always seems to turn into a Republican rally." A sincere concern for traditional values clearly motivates many in the movement, but critics point to an apparent lack of concern for minorities and the poor. "There are more than 300 verses in the Bible on the commitment to the poor, to justice and righteousness, but they are silent on that," complains the Reverend Tom Skinner, a born-again black activist.

What seems to trouble such critics the most is the movement's inexorable reduction of religious and moral values into crude political options. "I would hate for evangelical Christianity to become a spiritual version of the National Rifle Association," says Dr. David Hubbard of the Fuller Theological Seminary, who worries about the possible exploitation of politically naïve evangelicals. And whatever it does to evangelicals themselves, the effect on the rest of society could be devastating. "If in order to be faithful you have to support a certain stand regarding Russia, what's the next step?" asks the Reverend Theodore Edquist of the First Congregational Church of Boise, Idaho. "It strikes at the very heart of the whole notion of religious pluralism and religious and political freedom."

"Mad as Hell"

The movement's leaders insist that such worries are wildly overblown. "We're not religious fanatics who have in mind a Khomeini-type religious crusade to take over the government," says Falwell. "We support the separation of church and state . . . we want influence, not control." For the activist liberal theologians who have been in politics for years — fighting for poverty programs, urban aid, and an end to the Vietnam war — that argument is hard to dispute. "This is a populist reaction of resentment," says Worldview's Neuhaus. "These are very ordinary Americans and they are mad as hell. It's arrogant and self-defeating for those of us whom they are mad at to pretend they will just go away."

The challenge of the New Christian Right may stir more activism among liberals. But attention will have to be paid to born-again sensibilities. "No group on a crusade is willing to moderate its demands until it feels secure of its place, until it feels recognized as a power to be dealt with," says Neuhaus, adding that many of the liberals who propound the separation of church and state have gone beyond that to the separation of moral judgment from public policy. "They are the ones who have driven us into this current dilemma by trying to purge American life of religion and values — by creating a 'naked public square' where anything goes." What is clear on both the philosophical level — and in the rough-and-tumble arena of politics — is that the Falwells of the nation and their increasingly militant and devoted flock are a phenomenon that can no longer be dismissed or ignored.

A $1 Million Habit

In his dark three-piece polyester suits, the Reverend Jerry Falwell always looks dressed for church. He has to. As chief pastor, executive officer, and full-time salesman for his own evangelical empire, Falwell is rarely out of the pulpit. Like a prophet seeking honor in — and for — his own country, Brother Jerry has moved beyond his Lynchburg, Virginia congregation to seize vocal leadership of the emerging Christian right, constantly pouring forth a torrent of Biblical rhetoric on behalf of his own conservative vision of a moral America.

To those who know him best, Falwell is a cool, tireless organizer and past master at riding evangelism's new electronic circuit. In a whirl of nineteen-hour days, he darts from board meetings to televised prayer services, jets from political rallies to church conferences, gulps down a dozen cups of coffee daily and rarely misquotes a Bible verse or a financial statistic. His hometown church claims 17,000 members — more than a quarter of Lynchburg's population — but his real constituency is an estimated 21 million faithful who listen to his broadcast sermons every week and support his pyramid of enterprises. Falwell's Sunday service, the "Old-Time Gospel Hour," is carried by 681 TV and radio stations. The yield from this and other fund-raising operations ($1 million each week) supports what is, in effect, Falwell's own Christian denomination — including a children's academy, a Bible institute, a correspondence school, a seminary and Library Baptist College, an as yet unaccredited campus with nearly 3,000 undergraduates (and a former major-league pitcher as baseball coach). To this complex, Falwell last year added Moral Majority, Inc., a political-action organization aimed at unseating politicians who reject his recipe for a righteous republic.

Lapel Pins: Falwell's multifaceted ministry depends on a variety of marketing techniques. Once true believers send in for such premiums as Old Glory lapel pins, their names are added to his massive computerized mailing list. Regular donors (average weekly gift: $12) become Falwell's "faith partners" and are subject to regular computerized pleas for more. In terms of what he calls his "gross ministry," Falwell says he is "neck and neck with Oral Roberts." And by 1981, he predicts, Falwell ministries will lead the evangelical pack.

A driving need to succeed is as much a part of Falwell's pulpit power as his business acumen and folksy fundamentalism. Young Jerry's family was a brawling bunch; his father killed one of Jerry's uncles in a family feud and later died from alcoholism. But Falwell excelled in the classroom and on his high-school football team. He was prevented from delivering the valedictory address only after auditors discovered that he and other ahtletes had eaten free for a year on bogus lunch tickets. Jerry didn't get religion until a wintry Sunday in 1952 when he went to church in search of girls and found both Jesus and a pretty organist named Macel Pate. In 1956, after dominating the student body at a Bible college in Missouri, Jerry returned to Lynchburg to found his own independent Baptist church, in an abandoned popbottling factory, and continued courting Macel—whom he later married. Six months later he aired his first religious show on local television.

At times his knack for fund raising has caused problems for Falwell's empire. Seven years ago the Securities and Exchange Commission sued his Thomas Road Baptist Church for issuing allegedly fraudulent bonds; after an acrimonious trial Falwell agreed to institute more rigorous financial discipline. And some questions still shadow his financial operations. Falwell says, for example, that he spends only 17½ cents to raise every dollar he takes in, but some former financial employees and advisers insist the actual figure is three to four times higher—well above the norm for most charitable causes. Others criticize Falwell's borrowing from Peter to pay Paul—specifically borrowing up to $1 million from the college (with approval of the school's board) to pay his TV expenses.

"Their Way Out": Falwell also makes periodic pitches for money to support specific causes such as the Cambodian refugees in Thailand. There is no way for donors to know how much money such appeals bring in — or where it all goes. Says the Reverend David Brown, who served as controller for the "Gospel Hour" last year: "Jerry would say in his promotional literature that the money raised would be used for a project *and* for other operating costs of the ministry. That last phrase in fine print was their way out." "There's only one problem with a ministry like Jerry's," adds a prominent Lynchburg banker. "He can't stop raising money; if he does, it all falls apart."

There is no evidence that Falwell has ever siphoned off any money for himself. Still, at forty-seven, he lives in comfort. His home (which is owned by a wealthy follower) is a twelve-room Southern mansion complete with portico, swimming pool, and verdant lawns—all protected by a high wall and a Bible-quoting guard. Although his salary is only $42,500, Fallwell enjoys the perquisites of many big-time entrepreneurs: His ministry affords him an expense account, free life insurance, and a private jet that enables him (and often one of his three children) to take in diversions such as World Series games while traveling on "church business." Falwell is hardly embarrassed by these wordly appurtenances. Material wealth, he says, "is God's way of blessing people who put him first."

THE MEDIA AND POLITICAL CONSULTANTS

Chapter Three

The First Amendment's guarantee of freedom of the press both reflects and protects the political power of an institution that has always played an important role in the nation's politics. The publishers and pamphleteers of eighteenth-century America considered freedom of the press a natural liberty, and acted accordingly. Their criticisms of British and colonial authorities helped to plant the revolutionary seed in the minds of the colonists. Colonial governors were aware of the dangers of a free press, and sought unsuccessfully to control it by requiring government licenses for printing. Moreover, the authorities did not hesitate to bring charges of seditious libel against journalists who criticized the government.

The freedom of the press that was won in the eighteenth century created an environment in which political journalists could and did flourish. Reporters could build successful careers by covering politics at state or national levels, although Washington inevitably became the mecca for the political press.

By the time of the New Deal, the Washington press had become a firmly entrenched establishment force in the nation's capital. Jonathan Daniels, an experienced Washington hand who had served as President Franklin D. Roosevelt's press secretary, commented, "It would be difficult to find a body of men who more clearly represent Washington than the gentlemen of the press who report it. There are notions, carefully cultivated, that they are in Washington but not of it, and that they stand in scrutiny but also in separation. Actually, of course, they are probably more representative of the good and the bad on the Capital scene than any other body of bureaucrats. As they stay in Washington, which most of them hope to do, they are at least as remote from the country as the administrators are."[1]

The media is a powerful political force at all levels of the government. A century before the advent of radio and television, Tocqueville pointed out that the diversity and power of the press is a major characteristic of democracy, and particularly of a government such as that of the United States, which contains so many political subdivisions. "The extraordinary subdivi-

[1]Jonathan Daniels, *Frontier on the Potomac* (New York: Macmillan, 1946), p. 159

127

sion of administrative power," remarked Tocqueville, "has much more to do with the enormous number of American newspapers than the great political freedom of the country and the absolute liberty of the press."[2] Newspapers, concluded Tocqueville, can persuade large numbers of citizens to unite for a common cause. Moreover, "The more equal the conditions of men become and the less strong men individually are, the more easily they give way to the current of the multitude and the more difficult it is for them to adhere by themselves to an opinion which the multitude discard[s]. . . . The power of the newspaper press must therefore increase as the social conditions of men become more equal."[3]

The press has always attempted to create, in Tocqueville's terms, associations of citizens to back causes and candidates. The press attempts to be the kingmaker for many of the ten thousand or more elected offices throughout the nation.

The growth of the electronic media, radio and television, added a new dimension to the traditional political role played by the press. While newspaper publishers and correspondents are free to express their political views, supporting whatever candidates they choose, the electronic media are in an entirely different position. The airwaves used by the electronic media to communicate information are technically "owned" by the public. The government licenses broadcasting stations for a three-year period, after which it reviews the licensee's conduct in relation to statutory and administrative standards to determine whether or not the license is to be renewed.[4] One of the regulatory standards governing broadcasting requires impartiality in the expression of political views. When a station editorializes it must give "equal time" for the presentation of opposing opinions. Broadcasters, unlike publishers, do not often endorse political candidates.

While broadcasting is supposed to be politically neutral, it is inevitably drawn into partisan politics. All news and public affairs programs have a slant, which indirectly shapes citizen attitudes on important issues. Statements about public policy are often made simply by the choice of subjects to be covered. The White House, which is so frequently the focus of media attention, complains constantly that it is not being treated fairly. Republicans attack the "Eastern liberal establishment" press, while Democrats always echo President Harry S. Truman's lament: "I was sure that the American people would agree with me if they had all the facts. I knew, however,

[2]Alexis de Tocqueville, *Democracy in America*, Vol. 2 (New York: Vintage Books, 1954), p. 121. Tocqueville's volumes were first published in 1835.

[3]Ibid., p. 122.

[4]In fact, almost all license renewals are automatic, making the licensees virtually permanent owners of their stations.

that the Republican-controlled press and radio would be against me, and my only remaining hope of communicating with the people was to get the message to the people in a personal way."[5]

However much politicians may criticize the media, they increasingly depend upon it to project their personalities and communicate their views to the electorate. Political consulting has become a major industry.[6] By 1952, 45 percent of households owned television sets, and not surprisingly, that year marked the advent of political television in a big way in presidential campaigns.[7] General Eisenhower, portrayed as the simple and sincere man from Abilene, easily won over the sometimes acerbic but always witty Adlai Stevenson of Illinois. The Stevenson campaign spent only $77,000 on television, compared to a Republican expenditure of $1.5 million on its media campaign. The use of media consultants and the expenditure of large sums of money for public relations has been considered de rigueur for almost all political campaigns, presidential, congressional, and at the state level, as television has become the principal political medium. Media consultants are the new political gurus.

The vignettes in this chapter reveal the character and the style of two powerful political consultants on opposite sides of the ideological spectrum and the way in which one presidential press secretary attempted to manage the news during a national crisis.

[5]Harry S Truman, *Memoirs*, Vol. 2 (Garden City, N.Y.: Doubleday, 1956), p. 175.
[6]See Larry J. Sabato, *The Rise of Political Consultants* (New York: Basic Books, 1981).
[7]Ibid., p.113.

COLORADO SENATOR GARY Hart's strong bid for the presidential nomination of the Democratic party in 1984 surprised many political observers, who thought Walter Mondale and his organization were invincible. But the political cognoscenti underestimated both Hart, and perhaps more importantly, his pollster and political consultant Patrick Caddell.

Consultants and pollsters have become a permanent part of the political scene. No creditable candidate can do without expert advice as he or she attempts to assess public attitudes, raise money, and deal with the complex world of the media. The ever-growing consultant corps adds a new dimension to the traditional political world of politicians, parties, and elections.

The professional political consultant as a hired gun first appeared in California in the 1930s. A Sacramento newsman and press agent, Clem Whitaker, joined forces with public relations specialist Leone Smith Baxter, establishing a San Francisco consulting firm that for over two decades boasted a 90 percent success rate in seventy-five major campaigns.[1] Imitators followed Whitaker and Baxter's lead, as established advertising firms undertook political consulting. The professional consultant corps itself did not grow significantly until the 1960s and 1970s.[2]

By the 1980s, all candidates would agree that, with respect to political consultants, they would not leave home without one. Although many consultants are hired guns, a number have their own political identification and do not work for candidates who do not conform to their ideological views. Richard Viguerie, for example, the direct-mail specialist, is a New Right leader who would not think of working for liberal candidates. (See selection 12.) By contrast, Patrick Caddell is strongly identified with the Democratic party, where he works for liberal and middle-of-the-road candidates. Caddell, like many of his colleagues, puts candidates through a screening process. He seeks "real patriots in the sense of really caring about the country. If I were to apply one single criterion, it would be whether the individual really gives a good damn about what happens to the United States. Large numbers of politicians, frankly, could care less as long as they stay in office."[3]

Caddell believes that his polling and consulting services must be used to support not only viable candidates, but those who will make, in his opinion, an important contribution once elected. "Today there is a crisis of public confidence," he says, "not merely in specific officeholders, but in the functioning of government itself; not merely in bad policies, but in the entire process of policymaking. It is a crisis of confidence in the political process and the future of the nation."[4]

Caddell is one of many political consultants who have injected their own personalities and values into the political process, helping to determine the kinds of candidates that run and even the

---

[1] Larry J. Sabato, *The Rise of Poltical Consultants* (New York: Basic Books, 1981), pp. 11–12.
[2] Ibid., p. 13.
[3] Ibid., p. 31.
[4] Ibid., p. 74.

policies they work for once elected. Consultants are becoming an important political elite in their own right.

Caddell's search often leads him to offbeat antiestablishment candidates.

The following selection portrays how he "found" Gary Hart, and the role he played in Hart's campaign for the Democratic presidential nomination in 1984.

11 Ralph Whitehead
FOR WHOM CADDELL POLLS

For much of 1983 the wunderkind of American electoral strategy roamed the corridors of the Democratic party, searching for a presidential candidate who could expose the House of Mondale as a house of cards. Bumpers and Biden and even Markey turned him down before he was finally welcomed into the Hart campaign, then struggling for survival. The invitation was not without significance: Patrick Caddell has been the winning pollster for every Democratic nominee since 1972. He is the backroom general who can plot campaigns six moves in advance, the political psychologist who plots voters along the axes of the American psyche. His uncanny knack is for turning raw survey numbers into abstract insights, and insights into usable tactics. In a word, he's good.

He is also abrasive. Once an *enfant terrible*, he has ripened with the seasons into a full-blown prima donna. He plays a maddeningly high hand with his candidates and their campaign staffs. Charming and engaging at first meeting, he has turned scores of admirers into detractors. A falling out with partners at Cambridge Survey Research a few years ago led to a bitter fight that is still going through the courts. Caddell and Walter Mondale saw the world very differently during their years at the Carter White House and some wonder how much of Caddell's 1984 posture is vendetta.

Opinion on Caddell splits sharply. For some he is the Merlin of the highly volatile electorate of the 1980s and must be heeded by all who would draw the sword from the stone. To his critics he is a bomb thrower, a nihilist, a manipulator, a man who sets fires in the electorate just to watch them burn. He can tear down the establishment, the incumbent, the front runner, but what, ask his critics, can he build? They wonder whether Caddell was responsible for inflicting Jimmy

From *The Boston Observer* (April 1984), Vol. 3, No. 4. Copyright © 1984 by The Boston Observer Company. All rights reserved. Reprinted by permission.

Carter on the American people and whether he is about to do it again with Gary Hart.

Over the years, I've worked with Caddell and I've worked against him. And, for all his faults, I think he's on to something fundamental: a realignment with the Democratic party.

Pat Caddell is what naturalists call an edge species. These rare strains of plant life flourish on nature's edges, where the forest meets the tundra or the ocean washes the land. They eventually die if they move off these narrow margins, but their life on the edge gives rise to newer and hardier forms of life that *do* survive far from the margin. The edge species is one of nature's innovators.

Caddell sits at the edge of our political landscape. On one side looms the rocky face of the political establishment: the White House, the Congress, the special-interest lobbies, and the grand old men of the Democratic party. Caddell has sniffed the establishment's brandy, savored its food, diverted its women, taken lots of its money, sampled the townhouses, the private jets, and the celebrity. He has scaled these heights but hasn't taken root there.

On the other side sprawl the fields of the American electorate, which Caddell has laboriously surveyed. Through the force of his imagination and the magic of probability theory, he can run those green-and-white printouts through his fingertips and divine the fears and hopes of millions. What he has found is a deep undercurrent of distrust of establishment institutions that touches, even unites, voters on the left and right. He finds in these fields fertile soil for a candidate who can plant the seeds of hope and idealism, a candidate who gives voice to their suspicions that establishment politics are a "consensus of cynicism . . . that has lost faith in the American people — lost faith in their ability to discern carefully or choose wisely, lost faith in their enduring commitment to idealism and compassion, and lost faith in their strength of character to respond to hard truths or call for shared sacrifice."

The enduring picture of Caddell is that of the outsider. He was the Irish Catholic kid from Massachusetts who grew up on the edge of cracker culture in the Protestant Florida panhandle. As an undergraduate at Harvard, he had one foot in the campus and the other in his own commercial polling firm. He thrives today on underdog or insurgent candidacies: New York's Mario Cuomo and Chicago's Harold Washington were recent clients.

"Pat came to me as a junior tutorial student in the fall of 1970," recalls Josiah Lee Auspitz, then a graduate student in government at Harvard. "He wanted to do a paper on the Wallace vote." As a third-party insurgent in the fall of 1968, George Wallace had reached double digits; the Nixon forces had set these third-party voters as their prime target by the fall of 1970. Caddell, even at the outset of Nixon's campaign, understood that it would fail. He had surveyed these people in Florida and felt that he knew them. "He told me that Wallace voters aren't racist, they're frustrated and they're antiestablishment," Auspitz recalls. Caddell was on to something, and the 1970 returns showed it. The Republicans didn't get the southern gains they sought, and the successful candidates in the South, such as Jimmy Carter of Georgia, shared one quality: They were relatively new faces with strong convictions.

For most of his junior and senior years, Caddell studied these voters. Auspitz helped him to look past the numbers and into the depths of the southern culture, especially its religious heritage. "He was doing finely tuned studies of how Baptists and Methodists differed in their histories and views of the world," says Auspitz. Up North, Caddell paid particular attention to pockets of Wallace strength in industrial cities like Manchester, New Hampshire, and in liberal states such as Wisconsin. It is no coincidence that in 1972 McGovern confounded the expectations of the political establishment in New Hampshire and broke the race open in Wisconsin. His young pollster was Pat Caddell.

If you're a seasoned Massachusetts voter, you've probably got some of Caddell's furniture in your cognitive attic. If you were fed up with traditional Democrats and Yankee Republicans and felt that Mike Dukakis should be governor, then you and Caddell have met somewhere in the printouts, for he was feeding your purifying impulses back to you through his advice to the 1974 Dukakis campaign. If you regard Kevin White as cold and aloof and crooked, a loner in love with himself in the baronial vastness of the Parkman House, then you qualify as a collector — Caddell positioned Joseph Timilty on this score in his 1975 campaign for mayor. Similar themes were writ large, of course, for the 1976 Carter campaign.

Caddell's trade secret is a simple one. Most voters regard politics now as a craft specialty practiced somewhere far from the cultural and economic rhythms of their own lives. A Caddell campaign tries to connect a candidate with those rhythms. And the rhythms he senses in the electorate this year reveal a profound anxiety over the future: "We tried Carter and that didn't work. We tried Reagan and it isn't working. What next? Who next?" Enter Gary Hart.

The official Caddell literature, so to speak, consists chiefly of three long papers.

The first, written just after the Carter victory, warns the president that he takes office in the wake of "the breakdown of party and the failure of ideology," following a campaign that provided no mandate on policy. Caddell's recommendation is for a continuing campaign marked by inaugural strolls, town meetings, and fireside chats. The idea was to build support for policies by keeping public attention positively focused on antiestablishment themes — keep tapping into those rhythms. A parenthetical note from the memo is often quoted by Caddell's critics: "The old cliché about mistaking style for substance usually works the reverse in politics. Too many good people have been defeated because they tried to substitute substance for style; they forgot to give the public the kind of visible signals that it needs to understand what is happening."

Caddell's second paper lives in infamy as the "malaise memo." I have never read it although it has been described to me briefly by its author and others. It was the basis for Carter's week-long retreat to Camp David and his speech upon his return. Its premise: We've got a problem that takes two forms. One is literal — long lines, shrinking supplies, rising prices. The other is symbolic and psychic — our national spirit is running on empty. By solving the energy crisis we can rescue our economy and restore our morale.

The trouble was that while Caddell's themes were compelling, the energy proposals themselves were strictly business-as-usual. Big Government and Big Business would move in a Big Way, but there were few roles for the ordinary citizen. The problem articulated by Carter was rooted in the culture and the economy but the proposed solutions fell to the policy specialists in Washington. Caddell has a one-sentence explanation for this contradiction: "Mondale controlled the policy."

It is not surprising, then, that Caddell's third major paper, "Caddell '83," takes direct aim at Mondale and stresses innovative, populist policies to advance antiestablishment themes. Its 150 pages contain a campaign strategy in search of a candidate, but it holds many other things besides: a diatribe against interest groups, a shrewd critique of the Democratic party's delegate selection rules, a pastiche of speech drafts, a compendium of applause lines, a withering view of the Mondale campaign, an indictment of Reagan and a credible blueprint for beating him, a portrait of the surging activism and importance of minorities and younger white voters. Written in October 1983, it contains a step-by-step strategy of how the Mondale juggernaut could be stopped and how an insurgency candidate might capture the momentum and "rekindle the dry tinder of idealism." Read today, in full view of the Hart phenomenon, it can only be described as remarkably foresighted.

Caddell wrote his memo to prompt a left-of-center, antiestablishment candidate into the presidential race because none of the announced Democratic candidates fit Caddell's bill, *including Gary Hart.* By Caddell's analysis, Hart's was *for* new ideas and *against* interest-group politics, but his candidacy had not been infused with sufficient populist zeal to get the voters stirred up or give an edge to his themes. Nonetheless, at the outset of 1984, with the filing deadline for the New Hampshire primary having passed, Caddell's effort to bring a fresh face into the Democratic field had failed. Hart called Caddell and asked for some help. Although they approached each other warily, they each realized then that the other was the only game left in town.

In the ensuing months, Caddell provided a script for the story line that Gary Hart had created. Hart had long before declared himself the candidate opposed to old formulations and solutions. But it was Caddell who prodded Hart to root his appeal in the cultural and social rhythms of his own experience and appeal more directly to a generation whose political attitudes were shaped by the peace movement, the civil rights movement, the woman's movement, the environmental movement. Simply put, it was that appeal which brought Hart enough caucus votes in Iowa to establish him as *the* alternative to Walter Mondale. And as Caddell and others had predicted, the House of Mondale began to crumble.

Pat Caddell is trying to define the two faces of the Democratic party for the 1980s. Michael Barone has divided the party into Traditional Democrats and Trend Democrats. Bob Squier, a political consultant, has divided it into an institutional wing and a problem-solving wing. Caddell doesn't draw his formulations so crisply, nor does he highlight them with opposing phrases. But let me try to do it for him: We have Hardware Democrats and Software Democrats.

The Hardware Democrats are elitist. This isn't because some of them are graduates of Choate, but because they view the world as being run chiefly by institutionally-backed elites. Consider, for a moment, national security. Walter Mondale has the Trilateral Commission and the Council of Foreign Relations just as Chernenko has the Politburo. Until recently, the terms of the nuclear arms race were based on this elitism. Nuclear policy is driven by superpower strategy and this strategy requires strategic secrets. If there are secrets, then there are a few people who are in on the secrets. Thus the Soviet elite sustains the American, and vice versa. Mainframe talks to mainframe.

Software Democrats are populist. This isn't because they all grew up behind mules in South Dakota, but because they've grown up distrusting the establishment and trusting their own experience. They are working through the freeze movement to democratize our policies for preventing nuclear war by overturning the notion of the nuclear secret. They believe that the critical piece of evidence in the nuclear debate is our own anxiety. Our nightmares are our software.

The Hardware Democrats are bureaucratic. This isn't because their souls are cut from red tape, but because they fear the future as a time of vast uncertainty. Bureaucracies create certainty — not always the certainties we'd like, but certainties. Bureaucracies slow down the rate of change; bureaucrats are the peasants of postindustrial society. Through bureaucracy, tomorrow is daily cast into the mold of yesterday. You can't beat the bureaucratic machinery unless you come up with a superior method for creating certainty.

The Software Democrats are idealistic. They have confidence in the energy of ideas and values. For them, these qualities do create a sense of certainty. They can look at the blueprint and visualize the house (bureaucrats look at blueprints and visualize change orders and cost overruns). If we change our ideas, Software Democrats believe, we change realities.

The Hardware Democrats take what sociologists call an ascriptive view of our status and role: We are pretty much what others say we are. The world creates roles and defines us by bringing us into them. To fight for justice and change is to add to the supply of these existing roles: more entitlement lines, more affirmative action slots, more union jobs. This is our social and economic infrastructure. The Hardware Democrats have built it.

The Software Democrats believe we define ourselves. It isn't enough to add to the supply of exisiting roles; we've got to equip people to create all kinds of new and distinctive roles. The infrastructure doesn't define women or gays or blacks or browns. They define themselves, control their own history, and choose their own fate. Hardware Dems value status because it is the means for gaining security; Software Dems value equity as the means. A union card is status, but a college education is equity: It is mobile, it can be improved upon, and it's usually pretty liquid.

Caddell believes the electoral weight of the party now favors the Software Dems. Here's how he puts it in his 1983 memo:

> Presidential elections are always forays into the future — historically, socially, psychologically, and although inextricably linked to the past, their sustenance is future hope, future aspirations, future acts; they are the future while it happens. Conventional wisdom is always, at best, a consensus about the past, shaped against the rocks and stones of past events, past prejudices, past experiences as they are analyzed from hindsight. In politics, there is no real present, only an "apparent present" . . . squeezed between the grinding wheels of past and future.

More than anything else, "Caddell '83" is a ghost story. The shades of two men can be felt on every page and their voices heard in every paragraph. They are Robert Kennedy and Martin Luther King, Jr. The promise they brought to America's public life is clearly what drives the best in Pat Caddell.

Had these men survived, they might have formed an alliance for the 1968 election. Wiretaps aside, they had a relationship of several years' standing. Surely the tides of the year would have drawn them together. For civil rights. For peace. For a shift from guns to butter, hardware to software. For new sense of national purpose.

The passions stirred by the promise of 1968 later moved in at least two directions following their assassinations. They fell into the channels of older institutions such as the NAACP and the Urban League, the activist churches, and the industrial unions such as the UAW. Or they kept some of the volatility and scattered in the wind, into the Wallace movement (and hence Caddell's original interest in it), the antiwar movement, the precursors of the New Right, perhaps even today's freeze movement. Caddell chose to turn his eyes off the beaten path and watch for the crackling of heat lightning.

Obviously, the ghosts of 1968 animate the Democratic field of 1984. The heir to Hubert Humphrey. The aide to Martin Luther King, Jr. The aide to Bobby Kennedy. For better or worse, Caddell has been writing the 1984 script for a long time. All he did last October was put it down on paper.

THE 1986 FLORIDA RACE FOR the United State Senate was one of the most hotly contested in the nation. Popular Democratic governor Robert Graham challenged Republican senator Paula Hawkins, whom the voters had elected to her first term in 1980 by a small 52 percent margin over a relatively ineffectual opponent. Reagan's coattails, and substantial financial and other assistance from the national Republican party, helped Hawkins in 1980. The national Republican party promised to be an important factor again in 1986. Moreover, a highly popular incumbent president Ronald Reagan gave more substantial and effective support to Hawkins than he was able to do as a presidential candidate in 1980.

Hawkins' senate record paid close attention to Florida's agricultural and other economic interests. She also gained national attention as the sponsor of the Missing Child Assistance Act, and for her efforts to deal with the newly recognized problem of child abuse. Although voters could find much to praise and little to criticize in her senate record, Hawkins entered the 1986 race as an underdog. Her opponent was one of the most popular governors in the state's history. The seat itself even seemed to be jinxed as no incumbent had been re-elected to it since George Smathers' 1982 victory. Both candidates poured millions of dollars into their campaigns. The following selection portrays the high-powered political consultants they hired to plan their strategies.

12 Bill Peterson
POLITICAL CONSULTANTS: THE $2 MILLION MEN IN THE $11 MILLION RACE

The first big fight of the 1986 Florida Senate campaign came between consultants, not candidates. And it wasn't surprising.

Consultants are the new bosses of American politics, the stage managers of democracy. They travel from state to state, and sometimes from party to party, helping to elect candidates and reshape the political landscape.

The Florida Senate race pits some of the biggest names in the political-consulting business against one another. It is in some ways as much a test of their skills and talents as of the candidates'. The stakes are high.

Senator Paula Hawkins, a first-term Republican, and her challenger, Governor Robert Graham, a second-term Democrat, are expected to spend a total of more than $11 million on their campaigns. This means a handful of political image-makers, pollsters, and strategists will share about $2 million in fees.

Late last year, with the election still a year away, the Hawkins team made the first move, preparing a wave of television ads. The commercials were the joint product of media adviser Robert Goodman, one of the nation's zaniest and best known political admen, and pollster Richard Morris.

The two men view politics differently. "Morris deals with facts; I deal with emotion," Goodman says. "I am into feelings. I am for something that is moving, that has drama and is cinematographic. We [his firm] like real-life drama, to touch people where they live. I think love is the most powerful thing going in politics. . . . Dick thinks elections are referendums on issues."

Goodman, 56, has hired orchestras, chartered helicopters, written jingles, and even strapped a portable toilet to a donkey to create emotion in his ads. He tends to see a hero in every client. To him, George Bush was "the American eagle . . . a president we won't have to train" and Spiro Agnew was "my kind of guy."

The Hawkins ads were full of Goodman touches. One had helicopters hovering over a South American marijuana field; another featured an abandoned mother trying to make ends meet; a third pictured an ambulance arriving at a hospital with its siren screaming.

The ads were designed to showcase Hawkins' unusual Senate agenda: programs to find missing children, help displaced homemakers, and curtail the shipment of illegal drugs into the country. Morris supplied the larger-than-life slogan:

"Paula Hawkins: Unique, Irreplaceable."

Graham's pollster, William Hamilton, and his media adviser, Bob Squier, had been predicting for months that Hawkins would launch an advertising blitz in the fall of 1985. Like Hawkins' consultants, they are professionals, part of a close-knit fraternity, a controversial political elite.

"There is no more significant change in the conduct of campaigns than the consultant's recent rise to prominence, if not preeminence," writes Larry Sabato, a University of Virginia political scientist. "[They] have inflicted severe damage upon the party system and masterminded the modern triumph of personality cults over party politics in the United States."

To consultants, politics is a giant chess match, and campaigns, a series of moves across a giant chess board. The early commercials were easy to anticipate. Public-opinion polls had shown that both candidates were popular as individuals, but when it came to choosing between them, Graham had a large lead — ranging from nine to 23 percentage points — over Hawkins.

To keep raising the money needed to make the race competitive, Hawkins had to close the gap in the polls. A wave of advertising was the obvious answer.

The Graham team had also been at work. Hamilton had set up a series of "focus groups," small groups of Floridians asked to talk about the strengths and weaknesses of both candidates; Squier had shot some film of Graham for future ads and prepared a memo in which he proposed a campaign slogan: "Bob Graham. You know what he did in Florida. Think what he could do for Florida in Washington."

Both Hamilton and Squier have emotional ties to the race and consider it symbolic for their careers.

Hamilton, 46, grew up in Florida, received his first training in polling techniques at the University of Florida, and started his firm of William R. Hamilton & Staff Inc. in the state. He has conducted 250 polls there.

He is among the most widely respected pollsters in the Democratic Party. His reputation rests largely on his work in southern and border-state campaigns. Among his former clients are Jimmy Carter (in his 1970 race for the governorship of Georgia), Maryland Senator Paul S. Sarbanes, Missouri Senator Thomas F. Eagleton and Kentucky Governor Martha Layne Collins.

But Hamilton had a bad year in 1984. His presidential candidate, Democratic Senator John Glenn of Ohio, was an early loser in the primary season; he says his firm's only victories were in House races.

Win/loss records aren't as important to pollsters as other consultants. Pollsters, Hamilton says, are basically researchers who "don't have black boxes. . . . Media and organizational consultants promise they're going to deliver something that wins. We promise we'll get the data and make the best out of data in terms of strategy. We hope we can make the difference, but we can't promise."

According to a *National Journal* survey, Squier had the best year of anyone in the business in 1984, winning five of six races. He has worked for scores of winning and losing politicians, including Carter and the late Hubert H. Humphrey.

He helped elect one Democratic candidate, former Virginia governor Charles S. Robb, with ads showing him firing a pistol at a target range; another, former Mississippi governor William F. Winter, by putting him atop a National Guard tank; and another, former Kentucky governor John Y. Brown, Jr., by putting him on television with his photogenic wife, Phyllis George, a former Miss America.

But Squier and Graham have a special relationship. Squier helped make Graham governor; Graham helped make Squier rich.

"He is the franchise," says Squier, 51. "There's no question that Bob Graham invented this company. You have to remember, his was a race that wasn't supposed to be possible."

Squier, a commentator on NBC-TV, is treated like a visiting celebrity by Florida politicians. At a state Democratic Party banquet in Hollywood in November, he was introduced as "the guru of media, the man who is responsible for bringing Bob Graham to this point."

Graham was an obscure liberal state senator from Dade County with a penchant for putting audiences to sleep when he hired Squier three years before the 1978 governor's race.

"He was the perfect candidate," says Squier. "He trusted me, and he trusted the new campaign technology. He was willing to sit down at one point in the campaign and write a check for $250,000 to keep us going."

Squier's strategy was to put Graham, a multimillionaire, to work in 100 different jobs — from bellhop to chicken plucker. It was political gimmickry. And it worked.

The work days became Graham's trademark, and he has continued them ever since. Squier has remained his media advisor, producing ads for the governor's reelection campaign and several Graham-supported referenda.

The 1986 Senate race will be lucrative for Squier. His firm — The Communications Company, charges a $60,000 consulting fee, plus a 15 percent commission on every dollar spent on television or radio advertising. If Graham spends $3 million on ads, a conservative estimate, Squier's commission would be $450,000. Hamilton, by contrast, receives no commissions; he is paid a consulting fee and is paid for each poll he conducts.

On the wall of Charles R. Black's expensively furnished office in the Washington suburb of Alexandria hangs a photo of Hawkins. "To my good friend, and soldier of fortune," the senator wrote on it.

It is an apt description. Black, 38, a long-time friend and political adviser to Hawkins, is one of the most successful political operatives in the Republican Party.

His firm — Black, Manafort, & Stone — could receive more than $500,000 in fees from the Hawkins campaign. This is based on a retainer — normally $75,000 to $125,000 per race — and a commission for placing television and radio advertising. He charges a lower commission than Squier's 15 percent, but the Hawkins campaign is expected to spend more than Graham's on advertising.

Black is the general consultant to Hawkins' campaign. "I put the whole thing together. I do the planning, the strategy. I help hire the other professionals and the campaign staff," he says. "Basically, I'm the bottom line. When I wake up in the morning, I have to make sure what's supposed to happen in the campaign that day happens."

Black is also a lobbyist. His considerable political connections are obviously an asset. Among his former Republican clients are President Reagan, four Senate committee chairmen, Senate Majority Leader

Robert J. Dole of Kansas, Representative Jack Kemp of New York — a 1988 presidential hopeful, and Senator Phil Gramm of Texas.

Black says he doesn't lobby Hawkins or any other current client. But he adds: "We have a lot of friends up there [on Capitol Hill], and we give a lot of free political advice to people. I don't have any compunction about lobbying them if they're calling me for advice or help in fundraising. Just like the White House. I was a total volunteer in the [presidential] campaign. So today, if they [White House officials] call me for a little favor, I don't mind lobbying them because it's not a professional relationship."

Black's roots are in the right wing of his party. He has been a Senate aide and campaign adviser to Senator Jesse Helms of North Carolina, executive director of Young Americans for Freedom, a conservative student group, chairman of the National Conservative Political Action Committee, political director of the National Republican Committee and Reagan's 1980 campaign (a job he resigned when Reagan fired campaign manager John Sears), and "senior consultant" to the Reagan-Bush 1984 campaign.

Black's teammates in the Hawkins campaign are an eclectic lot. Goodman is a moderate Republican, who sometimes works for Democrats; Morris a registered Democrat who sometimes works for Republicans.

Goodman's background is in commercial advertising; his Baltimore agency was in business seven years before it did its first political race in 1966. Since then, it has worked on about 100 races; 13 U.S. senators are current or former Goodman clients. Republican Senator Pete Wilson of California was the best man at Goodman's wedding.

Goodman is known for his "feel-good" approach to politics; Morris, a relative newcomer to national politics, for his ability to go for the jugular.

Morris, 38, is a self-taught pollster. His roots are on the issue side of New York Democratic politics. He envisions himself as much a strategist as a pollster. He describes most other pollsters as "diagnosticians." "They don't prescribe drugs; they just tell you that you have cancer," he says. "After working with me, getting data from other pollsters is like getting data from a vending machine."

Morris' first big break came in Massachusetts in 1978 when he helped mastermind the upset victory of Edward King, a conservative Democrat since turned Republican, over the incumbent, Democratic Governor Michael S. Dukakis.

The following year he approached Hawkins, who had just stepped down from the state Public Service Commission, with polling data he used to persuade her that she could be elected to the Senate. He and Black were the strategists behind her upset 1980 victory.

"Dick is a great guy to have around when the grenades start to drop," Goodman says.

"I throw them back," boasts Morris.

A classic example of this occurred in the 1983 Mississippi gubernatorial race. Morris and Goodman were working for the Democratic candidate, William A. Allain. Three weeks before the election, Republican supporters of Allain's opponent, Leon Bramlett, called a news conference during which three black transvestite prostitutes claimed Allain had engaged their services.

In a single day, Allain dropped 60 percentage points in Morris' polls. But Morris had gotten early word of the allegations and had prepared a wave of ads to counter them.

"There's a new word in Mississippi. The word is smear," said one ad. "We're being asked to believe the worst, the absolute worst about a man we've known and trusted for 25 years. Who are the people who are doing the charges and on whose say-so — three prostitutes, three transvestites, each with long criminal records, each who admits they were paid $1,000 and $50 a day to keep up the story. We're a lot smarter than that in Mississippi."

Allain won the election.

The recent Hawkins ads impressed many Florida Democrats. "Hawkins is unique. That's been one of her problems: She is almost falling off the edge," says one party leader. "They've taken something bad and made it good. They're saying total concentration on something like missing children isn't weird. That's smart."

The ads caught the Graham team in limbo. The governor has formed a fund-raising committee, opened an office and hired a campaign manager, but he has yet to make a formal announcement of his candidacy.

Meanwhile, his office has been plagued by management shifts. His chief of staff, press secretary, and speechwriter have left during the past five months.

The campaign's response to the Hawkins commercials was a bit of guerrilla warfare, stage-managed by Squier. He was helped by two accidental events. One was a statment by John Walsh, star of a Hawkins ad about missing children, that he would do a similar commercial for Graham, if asked. Walsh has crusaded on behalf of missing children since his six-year-old son was murdered in 1981.

The other event occurred one night in mid-October when Squier's son Mark happened to be at work in a Philadelphia video-processing firm, where copies of the Hawkins ads were being reproduced. By mistake, the ads appeared on a television monitor in a room where Mark Squier was eating a carryout Chinese dinner.

The young Squier told his father about the ads. "If I hadn't, he would have fired me," he says. Bob Squier promptly informed reporters that Hawkins was about to launch an ad blitz, something the campaign had repeatedly denied that it was planning.

"I thought I was doing a public service," he says.

Goodman was furious about "the babbling to the press." He says it caused him "pangs of discomfort," "embarrassed a lot of people," and created "real shell shock" within the Hawkins campaign.

The ads, however, accomplished their mission. A Florida newspaper poll taken after the million-dollar blitz found Hawkins had drastically reduced Graham's lead, to 48 percent to 41 percent. In a poll by the same group of newspapers in March 1984, Graham led Hawkins by 22 percentage points.

"This is going to be a long and woolly affair," Morris says.

S UCCESSFUL POLITICAL CANDI-
dates learn to deal with the media
from the day they run for office
until they retire. The grist of the reporter's mill is information, and sometimes
misinformation. Reporters follow political candidates like hawks stalking their
prey, hoping that in one fell swoop they
will be able to capture information that
will command a front-page headline or a
spot on the nightly television news. At
least that is the view of the press held by
many politicians.

The focus of the most intense press
attention is, understandably, presidential politics, both running and governing.

Before Richard Nixon boarded over
the indoor White House swimming pool
to make a press-briefing room, presidential aides going to their offices in the
West Wing walked through a press
lounge. There, one White House aide
told the author, the "piranha" eagerly
waited to devour White House staffers.
In the paranoiac atmosphere that so frequently pervades politics, the press is
always the enemy unless it is controlled.
Every president in the modern era, from
Franklin D. Roosevelt to Ronald Reagan,
has attempted to manage the news. William Safire defines managed news as "information generated and distributed
by the government in such a way as to
give government interest priority over
candor."[1]

The media are, to use the phrase of
Douglass Cater, the fourth branch of the
government.[2] The press, which now includes the electronic as well as the print
media, has appointed itself guardian of
the public interest. Although many

members of the press have a cozy
relationship with public officials, upon
whom they depend for valuable information, the theory of the press that is
taught in journalism schools requires
reporters to distance themselves personally from the subjects of their stories.
The adversary relationship between investigative reporters and the government
enables a reporter to ferret out the facts
no matter how unpleasant they may be.

While the Washington press includes
reporters like Bob Woodward and Carl
Bernstein, whose investigations of the
Nixon White House's coverup of the
break-in at the Democratic National
Headquarters in the Watergate office
complex led to impeachment proceedings against the president and his
resignation, they are exceptions and not
the rule. Understandably, the seductive
Washington environment, in which
power and status mean everything, has
co-opted many reporters. The press has
become part of the Washington establishment because it has learned to
play the game of power politics itself.
The Gridiron Club, an old and exclusive
organization of newspaper people, symbolizes the press elite. Annually it invites
members of the political establishment
to join it in a fun-filled session of humor
and satire. The spirit of camaraderie that
prevails at such a gathering can best be
appreciated by those on the inside. President and Mrs. Reagan were the highlights of the club's meeting in 1982, as
the First Lady skillfully performed a skit
that satirized the prevailing press view of
her activities.

The Gridiron Club may roast politicians, but its members recognize that the

[1] William Safire, *Safire's Political Dictionary* (New York: Random House, 1978), p. 397.
[2] Douglass Cater, *The Fourth Branch of the Government* (Boston: Houghton Mifflin, 1959).

press and the politicians are in the same broader club of the politically powerful. Washington reporters recognize that to be at the top of the newspaper profession they must have access to the top of the political world. The linkage between success and power often softens the adversary stance of the press.

Washington's political centers of power recognize that the press is an important fourth branch of the government. Presidents, members of Congress, and even Supreme Court justices know that managing the news will buttress their power and may even be a key to survival. Presidents, especially during their first few years in office, feel besieged by a press that they consider hostile and unfair. Even before he became president, John F. Kennedy went out of his way to warn an aide about the press,

"Always remember that their interests and ours ultimately conflict."[3]

Kennedy cultivated political reporters, and his good press relations not only helped him to win the presidential election in 1960 but also buttressed his presidency. Richard Nixon blamed his 1960 defeat on an unfair press, an attitude that was intensified after he lost his race for the California governorship in 1963. Nixon understandably put managing the news at the top of his agenda when he became president.

All presidents would like to manage the news, which, in the view of Jimmy Carter's press secretary Jody Powell in the following selection, gives the White House the right to lie when national security is at stake.

13 Jody Powell
THE RIGHT TO LIE

Since the day the first reporter asked the first tough question of a government official, there has been an ongoing debate about whether government has the right to lie.

The debate took on its present form one day in 1963, when then Pentagon spokesman Arthur Sylvester, for reasons known only to himself, responded to the question officially and honestly. "Yes," he said, "under certain circumstances I think government does have the right to lie."

The resulting furor has made every sitting press secretary and senior government official leery of the question from that day since. Like all my predecessors, I was always careful not to give a direct response. It was

[3]William Safire, *Safire's Political Dictionary*, p. 397.

one of those questions for which you prepare and keep on file a standard evasion.

But Sylvester, of course, was right. In certain circumstances, government has not only the right but a positive obligation to lie. For me, that right-obligation flows directly from two other principles:

First, that government has a legitimate right to secrecy in certain matters because the welfare of the nation requires it. In other cases, individuals, even public figures, have a certain right to privacy because common decency demands it.

Secondly, the press has a right to print what it knows within very broad limits, without prior restraint, because the survival of democratic government depends on it.

Those two principles are often in conflict. Fortunately, the confrontation is not usually irreconcilable. Questions can be evaded. Answers can be devised that may mislead, but do not directly misrepresent. A "no comment" can sometimes be used without its being taken as a confirmation. Or the reporter can be sworn to secrecy himself and told why it is that certain information would be terribly damaging if published.

That is usually the case, but not always. Occasionally, the conflict is so sharp and the matter involved so important that there is no way to slide off the point. There is simply no answer that is both true and responsible. In such cases, the only decent thing to do is to lie and, I would argue, to make it the most convincing lie you can devise.

In my four years in the White House, I was only faced with that type of situation twice.

The first involved a question from a so-called reporter who was noted for trading in gossip and personal scandal, and who worked for a publication that had an even worse reputation in that regard.

The question involved the personal life of a colleague and that of his family. To have responded with what I believed to be the truth would have resulted in great pain and embarrassment for a number of perfectly innocent people. Beyond that, I could see no reason why the matter should be of public interest.

I had little doubt that an evasion or "no comment" would be taken as more than adequate confirmation by this particular writer, and no doubt whatsoever that there was no hope of successfully appealing to a sense of compassion and fair play. So I lied.

I did not just deny the allegation, but went to some trouble to construct a convincing argument as to what I suspected to be the case. Apparently, it worked, probably because others who were asked responded in much the same way I did. In any case, the story never appeared in print anywhere that I know of.

I have absolutely no regrets for what I did, and can say without hesitation that I would do the same thing again if similar circumstances arose. Quite simply, it seems to me that to the extent journalism insists upon the right to probe into matters that can destroy families and ruin careers, but which in no way involve a breach of public trust, it must also grant the right to those who become targets to defend themselves by the only means available.

Moreover, there will inevitably be a disputed area between journalists and public figures over what is, and what is not, a legitimate matter of public interest. In some cases, the answer may not be clear, even to the most unbiased observer, except in retrospect. And it hardly needs to be said that a *post hoc* decision that a personal matter should have remained private is of absolutely no benefit to those who have been hurt by its publication.

The other situation in which I believed, and still believe, that I had an obligation to lie occurred in April of 1980.

Following the collapse of the first of two attempts to negotiate an agreement with the Iranian government to secure the release of our hostages, because those nominally in positions of authority either could not or would not live up to their promises, the president began to look more seriously at a military rescue operation.

He had given orders for work to begin on such an option as soon as the hostages were seized. At that time, there seemed to be no feasible way to go about it with a decent chance of success. In the intervening months, as the Pentagon studied, planned, and trained, and as we learned more about the situation in the embassy compound through intelligence operations and the news media, the chances for a successful attempt began to increase.

Although I knew the work was being done, I knew nothing about its specifics, and indeed did not want to know, until March 22, 1980. In a meeting at Camp David to review our options following the disintegration of the first agreement, Secretary of Defense Brown and Joint Chiefs of Staff Chairman General David Jones presented a full briefing on their plans for a rescue operation.

It was impressive, both because of the work that had gone into it and the intelligence that we had managed to gather, and because the detailed consideration of such an option inevitably has a powerfully sobering effect on anyone with a say in whether or not it will be implemented.

Still, no one seemed to feel that this was the correct choice at the time. There were some questions raised about whether some aspects of what was necessarily a complex plan could not be simplified. More important in the decision not to go ahead then was the willingness, although reluctant, to give diplomacy one last chance. No one doubted that there would be American casualties, even in a successful operation. One

Israeli soldier and three hostages had been killed at Entebbe, and the problem that faced our planners, and would face the strike force, were many times more difficult than anything the Israelis had confronted. There had also been messages from our intermediaries, and indirectly from Iranian officials, almost begging for a chance to put the negotiated agreement back on track.

Even though no one argued that day that we should choose the rescue option, I left the meeting feeling that we were heading down a road that would soon bring us to that choice unless the Iranians suddenly came to their senses. Despite my agreement with the decision to try the diplomatic approach again, I had to admit to myself that the odds seemed to be against the Iranians' implementing the agreement they had already reneged on once.

On the morning of April 11, shortly after that second diplomatic effort had indeed collapsed, the president called me into his office a few minutes before the regular Friday morning foreign-policy breakfast was to begin. During most of the administration, I had not attended these breakfasts on a regular basis. When the president felt that the agenda required my presence, he would let me know. Occasionally, I would ask to be included if I had a point I wanted to raise, or if I felt the need to listen to the discussion on a particular topic.

Once the hostage crisis began, however, I asked to attend on a regular basis, so that I could keep abreast of the latest thinking by the decision makers, as well as the often fast-breaking events. The president readily agreed. So I was somewhat surprised that morning when he said that he wanted to talk to me about whether I should attend the breakfast.

Then he explained that one of the topics, not included on the written agenda, was the rescue mission. I could tell, or thought I could, by his tone of voice and expression that this had now become a serious option for him.

Was this something I would rather not know about? the president asked. Would it make my job easier if down the road I could honestly claim to have had no knowledge of this option?

I replied that I had given some thought to the matter since the Camp David session. It seemed to me that if he decided to go ahead with the rescue option, we would need an aggressive effort to protect its secrecy. That might involve purposely misleading or even lying to the press. If it did, I was the person to do it. And if I did it, I wanted to have the information necessary to make my effort successful. Since I was also being asked about the Iran crisis almost every day, I said, there was the chance that I might inadvertently compromise the mission unless I knew exactly what activities were the most sensitive.

The president said he had expected that would be my response, and he agreed with it, but he had wanted to hear it from me.

Then he added with a hint of a smile, "If you have to lie to the press, I may have to fire you when this is all over, you know. I'm not sure I can have a press secretary who won't tell the truth to the press."

"That," I said, "would be doing me a real favor."

"And an even bigger one for the country," said the president with what I hoped was a smile, as he turned to walk to the Cabinet room, where his foreign policy team was waiting.

The briefing, on which I took no notes, was much the same as the earlier session at Camp David. Maps and charts were positioned on an easel and occasionally spread on the table for closer examination. The questions and suggestions from three weeks earlier had been taken into account, and the military planners had come up with a few new wrinkles on their own.

By the time it was over, I sensed that the men around the table, including the president, were leaning strongly toward ordering the plan to be implemented. The comments that followed confirmed my hunch. I added my endorsement, and emphasized again my feeling that we would need to give some thought to cover stories and an aggressive effort to protect the secrecy of the mission if the president decided to go ahead.

The only partial demurral came from Deputy Secretary of State Warren Christopher. Although he was inclined to recommend that the president order the mission, as he made clear later, he did not know how Secretary of State Vance (who was taking a brief and well-earned vacation) would react and did not feel that he should express a personal opinion.

The president said he was tentatively inclined to proceed with the mission, but would defer a final decision until he had discussed it with Vance.

As we got up to leave the room, I found myself standing next to Harold Brown. "Mr. Secretary," I said, "the president is going to go with this thing, I can sense it. If we can bring our people out of there, it will do more good for this country than anything that has happened in twenty years."

"Yes," said Brown, "and if we fail, that will be the end of the Carter presidency."

"But we really don't have much choice, do we?"

The Secretary shook his head no as we walked out the door.

A moment later, Helen Thomas, of UPI, walked around the corner from the press room on the way to my office.

"Big meeting, huh?" she called down the short corridor. "You guys decide to nuke 'em?"

Brown and I both nodded yes, and I offered to let Helen and her colleagues know in plenty of time to be on the scene when the warheads struck.

If she only knew, I thought.

In fact, one of the problems we faced, once the president made his final decision four days later, was the number of press people in Teheran. As part of his objections, Cyrus Vance had warned that the Iranians might seize some of the several hundred Americans still in Teheran, thus leaving us with more hostages to worry about, even if the mission was a success. A fair number of this group were journalists.

I told the president that I saw no way for us to make the reporters come home, short of telling the news organizations what was about to happen, and that was clearly out of the question. Still, he felt an obligation to try. The president's first inclination was to order them home. I argued against this. There was no way to enforce the order, and I suspected that the attempt would so enrage the news executives that they would insist on keeping people there who might have been planning to come back anyway.

"Some of them are so ornery that they might just send an extra correspondent over to prove they can do it," I said.

In the end, we decided to use the increasingly volatile situation in Iran as an excuse to try to get journalists and other Americans to come home.

At a news conference on April 17, the president announced that he was prohibiting all financial transactions between Iranians and Americans and barring all imports from Iran. Then he stated that "to protect American citizens," he was banning all travel to Iran.

These steps, he said, would "not *now* be used to interfere with the right of the press to gather news."

"However," he continued, speaking slowly and precisely, "it is my responsibility and my obligation, given the situation in Iran, to call on American journalists and newsgathering organizations to minimize, as severely as possible, their presence and their activities in Iran."

As we had feared, the only effect was to provoke angry calls, particularly from the networks. After listening to Washington bureau chiefs and presidents of news divisions berate us for trying to repeal the First Amendment and stifle news coverage for political ends, I finally lost my temper with Sandy Socolow of CBS.

"Look Sandy," I said, "the president told you what he thinks you ought to do, and I have nothing to add to it. I warned him that you people would get on a high horse, but he wanted to do it anyway. I personally don't give a good goddamn what you people do. If I had my way, I'd ask the fucking Ayatollah to keep fifty reporters and give us our diplomats back. Then you people who have all the answers could figure out how to get them out."

As soon as I hung up the phone, I regretted having lost my temper. Not because I feared that I had hurt Socolow's feelings — he is not an overly sensitive fellow — but because I was worried that my angry response might have implied that something dramatic was about to happen. I had come that close to saying that he would have to accept the consequences for what happened if he ignored the president's warning, but had caught myself in time. I vowed to keep my temper in check, at least until this operation was complete.

The president's statement of April 17, in addition to being a futile attempt to get Americans out of Teheran, also fit into our cover story. By announcing additional sanctions, he implied that there would be a period of time during which we would wait and see if they would work before any other actions were taken. I, and others who knew what was actually afoot, strengthened this impression with background briefings.

We also suggested that if we were forced to consider any sort of military option, it would be something like a blockade or mining of harbors. This was the cover story we had devised for the military movements necessary to prepare for the rescue mission. On several occasions I speculated with reporters off the record about the relative merits of a blockade as opposed to mining.

We had, in fact, ruled out both of these options. They were unlikely to force the Iranians to yield, and once attempted would have to be followed up by an escalation of military force if no response was forthcoming. We would thus be starting down a road the end of which no one could see. We also believed that once any sort of military move was made, the Iranians as part of any general reaction might tighten security around the embassy, which we knew to be extremely lax, or disperse the hostages, thus denying us the rescue option.

The problems associated with the blockade were much the same as those associated with bombing power stations or other valuable targets in Iran — ideas that were being advanced by several columnists and commentators. I had suggested to the president earlier that what he ought to do was "bomb the hell out of every dam and power station in Iran. Let the Ayatollah shoot two hostages and call on the Russians for help, then turn the whole thing over to Agronsky and Company to handle."

His response is not printable.

By the week of April 20 it was becoming clear that our cover story was working too well. All the talk about mining and blockades was making some people nervous and everyone curious. That presented a problem. We did not want anyone, even on the White House staff, snooping around in an effort to find out what was going on. They just might stumble on something. In addition, once the staff begins to talk a great deal about anything, it is only a short time before the press gets interested, too.

But this also presented us with an opportunity to reinforce our cover story. On Tuesday, April 22, little more than forty-eight hours before the Delta Team would enter Iranian air space, Hamilton called a staff meeting to address the concerns that were buzzing about the staff. He assured them all that we had no plans, at the moment, for mining or blockading. When asked about a rescue mission, he lied.

As soon as I heard what had taken place, I began to prepare for a press call. It came less than ninety minutes after the meeting ended. Jack Nelson, bureau chief of the *Los Angeles Times*, wanted to talk to me about something he had heard from a "pretty interesting staff meeting you people had this morning." I said I had not been there but would check with Hamilton.

I then called Hamilton to tell him what I was about to do. I hated to do it to Nelson, who was one of the more decent journalists that I had gotten to know since coming to Washington, and one who would become a good friend once the administration was over. But I did not feel that I had any choice. I knew what he wanted to talk about. It was an opportunity to reinforce the web of deception we had constructed to protect the rescue mission.

When I called Nelson back, he said he had heard that some staffers had expressed concern that we were about to take some action that might "involve us in a war." I confirmed this report and repeated Hamilton's assurances that we were planning no military action whatsoever, and certainly nothing like a rescue mission.

Later that day, Nelson came by my office to continue our discussion. Toward the end of that conversation, he asked, "You people really aren't thinking about doing anything drastic like launching a rescue mission, are you?"

This was the moment of truth, or, more accurately, of deception. Up to this point, I had only repeated false statements made by others, and admittedly fine distinction, but a distinction nevertheless. Now I was faced with a direct question. With a swallow that I hoped was not noticeable, I began to recite all the reasons why a rescue operation would not make any sense. They were familiar because they were exactly the ones that it had taken four months to figure out how to overcome.

"If and when we are forced to move militarily, I suspect it will be something like a blockade," I said, "but that decision is a step or two down the road."

I made a mental note to be sure to call Jack and apologize once the operation was completed, hoping he would understand.

The result was a story in the *Los Angeles Times* reporting Hamilton's assurances to the staff that no military action was in the offing, and that a rescue operation was still considered to be impractical.

When I read it the next day, I remember hoping that some Iranian student at Berkeley had enough loyalty to the Ayatollah to phone it in to Teheran.

Two days later the hostage rescue attempt ended in disaster. Nelson, to his credit, seemed to understand what I had done, even though he could not explicitly condone it. Most other reporters reacted in similar fashion when the story of my deception came out. A few even stopped by to say privately that they would have done the same thing in my position. A few others were quoted, anonymously, as saying that I had destroyed my credibility and ought to resign.

The issue quickly faded as we dealt with the spectacle of Iranian leaders boasting over the bodies of American servicemen, the tortured but eventually successful efforts to secure their return, and the ceremonies honoring their courage and dedication to duty.

There were a few attempts to exploit the situation for political purposes: Stories were planted with reporters that the mission had been discovered by the Soviets and a call from Brezhnev had brought about the cancellation, and that the military commanders had wanted to go ahead after the loss of three helicopters but the president had lost his nerve and ordered them to turn back. These attempts at disinformation were largely unsuccessful. Later, as we shall see, those responsible for these efforts were able to find journalists whose indifference or incompetence made them useful political tools.

In October of 1983, . . . controversy flared again between the White House and the press over the relative rights and responsibilities of the two institutions. The occasion was the American invasion of Grenada, and there were several reasonably separate issues involved.

The first was the same one that I had dealt with three and a half years prior: the right of government to lie. On the afternoon before American forces landed in Grenada, CBS White House correspondent Bill Plante learned from a reliable source that an invasion would take place at sunrise the next morning. He checked with the White House Press Office and got a flat denial. "Preposterous," said spokesman Larry Speakes. Other reporters got the same response from other government officials.

The decision by the Reagan administration to deceive journalists rather than risk the possibility that the invasion plans would be disclosed seemed to me to be eminently defensible.

When I asked Plante later what he would have done if the White House had confirmed the invasion plans, his response was "I don't know; we would have tried to find some way to use what we knew without endangering the operation."

That in itself would seem to confirm the wisdom of the White House judgment. You cannot expect government to leave such questions in the hands of the fourth estate. The consequences of an error are too severe.

Moreover, given the extent of eavesdropping capabilities in Washington, it would be an unacceptable risk to have Mr. Plante and others at CBS chatting at some length over open telephone lines about how they would use the information. By the time their decision was made it most likely would be moot.

Some journalists were willing to agree privately that this situation was one of those in which there was no other choice but to lie. Most, however, were unwilling to endorse publicly the idea that lying could be condoned under any circumstances, feeling that government does enough lying as it is without any encouragement from them.

They make the very valid point that once you step away from the categorical, there is no easily discernible place to draw the line.

Still the essential dilemma remains. What about those situations where an evasion simply will not work, where a "no comment" is almost certain to be taken as a confirmation? If, at the same time, the information to be protected is of sufficient importance, if lives are at stake for example, a lie becomes in my estimation the lesser evil of the choices available. It is ludicrous to argue that soldiers may be sent off to fight and die, but a spokesman may not, under any circumstances, be asked to lie to make sure that the casualties are fewer and not in vain.

Churchill made the point with his usual flair in 1943. "In wartime," he said, "truth is so precious that she should be attended by a bodyguard of lies."

Unfortunately, once one steps onto the slippery slope of relativism, firm footing cannot be established, even on the basis of "wartime" or "lives at stake." There are other dilemmas that can and do arise, where calculated deception might be appropriate.

Although I never faced it personally, the protection of an important intelligence source or method, even in peacetime, might be one.

And what about the protection of an important diplomatic initiative? I almost faced such a situation at Camp David when reports of bad blood between Sadat and Begin arose and when there were leaks about Sadat's threat to break off the talks. . . . I was able to deal with those problems without telling a bald-faced lie, but that was mostly a matter of luck.

In the midst of the Grenada controversy, a columnist revealed that the premature publication by Jack Anderson of a story about Henry Kissinger's secret diplomatic initiatives had damaged, although not fatally, the movement toward normalization of relations with China. That initiative became arguably the most significant strategic event since the Second World War. Would lying have been appropriate in an effort to keep it on track?

In the early months of the Carter administration the *Washington Post* published accounts of secret payments through the CIA to King Hussein of Jordan. The story appeared on the day that Secretary of State Vance arrived in Amman to discuss a Middle East peace initiative with Hussein. Needless to say, the result was a less than positive environment for the talks.

In that case, we had chosen to be candid with the *Post* and appeal to their sense of responsibility. From our point of view the effort was a failure. Although we had not asked them not to publish the story, feeling that such a request would be futile, we had requested a delay. When it came out at the most unfortunate of all possible times, we felt the *Post* was guilty of bad faith. The *Post* maintained that the timing was a result of a misunderstanding.

In any case, the question remains. In our judgment the *Post* had enough information to go with the story whatever we said. But what if we had concluded that it was possible to kill the story with a lie, would we have been justified in doing so?

To take another step down the slope, what degree of deception would be acceptable from a Justice Department official trying to protect the rights of an innocent person whose name had cropped up in an investigation?

Or what about a spokesman at Treasury attempting to avoid the premature disclosure of information on a financial decision that could lead to severe damage to innocent parties and great profits for those in a position to take advantage of the leak?

The problem becomes, as noted above, where precisely to draw the line. There is no convenient place. About the best one can do is to argue that it must be drawn very tightly, for practical as well as moral considerations. Distinctions may be difficult at the margins, but we can all tell the difference between mountains and molehills. If government does have the right to lie in certain situations, that right is as precious as the truth it attends. It must not be squandered on matters of less than overriding importance.

Which brings us to another issue in the Grenada controversy. Many correspondents said that the exchange between Speakes and CBS was not the cause but the catalyst for their outrage. They charged that the administration had repeatedly lied to them on matters that were in no way vital to national security or the protection of lives. They listed examples that ranged from the dates of resignations to travel plans to attempts to square the facts with some off-the-cuff presidential remark.

They also pointed to a history of efforts to curtail the flow of information from the screening of calls to White House officials from reporters by the communications and press offices to proposals for the review of anything written by thousands of government officials after they leave office. (At this writing, Congress has wisely blocked this last absurdity, but the administration has vowed not to give up.)

That attitude was not unanimous, but it was clearly shared by a large number of White House correspondents. And that is a dangerous set of circumstances for the administration and potentially for the nation. The danger for the administration is that it will find itself lacking credibility across the board, that no explanation will be accepted at face value and every action will be subject to the most unflattering interpretation.

For the nation, the danger lies in the fact that an administration that is generally believed to be dishonest will not command the respect necessary to protect legitimate secrets. There are many cases in which truths less vital than the timing and objective of military operations are protected by successful appeals to reporters not to publish. The full and exact reasons for such requests cannot always be disclosed, because they too may be quite sensitive. Needless to say, such appeals — which amount to a request to "trust me" — can only be effective in a climate of mutual trust.

To the extent that this climate was placed in jeopardy following the Grenada controversy, the problem was not primarily a conflict over government's right to lie about issues of ultimate importance, but a perceived pattern of deception solely for the sake of convenience — of lies designed to protect and promote nothing more precious than someone's political backside.

Even during the Grenada operation, there were lies from the government that were difficult to justify by any reasonable standard. Claims that coverage was curtailed, after the invasion had begun, because of concern for the safety of reporters were poppycock. Even experienced spokesmen had a hard time making that argument with a straight face.

Similarly, attempts to blame the decision to restrict coverage on "military commanders" were deceptive and cowardly and dangerous. There is no doubt that many uniformed military officers hold the press in less than great esteem or that the restricted coverage was completely in line with their preferences. But that is not the point. Such decisions are always subject to White House review. And they were repeatedly brought to the attention of White House officials. If the preferences of the military commanders were honored, it was because the president and his men agreed with them.

This refusal to accept responsibility for one's own actions was dangerous in this case because it served to exacerbate tensions between the military and the fourth estate, to heighten mutual distrust on both sides. These tensions are already high enough and that problem is going to be with us for the indefinite future. Already it works against responsible and accurate reporting of national security issues. It also promotes an unreasoning distrust of all things military in our society. There is, in my view, no excuse for an administration's hiding behind the armed forces simply to avoid facing ticklish questions.

A related issue has to do with how much the White House press secretary should be told in situations such as this. It very quickly became clear in this particular case that the press secretary and the press office had been kept in the dark until the invasion was under way. Mr. Speakes and his people were not intentionally lying themselves when they denied the reports from Plante and other newsmen; they were merely passing on what they had been told by members of the National Security Council staff.

This quickly became a bone of contention within the White House. Mr. Speakes and his people were none too happy about the way they had been treated. One deputy resigned as a result. However, more senior White House officials declared themselves well pleased with the procedure and stated that they would handle things the same way if similar situations arose in the future.

Mr. Speakes made it clear that if a lie was required and he was to be sent out to tell it, he wanted to know what was at stake. And he was exactly right. Keeping the press secretary in the dark can create serious problems.

First, it inevitably erodes the press secretary's effectiveness. It costs him in prestige and status, factors that may mean more than they should in Washington, but still cannot be ignored. The press secretary's job is tough enough as it is; he deserves every break his colleagues can give him. Putting the guy whose business is information in a position that makes him appear to be uninformed, out of touch, and not trusted makes no sense over the long haul.

Beyond that, if a secret is worth lying about to protect, it makes sense to come up with the most effective lie possible. Most sensitive operations are accompanied by a cover story, designed to provide an innocent explanation for bits and pieces that might leak out. Since the first group of people that such a story must convince is the press, having the press secretary involved in designing the story is not a bad idea. He more than anyone else is likely to know what will be convincing and what will not.

Furthermore, the use of the story, if it ever becomes necessary, is likely to be more effective if the person who puts it out knows exactly what he is trying to do. Dealing with the press, particularly in ticklish situations, is very much an art. You cannot treat the press secretary like a robot and then expect him to perform like an artist.

Another danger in keeping the press secretary uninformed comes from the way in which a press office operates. When a new question arises or an issue looks like it is going to get hot, the press office begins to function very much like a news organization. Deputy and assistant and deputy assistant press secretaries immediately get to work calling all over the government to try to find out what is really going on and where it may lead.

As information is gathered, it is often passed on to the reporter who has made the query in bits and pieces as part of a continuing exchange of information and ideas. Needless to say, if there is something highly sensitive that has to be protected, the press secretary needs to know about it. Otherwise, this process could stumble into and lead to the uncovering of information that should be kept secret.

In matters large and small, keeping the press secretary in the dark is risky business. If he cannot be trusted with sensitive information, he should be replaced. Failing that, he ought to be given the information he needs to do his job effectively.

Having said all that, however, I suspect that the most important lesson from this episode is to be found in the fact that the press was a clear loser in its fight with the administration over Grenada. It lost in the court in which such matters will eventually be decided — the court of public opinion. In the immediate aftermath of Grenada it was sometimes difficult to tell which the American people enjoyed more, seeing the president kick hell out of the Cubans or the press.

And the reasons the fourth estate lost were to a large extent its own fault.

The strength of the public reaction in favor of the administration's policy of denying access to the press was a shock to many Washington journalists. The more thoughtful were concerned as well as surprised.

It is true that the press is particularly vulnerable among our major institutions because it is so often the bearer of sad tidings, the forum for criticism of ideas, individuals, and institutions that Americans hold dear. It is also true, as journalists are fond of pointing out, that their job is not to win popularity contests. But the vocal and sometimes vicious public reaction against the press in the wake of Grenada was more than just some sort of "shoot the messenger" syndrome.

In part it sprang from the way the fourth estate handled the terrorist bombing of our marine headquarters in Beirut, which occurred just prior to the Grenada operation. The behavior of some news organizations was not the sort that would inspire public confidence in their judgment or self-restraint.

There was, for example, the repugnant spectacle of CBS camped ghoulishly at the home of parents awaiting word on the fate of their marine son in Beirut. And they hit the jackpot. The boy was dead. So they got to film the arrival of the casualty officer and the chaplain bringing the tragic news to the parents.

The tragic scene, for which every standard of good taste and decency demanded privacy, was then offered up to satisfy the voyeurism of the worst segments of the American television audience and the demands for the higher ratings that are believed, with some justification, to come with sensationalism.

Nor was this sort of gross insensitivity confined to television. A few days after the Beirut bombing, readers of the *Washington Post* were treated to the incredibly insensitive comments of a *Newsweek* executive describing at some length what a wonderful thing the tragedy was for his magazine:

"We are exhilarated by this. It's the sort of thing *Newsweek* does best — react to a big story in a big way. We'll be pulling out all the stops. . . . one hell of a story . . . pursuing a variety of angles . . . expect a lot of competition, it's the biggest story of the year."

If the tasteless coverage of the Beirut tragedy was a factor in the public's reaction to Grenada, it was by no means the whole of it. The attitudes reflected did not develop over a few days or weeks.

If the government has in this and other instances been guilty of excess in the exercise of what I believe to be its legitimate right to mislead and even deceive on matters of vital import, the fourth estate has also been guilty of excess in its cavalier insistence on the right to do as it pleases with little regard for good judgment, good taste, or the consequences of its actions — and the American people know it.

One consequence of the information explosion has been that more and more Americans have had the opportunity to see news coverage of incidents they knew something about. And they have come away disillusioned, and sometimes angry, because of the wide gap that too often existed between what they knew to be the case and what was reported.

And if they were foolish enough to try to set the record straight by appealing for a correction, they also ran head on into that determination never to admit a mistake, much less do anything about it.

The public's reaction to Grenada ought to be a danger signal for journalism. The question . . . is how the fourth estate will react. The greatest danger is that the reaction will be defensive, a renewed determination to pretend that nothing is wrong except the shortsightedness and lack of sophistication of the American public.

I N THE FOLLOWING SELECTION, one of America's best-known reporters in the White House Press Corps gives *his* side of the story. Readers have a unique opportunity to appear behind the scenes of the White House press as Sam Donaldson depicts both the exhilarating and frustrating aspects of his work.

14 Lee Michael Katz
PRESSING MATTERS: An Interview with White House Correspondent Sam Donaldson

Sam Donaldson, 52, is known to millions of television viewers across America for his booming voice and willingness to confront the president of the United States. A national fixture on ABC's nightly news, *This Week with David Brinkley*, and as Sunday evening anchor, Donaldson is known as a tough, aggressive, and often abrasive reporter. Although his peers are quick to note his legendary personality quirks, they have also again selected him as the top White House correspondent in a *Washington Journalism Review* poll.

The El Paso, Texas native began his television career with KRLD-TV in Dallas in 1959. He came to Washington as a local television reporter in 1961, joining ABC News in 1967. Donaldson has covered every political convention since 1964, went on special assignment to Vietnam in 1971, and covered the House and Senate before roosting at the White House.

By his own admission, Donaldson's persistence earns him the enmity of the Secret Service and often his colleagues. A reformed smoker, Donaldson led a zealous, though quixotic, battle to ban smoking in the White House press room. Feuding with longtime friends, Donaldson finally settled for the installation of an expensive filter to keep the smoke out of his way.

Friends say he has mellowed since his recent marriage to his third wife, Jan, a television producer — but only slightly.

For several years, Donaldson has been insisting he wants to leave the White House beat, but ABC has been reluctant to give in. In the following interview, he describes some of the professional rewards and frustrations he has experienced dogging the president of the United States.

CC: What are the changes you've seen in the time you've covered the White House?

DONALDSON: The change that has impressed me most between the

Carter administration and the Reagan administration is that the Reagan people seem to believe that the press ought to be an adjunct of their public relations image department. They really, I think, have a basic misunderstanding or contempt for the traditional role of the press as some sort of oversight mechanism which may be troublesome to them. I think this crowd doesn't really appreciate that [role] and they get very upset, angry, and feel betrayed in some sense when either circumstances or better reporters than I am diligently ferret out news that doesn't suit them.

CC: Have you noticed any examples where they've actually tried to suppress news, or is it more sophisticated?

DONALDSON: I think it's a very sophisticated thing. I personally have never been asked by a person in this administration to withhold a story which I had and told them I was going to do.

[But] almost everything Ronald Reagan does that the press gets to see is done first and foremost with the PR aspect in mind.

When you press them and probe in an attempt to go beyond that information, you hit the stone wall or the kinds of tactics which just shut things down. We had a big contretemps last summer over a skin swatch on the president's nose, which seemed to culminate in a piece of paper distributed from the press office which said, on the authority of the White House physician, that the skin swatch was checked for infection.

In fact, we subsequently learned that a biopsy had been performed, and the story is that Mrs. Reagan felt strongly that that news should not be disseminated and urged in the strongest terms — and when the First Lady does it, that's the law — that it not be disseminated.

And so we have public relations people and press secretaries nimbly attempting to stay afloat above that fine line of telling bald-faced untruths, and simply dodging questions, and withholding information. That piece of paper, in my estimation, put them under.

CC: How much power does Nancy Reagan wield?

DONALDSON: Tremendous power. When it comes to the physical or political safety of her husband, she is more powerful than anyone.

CC: Is she sort of an unelected co-president?

DONALDSON: No, not at all. She's just a very strong-willed woman who has the best interests of her husband at heart, and he knows that and he trusts her, obviously, and loves her. And I think if you got on the fighting side of Nancy Reagan, you might as well hang it up when it comes to dealing with the Reagan presidency and the White House.

CC: Speaking of which, you make references to her every now and then on the *This Week with David Brinkley* show. Do you think she hates you?

DONALDSON: You'd have to ask her. She's never said that to me. George Will is the person on the Brinkley show who is a personal friend of Mrs. Reagan, according to the public print, and I will not quarrel with that. I don't know her well at all. I see her infrequently at those few press receptions where the press is invited and couldn't pass a judgment on whether she even thinks at all about me, much less what she thinks.

CC: Are there many examples where you simply have to dish out the White House line because you don't have enough time or you're in a situation where that's all you get?

DONALDSON: Oh, sure. Most of what I tell the ABC viewers from the White House is material that has been imparted to me, usually in the mass briefings, by a press secretary or an official. I carefully label it that way. I will say, "Administration officials say, . . ." and if there is controversy over the facts, I will say, "Administration officials insist such and so, although . . ." and then I will name the others, "maintain such and such." But most of the time I don't see all of the camel that's been put together by some committee. I get the left leg or I get the hump or something.

CC: Let's take an easier example where it might be obvious that they're just laying on the bull, so to speak. Let's take someone like Margaret Heckler where one day the White House says there's full faith and confidence in her, and the next day she's on a boat to Ireland.

DONALDSON: Everyone understands that and it's hardly worth spending a great deal of time attempting to discredit in the name of truth. Maybe I have more faith or a more sophisticated view of the television news audience than a lot of people, but I don't think people out there watching television news — as opposed to people who may not be interested in the news — are so dumb that they don't understand that throwing Mrs. Heckler out of her cabinet post as secretary of Health and Human Services and into the post of ambassador to Ireland is a demotion. They understand that.

CC: Or full faith and confidence in Raymond Donovan. You and I might understand the intricacies of what the language of White House-speak is, but do you really think that Joe Sixpack out there in Peoria does?

DONALDSON: But that's part of your job as a reporter. What you have to say — and you can say it without being a biased, prejudiced reporter — is to explain the circumstances of what press secretaries and presidents from time immemorial have always had to say they felt in conditions like this, that first of all they stand by their person. You can almost go by all of these scandals, they have a six-day life almost, and the first day they deny that anything has happened. The second day they suggest that something has happened, but it's certainly not what the critics are charging. The third day they admit that the critics have a case and so-and-so is taking a leave of absence, but the president still has confidence and we can never convict someone until they've been judged by a jury of their peers. On the fourth day they accept the person's resignation with regret. By the fifth day in the back channels they're telling all the reporters how glad they are to be rid of that political burden.

I've seen this come and go, and you kind of can report each day, and then the sum total tells the full story. And I don't have to predict the first day, when charges are made against an administration official, what the outcome is going to be to my audience.

CC: It seems like there's been a fairly high amount of scandal and turnover in cabinet and sub-cabinet positions in the Reagan White House since 1981, yet none of it seems to have any effect or make the slightest chink in the White House armor. The secretary of Labor can be under indictment and it doesn't seem that President Reagan is held accountable for it.

DONALDSON: It's part of the Reagan mystique. If I tell them that Ronald Reagan doesn't know the following things as demonstrated by what he says and does, if the television audience and the American public says, "It doesn't matter to me. I don't care that he doesn't know anything about arms control or he doesn't know where the Soviets have their warheads. I still like him and I'm going to vote for him." Frankly, it's okay with me.

CC: What are his deficiencies?

DONALDSON: He does have great areas of ignorance about things in which he is not interested or frankly leaves to others to learn the details about. Reagan has a good mind when he applies that mind, and we continually watch him — he'll be 75 shortly — to see if it's failing. I find that it is not. The trouble is he doesn't seem to apply it or show an interest in things which conventionally are matters that the president of the United States ought to personally engage himself in.

He trusts his staff. They bring him the options, having thrashed it out. He prefers that they bring him a consensus so that he can just check off, but when they finally have to bring him some disagreement, he then makes the judgment. He makes that judgment based to a large extent on his ideology, on his firm convictions, some of which are based on a world which no longer exists — but who's to tell him that — but he makes it.

CC: Who do you think was the better president — Reagan or Carter?

DONALDSON: In the short run, Reagan is certainly a president who commanded the office better than Carter, who has provided an esprit, which is part of being president, better than Carter and who has apparently dealt with the day to day problems, albeit through the staff system, better than Carter. But my hunch is that in the long run Jimmy Carter will certainly be counted a stronger, better president than the voters thought in 1980. Whether he eclipses Ronald Reagan is going to depend on what happens to Reagan and his policies. Supply-side economics has clearly done two things. It helped revive the economy through a recession, but it laid the foundation, unless dealt with now, for an even worse cataclysmic fall in the future. He sold today quickly so that tomorrow would have to pay for it.

Ronald Reagan, the man of all these puritan values, in fact tried to tell us that there is a free lunch. Well, there is no free lunch. Now, can he save himself? You never count Reagan out because they call it luck, they call it whatever it is, events. Two-hundred-forty Marines got blown up in Lebanon on a Sunday. If that had happened to Jimmy Carter, we would have been all over him. But by Tuesday Reagan invades Grenada and it's a triumph. Reagan may escape all of the seeds which his policies, in my view, have put at the ground.

CC: Do you think that Ronald Reagan has sufficient grasp or interest in the issues? You cover the White House. Does he work a full day?

DONALDSON: He doesn't work a full day in the traditional sense — 9 to 5, 8 to 6. Jimmy Carter, 7 to 7. No. His day is measured and paced. There's built-in down time. His schedule, except on occasion, is not a taxing one physically or mentally, but he does work. He does do things. One of the most visible things he does, of course, again, is the public relations image for his own administration, a picture with a poster girl in the Rose Garden at some ceremony, out in the stumps selling tax reform, if you will. His aides insist that he works hard behind the scenes, but since I'm never allowed behind the scenes to see that, I'll just have to pass along to you what they say.

CC: If you look at presidential press conferences, even under Eisenhower, who wasn't really known for them, and Nixon, who didn't seem particularly to care for them, it seems of all the presidents in the modern era, President Reagan comes out holding fewer news conferences than anyone.

DONALDSON: It's abysmal. It goes back to what I said to you earlier. They really believe the press's main function or only function ought to be simply as a conveyor belt — garbage in, garbage out — of whatever they want to say. And they want the president always to be presented in a structured way that they can control . . . They don't like to present him in an unstructured situation because Reagan is a very self-assured guy. He wants to answer questions, be it anecdote, or figures that aren't correct, or an assertion about Social Security's interplay with the deficit, which he often gets wrong.

But the staff worries about this because even though we've talked about the American people overlooking those kinds of lapses or ignorances on the part of Ronald Reagan, there's that nagging fear that someday, either through accumulation or something he says that's very egregious or bad timing, it could all blow up.

CC: You're aware, obviously, that you're a pariah in many ways, the skunk at the garden party, badgering and badgering the president. Does that make it hard to do your work? And do you think people understand what you're trying to do, or do you think they just view you as a giant pain in the ass?

DONALDSON: I don't know. I won't embrace any of your description, but I'll try to answer the thrust of it.

I think people understand what I'm trying to do and [what] other reporters at the White House [are trying to do]. I think the political partisans of Ronald Reagan don't like it one bit and let me and others know about it, and say that I'm unfair and vicious, and clearly out to destroy the president because I am, the kinder ones say, just a super-liberal (the unkinder ones say I'm a conscious agent of the Kremlin, whatever, fill in the blank).

But I think it's a very small number of people, just the fringe. I think most people understand that they're a little disquieted about the way we work because they get to see how television reporters work. A print reporter goes up to the door, knocks on the door, someone comes, and he says, "Madam, we're so distressed that your son was killed today in Lebanon. Could we come in and talk to you about it?" No one sees that. A television reporter goes up and says it and everyone sees that, so we're, as you say, we're the skunk.

I get a lot of letters which call me all sorts of names, and some letters from thoughtful people who point out mistakes I make. The vast majority of the mail I get, believe it or not, is from people who say, "Keep it up," and some of them, of course, are just as unfair the other way, because they clearly hate Ronald Reagan and they let me know in one respect or another. They assume I do too, falsely. But the vast majority of the mail in the middle is just people who say, "Ask him the question, ask him about this, what about that," and I think they understand.

But when people see the process and they see me or others yelling at the president from a ropeline as he's going to and from his helicopter, it seems rude and unnecessary to them. "Why are you yelling at that nice man?" The answer, of course, is that that nice man, who is the person I cover, never comes close enough for me to speak in a calm voice and ask a reasonable question, except under the most rare and unstructured circumstances.

So the alternative is, when I have the opportunity to see him in public, to ask him nothing or shout it. And in fact he answers many questions with the answer, whatever it may be that he wants to give.

CC: Do they use the Secret Service as protection to keep you hounds at bay?

DONALDSON: Absolutely. The Secret Service attitude toward the press between the Carter and Reagan administrations is almost, not quite, but almost day and night. In the Carter administration the Secret Service understood what we were doing. We understood what they were doing.

And the Secret Service would say to us in off the record moments, "Let's face it, folks, we're glad you're there because if an attack is made on the president, you're in the way. And we don't wish you any harm, but you're kind of a protective shield." In those days, the Secret Service knew that its job was the physical protection of the president, not the political protection.

But the Secret Service today, since the Hinckley shooting, and since people in the Reagan administration have taken a different view of the press, see it as their job to do precisely what the staff tells them to do, willy-nilly of whether it's for the physical or political protection of the president; and many of the agents and many of the supervisors, although not all, dislike us quite clearly. They have said as much to me and their actions demonstrate it. They will make every effort to harass us if they can.

CC: Do you know what story you're going to do every day?

DONALDSON: No. Often we do because the agenda is set by the White House senior staff. They hold a story conference every morning and decide what they will do and allow the president to be seen doing. The president has five things on his schedule, but the only time you see him is for the second thing.

There is a tendency by television, since we are a visual medium, thank you very much, to be sort of pushed in the direction of that particular story, and of course the things that we perhaps are more interested in, the behind the scenes maneuvering, we never see at all.

Take the campaign of '84. We could have taken the view that since Ronald Reagan's campaign consisted of, as I pointed out in so many words, often, balloons, the American flag, Lee Greenwood singing "God Bless the USA," hand-picked people admitted by ticket only in the crowds wearing the right buttons, waving their own little American flags passed out by Reagan volunteers, then we ought not to put it on the air after we did it once, right? One definition of news is deviation from the norm, and that is the norm. But the pressure of a political campaign with Mondale making charges and making statements every day, arguably of trying to attack the issues, was such that had we not tried to cover the Reagan campaign, whatever it happened to be, I think we would have legitimately been charged with total unfairness.

CC: Do you think that there's a kind of self-censorship, particularly covering campaigns, but covering the White House also, that exists in which all the reporters are in the same plane, you're all in the same hotel, you get all the same amount of access to the same event, and most of the time the only people you talk to is yourselves?

DONALDSON: Is this self-censorship or is this just developing a story by interviewing reporters, which is one of the fine techniques of the business? I've indulged in it myself from time to time.

CC: But is there a problem? You're probably going to the Washington Press Club dinner tonight, in which all of you compete to see who's the fanciest administration official you can parade around at your dinner table. Isn't it hard to break bread with them and then break their —

DONALDSON: I don't compete that way. I hate to sound holier than thou, but one of the things I've been preaching for years is I don't want to be social friends with the people I cover. When I first came to Washington in '61, everyone wanted to be. I don't want to be because there's a difficult problem there and you just identified it.

Yes, I can go to the Press Club dinner tonight. I don't know who I'm going to be sitting next to at the ABC table. If it turns out to be the ambassador from Israel, who's one of the ABC guests, I'll talk to him and he'll talk to me, I hope. But I don't think that compromises my coverage of him in any respect or the State of Israel. But if I start trying to make a social friend out of him and vice-versa, we go fishing together, exchange presents at holiday seasons, think of [ourselves as] social friends, I think that would be very difficult, and I think it's wrong, and I don't try to do it.

CC: Are there a lot of journalists who cross that line, get too close to their sources?

DONALDSON: Some columnists, but I think they're a special breed who clearly get very close to their sources, but usually they acknowledge it. In the old days Theodore White was Lyndon Johnson's special columnist. George Will makes no secret of the fact that he has the Reagans to his house for dinner once a year. Well, once a year isn't that much. He dines with Mrs. Reagan at lunch frequently and he's on the record as a friend of the president and Mrs. Reagan.

CC: Due to the nature of the Washington press corps, do you think that there is as much enterprise reporting as there could or should be?

DONALDSON: No, of course there isn't, particularly at the White House, particularly by me and other television correspondents.

We'll dig and we'll come up with a quote, a background quote that helps throw some light on the story that we got at the press briefing that was on the record, and we pat ourselves on the back and say, "What a good boy I've been, really done a good job," but it's not the same thing as breaking a new story in the public interest. We don't do enough of it. You're right.

CC: Do you think people understand exactly how you report from the White House? People might think you get a good story and wander over to [Chief of Staff] Don Regan's office and say, "Well, Mr. Regan, what is the White House's position on that?" or you wander over to someone else's office and ask them these questions and you have free access to roam the White House. What is the actual reality?

DONALDSON: The reality is you hear press briefings in the press room from Larry Speakes. Beyond that, you make phone calls which may or may not be returned. At times of crisis, often they are not returned. During the two-or three-or four-day period when it looked like the president's tax-reform bill might go down the drain in the House of Representatives, thanks to the Republican Party's opposition in the House, I put in a daily call to Donald T. Regan. He did not return my call once. There have been other occasions when I've heard from Donald T. Regan, but it was not as pressing an occasion or as pressing a news matter.

They control access to their thoughts and to the leaks that they wish to give us absolutely. I have never, to the best of my memory, gotten a story at the White House because I have overheard someone say something when they didn't know I was overhearing them.

Now you say to me, "Sam, I read in the major newspapers stories from the White House clearly that are on target, which come from informed sources quoting senior administration officials. I seldom hear you do those stories the night before. You get beaten day after day. Why is that? Is it because you don't have the sense to call or you're too lazy to call?"

CC: Because they chose to leak it to the *Washington Post* rather than ABC News.

DONALDSON: Thank you for answering the question. Exactly right. What do you do? Do you stand up and scream and yell? Do you fall down on your stomach and beat your hands and legs like a small child? No. You just keep in there pitching.

Well, what do you do on a story like that? We all chase it, we all pass along information that's been reported even though we ourselves cannot confirm it, do not have any firsthand knowledge of it. That's the incestuous part of the news business.

CC: Are these self-serving leaks by the administration back-handed ways to get their message across?

DONALDSON: Oh, sure. Leaks have a purpose. Very seldom does someone leak inadvertently. It's a two-edged sword. Leaks are a good thing to let the public know what they're thinking. I think it's smarter to float an idea to see what the reaction is before you stand up in public and say, promulgate, as Jimmy Carter did, an ambitious energy plan which had no chance of passage in the United States Congress because they hadn't taken their soundings properly.

On the other hand, clearly they may have very bad motives, to get someone else in the administration that is your enemy, to plant false information to embarrass, or defame someone who is your opponent on the policy level.

CC: There has been a rather overt and some would say heavy-handed move to punish so-called leakers in which it's even been suggested that every significant administration official take a lie detector test. Do you see this as chilling at all?

DONALDSON: Yes. I want to say it's silly, but I think there's just enough hardnosed desire behind it to do it than to dismiss it as being silly. [Secretary of State] George Shultz is right — forget the business that it's an infringement on what I think is someone's personal constitutional right to be let alone in those matters, but lie detector tests are unreliable. To use them as a device to try to demonstrate someone's patriotism is ridiculous.

CC: What do you think was the real reason behind the quest for lie detector tests?

DONALDSON: I think that many of these people really think that these leaks are harmful to the national security. But almost all leaks are things that have nothing to do with true national security but with covering up mistakes on the part of the bureaucracy or of the political people who are elected to office or appointed to office.

The president once said he was up to his keister in leaks, and who's doing it. Well, his own people are doing it.

CC: It seems like one of your biggest problems is, will you, Sam Donaldson, report every act of terrorism on "Nightline" on the news?

DONALDSON: We've got to report everything that happens. If it's so-called terrorism, then we report that. If it's an act that is newsworthy and has blood and carnage, it's not my job to make an editorial decision that this isn't good for the American people because, after all, it's a terrorist and we're just playing into their hands when we give them the exposure they want, that they counted on, and may be the very reason for their act. If I get into the censorship business, and decide what's good for the American people, that, of course, is the antithesis of what we think the news business is all about.

CC: You never feel like a stooge, like you're giving them what they want?

DONALDSON: A stooge? Larry Speakes comes out to the pressroom and says, "This is what we want the American people to know about what the president did today." Am I a stooge because I give Larry Speakes what he wants? I'm a reporter. I cover that story.

It's the news, and reporters and broadcast organizations ought to never get into the business of deciding that something isn't good for the American people or that those who perpetrate an act that is newsworthy have a motive that we don't agree with, and therefore censor the story.

Are you suggesting that someone or some group of people who understand how to manipulate the media — that we shouldn't put those people or those causes on the air? If that's what you're saying, we couldn't cover politics in the United States. I couldn't be a match against Deaver, let alone the Amal.

CC: The situation that's set up now calls for a pool of correspondents to be chosen at random and taken to a secret place in the event of something like the invasion of Grenada. Do you agree with these pools?

DONALDSON: I don't agree with the pool; I don't agree with what's happened. I don't say the military is under an obligation to take reporters and photographers in with the first wave, with the first pathfinder paratroops that drop into an enemy zone at the beginning of some military action. I think, in fact, that would be silly and probably, as someone who is no braver than the next man, I'd be scared to death to do it.

What I say is that at some point early in a military operation, the rule of reason should apply from the standpoint of admitting the press.

What the military is afraid of is people seeing either the very fact of war — the blood, the dying, the carnage — or as attends every military operation, mistakes — blowing up that mental hospital in Grenada. In any war those things happen.

CC: So in any future wars the press will be shut out?

DONALDSON: My hunch is that we won't be. I think, on balance, the American public will demand the kind of press access under reasonable rules and under reasonable conditions to any future wars, or "armed conflicts" that we engage in. We'll not be satisfied just to get the body bags every week.

CC: For the rest of its term, do you think the White House will run roughshod over your attempt to cover it?

DONALDSON: Ronald Reagan will leave office in three years. The Reagan administration will not go on forever. The press will.

Up Close to Sam Donaldson

If I've learned one thing in my life, it is: That the conventional wisdom is usually wrong. The time to really question something is when everyone says it's true.

My best asset is: A sort of aggressiveness. The problem with using the word "aggressive" [is that] it can be destructive aggressiveness. And I argue that I neither mean to be nor am destructive.

My biggest fault is: I don't listen enough — I'm usually doing the talking.

I love to read: History and biography.

The latest book I read was: The autobiographies of test pilot Chuck Yeager and Chrysler baron Lee Iacocca.

The person who influenced me most: I suppose it would have to have been my mother.

If I weren't covering the White House, I would like to cover: There is not something that I'm just dying to cover which I haven't had the opportunity to cover. Every time I go to Roone Arledge [group president of ABC News and Sports] and tell him that I want out of the White House, he asks me that question. I fall mute because the one or two jobs that are better than mine at this network are filled at the moment by very good people. [Peter Jennings and Ted Koppel].

If I weren't a journalist, I'd like to be: Something that uses some of the same talents that I use in my business now. Maybe a trial lawyer?

My most memorable moment covering the White House is: The peace treaty between Israel and Egypt in 1979.

I'd never have gotten as far without: Hard work. Other people may think I'm lazy, but I don't think the record shows that.

I wish I'd been there when: What am I supposed to say? I would like to have been there at moments of tragedy on the American scene that I didn't cover? No, I'm not foolish enough to say that, although in my heart of hearts, you know, we all like to cover [the big] stories, right?
I really wish I'd been there when Lincoln delivered his Gettysburg address. I wonder if I would have been able to recognize that it was something worth reporting.

If I were president for a day: My policy would be that we had to pay for what we spend. And that means we would have to raise revenue. I would stop selling the idea that there is a free lunch.

I always try to remember: That if I ever start believing my press, I'm lost.

The one thing that really drives me crazy: Incompetence. My own and others'.

I N 1959 THE DEAN OF POLITICAL journalism, Douglass Cater, Jr., labeled the Washington Press Corps the fourth branch of government.[1]

A vital ingredient of political power is information about both opponents and potential supporters, knowledge of their comings and goings, positions, the policies they are likely to support, and the constituencies which back them. To a considerable extent, reporters are the conduits of this kind of information *within* government as they touch base with politicians and officials on their beats, prying for, but also supplying them with information, all in the process of informing the public. Washington power-seekers also know the importance of the well-planted leak to gain publicity for themselves and their policies.

As reporters ply their trade they, as the politicians they cover, find participation in Washington's social world to be indispensable. Henry Kissinger, former national security advisor and secretary of state to Richard M. Nixon, described social life in Washington much as Metter-

nich, whom he so much admired, depicted international relations and power machinations among nation-states in the early nineteenth century. "The criteria of this social life are brutal," wrote Kissinger in his memoirs, "they are geared substantially to power, its exercise and its decline. A person is accepted as soon as he enters the charmed circles of the holders of power." Social life "provides a mechanism for measuring intangibles and understanding nuances. Moods can be gauged by newspapermen and ambassadors and senior civil servants that are not discernible at formal meetings. It is at their dinner parties and receptions that the relationships are created without which the machinery of government would soon stalemate itself."[2]

The following selection describes how Washington reporters have become an integral part of the capital's social world, where the political elite meet informally to plan strategies over cocktails and canapés.

15 Charlotte Hays and Jonathan Rowe
REPORTERS: THE NEW WASHINGTON ELITE

Thumbing through his engagement book, *Los Angeles Times* Bureau Chief Jack Nelson surveys an impressive array of entries — a gala affair for King Fahd, dinner at the Canadian Embassy, *U.S. News and World Report*'s party for retiring Editor Marvin Stone, cocktails for the Chinese

[1] Douglass Cater, *The Fourth Branch of Government*, (Boston: Houghton Mifflin Co., 1959).

[2] Henry Kissinger, *White House Years* (Boston: Little, Brown & Co., 1979), p. 20.

ambassador, and several movie screenings. "Spring is the worst time of year," complains Nelson. "You could just look at your schedule and see that you had too much to do. There were about eight black-tie things."

Nelson is not unique. He represents a pervasive phenomenon on the Washington scene: the Socialite Journalist. Washington editors, and even reporters, enjoy a status that would shock their counterparts in Cleveland or Chicago; no party today is complete without its representatives from the media. "When we're putting together a guest list," says Betsey Weltner, a publicist with Gray and Company, the public relations firm, "including a journalist is just as important as including a diplomat or a Cabinet member."

"We invite jobs, not people as individuals," admits Sandra Gottlieb, the socially savvy wife of the Canadian ambassador. Asked for a list of status positions, Mrs. Gottlieb ticks off the editor of the *Washington Post*, a Supreme Court Justice, the bureau chief of the *Los Angeles Times*, and a vague category called "opinion makers."

Ambassador and Mrs. Gottlieb frequently entertain Meg Greenfield, the Joseph Krafts, the Tom Bradens, the James Restons, and Ben Bradlee and Sally Quinn. A writer and *Post* columnist herself, Mrs. Gottlieb also gives less official "smart lady lunches." *Women's Wear Daily*'s Susan Watters, Abigail McCarthy, Barbara Matusow (Mrs. Jack Nelson), and *Washington Weekly* publisher Joan Bingham have been to smart lady lunches.

Journalists in Washington have become what bankers are in Pittsburgh or Tulsa: the straws that stir the drink. "Washington is fundamentally like Hollywood," says Richard Cohen, a *Post* columnist who is himself something of a "catch." "It doesn't make steel, and it doesn't make computers, and it doesn't deal in high finance." Washington makes news, and the life goal of the powerful here is that others think well of them. For this to occur, the press must think well of them first.

Ali Bengelloun, Ambassador of Morocco, recalled for the *Washington Journalism Review* how he stopped by the *Washington Post* to visit Executive Editor Ben Bradlee immediately after presenting his credentials to President Carter. "I consider Bradlee a personality who plays a big role in Washington," Bengelloun explained. And he added, "I consider it very important to have journalists to my home, just as I would want to meet a member of the Cabinet face to face." Tell that to a journalist often enough, and he'll start to believe it's true.

In a city where the elected powers come and go, the press has become a part of the permanent social establishment, valued for its store of lore and wisdom. More than one new senator or Cabinet secretary has huddled with a veteran pundit to find out how to deal with the Appropriations Committee chairman or where the bodies are buried at State. Journalists, for their part, scrutinize a new administration a little the way the denizens of Palm Beach size up the family that bought the mansion down the drive. In contrast to the permanent pillars of Washington journalism, says Mrs. Gottlieb, "a Mr. Secretary today is a Mr. Has-Been tomorrow."

Socializing with the Washington media becomes a priority even for the very highest. President Jimmy Carter, for example, showed up for the 1980 opening of the *L.A. Times's* new bureau on I Street. Nelson, who knew Carter when he was a reporter with the *Atlanta Constitution*, sees nothing extraordinary about the president of the United States stopping by a newspaper party. "I don't see any reason why we shouldn't consider ourselves on equal footing with those we cover," he says.

All of this sounds a bit strange if you still think of journalists as the hard-boiled types who do most of their socializing in bars. It's equally curious to a journalist from another country. Christopher Hitchens, the British-born correspondent for *Nation* magazine, says, "If you said in London, 'You must come to dinner. I've got the features editor of the *Observer*,' everybody would laugh."

New Deal Seduction

Asked to check her guest list, Polly Fritchey, wife of columnist Clayton Fritchey and one of Georgetown's leading hostesses, finds that about half of the people at her last party were journalists. Would the press have figured so prominently on such a guest list 20 years ago? "Oh, God, no!" exclaims Hugh Sidey, the columnist and Washington bureau chief emeritus of *Time*. "It amazes me even today."

When Sidey came to Washington during the Eisenhower years, the social life of reporters here — even the relatively privileged ones at *Time* — was far more modest than today. "We didn't make much money, and I lived in a small apartment on Pook's Hill with my wife and child," recalls Sidey, who wrote books on the weekend to help make ends meet. He donned white tie for the first time in his life for the second Eisenhower inaugural, but he was totally unfamiliar with the capital's social elite. "I whispered to somebody, 'Who's that very handsome woman,' " he recalls. "It was Mrs. Merriweather Post, but I didn't recognize her."

One day earlier this year, Sidey's upcoming social calendar included such events as a dinner at the F Street Club for Clare Booth Luce hosted by Henry Grunwald, the editor-in-chief of all Time, Inc. publications. Ronald Reagan was one of the invitees expected to attend. On another evening, Sidey was due at the Chevy Chase Club for a dinner in honor of Count von Stauffenberg.

As Sidey's experience indicates, the social debut of the Washington journalist is a fairly recent occurrence. A handful of lions, such as Walter

Lippmann, have always supped with Cabinet secretaries and ambassadors, but ordinary reporters and bureau chiefs, even for major publications, have traditionally been minor characters on the social scene.

In the late nineteenth century, Washington reporters were widely associated with rough-and-tumble congressional politics and influence peddling. Some correspondents supplemented their meager salaries by working as staff members for the same legislators they wrote about. The champion in this regard was probably one Uriah Painter, for 25 years a correspondent for the *Philadelphia Inquirer* and described as "one of the few newspapermen in Washington who died wealthy." Painter played all the angles, coming out against bills so he could be bought off, as well as doing freelance lobbying on the side. One congressman of a progressive bent complained that within six months of their arrival in Washington, reporters could be found "eating out of every official hand between the White House and the Capitol."

Through the 1920s, Washington was a pretty sleepy place, ignored by the rest of the country, and small enough for a single correspondent to cover. Presidents such as Warren Harding and Calvin Coolidge didn't cause many late hours for the press corps here. Herbert Hoover, a man of greater talents, held himself aloof from journalists; fraternizing would have been beneath his dignity.

All that changed with the election of Roosevelt, who brought with him both intellectuals and action. Covering the important events of the New Deal, journalists became more important, too. Roosevelt understood, moreover, that the journalists could help make FDR.

The Depression was still the era of the tyrant publishers, men such as William Randolph Hearst, who presided over what critics of today's "liberal" media must think of as journalism's good old days. "The publishers didn't just disagree with the New Deal," wrote William Rivers, a historian of journalism. "They hated it." Roosevelt quickly concluded that to get favorable coverage, he would have to court the reporters — who often disagreed with their employers — the way his Republican predecessors had courted the publishers.

Before FDR, reporters had gone notebook-in-hand to White House social functions, hangers-on rather than participants. Roosevelt invited them as guests. He developed a sense of professional camaraderie with reporters, suggesting during interviews, "If I were writing that story. . . ." He also initiated the custom of the president's holding frequent press conferences, which gave reporters presidential quotes and kept FDR at the center of attention. Even Mrs. Roosevelt held press conferences — the first First Lady to do so. Mrs. Roosevelt's close friend, Lorena Hickock, was a journalist.

By extending reporters a measure of presidential solicitude, Roosevelt began their transformation from raffish operators to members of Mrs.

Fritchey's guest list. According to Hope Ridings Miller, former editor of the *Post* society page, "Reporters have only been socially acceptable since the Roosevelts."

Redecorating with Jackie

Still, the press's position in Washington high society remained relatively minor through the late forties and fifties. Neither Truman nor Eisenhower felt at home with reporters, nor understood how they might be used to forward White House policy. And in the newsroom of the old *Washington Daily News*, says Tom Kelly, a reporter for the *News* in the fifties, staff members still socialized with cops rather than high-ranking bureaucrats or diplomats. "You drank beer and whiskey," says Kell, "and if you'd come on about wine you'd have been laughed out of the room." Correspondents for major out-of-town newspapers had more standing than the reporters for the local tabloid, but they were still more at home in bars than in the parlors of Georgetown.

It wasn't until the emergence of John F. Kennedy, another glamorous, charming Democrat, that reporters resumed their upward march in status. And they were waiting for the call.

By the 1960s, many more reporters were college educated and from middle-class backgrounds. Edward R. Murrow, meanwhile, had defined a new role — the reporter celebrity — with his World War II radio broadcasts from Europe. Through television, newsmen were gradually becoming as well known as the public officials they covered.

With his father's help, Kennedy had courted the press diligently from the very beginning of his political career. Long before he reached the White House, JFK came to appreciate the influence of publications such as *Time*, *Life*, and *Look*, which were then the predominant vehicles of national celebrity. Flattering photographic depictions of what appeared to be Kennedy's private life appeared frequently — and not by accident. When, for example, the dashing young senator took Jacqueline Bouvier to Hyannisport for the first time, a *Life* photographer happened to be lying in wait to record this spontaneous occasion for posterity. *Life* ran the pictures under the title "The Courtship of a U.S. Senator."

Like Roosevelt, Kennedy was well versed in the world of newsroom politics and deadlines. Also like Roosevelt, JFK charmed reporters with personal attention. One *New York Times* reporter said after the election that it was as though "one of us" had made it to the White House. On the eve of the inaugural, the person Kennedy chose to visit was Joseph Alsop, the columnist.

In contrast to FDR, Kennedy honored the press in public. The first president to hold regular televised news conferences, Kennedy showed an entire nation of viewers that he took reporters' questions seriously, that they were welcome participants in an exciting, renewed Washington.

The demise of Hearst and other autocratic, ideological publishers had given Washington editors and reporters an unprecedented amount of freedom. Major newspapers increasingly sought respectability through "objectivity." Publishers and owners saw themselves as stewards, concerned about turning a profit; the old-style conservative crusading was seen as undignified. In the 1930s, more than half of the Washington reporters responded in a poll that their stories had been "played down, cut, or killed for 'policy reasons.' " By 1962, less than 8 percent reported such problems.

Kennedy realized that, even more that in Roosevelt's time, the people to invite to dinner were no longer the publishers, but the reporters and editors who actually produced the news. And, as with his press conferences, Kennedy often entertained his journalist friends in front of a conveniently positioned camera. In his admiring account of the Kennedy presidency, entitled (suggestively in this context) *Conversations With Kennedy*, Ben Bradlee recounted numerous intimate family dinners at the White House. This was Bradlee the *Newsweek* bureau chief before his jump up to the *Post* editorship.

"Kennedy swept us into a world we'd never seen before," Hugh Sidey reminisces. "Suddenly here you were at Hickory Hill with the 'beautiful people' you'd only read about. You were on the Honey Fitz, or taking a nude swim with the president of the United States. Or Jacqueline Kennedy called you about a story on redecorating the White House. That's the stuff novels are written about. Kennedy brought us onto the magic carpet with him."

Camelot passed, but the prominence of reporters continued to increase. When a distraught Jackie Kennedy needed support in the hours just before her husband's death, she called on two trusted friends: Ben Bradlee and his first wife, Toni. Theodore White captured that scene in a widely read article for *Life*, reminding Washington of where journalists stood in society.

If Kennedy, following Roosevelt's example, conferred new power on reporters, Ralph Nader demonstrated the extent of that power. Working not from the White House, but from rag-tag offices and even pay phones, Nader used the Washington press corps to build a movement. With late-night telephone sessions and dead-eye news tips, Nader sold consumerism to the reporters. They sold it to the country, giving Nader's Capitol Hill appearances lavish coverage and making his young "Raiders" well-known Washington characters. Journalists became fellow crusaders; no longer just scribes for the first draft of history, they were becoming protagonists in their own right. When Nader began appearing in news magazine surveys as one of the ten "most influential" people in America, the press that worked with him shared some of that glory.

During the same period, the "New Journalism" elevated the humblest and most ephemeral of literary forms to the status of literature. Journalists would now be able to "express themselves" — be somebodies — and even Truman Capote was doing it. Then came Watergate, in which the personas of two *Washington Post* reporters merged with those of Robert Redford and Dustin Hoffman. Journalists were the heroes in the slaying of an evil president. Describing the filming of *All the President's Men* in the *Post* newsroom, Sally Quinn observed in her Style article, "Lights, Cameras . . . Ego," that the actors were awed by the journalists, not vice versa.

Just 400 of My Close Friends

When Franklin Roosevelt was first courting the press, few would have guessed that half a century later one of the three or four best invitations in town would be an evening with a *Washington Post* editor and a former social reporter — namely, Ben Bradlee and Sally Quinn. "If Ben and Sally gave a party for their cleaning lady," says one veteran observer of Washington society, "everybody would want to come." At a party this January for two reporters, Elizabeth Bumiller of the *Post*'s Style section and her husband Steven Weisman of the *New York Times*, the guests packed into the $2.5 million Bradlee-Quinn mansion included the Michael Deavers, the James Bakers, and the Richard Darmans.

It's gotten so that journalist socialites compete openly. "We put on a hell of a good Christmas party," brags Jack Nelson, whose entertainment budget is generous. "Everybody in town knows that the *L.A. Times* puts on a good Christmas party." (Deaver and Baker were among last year's guests.) Since *L.A. Times* reporter Sara Fritz is president of the Washington correspondents' association, the bureau offered to pick up the $30,000 tab for the group's recent dinner at the Hilton.

The elite of Washington journalism, including Nelson, annually celebrate their own importance at the Gridiron Club dinner. Traditionally, top editors and bureau chiefs would orchestrate an off-the-record evening of skits and laughter attended by their publishers and suitably high-ranking administration officials, Congressmen, and lobbyists. In more recent times, the heavyweight correspondents have come to dominate the Gridiron festivities, and it is to their invitations that the White House staff responds. The *Post* Style section unfailingly provides detailed coverage of the event, even though its reporter is made to stand outside the banquet hall, where she scrambles for quotes from the celebrity journalists in attendance.

In 1982, Nancy Reagan indicated the importance of the Gridiron dinner when she chose the event as the spot to launch her counterattack against her image as a rich bitch. Mocking her media persona, Reagan performed in her own skit, dressed in Salvation Army cast-offs and singing an original number called "Second-Hand Clothes" (to the tune of "Second-Hand Rose"). It was not the sort of performance our First Lady would put on for social inferiors, and participants observed that Mrs. Reagan was noticeably nervous during rehearsals. "It was a tribute to the press," says Sheila Tate, then Mrs. Reagan's press secretary, "that Mrs. Reagan cared enough about them to do that, and that she went to their own forum."

These days, however, you don't even have to be the Gridiron to attract that kind of attention. When *The New Republic* last year threw itself an elegant black-tie affair at the National Portrait Gallery in honor of its 70th birthday, it turned out to be a *very significant bash.* The party was covered by the *New York Times* and led the Style section. The *Post* accorded the glitzy event gargantuan headlines and photographs but teased *New Republic* publisher Martin Peretz between the lines: "Martin Peretz hugged Gary Hart. Then Martin Peretz hugged Henry Kissinger. And there you have it." In addition to Hart and Kissinger, the 400-person guest list included Jeane Kirkpatrick, Daniel P. Moynihan, Irving Kristol, Eugene McCarthy, Jerry Brown, and Barney Frank.

Ambience is one of the more visible signs of the new social status of journalists. Where once reporters pecked away at their Royal manuals in dark cubby-hole offices in the old National Press Building, many now toil in bureaus bordering on the luxurious. It would be hard to distinguish *Time's* new bureau on Connecticut Avenue from the law firms that occupy the rest of the towering marble and glass building, except that the magazine's pink labyrinth of thick carpets and sculpted greenery is, if anything, more elegant.

The *L.A. Times's* new 32-person bureau was designed with entertainment in mind. It includes a magnificent brass wet bar in the conference room, above which are photographs of the dignitaries who have supped there. (Sandra Day O'Connor posed for a group shot with the women reporters of the bureau.) "We used to use styrofoam cups," Nelson recalls. Now, Ridgewells, an upscale local firm, caters with real china.

Tracking the Elusive Gaffe

The implications of the social ascension of the capital's press corps are far from pernicious. Many reporters are perfectly capable of earning good salaries, attending fancy parties, *and* digging hard for tough stories. More secure in their status, reporters here no longer stand in awe of the powerful people they cover. The days of Roosevelt's "Giggle Gang" — the reporters who sat in the front row at his press conferences and laughed at all his jokes — are probably gone forever.

But the evolution of the journalist socialite also has the potential of taking a toll on the news product. The symptoms are subtle but real. Reporters and editors who see themselves as part of the Georgetown elite risk drifting out of touch with the rest of American life — and their own readership. Ben Bradlee has been an inspirational leader in the *Post* newsroom, but as one veteran Washington reporter points out, "The question is, where does Ben Bradlee get his car fixed? Does *Ben Bradlee* know where Ben Bradlee gets his car fixed?" Given Bradlee's lifestyle, the reporter asks, "How can he identify with average people anymore?"

"One's impression," Daniel P. Moynihan wrote in the early 1970s, "is that 20 years ago the preponderance of the 'working press' — as it likes to call itself — was surprisingly close in origins and attitudes to working people generally. They were not Ivy Leaguers. They are now or soon will be. Journalism has become, if not an elite, a profession attracted to elites. This is noticeably so in Washington."

As pay scales escalate, as newsrooms fill up with prestigious specialists on foreign policy and the money supply, reporters naturally become more remote from the people who read or watch the news. "You find more people who have Ph.D.s from Harvard in Slavic languages and don't keep a flask in their desk drawers," as Richard Cohen puts it, almost wistfully.

Cohen admits he's not comfortable with his status as a well-known Georgetown guest. "I know it's the only way the town can function, but sometimes I feel like picking up my fork . . ." he says, stabbing an imaginary fellow diner. Ambivalent though he is, Cohen still uses "a recent Washington party" as the social context for some of his columns.

According to Cohen's familiar view of "the only way the town can work," a crucial place to get your administration and State Department sources relaxed and talking is in someone's comfortable living room, during the cocktail hour. This is where "inside" information changes hands. Several dangers, however, arise in this setting.

First, journalists can be seduced into participating in relatively insignificant political turf battles involving their fellow party-goers. Mary McGrory, another *Post* columnist, calls journalist-source socializing "calculated." The fact is, a lot of "inside" insight consists largely of high-ranking officials' grinding their axes in hopes that their reporter friends will plant them in a competitor's back. What makes juicy gossip on Saturday evening too often makes page one or the op-ed page as "analysis" Monday morning. Conversely, any number of accomplished reporters and commentators — David Broder, for example — manage to avoid fancy socializing without suffering from a noticeable lack of "inside" information.

There's nothing wrong, of course, with getting a helpful tip from a friendly assistant secretary of Defense just because you meet during a fancy social hour. But what he's likely to reveal will rarely be the whole story, or even the most important angle. The great recent advances in reporting on complex topics, such as military procurement, stem in large part from reporters, many based in Washington, picking themselves up and traveling to the test ranges to see if our guns and tanks really work. Across a wide range of subjects, the best Washington sources are the mid-level congressional staff members and frustrated agency bureaucrats, most of whom you will not find at the choice parties.

A second cause for worry is what might be called the Agronsky & Co. syndrome. As valued guests at Washington social events, journalists come to view their every passing thought on the "news behind the news" as worthy of wide attention. Jennifer Phillips, a well-known Georgetown hostess whose family is connected with the Phillips art collection, explains that "if something like Bitburg happens, you just can't wait to get with a group to analyze it and figure out the implications. It makes for a wonderful, exciting social atmosphere."

"We're the Marco Polos of our day," quips Hugh Sidey. Any dinner guest who seems to know who really wears the pants on the White House staff or what the Geneva arms control negotiators do in their spare time is likely to be a welcome adornment to Mrs. Phillips's salon.

Such chattering has actually been elevated to a journalistic form all its own — the Agronsky-style Washington talk show. Eminences of the trade sit around and trade speculation on the administration's latest public relations blunders and who's likely to run for president in 1992. Frequently, the same pointless navel contemplation goes on in the news pages and on the networks as well. Michael Kinsley of *The New Republic* calls it "gaffe-ology," — and he's right in arguing that it's of little interest to those outside of journalism and government — certainly few people outside of the Beltway.

In the end, this may be the worst result of reporters becoming social bigwigs: the press tends to get boring when it sees itself as too important. One Washington hostess told *Vanity Fair* recently, "You've got the *Washington Post* Style section, and you use that to write about yourself and your friends. You can tell yourself you're setting the tone for Washington, and I suppose in some ways you are. You're famous because you write that you're famous. This is off the record, of course, because I have to live in this town."

THE
PRESIDENCY

Chapter Four

The administrations of Lyndon B. Johnson and Richard M. Nixon changed the perspective of many Americans about the presidency. In spite of the bitter partisanship that always precedes presidential elections, the office of the presidency had before Lyndon B. Johnson always been treated with great reverence, which often led to reverence for the man who occupied the White House. This is not to suggest by any means that presidents had always been extolled for their virtues and placed on a kingly throne, for anyone familiar with American history knows that there have always been bitter personal attacks on presidents by a wide assortment of critics. And these presidential critics were not above calling their prey "mentally unbalanced." Nevertheless, most presidential biographies concentrated on the heroic and not the neurotic qualities of their subjects. An eloquent illustration of this was Carl Sandburg's biographical volumes on Abraham Lincoln. All the resources of the poet were directed toward enshrining President Lincoln in the Temple of the Gods. Contrasting Carl Sandburg's biography of Abraham Lincoln with more recent works on presidents by such authors as James David Barber or Doris Kearns, not to mention Bob Woodward and Carl Bernstein, reveals the major differences between past and present approaches to assessing presidents.[1]

Although the administration of Lyndon B. Johnson seemed entirely rational to his supporters, other persons, particularly critics of the Vietnam war, believed the president to have relentlessly, single-mindedly, and more importantly *irrationally* embarked on a highly destructive policy. David Halberstam began an extensive study of the history of the war in order to determine how the United States became involved. His bestselling book, *The Best and the Brightest,* published in 1972, emphasized the role of personalities, not so much of the president himself as of his top level advisers, in making the critical decisions committing the country to the

---

[1]See James David Barber, *The Presidential Character* (Englewood Cliffs, N.J.: Prentice-Hall, 1972); Doris Kearns, *Lyndon Johnson and the American Dream* (New York: Harper & Row, 1976); Bob Woodward and Carl Bernstein, *The Final Days* (New York: Simon & Schuster, 1976).

war.[2] In the same year, political scientist James David Barber published his ground-breaking book, *The Presidential Character,* in which he made personality profiles of a variety of presidents in order to determine the effect of presidential character on performance. With the publication of Barber's book, psychopolitics came of age.

James Barber attempted a complex classification of different character types, and came to the conclusion that the best presidents were what he termed "active-positive." The active-positive president is achievement-oriented and productive, and has well-defined goals. He is rational, "using his brain to move his feet." Above all, he is flexible; he can change his goals and methods as he perceives reasons for altering his course of action. He has a sense of humor about the world and, more importantly, about himself. John F. Kennedy was, according to Barber, an ideal active-positive president.

Perhaps even more significant than the active-positive presidents are the "active-negative" presidents. These are the presidents that may do irreparable damage, according to Barber. They have a compulsive need to work because of personal problems and a misguided "Puritan ethic." They are ambitious and power hungry but lack goals beyond that of rising to power. They tend to be politically amoral, as was Richard Nixon, but may take on false and misleading goals, such as making the world safe for democracy, as did Woodrow Wilson. The great energy of the active-negative type is frequently directed in irrational ways, and once set in a course of action the active-negative president tends to become very rigid, especially in the face of opposition and criticisms from the outside. Because of personal insecurity, the active-negative president surrounds himself with yes-men in order to fortify him in confrontation with the hostile world outside. Barber's portraits of various active-negative presidents, including Richard Nixon, when taken in conjunction with the portrait of President Nixon in Bob Woodward's and Carl Bernstein's *Final Days,* is truly frightening. Because of the enormous power that presidents possess, it is especially important to examine their characters and styles, which set the tone of presidential administrations.

The selections in this chapter illustrate various dimensions of presidential personality, and what is frequently overlooked, the way in which the personalities and styles of the president's staff can influence the political process.

[2]David Halberstam, *The Best and the Brightest* (New York: Random House, 1972).

D URING HIS FIRST TERM, Ronald Reagan was clearly a positive president, although whether or not he was, in James David Barber's terms, active or passive can be debated. Before the 1980 presidential election Barber had characterized Reagan as passive-positive. He predicted that "his would be a rhetorical presidency. Reagan's style is centered on speech making. He has been a speechmaker ever since, as a young college freshman, he made a dramatic speech that won great support on the campus. He can move and act to capture an audience."[1]

Barber typed Reagan as a passive-positive personality because he "has always been a kind of booster, an optimist, a conveyer of hopefulness. He is passive in the sense that he has a long record of saving his energy, of not working too hard. He was a nine-to-five governor, and as a campaigner he takes it pretty easy. The danger is that people with this kind of personality give in to pressure too quickly."[2] However, concluded Barber, the time might be right for a Reagan presidency because the country "is in need of a rest. . . . In that environment, Reagan might prove somewhat of a unifying figure, conveying a folksiness that's less electric and dramatic than what we've been through. His presidency might be a kind of Eisenhower second term, where the danger is drift and inaction but the plus is a kind of healing and recovery."[3]

Reagan's personality and style won him public affection during his first term, even with some groups that did not approve of his policies. The following selection portrays his positive personality and upbeat presidency, which, combined with his mastery of the media, made him seem electorally invincible.

16 Steven R. Weisman
RONALD REAGAN'S MAGICAL STYLE

Americans like him. Amid the whir and clank of machinery at a Ford Motor Company assembly plant in Claycomo, Missouri, a few weeks ago, even the men wearing "Mondale" baseball caps joined in cheering Ronald Reagan. In New York City, he told Jewish leaders some things they didn't want to hear about Israel. Then he grinned and wished his audience a joyful Pesach, and they responded with appreciative laughter and applause.

When a president runs for reelection, conventional wisdom holds that he runs on his record. Across the country, voters are surely sizing

[1]U.S. *News and World Report*, October 27, 1980, p. 30.

[2]Ibid.

[3]Ibid.

up Mr. Reagan's performance on the economy and foreign policy. But presidents must also strike a personal chord and they must embody the dreams and values of the nation. "You cannot be a successful president unless you can project a vision about the purpose of America," says Thomas E. Cronin, a leading scholar of the presidency. And it is becoming clear that this year, to a degree unmatched in modern times, the public is being swayed by these intangibles. One of the most astonishing features of Mr. Reagan's political success is that, whether or not they agree with him and his policies, Americans *like* him.

As a candidate, President Reagan still benefits from the public's yearning for a take-charge leader after the succession of national traumas from Watergate to the Iran hostages. His political fortunes have been helped by the expanding economy and by the vitriolic Democratic primary campaign. Yet the White House's own political experts say that Mr. Reagan's greatest political asset is his ability to project himself as a man of conviction, genial self-confidence, optimism, and old-fashioned values. It has enabled the president to weather countless political storms largely unscathed.

He has committed untold public bloopers and been caught in dozens of factual mistakes and misrepresentations. He has presided over the worst recession since the Great Depression. The abortive mission in Beirut cost 265 American lives, and there has been a sharp escalation in United States military involvement in Central America. An extraordinary number of Mr. Reagan's political appointees have come under fire, with many forced to resign, because of ethical or legal conflicts. Yet he is The Man in the Teflon Suit; nothing sticks to him.

Millions of voters do approve of Mr. Reagan's conservative policies, and millions more don't concern themselves about policy issues. That is to be expected. What is extraordinary is the president's support from another quarter. Opinion polls show that he wins substantial allegiance among those very people who worry about his record-breaking deficits, who fear that his actions could lead to war, and who believe that his economic program has clobbered the poor.

Says Fred I. Greenstein, professor of politics at Princeton University: "He is more successful than any recent president in establishing space between himself and his policies."

Clearly, the creation of that space has been a major goal of the administration. Richard B. Wirthlin, the Reagan campaign polltaker, puts it in terms of a "social contract" between the president and the public — "the giving of a stewardship to a president based upon trust, confidence, and congruence with a system of beliefs, rather than a congruence with a set of articulated policies." Mr. Reagan's unmatched skills as a communicator of basic values have been applied to achieving that end.

It remains to be seen, of course, whether Mr. Reagan's magic will prevail in this election year. A series of foreign-policy setbacks might well tarnish his public image. He suffered a stunning defeat earlier this month when the Republican-controlled Senate overwhelmingly repudiated CIA participation in the mining of Nicaraguan ports. A major disaster in Central America might turn the race around. And his popularity could be damaged if the economy sours.

Yet it seems evident that, given the success of his strategy to date, the political marketing of Mr. Reagan's personal qualities may change the nature of the 1984 campaign. To a degree unknown in recent elections, the challenger will have to meet the incumbent's personality head on, matching his style and countering his overarching message with one of his own.

The Reagan approach may also have a more lasting effect. He has fashioned a new chemistry of image, message, and personality — a presidential persona — that could change the boundaries of the American presidency itself.

In his book *Why Not the Best?* Jimmy Carter quotes a line from Reinhold Niebuhr that summarizes the former president's view of the world and of his trade: "The sad duty of politics is to establish justice in a sinful world."

Americans in this century have tended to elect presidents who represented change rather than continuity. John F. Kennedy's youth and vigor were an antidote to the era of Dwight D. Eisenhower. Jimmy Carter, like Mr. Reagan, based his appeal on his persona, offering the nation integrity in the aftermath of Watergate. But the contrasts between Mr. Carter and his successor are particularly illuminating.

Mr. Carter bore the burdens of office like a cross. He identified personally with his administration's traumas, and told Americans that there were no simple answers. The apotheosis of his martyr presidency came with his refusal to set out on the campaign trail in 1980 because of the Iran hostage crisis. Clinging to the Rose Garden, he succeeded in turning the White House into a kind of prison.

He also regarded the mastery of the details of his job as crucial to his leadership. During the Middle East summit meeting at Camp David, he got down on hands and knees to study maps of the Sinai. He read volumes of Russian history before meeting with Leonid I. Brezhnev, the Soviet leader. He sought to educate Americans to nuances. Discerning a "crisis of confidence" over energy shortages, he consulted leading intellectuals on their view of the national malaise. He called on Americans to accept limits on future growth.

On every count, Ronald Reagan's approach to the presidency is dramatically different. Mr. Reagan positively enjoys the job, keeps his distance from crises, ignores details both as Chief Executive and Chief Communicator. No matter how grave things look, his attitude is invariably upbeat and reassuring.

Some of the differences were inevitable, given the nature of the two men. More significantly, Mr. Reagan and his aides perceived the style of the Carter administration as wrong-headed and doomed to fail. They had altogether new and different ideas about how to present the president to his people.

Every administration for a generation has spent substantial time and energy seeking to make optimum use of television and the print media in the president's behalf. But as the candidate of the minority party and a president whose legislative plans represented a dramatic break with the past, Mr. Reagan had a special need. And because of the long history of presidents driven from office or defeated for reelection, White House aides were also determined to use the media to strengthen the institution of the presidency itself.

To an unprecedented extent, Mr. Reagan and his staff have made television a major organizing principle of his presidency. His day is planned around opportunities for television coverage. Every effort is made to assure a constant flow of positive visual images and symbols from the White House.

In 1982, as unemployment soared and the president was accused of lacking compassion for those out of work, Mr. Reagan avoided appearing in public and before the television camera in black tie. Instead, he showed up for events concerned with unemployed teenagers, dock workers and others being trained for new jobs. When disaster strikes a community, Mr. Reagan doesn't stop at sending relief funds — he makes a detour, as he did to flooded-out Louisiana last year, to be photographed stacking sandbags. When a presidential journey overseas is in the works, producers from the television networks accompany White House aides on the advance trips. The two groups jointly figure out the best photo angles of the president — staring into the demilitarized zone from South Korea, gazing grimly across the Berlin Wall. Plans for the president's trip to China were similarly television tailored.

This administration's exceptional ability to manipulate the media is impressive. One means of assuring that the cameras stay on the president, for example, is a White House policy that has Mr. Reagan himself making important announcements on television. For details and analysis, the news media are handed over to Treasury Secretary Donald T. Regan, Defense Secretary Caspar W. Weinberger or other top aides — but under ground rules whereby that may not be identified in news accounts. As a result, the only person who can be shown on the 7 o'clock news coverage of such announcements is the president himself, offering broad, positive precepts.

Another goal is to keep Mr. Reagan's image as far from bad news and negative discussion as possible. Sometimes the president disappears altogether. The momentous announcement of the withdrawal of the Marines from Lebanon was made in a written statement distributed late in the day, minutes after Mr. Reagan had left for his ranch in California. There were no senior officials immediately available to the press to explain why the withdrawal was ordered.

The White House communications staff is nothing if not imaginative. Last year, former Interior Secretary James G. Watt stirred up a hornet's nest of rock-and-roll lovers after he ousted the Beach Boys from their July 4 concert on the Mall. Mr. Watt was summoned to the White House and handed a large plaster foot that had a bullet hole in it, a brilliant device for making light of the incident. Later, it was learned that David R. Gergen, director of communications at the time, had commissioned the making of the foot weeks before, with the thought that it would come in handy if someone in the Administration happened to make a gaffe.

A sense of timing showed up on a more serious topic last December when the White House learned that the Pentagon was about to release a report criticizing the administration for alleged failures in the massacre of marines in Beirut. White House officials preempted the negative impact of the report by leaking Mr. Reagan's reaction to the charges the day before the report was made public.

The mastery of media techniques has been placed in the service of a president with a remarkable approach to political discourse.

According to Aristotle, the art of persuasion requires more than logic and argument. One of a speaker's most important tasks, he wrote, is to understand the psychology, the "ethos," of his audience. Instead of lecturing his audiences about limits, President Reagan offers good news. There is no limit, he says, to what the nation can accomplish. He talks of heroes on the battlefield and tells Americans that if they work hard, pay taxes, and seek a better life for their children, they are heroes, too. It is a message — known among his advisers in the 1980 campaign as the "can-do-America" theme — aimed at a public that has felt the nation floundering through years of economic and foreign-policy crises. It is particularly potent in its appeal to blue-collar ethnic Roman Catholics in the Northeast and Middle West and to fundamentalist Christian groups in the South.

Mr. Reagan keeps his message simple. Campaign aides speak of a hierarchy of public feelings: A voter has an "opinion" about money for a new B-1 bomber and an "attitude" toward increasing military spending, but he regards the defense of freedom as a "value." As much as possible, Mr. Reagan seeks to appeal to "values." And as his aides say, for all his ability as a performer, his appeal would not work except for the fact that he is a true believer.

"He operates on a separate plane from the rest of us," says a senior Republican in Congress. "We may find him flawed because he doesn't know the details and can't analyze them. But he can have a simple dialogue with the voters. It's raw personality. Jimmy Carter agreed with you, and you didn't like it. This guy can dissagree and you think he's great."

As much as possible, the president tries to prevent his message from being undermined by the details of political issues. For example, he seeks often to transform a debate over the effects of his programs into a broader issue of his personal compassion. Asked at news conferences about his civil-rights record, the president speaks less of his policies than of how he campaigned as a radio sports announcer to integrate baseball. His parents, he says, wouldn't allow him to see "The Birth of a Nation" because it was a racist film. Accused of being indifferent to the hardships suffered by the unemployed, he tells of the pain he felt when his father lost his job on Christmas Eve during the Great Depression.

Sometimes, the president transcends the details of an issue by focusing on a single element with all the force of his persuasive powers. In 1982 and 1983, Europe was roiled by protests over American plans to place new missiles on that continent. Rather than devote his time to the intricacies of his arms-control policies, the president addressed the issue generally. With utmost sincerity, he spoke of his commitment in principle to arms control, and of his fervent wish that nuclear weapons could one day be banished from the face of the earth. The speeches helped ease European fears, clearing the way for the missiles to be installed on schedule.

Mr. Reagan has used a similar approach — ignoring the elements of an issue to concentrate on general principles — in talking about the Middle East. "How many people follow the ups and downs in Lebanon closely?" asks a top Reagan adviser. "It's probably less than 20 percent. But how many people understand that his attempt to establish peace was the major objective? You're getting closer to 50 percent."

If positive communication with the mass of the public is the goal, Mr. Reagan seems to achieve it. He seems to know intuitively how to communicate on the right plane for his larger audience, even when doing so involves skirting over the nitty-gritty of an issue.

In political terms, the president thus enjoys remarkable freedom from attack on the frequent occasions when his statements are at variance with the record. Even the press is less inclined than it once was to pay much attention to such statements.

Mr. Reagan claims that the government is spending more on those in need than ever before. But he fails to note that inflation has eroded the value of most such government programs: Food stamps, for instance, buy less food today than they did a few years ago. Moreover, he has made many poor people ineligible for federal aid.

In defending his domestic programs, Mr. Reagan typically makes two claims. He leaves the clear impression with his audiences that there have been no outright budget cuts in major programs, and that where cuts have occurred the poorest families have not been affected. In fact, the funds budgeted this year for the Environmental Protection Agency, job programs, aid to families with dependent children, social-services block grants for the poor, and aid to elementary and secondary schools are less today than in the 1981 fiscal year, even without including the negative effects of inflation. And according to the nonpartisan Congressional Budget Office, about 40 percent of the reduction in benefit payments has fallen on families making less than $10,000 a year.

The president's willingness to stretch the facts takes a variety of forms. In 1982, he portrayed his program of tax increases as a corrective measure to eliminate loopholes and "ornaments" others had hung on his 1981 tax cut. In fact, Mr. Reagan had placed those ornaments himself to corral enough votes to get the legislation passed.

After seeking to weaken key enforcement provisions of the Voting Rights Act, he finally signed the strengthened version demanded by Congress. Then he announced: "This legislation proves our unbending commitment to voting rights."

More often than not, such presidential comments attract scant public attention. Even when they are reported in the print media and on television, they apparently have little negative effect on Mr. Reagan's public image. The voters seem to have come to recognize that the president is absolutely sincere in his statements. What might be construed as deviousness in another politician is accepted in his case as a simple mistake or a mistaken simplification or nitpicking on the part of the press. Moreover, there is evidence that the public is willing to draw a distinction between Mr. Reagan and his personal beliefs, on the one hand, and his government policies, on the other. According to a mid-March Gallup Poll, 55 percent of Americans approve of Mr. Reagan's performance in office. Yet several other polls show that they give his policies in Lebanon and Central America substantially lower ratings.

Though much is made today of Mr. Reagan's years as a film actor, in fact he was not as well known on the movie screen as he was on television. As Christopher J. Matthews, a top aide to the Speaker of the House, Thomas P. O'Neill, Jr., has pointed out, it was not until Mr.

Reagan took over as host of the General Electric Theater that he became the proverbial household word. He was known throughout the nation as a genial host who was not a GE official, but a kind of mediator between the company and the audience.

In Mr. Matthews's view, Mr. Reagan has found a similar spot for himself as President. He is, says Mr. Matthews, "not in government" but "at some unique point — previously uncharted — between us and government." He presents himself as independent of whatever problems may be vexing the nation — a kind of genial host to the whole country.

At press conferences, Mr. Matthews notes, the president consults a seating chart that helps him to call on reporters by their first names as though he were the host of a friendly get-together rather than an adversarial press conference. Delivering the state of the union message, he introduces heroes in the audience — Lenny Skutnik, who saved a man from drowning in the icy Potomac River, or Stephen Trujillo, an Army sergeant who performed bravely in Grenada. He uses radio and television addresses to salute such developments as the efforts to combat drunk driving or to arrange for organ transplants.

As the nation's host, Mr. Reagan can fully exercise his profound skills as a communicator. His charming manner and his oratorical gifts are seen and heard to best advantage. (His greatest gift is for narrative: The strongest speeches, such as the one last September after the downing of a South Korean airliner, or the one in October after the invasion of Grenada and the truck bombing in Beirut, were masterpieces of storytelling.)

But the president's public stance apart from his government has another, more significant advantage. It removes him from the firing line, softening public anger toward him personally over unpopular or mistaken policies. In 1982, he addressed rallies on Capitol Hill, denouncing the members of Congress as though he were just another citizen with a bill of grievances. In fact, incongruous as it may seem, Mr. Reagan — four years after being elected Chief Executive — continues to blame many of his problems on those he calls "the people in Washington."

Strategy and technique help explain President Reagan's ability to make himself liked by Americans, but his efforts to project himself come easily. Backstage, by all accounts, Mr. Reagan is the same person he is out front.

To be sure, there are certain anomalies about the president's public image. For many voters, he embodies an old-time America of tightly knit families, small-town neighborhoods, and God-fearing values. Yet he came of age in show business, became the first divorced man to serve as president, has had an often-troubled relationship with his children, rarely goes to church, and, though he has publicly praised the notion of tithing, doesn't personally come close.

On most counts, though, Mr. Reagan is much the way he presents himself. Dwight Eisenhower had some of Mr. Reagan's public qualities — the infectious smile, the mangled syntax, the relaxed working habits — but Mr. Eisenhower struck many of those who knew him privately as a crafty operator and a demanding boss. Close associates of Mr. Reagan describe him as "guileless" and an "undemanding" person to work for.

Mr. Reagan's old-school, noblesse-oblige quality also shows up even with his staff. On a sweltering afternoon in the Oval Office in 1981, for example, a close aide suggested that the president might want to remove his jacket; after all, the two men were alone. Mr. Reagan was shocked at the suggestion.

Mr. Reagan extends myriad courtesies to his staff, autographing pictures for them, remembering their birthdays, and greeting their families in the Oval Office. He goes out of his way to assure adversaries that he does not hold grudges or take their criticism personally. He seems to recognize that graciousness is the best policy politically, as well.

In 1982, while on his way to Bogota, Mr. Reagan learned that President Belisario Betancur of Colombia was going to denounce him in a speech. Mr. Reagan's aides debated what action to take until he finally announced, "We're going to smother him with kindness." Mr. Betancur's tongue-lashing took place as expected, but the relationship between the two men flourished. Before seeing Mr. Reagan off at the airport, the Colombian president commented with some amazement: "You are such a friendly man."

More recently, White House aides were divided over how much hospitality to show the Reverend Jesse Jackson and the downed Air Force pilot he brought back from Syria. Mr. Reagan cut short the debate by saying: "The only way we can lose is if we're not gracious."

When Mr. Reagan was seventeen years old, he wrote a poem for his high-school yearbook in Dixon, Illinois, containing the following passage:

> I wonder what it's all about, and why
> We suffer so, when little things go wrong?
> We make our life a struggle,
> When life should be a song.

That upbeat message is still part of the president's personality. "He is an absolutely unstoppable optimist," says one administration official. Throughout the 1982–83 recession, for example, Mr. Reagan saw each new economic development as a sign that prosperity was on its way back. During a hopeless moment in the negotiations to prevent a war over the Falkland Islands, Mr. Reagan counseled aides in the Situation Room not to despair. The United States, he said brightly, could be "the envy of the world" if it could broker a solution.

Like the president's graciousness, his optimism is a useful quality in building support for his programs. All presidents come to recognize that persuasion is their principal task, and Mr. Reagan is typical in that regard. White House aides estimate that he spends 80 percent of his time selling his programs and only 20 percent of his time actually shaping them. Optimism is the hallmark and chief technique of a successful salesman.

But congressional critics charge that the president's optimism keeps him from giving policy problems the rigorous analysis they deserve. Repeatedly, for example, Mr. Reagan has rejected the pessimistic warnings of key economic advisers of what might happen if the federal deficit is not reduced drastically.

And while the situation in Lebanon deteriorated, the president continued to tell congressional visitors that prospects were good for a settlement. Speaker O'Neill, for one, said later that he felt deceived. Some senior administration advisers now admit, in fact, that Mr. Reagan's optimism may have prevented him from seeing that events were undermining his original assumptions in sending American troops to Beirut.

The picture of the president's decision-making process, as painted by his aides, makes for a sharp contrast with what is known of most of his predecessors.

For one thing, Mr. Reagan enjoys the job. He never complains about the loneliness of making difficult decisions that has for generations been a staple of presidential leadership. Typically, Mr. Reagan puts in an eight-hour day, does homework in the evening, and takes the trouble to master material for meetings and trips.

But a vacation is a vacation: Last February, he was on his way to his ranch in Santa Barbara when — in the course of a few days — the Lebanese government virtually collapsed, his decision to withdraw the Marines from Beirut produced an uproar, and Yuri V. Andropov suddenly died in Moscow. Mr. Reagan refused to interrupt his holiday to return to Washington. His personal inclination fit with his aides' aversion to having the president seen as a super crisis manager — another break with the attitudes of previous administrations. "If he had come back and held a bunch of meetings," a White House official explained, "the public might have developed unrealistic expectations about what could be accomplished."

The distaste for details is a trademark. In his memoirs, Jimmy Carter offers an incredulous description of the briefing he gave Mr. Reagan on the hostage crisis just before his inauguration; Mr. Reagan took no notes. Nor does President Reagan have much of a memory for details. In 1982, he toasted the people of Bolivia when he was in Brazil. During a recent meeting, he referred to his administrator of the Environmental Protection Agency, William D. Ruckelshaus, as "Don." (Later it became clear he had mistaken him for Donald H. Rumsfeld, the Middle East negotiator.) In front of reporters at his ranch, he called his own dog by the wrong name.

If Mr. Reagan receives a sheaf of papers with a short covering memorandum, he generally reads the memorandum. On the eve of the Williamsburg economic summit conference last year, he set aside his stack of carefully prepared briefing documents to watch "The Sound of Music" on television and never got back to the papers.

To refresh his memory on the points he wants to raise, the president uses cue cards in meetings with foreign leaders and others. Although some call the cards a distraction, Mr. Reagan seems not at all embarrassed.

An aide recalled that at a White House session last year, the president sat down at the cabinet table with a group of educators. Their spokesman confessed that he was quaking with nervousness; would the president mind if he read from his notes? Mr. Reagan told him not to worry. With a grin, he held up his own cue cards.

More serious problems arise, however, from the fact that the president rarely puts aside significant amounts of time to look into subjects he knows little about. He doesn't devour books, engage in intellectual argument, or seek out information from unofficial sources. If he is seated at dinner with a stranger who might be an expert on a topic Mr. Reagan knows little about, the president prefers to banter about sports or show business. In general, he relies more on what he hears and observes than what he reads. He is not one to reach out for ideas. "The possibility that you can teach him is not there very much," says a former foreign-policy adviser. "You get the feeling that his mind is pretty much made up."

The president's approach can lead to significant confusion. He astounded associates recently with an admission: Not until last fall, he said, did he realize that the Soviet Union has 70 percent of its strategic nuclear warheads placed on its land-based missiles, whereas the United States has only 20 percent of its strategic warheads on such missiles. Not until then did he realize why his original proposal for Russian cuts in land-based missiles, without similar American concessions, had been perceived as one-sided. The failure to master such basics has prevented him from resolving philosophical divisions in his administration over arms control.

A top White House official likens a policy session with Mr. Reagan to a meeting between a client and his lawyers: He focuses less on minutiae than on the extent to which a proposal is consistent with his personal guidelines. Before asking the president to make a decision, his aides try to achieve a consensus among themselves, but, like any client, he sometimes rejects even unanimous advice. Mr. Reagan took that tack when he dismissed the striking air traffic controllers in 1981 and when he refused to entertain the idea of tax increases in early 1982.

Close aides concluded long ago that it is often useless to try to persuade Mr. Reagan to support something he cannot believe in. In fact, as his aides recognize, his success in communicating an idea to the public is in part a function of his genuine emotional commitment to that idea. "So many politicians tire of that stump speech," says an adviser. "Reagan is willing to repeat it again and again because he believes every word of it." A Republican ally in Congress adds: "If he gets an idea firmly fixed in his head, he uses it forever."

Sometimes, though, the president's aides feel that he must be made to see the light on a particular issue. Then they may try to administer what they call "reality therapy." It usually takes the form of a visit by congressional leaders who agree with White House aides that the time has come to urge Mr. Reagan to be more flexible.

White House aides avoid appealing directly to the president on political grounds. "You argue from weakness if you go in there and tell him, 'If you don't do this, you're going to suffer a loss in your job approval rating,'" says James A. Baker, 3d, the White House chief of staff. But Mr. Baker and others admit that they cannot ignore their mandate to help win legislative approval for administration programs, or to strengthen Mr. Reagan's political standing. If the political stakes are high enough, they find a way to get his cooperation.

Their time-tested technique is to persuade the president that he is not reversing course even if that is precisely what they want him to do. Mr. Reagan truly does not believe that he changed policies significantly when he accepted a tax increase in late 1982, or when he dropped his efforts to delay construction of a natural-gas pipeline from Siberia to Europe, or when he decided to withdraw American troops from Lebanon.

White House aides say that Mr. Reagan is a genius at boiling abstractions down to concrete concepts that the public will understand. Often, his staff may look over the draft of a speech he has been working on and point out that a statement is incorrect. "How can we state it so that it is correct?" he will reply and prod his aides to find the down-to-earth facts and images to support his notions. He seizes on any bit of information that comes to him if it reinforces something he already believes.

Mr. Reagan, himself, skims the leading newspapers each day in search of telling anecdotes. He also seeks them in letters he receives and in articles in such publications as *Human Events*, the ultraconservative magazine. The stories tend to be about people who use food stamps to buy vodka or who falsify papers in order to obtain disability payments.

Mr. Gergen, the former communications director, calls them "parables," arguing that the public cares little about their authenticity. But press attention has forced the White House to "scrub" the stories for accuracy before Mr. Reagan uses them. "I always think that if we can get through a press conference without some disaster, it's a success," says a senior White House official.

More problematical are what the president's aides refer to as "notions." These include his debatable statements that the Great Society caused poverty to increase in the 1960s or that the United States actually decreased military spending in the 1970s. Asked recently why the president says things that are untrue, a long-time adviser laughed and said: "I don't know. He's been doing it for years."

The role of Mr. Reagan's staff is much debated in Washington. Some fear that his refusal to become involved in the intricacies of policymaking leaves him vulnerable to manipulation. Moderates claim, for example, that the president was persuaded to approve a crackdown on "leaks" to the press last fall without realizing that it called for lie-detector tests for his cabinet and staff.

Other critics charge that the White House staff is not activist enough, that they are cowed by Mr. Reagan's strong positions on some issues. Despite briefings from budget experts, Mr. Reagan resists accepting the idea that his programs to cut tax revenues and increase military costs have widened the federal deficit. His aides no longer push the point. One comments: "He doesn't like to be crowded or pushed hard by one individual."

The result of the staff's wary attitude toward Mr. Reagan is that, for all his geniality and attentiveness, he is not personally close to anyone. He tends to regard his closest aides at the White House as retainers or surrogate sons, but not as cronies.

Their manner toward him, in return, is highly deferential and respectful. Even Mr. Reagan's closest advisers find him to be basically remote, operating on a different plane and by his own lights — distanced from them. By all accounts, it is so rare for Mr. Reagan to confide in them, to share his darkest concerns or inner turmoils, that there is some doubt among his staff that he is troubled by any. Not until he was ready actually to announce his decision, for example, did Mr. Reagan tell even the members of his inner circle explicitly that he had indeed decided to run for reelection. Mr. Reagan is known to be similarly circumspect with his long-time friends in California. The only person with whom Mr. Reagan is known to share his inner feelings is his wife, Nancy.

Backstage at the White House, much as in his public persona, there is a wall of his own making between the affable president and his audience. The nation's host is a solitary man.

Long before the age of television, political experts complained about the electorate's limited attention span. In 1925, Walter Lippmann observed: "The public will arrive in the middle of the third act and will leave before the last curtain, having stayed just long enough perhaps to decide who is the hero and who the villain of the piece."

No modern president has exploited that tendency more effectively than Mr. Reagan. His performance inevitably raises questions about his prospects for reelection and the larger legacy he will have left as president.

The Democratic candidates hope to defeat Mr. Reagan by capitalizing on voter concerns about world tensions, fears that inflation, or unemployment may resurface or worries that Mr. Reagan will cut Social Security, Medicare, and other domestic programs.

And it remains to be seen how long the president's popularity would hold in the face of a barrage of policy reverses. The outer limits of his magic touch have yet to be tested. In the 1982 recession, for example, Mr. Reagan's approval rating dropped substantially. If there were a major increase in inflation or unemployment before election day, that rating might very well fall again.

Moreover, there is no way to be certain how the public will react to such events as the rebuke Mr. Reagan received April 10 when the Senate voted eighty-four to twelve for a resolution opposing American support of the mining of harbors in Nicaragua. Among those voting against him were the majority leader, Howard H. Baker, Jr., and forty-one other Republicans.

It was one of the worst setbacks Mr. Reagan has experienced in his relations with Congress, and one of the most serious rejections of a presidential policy since the Vietnam War. Administration officials state that the mining has ceased, and the future of all covert assistance to rebels in Nicaragua is now in doubt. But Mr. Reagan has a record of being able to carry his case to the public, bringing enough pressure on Congress to salvage much of what he seemed to have lost and preserving his popularity.

In January, when Congress returned after the holiday recess, Republican Congressional leaders informed Mr. Reagan that his policy of maintaining American troops in Lebanon had lost most of its support in Congress. The president withdrew the troops and his policy was widely described as a debacle. But his approval rating among the voters has been steadily rising ever since.

The president's astonishing political success to date suggests that the Democrats will have to do more than base their challenge on a catalogue of issues. They will have to run against the nation's host. Even now, Mr. Reagan's reelection strategists are planning some daunting presidential extravaganzas. Mr. Reagan plans to open such national celebrations as the World's Fair in New Orleans and the Olympic Games in Los Angeles. After returning from China, he will be off for a summit meeting in London and ceremonial stops in France and his ancestral home in Ireland.

Presidential pageantry gives all incumbents an advantage. But Democrats have a special problem because of Mr. Reagan's skills. Should they question his work habits and misstatements? The voters may continue to feel that these are simply unimportant. More likely, the Democrats will have to meet Mr. Reagan on his own terms, raising the political debate to a choice between two visions. Senator Gary Hart would be under more pressure to define his ideas. Former Vice President Walter F. Mondale would be under more pressure to give his ideas fresh urgency and drama. Any Democrat will have to find a way to convince the voters that he, like Mr. Reagan, is speaking from his heart.

What impact will Mr. Reagan's performance have on the presidency itself? It seems hard now to remember the days when much of official Washington patronized him as an amiable amateur. He ended up transforming the conventional definition of the job.

In part, he has avoided some traditional pitfalls. He has not allowed himself to be unduly awed by the trappings of power — he has not taken the obsessive personal interest of his predecessors in assigning seats at state dinners or aboard Air Force One or in deciding who can use the White House tennis court.

"The main problem with power is that the person who uses it has trouble holding onto his identity," says John P. Sears, who managed Mr. Reagan's campaign in 1980 before being dismissed the day of the New Hampshire primary: "I think Reagan really does believe he's just a temporary custodian. This is where his training as an actor comes into play. An actor realizes that he's out front, and that he might get credit if the movie is a hit or blame if it's a bomb. But he knows there are people behind him who are working to pull the whole thing off."

That perspective might well be emulated by future presidents, whatever their background. They may also be tempted to learn from Mr. Reagan's political success. By concentrating on general themes and by projecting an upbeat spirit he has minimized the political damage that comes with running a government. By formulating a compelling vision of national purpose and by breathing it into every act and statement, he has forced critics and would-be challengers to debate the issues on his terms. He has shown that it is not enough for a president in the modern age to have such a vision; he must also be willing to spend most of his time selling it — persuading, cajoling, and communicating.

Mr. Reagan may also have altered the experts' perception of the qualities required for the presidency. "We better take another look at the nature of the job," says Mr. Sears. "We've had an awful lot of intelligent people in the White House who have done a poor job at it. Sometimes intelligence in a president can lead to confusion of purpose. Simplicity, on the other hand, has its merits."

And its dangers. Some of the president's closest aides, in fact, are concerned that Mr. Reagan is too insulated. "His instincts are the right ones, but that doesn't mean they shouldn't be tested against reality," says a senior White House official. What's more, Mr. Reagan's aloof managerial style has left an enormous amount of power to be fought over by his staff and led to considerable confusion in arriving at the final decision.

But there are larger questions posed by Mr. Reagan's first term in office: How far should a president try to separate himself from the political consequences of his policies? Is it enough for a president to speak to the yearnings of an age if he fails to confront the electorate with complex, difficult choices? In November, the voters may provide some answers.

T HE FOLLOWING SELECTION continues the Reagan saga, explaining how his "directors" — political advisors and consultants — helped their talented client preserve his teflon armor during his second term as president. Reagan made the White House his own personal stage, brilliantly playing the presidential role that he had learned from Hollywood and history. When necessary he could easily speak the appropriate lines given to him by his advisors, but to their chagrin he often turned press conferences, political speeches, and ceremonial occasions into dramatic performances, sometimes embellishing facts and fictionalizing politics to please his audiences.

Reagan's dramatic talents also please James David Barber, the author of the following selection. He observes, "The bright side of presidential dramatics is inspiration." But he also expresses reservations, writing. "The dark side is the power of drama to overwhelm reason. the lure of illusion, the fracturing of logic, the collapse of political conversation. The dark side is the drift into the swamp of fantasy and on over the brink of disaster. Drama offers interest, but it risks political insanity. That process begins with contempt for the facts."

17 James D. Barber
THE REAGAN PRESIDENCY: CHARACTER, STYLE, AND PERFORMANCE

By the time Reagan reached the stage of the White House, he had more experience pleasing audiences than any American politician since William Jennings Bryan. He had mastered the arts of dramatic performance on the stage, in radio sportscasting and commentary, in the movies, in television, and in specialized and general platform oratory. No other candidate in 1980 or 1984 had anything like Reagan's professional experience in the modern media. And not since Harding had a happy-talk president's character and style fit together so nicely with the public's yearning for positive thinking in politics. The president had a terrific sense of humor, which he exercised regularly in what started out to be formal prep sessions by his staff. "Being dull," he said, "is very hard for me," and he loved Nancy especially for shielding him from boredom. He and Nancy let their emotions show: for all his general geniality, the Reagans are to be found weeping sentimentally on scores of occasions from one end of the biographies to the other.

The obvious combination of public personality and media talent made it surprising that it had taken so long for the Reagan "type" to appear in the age of media politics. Here was a man who, at his inaugural ball,

From James David Barber, *The Presidential Character: Predicting Performance in The White House,* 3rd ed., © 1985, pp. 490–496. Reprinted by permission of Prentice-Hall, Inc., Englewood Cliffs, New Jersey.

could do the apparently impossible: "Ronnie and Nancy danced intimately while thousands watched." He knew how to rehearse systematically for the apparently unrehearsed, spontaneous move, such as saying "There you go again" before giving one of his memorized responses (based on leaked Carter memos) in answer to Jimmy Carter in their campaign debate. He introduced the teleprompter to the English Parliament. He could steal FDR's finest lines — "rendezvous with destiny," for example — and make them sound his own. Painted by his opposition as a combination fool and knave, he knew how to turn those expectations to his advantage; he became one of those lucky politicians who get credit for being normal. As an entertainer/speaker at an Al Smith dinner, he could surpass any presidential candidate in sight — approximately as Rudolph Nureyev could surpass him at the polka. Reagan was specially adept at playing the injured innocent, the wounded bear, saying "I can't be angry . . ." when assaulted by a critic. The minor tricks were part of his nature by then — for example, knowing how to look and move slightly but expressively when the television camera finds you listening to your opponent's answer. To the television audience for presidential addresses, he spoke simple English and even used such homely but effective props as a dollar bill and 36 cents in change to make his point. His staging was superb, from his tan and tieless performance in front of the Statue of Liberty during the campaign, to his inaugural on the visually correct side of the Capitol Building, where he could gesture expansively at the monumental wonders of the Mall. The television networks followed him around like trained puppies, eager to put on the news shows good happy clips from Nancy's "surprise" birthday party for him on February 4, 1983, followed a few days thereafter by the president's foray into a drugstore to buy her a valentine. Even his administration's top people seemed to have been typecast as supporting players for the Reagan performance. Surrounded by such sober types, his mildly maverick manner makes him seem fresh and interesting.

The Fictionalization of Politics

That one can carry off an act like Reagan's without control and calculation — by just "being oneself" while strolling through the media minefield — is a myth beyond credibility. At least since his Hollywood days, he has been used to having his appearance managed by others. He approached playing Governor of California the same way, by following his directors. Then when trouble came, as when a homosexual clique was found in his administration, "Ronnie was told as much, but, as he always did in emotionally difficult and complex situations, he distanced himself from the realities and went on." When he finished being governor, a public relations firm, Deaver and Hannaford, took over the task of directing him. The same director/star relationship continued in his presidential politics.

What was made to look like a Reagan move was often a performance directed by others. For instance, there was Reagan's famous performance at the 1980 "debate" in New Hampshire, in which the audience saw an indignant Reagan stride onto the stage and insist that all the other candidates, not just George Bush, should have their chance to say their piece. That broke the agreed-upon rules, so the editor of one of the sponsoring newspapers asked that Reagan's microphone be turned off. Reagan the wounded bear turned on him and spoke: "I paid for his microphone, Mr. Green!" Bush looked foolish, Reagan looked simultaneously democratic and in charge. Political reporter David Broder turned to his colleague Lou Cannon and said, "Reagan is winning this primary right now." For that and other reasons, Reagan did go on to win big in New Hampshire: he got more votes than the other six candidates put together.

But the management of Reagan is all the more effective for being invisible. In this not untypical case, Reagan's manager John Sears got the idea of inviting the other candidates to the scheduled Reagan-Bush debate — and Sears went ahead and asked them without even telling Reagan, much less getting his okay, until noon of the day of the debate itself. When Bush, through his manager (and Reagan aide-to-be) James Baker refused to agree that the others should speak, here came grim-visaged Reagan, pacing up the aisle to the platform with the alphabetic four trailing behind him: Anderson, Baker, Crane, and Dole. Beside him, though, walked his aide Jim Lake, and to Lake, Reagan was saying, "What am I supposed to do? What exactly am I supposed to do?" Lake said, "We're going to go up there. You're going to make this statement that these guys should be allowed to speak. If they leave, you've got to stay and debate." Reagan walked up and sat down. Lake sent a Secret Service agent up with a note: "Give 'em hell, Governor. The whole place is with you." Scowling Reagan looked up a moment and gave Lake a wink. Then stern and indignant, he played out the part.

That is why thankful movie stars, receiving their Academy Awards, pay homage to their unseen but essential directors and producers.

The perfection of the Reagan act kept breaking down in the campaign because it was impossible to keep it completely under control; nosey reporters kept asking him questions, and his answers were too often downright flakey and thus newsworthy. Once in the presidency, managing the act was much easier. Media access to the president was radically restricted. By the midterm elections of 1982, Cannon was calling him "one of the most isolated chief executives since World War II." In the analogous period, Jimmy Carter had held three times as many press conferences as Reagan held, and Eisenhower, Kennedy, and Johnson had even more than that. Increasingly his staff kept reporters away from him at staged "photo opportunities" so as not to tempt him into spontaneity. Interviews were rare and controlled. Nancy would coach him, "You wouldn't know," "We're doing the best we can," or Ed Meese would come between questions and answer with "You don't have to answer that." On the other hand, the president repeatedly addressed the nation on television and put out a regular radio program, sometimes eliciting an opposition response which was almost never as well done as the Reagan original. Reagan was not about to be shanghaied by the press, if he and his attentive managers could prevent it. As always, he worked best when he could rehearse and a major Reagan address took hour after hour of rehearsal. Preparing for the climactic television debate in 1980, Jimmy Carter studied his briefing books. Reagan and his friends did that too, but they devoted hours to practicing the dramatics and studying videotaped playbacks of the trial runs.

Such control protects Reagan from a malady he has experienced repeatedly: getting carried away by an audience. Passive-positives are prone to that in part because they are more closely attuned to the here and now — the present, in-person audience — than others are. Nancy, his most worshipful audience, has been a steadying influence in that respect. She was away from his side when, on the spur of the moment, he told the California delegation to the 1968 Republican convention that he was a candidate for president. In 1962, Nancy reports, he suddenly changed his party registration from Democrat to Republican when, in the midst of one of his speeches a woman registrar interrupted to sign him up. In 1980 audiences kept inspiring him to excess. He added to a speech to the Veterans of Foreign Wars the startling idea that the war in Vietnam was a "noble cause." A group of reporters for religious publications inspired him to bubble up the thought that "creationism" ought to be taught alongside evolution in the public schools. At the Michigan state fair, a woman in the audience wearing a Carter mask needled him into saying he was happy to be there while Carter "is opening his campaign down there in a city that gave birth to, and is the parent body of, the Ku Klux Klan," a statement wrong in every particular. "I could have bitten my tongue off," Reagan said right after the speech as he recognized the mistake. An uproar followed. Reagan had to apologize to the appropriate mayor and governor. Nancy, reading the signs, got Stuart Spencer to join the campaign and keep him from flying off; "Okay, Stu, okay," said Reagan, "I'll stick to the script." In the presidency, Reagan could much more easily be restrained from audience-inspired blurts.

Other things being equal, such dramatic calculations and controls are all for the best. The modern presidency is of necessity a performance — a media performance — and the modern arts of president-playing are to be celebrated, not disdained. They make politics interesting and thus encourage participation. They translate complexity into simplicity, which, in real-world politics, is a prerequisite for action. At their best they enliven and expand the national classroom, where the lessons have to do with life and death. The bright side of presidential dramatics is inspiration.

The dark side is the power of drama to overwhelm reason: the lure of illusion, the fracturing of logic, the collapse of political conversation. The dark side is the drift into the swamp of fantasy and over the brink of disaster. Drama offers interest, but it risks political insanity. That process begins with contempt for the facts.

Reagan seemed to love facts. Unlike politicians who take their stand on the landscape of generality, Reagan was forever citing statistics and telling interestingly specific bits of history or biography. The trouble was that he very often said, with an air of resolute conviction, things that simply were not true. Reporters and opposing candidates collected the errors of Ronald Reagan by the notebookful. Far from trivial, Reagan's counterfactuals bore directly on major problems of public policy. If trees cause air pollution, if oil slicks help cure tuberculosis, if welfare cheats are rampant, if the Shah of Iran was a "progressive," if the Soviet economy is about to collapse "because they've already got their people on a starvation diet of sawdust," if there is more oil under Alaska than under Saudi Arabia, if billions upon billions of federal expenditures are "fat" — then follow various highly significant directions for the relevant policies. Not that his perceptions were random; they suited his rich friends far better than his poor victims. Richard Cohen reported that Reagan, at one spring 1982 press conference, "said Social Security was not 'touched' when in fact it had been cut. He said programs for pregnant women had not been reduced, but merely merged with others. They were cut — by about $200 million. He said the overall poverty budget was increased—it wasn't; the new money went for defense. But the frequency of Reagan's "slips," "gaffes," or "bobbles," was in itself amazing, especially given the heat Jerry Ford and Jimmy Carter had had to endure for far less significant blunders. More interesting, though, was Reagan's own apparent attitude toward his "mistakes": he did not seem to mind. Though he sometimes waxed indignant over accusations of inaccuracy, he typically acted like an actor who, having blown a line, has to forge right ahead without worrying over it. When a reporter quoted one of his strange statements back to him, he shrugged and said he did not remember saying that, but that he had "probably just read something from a piece of paper that had been put in front of me." Or he "would just smile pleasantly or shake his head in disagreement with his critics, as if mastery of provable fact were things on which gentlemen certainly could differ in goodwill." The gaffe story had developed its plot to perfection in presidential politics, from error to expiation — but Reagan would not play. He was, it seemed, literally shameless when it came to the question of factuality. As James Reston put it, "Give Mr. Reagan a good script, a couple of invisible TV screens, and a half hour on prime time, and he'll convince the people they have nothing to fear but the facts."

Like his dramatic skills, that attitude was rooted in his own theatrical experience. Arriving in Hollywood, he remembered being "filled with all the star-struck awe of one who had from childhood been entertained in the house of illusion — the neighborhood theater." He missed completely the GI cynicism of World War II, dwelling instead through those years in another house of illusion — making mythic films of patriotic puffery and acting in a musical comedy about the war. Fantasy in Reagan's life was not, as it might be for a reporter or historian, something to guard against, but rather a point of pride. The actor is meant to be an enthusiastic fantasist, a dreamer. "So much of our profession is taken up with pretending," he wrote, "with interpretation of never-never roles, that an actor must spend at least half his waking hours in fantasy." Reagan especially liked Carl Sandburg's slant on dreaming: "The Republic is a dream. Nothing happens unless first a dream." David Stockman summed up the White House system at one critical era: "Every time one fantasy doesn't work they try another one." Another staffer left the Reagan White House saying, "The whole administration's a fantasy that they have the power to maintain and define as normal . . . but they have no questions. It's an administration without questions." To Reagan, accusations of fantasy translate easily into praise for having the courage to dream great dreams and not to let a lot of piddling little facts get in the way. His conscience is easy — he didn't lie, he just made things up.

For years Reagan has been making up stories about himself — mythlets he seems to believe. "I'll never forget one game with Mendota," one such tale begins and goes on to describe how he lost a close football contest for Dixon High by confessing to the unseeing umpire that he deserved a penalty; though sorely tempted, "truth-telling had been whaled into me. . . . I told the truth, the penalty was ruled, and Dixon lost the game." But the fact is, as Cannon reports, that Dixon lost only one game that season — to Mendota by a score of 24–0. Then he tells the one about how his brother was persuaded to go to college because an old immigrant at the cement factory said to him, "Look at me — ve'll always vork together, chust you and me, and zomeday you'll be chust like me — isn't that nize." A cute story and according to Neil Reagan, total fiction. In 1983, Reagan told Hugh Sidey of a peak experience in his life — when, at Eureka, "I played Captain Stanhope in *Journey's End*. I never was so carried away in the theater in my life. I was in the war as far as that play was concerned." He added details about the cast and his role. The trouble is, he did not act in the play at all. He saw it performed when he was a freshman. Later he said that "in some strange way, I was also on stage." That psychological identification had overwhelmed the facts and he had moved from his seat to the stage. "He is forever reinventing his past," William Leuchtenburg writes, especially in juggling the history of his attitude toward Franklin Roosevelt to suit Reagan's current politics. As David Broder noted, "It is apparently President Reagan's belief that words can not only cloak reality but remake it." The past is raw material, to be shaped as needed for purposes of revealing dramatic truth.

Nor is Reagan's fantastic imagination devoted only to historical reconstructions. He thinks up stories he might act in in the future. After he lost to Ford in 1976, Betty Glad noted, Reagan fantasized about man-to-man confrontation with Leonid Brezhnev. As he told his son, Mike, after he lost to Ford in 1976:

> You know the real reason I'm upset? I was looking forward to sitting down with Brezhnev and negotiating the SALT II Treaty. I wanted to listen to the interpreter tell me for an hour and a half what Brezhnev wanted the president of the United States to give up in order to maintain friendship with Russia. Then, I was going to slowly get up, walk around the table and whisper in his ear, "Nyet." I really miss that. I don't think Brezhnev has ever heard that word before.

In July 1982 he was still at it, telling Laurence Barrett that:

> I often fantasize [about taking] Soviet leaders in a helicopter and just flying around, just kind of let them choose where we go, so it couldn't look like a planned tour, and be able to point down and say, "Yeah, those houses down there. Yeah, that house with a trailer and a boat on it in the driveway. That's a working man in America. Yes, he lives in that house. He has that boat. He drives that car to work." They could not show me comparable things in their country.

Nowhere does Reagan make this attitude clearer than in his story of how segregation ended in the armed services "in World War II . . . largely under the leadership of generals like MacArthur and Eisenhower": "When the Japanese dropped the bomb on Pearl Harbor there was a Negro sailor whose total duties involved kitchen-type duties. . . . He cradled a machine gun in his arms, which is not an easy thing to do, and stood at the end of a pier blazing away at Japanese airplanes that were coming down and strafing him and that [segregation] was all changed." A reporter told him segregation lasted at least until three years after the war when Truman ordered it stopped. Reagan replied: "*I remember the scene. . . . It was very powerful.*"

Reagan off-stage seemed to be engaged in creative fantasizing. Laurence Leamer notes that

> What was so extraordinary was Ronnie's apparent psychic distance from the burden of the presidency. He sat in cabinet meetings doodling. Unless held to a rigid agenda, he would start telling Hollywood stories or talk about football in Dixon. Often in one-on-one conversations Ronnie seemed distracted or withdrawn. "He has a habit now," his brother, Neil, said. "You might be talking to him, and its like he's picking his fingernails, but he's not. And you know then that he's talking to himself."

> "If people knew about him living in his own reality they wouldn't believe it," said one White House aide. "There are only ten to fifteen people who know the extent, and until they leave and begin talking, no one will believe it."

The uncoupling of the president from White House decision-making became a startling fact of life among his advisors. A former aide said that the president, facing a policy question, "will not go far into it because he is not really looking to make a decision. He is looking for lines to repeat when the time comes to sell. He thinks of himself not so much as the person who decides but rather as the person who markets." A current aide confessed how difficult it was to get the president to concentrate on policy specifics: "I have to prepare a script. Otherwise he will get me off the subject and turn what I have to say to mush. I have about six or seven minutes, and then he guides the conversation." Similarly abroad: Joseph Kraft noted that "foreign leaders repeatedly come away from sessions with the president claiming he is a pussycat, too nice even to mention disagreeable subjects."

The uncoupled quality came through also in public on those rare occasions when he spoke without a script. David Broder noted that "To hear him speak extemporaneously on domestic policy is to hold your breath in nervous anticipation of the unknown." Lacking firm anchoring in the mind of the president himself, policy in the Reagan administration lurched from one accident to another. The supply-side hocus-pocus was but the most evident of a series of inventions in which the logic of politics fell apart in the presence of the logic of the theater. Theodore White saw that the Reagan budget "defied common sense — almost as much as the illusion that by sheer power alone, people can learn to slide uphill." Stockman and Murray Weidenbaum slapped together figures from their "visceral computers" — their gut feelings. The Reagan people had thought to propose a 5 percent rise in defense spending, but Carter proposed that figure in his final budget, so the Reaganites upped theirs to 7 percent, the president explaining that "worldwide, what we're doing in defense must be seen as different from Carter. It must be a symbol of a change in the climate as regards to defense." Thus the figures had nothing much to do with actual guns and bullets, but with symbols, and so there was not much apparent need to get the figures right; the billions were tossed around with cheerful abandon. That was the dashing style in which much of the Reagan "program" got constructed, from governmental decentralization to missile development. One after another, the major new projects rolled out of the White House hangar: a new defense system, based in outer space, to turn back Soviet missiles, a new "zero option" aiming at total elimination of nuclear weapons, a new proposal for merit pay for school teachers — each enjoying its week or so in the sun before passing into the oblivion from which it had emerged. Cannon came to call the president "The Great Deflector."

PRESIDENTS DEPEND UPON their political advisors to develop policies and plan strategies. The White House staff is always the inner circle, but cabinet secretaries may also have the president's ear. The heads of executive departments are chiefs of state in microcosm. Their budgets exceed those of many nations, and their staffs are often greater than the president's in number if not in power. They enjoy many of the perks of heads of state, traveling about in luxurious limousines paid for by the government, commandeering military aircraft when necessary, and conducting diplomatic missions abroad representing their departments and the government. They may even, as Joe Califano did when he was Secretary of the former Health, Education, and Welfare Department (now the Department of Health and Human Services), pick a chef that will serve their favorite cuisine in their department's private dining room. Politically beholden to the president for their appointments, cabinet secretaries nevertheless have their own constituencies which, if managed and represented properly, give them a large measure of independent power.

The following portrayal of Ronald Reagan's treasury secretary, who was also his former White House chief of staff, reveals how one department head's personality and style shaped his relationship with the president and Congress.

18 Jane Seaberry and Anne Swardson
ON MANEUVERS WITH JIM BAKER

Shortly before 2 P.M. last December 17, Representative Claudine Schneider received an urgent telephone call asking her to attend a meeting in the Capitol with Treasury Secretary James A. Baker, 3d.

"When?" the Rhode Island Republican asked.

"In 10 minutes."

The House Ways and Means Committee's tax revision bill was near defeat on the House floor, and the House Republican leadership unanimously opposed it. So Baker, using the office of Minority Leader Robert H. Michel of Illinois, called a meeting of White House allies to try to bypass his own party's leadership.

Gathered for the meeting were nine members of Congress whom Baker knew well and who could be counted on to get the votes of particular blocs. Schneider, for example, was selected because she is a vote-getter in the Northeast, where GOP opposition to the tax bill had been strong.

Baker also selected ranking members of committees and influential senior members, such as William S. Broomfield of Michigan and Henry J. Hyde of Illinois. And, for their technical expertise, he drafted the few Republicans from the Ways and Means Committee who supported the bill.

After dividing up the lobbying chores, Baker began making personal appeals, negotiating compromises on the bill's fine points, and calling on legislators' loyalty to the president.

That night, a smiling Baker watched from the visitors' gallery as 49 Republicans joined 207 Democrats to defeat a motion to kill the legislation, 256 to 171. The measure then passed on a voice vote.

After a slow start in his first year as Treasury secretary, Baker has won some of the Reagan administration's toughest political battles. Those include maneuvering the tax bill through a Republican minefield; holding back — at least temporarily — congressional protectionist pressures; and devising a plan for handling the international debt crisis by increasing loans to hard-pressed nations while requiring them to adopt free-market policies. This is now known as the Baker Plan.

For Baker, however, his second year in the Cabinet may prove to be tougher. Some of this year's problems may be compounded by last year's compromises. In the tax area, for example, Baker won support for what essentially was a Democratic bill by promising a Reagan veto if certain changes were not made in the Republican-controlled Senate. But the Senate Finance Committee, which takes up tax overhaul in March, does not consider itself bound by those promises.

With a record trade deficit in 1985 and a congressional election campaign beginning in the spring, Reagan administration officials say they expect protectionism to become an increasingly hot issue. As the president's chief economic spokesman, Baker has led in devising solutions to the trade problem.

The continuing drop in world oil prices further complicates the international economic outlook and threatens the stability of many Third World countries that depend on oil revenue to survive. It also jeopardizes the Baker Plan, which already has been criticized for being too little, too late.

One high-ranking administration official says the Baker Plan will need to be modified because of the oil-price drop. The oil-exporting debtor countries will need to enforce even tougher austerity measures, which the Baker Plan was designed to ease; only then can those debtors improve economically or expect to get more bank financing, the official says.

If there has been a theme to Baker's first year at the Treasury Department, it is compromise, analysts within and outside the administration agree.

Soft-spoken and low-key, Baker, 55, works hard to stay out of the limelight. While some Cabinet officials are eating pheasant at glittery affairs in Washington, Baker is hunched in a blind on his Texas ranch hunting quail. During the high-tension December days when the tax bill was in jeopardy, he and his deputy, Richard G. Darman, spoke to no one as they walked through the halls of the Capitol, followed by a small army of reporters and camera crews.

In a recent interview, Baker declined to accept credit for the House turnaround on the tax bill. "I don't think I did that," he said. "The president did that."

"I worked on the phone," he added. "So did a whole lot of other people."

Repeatedly last year, as in the previous four years when he served as White House chief of staff, Baker was called on to be the president's point man during difficult times. Colleagues and combatants openly admire the skills of the intensely political Houston lawyer-banker, who is known for his smooth-talking, calculated manner, his policy of never going out on a limb, and his attention to detail.

Baker collects political chits by attending fund-raisers and other political events on behalf of congressional Republicans. His aides note that such actions helped achieve the House tax victory. They say that his contacts could aid Baker in pushing tax overhaul through a nervous Senate.

"He has helped a lot of us," Republican Senator Charles E. Grassley of Iowa says. "He was the drawing card at a fund raiser for me last fall."

Commerce Secretary Malcolm Baldrige, who worked with Baker on George Bush's unsuccessful presidential campaign in 1980, says Baker does not take extreme positions when he finds himself alone on an issue. "Jim Baker is a very practical man," Baldrige says. "He has an open mind. That means to me there's more than one way to skin a cat. It doesn't always have to be done just his way."

Baker's combination of savvy and muted ideology played a large role in last year's turnaround in the administration's policy toward international trade and debt issues.

High-ranking administration officials say Baker showed little or no interest in trade policy before last summer, despite pressure from the Commerce Department and the U.S. Trade Representative's office to deal with the issue at the White House level. When it became clear that trade was becoming a dangerous political issue for the president, Baker developed a sudden interest in devising a plan to douse protectionist fires, administration officials say.

In a matter of weeks last summer, Baker and his deputies devised a plan within the Economic Policy Council, which Baker heads.

From the start, it was clear that any serious effort to deflect protectionism would have to involve lowering the value of the dollar in relation to other currencies. The strong dollar was making U.S. exports expensive overseas. The White House, however, opposed tinkering with foreign exchange markets.

Warning of the need to head off rising protectionist sentiment in Congress, Baker managed to persuade the White House to make a 180-degree change in policy.

On September 22, Baker announced an agreement with France, West Germany, Britain, and Japan to coordinate efforts to push down the dollar. Since then, the value of the dollar has fallen about 13 percent against other major currencies.

Several high-ranking administration officials credit Baker with helping to move stalled trade-policy initiatives advocated for months by the Commerce Department and the U.S. Trade Representative. And they credit his influence in the decision to have Reagan make a major trade policy speech and to initiate unfair trading-practice complaints against some countries. The result: Legislation to impose a surcharge on imports languished in committee, and Congress made no attempt to override Reagan's veto of a bill to curb imports of textiles.

"There was a real push given . . . because of rising protectionist sentiment in Congress," Baldrige says. "That's something Baker really understood. That was true of a great many in the administration who hadn't been closely involved in trade before. What should have been done for their own sake was done because of the rising protectionist sentiment in Congress."

When they devised the monetary plan, officials acknowledged they knew it wouldn't be enough to change the world. But they also were certain it would deflect some criticism. This spring, Baker will have to come up with something else to quiet Congress, administration officials warn.

Baker also will have to produce a more convincing plan to settle another international problem: the Third World debt crisis. Late last summer, government officials from several Latin American countries complained to Baker that they were struggling under the burden of mounting debt and poor economic growth, and that their debt troubles threatened the stability of their fragile democracies.

With that problem in mind last fall, Baker proposed that commercial banks lend $20 billion to the 15 largest developing-country debtors during the next three years to help ease their problems in repaying loans to western banks. Multilateral development banks would add another $9 billion.

But criticism of the plan is mounting. Late last month, Mexico's finance minister, Jesus Silva Herzog, claimed that the Baker Plan was not enough to restore these 15 countries to economic health. Baker responds that his plan wasn't expected to work overnight and that the complainers should take steps to help themselves.

"I happen to believe . . . that it's important that the United States lead in international economics," Baker says. "We should lead where appropriate."

Other administration officials say the Mexicans, for example, will need to tighten their belts. But, because of falling oil prices, the administration doesn't know what it can do to help Mexico, one official says.

"Some people think the proper course is to write down that debt or write it off and not think in terms of additional capital flows," Baker says. "I think that would not be an alternative approach, but an admission of defeat."

Defeat remains a possibility for Baker on tax overhaul. He frequently reminds visitors that "no one ever said tax reform was going to be easy" and that the Senate is faced not only with restoring deductions and credits dear to senators, but with living up to the promises that Reagan has made to change the bill.

The promises, negotiated in part by Baker, helped reassure not only House Republicans but the president himself. In Cabinet meetings, Baker pushed for a quick presidential endorsement of the House bill as soon as it emerged from the Ways and Means Committee in late November. But other aides successfully urged that the president endorse only the general concept of tax overhaul because of substantive objections to the House bill.

The delay and the weak endorsement nearly killed the legislation, giving 164 Republicans political leeway to vote against bringing the bill to the floor. Only then was Baker's advice accepted and the intensive lobbying effort begun.

The promises, outlined in letters to Michel and Republican Representative Jack Kemp of New York, included a personal exemption of $2,000 for most taxpayers (the House bill would grant the full increase only to those who do not itemize); depreciation write-offs for business investment at least as generous as originally proposed by Reagan, and a top rate of 35 percent (the House bill would cut the current top rate of 50 percent to 38 percent).

These changes would cut federal revenue needed to keep the legislation from adding to the federal deficit.

Baker, who accompanied members of the Senate Finance Committee to their tax "retreat" in West Virginia last month, suggests that the panel look at such revenue-raising proposals as repealing the deduction for state and local taxes. The House ignored that provision of the Reagan plan, and the Senate seems likely to accept only a partial limitation of the deduction, at most.

In his legislative battles, Baker has been criticized by conservatives as not being ideological enough. Critics charge that Baker's compromising has helped give away too much, particularly regarding the agenda begun in the president's first term. Instead, they say, he should fight Congress on principle.

Many of these critics were appointed to Treasury posts during Reagan's first term, when Donald T. Regan was secretary and the department was the ideological locus of true-thinking supply-siders and strict monetarists, such as Norman Ture and Paul Craig Roberts.

Administration colleagues say many of the inflexible economic views of the first-term Treasury are gone, making it easier to discuss policy with Treasury subordinates. They point to the resignations of Roberts and Ture, and the departure of Treasury Undersecretary Beryl Sprinkel for the chairmanship of the Council of Economic Advisers.

Although Regan has been White House chief of staff for a year and most of his appointees have left the Treasury, comparisons continue between Baker and him in style and substance.

Where Regan would charge ahead on issues regardless of the political costs, Baker contemplates the consequences before deciding an issue's merits, top Treasury aides say.

Baker's low-key style with Congress also sets him apart from Regan. Regan enjoyed sparring at congressional hearings, even when confrontation with angry legislators was expected. Baker, by contrast, is deferential at hearings; he avoids conflict and prefers small meetings and backroom maneuvering, close aides say.

"He sees public hearings as more symbol than substance," a Treasury official says.

"I think there was some damage done when Donald Regan was secretary," says Democratic Senator David H. Pryor of Arkansas. "I think that if the president wants a tax bill, he ought to utilize Jim Baker. He is trusted by the committee. He's practical. He listens. He's open-minded."

"The bottom line is: too much politics and not enough economics," economist John Makin of the American Enterprise Institute says of the changes Baker made and accepted in the tax plan. But Makin agrees that Baker would have been "dealt out of the game" if he had resisted the tax legislation on ideological grounds.

Economist Alan Greenspan, who has observed Treasury secretaries during the past two decades, says Baker has the potential to follow in the footsteps of such great secretaries as George Shultz, currently secretary of State, and Robert Anderson, who served during the Eisenhower administration.

However, the challenges of Baker's second year — taxes, trade, and debt — are tougher than those faced by his predecessors, Greenspan says.

"He's in a period when international financial problems and other areas [in which] the Treasury functions have become critical," Greenspan says. "At this point, he has at least attained the status of average, and could very well, depending on how the rest of the term transpires, become one of the best."

T HE WORLD OF THE WHITE House staffer is unique. In the rarefied atmosphere of the West Wing of the White House the president's press secretary, national security adviser, top personal assistants and troubleshooters, and other staffers who are particularly close to the president work near the Oval Office. Occupying physical space that is near the president is of enormous symbolic significance, being generally taken to reflect a close relationship with the president himself. Not all of the White House staff works in the West Wing; many occupy offices in the old and new executive office buildings, which are respectively adjacent to and directly across Pennsylvania Avenue from the White House. The formal office of the vice president is in the old executive office building with a view directly overlooking the West Wing. President Carter moved Vice President Walter Mondale into an office in the West Wing to symbolize a close presidential–vice presidential relationship (the former vice president's office is occasionally used for ceremonial functions and stands ready to receive vice presidents in the future).

The White House staff is a relatively new institution; President Roosevelt created it in 1939 as part of his reorganization plan establishing the executive office of the president. The White House staff, however, did not come into its own as an independent force until much later. While it always included powerful and influential persons, its original purpose was best expressed by Harry Truman: "The presidency is so tremendous that it is necessary for a president to delegate authority. To be able to do so safely, however, he must have around him people who can be trusted not to arrogate authority to themselves."[1] Truman continued, "Eventually I succeeded in surrounding myself with assistants and associates who would not overstep the bounds of that delegated authority, and they were people I could trust. This is policy on the highest level: it is the operation of the government by the Chief Executive under the laws. That is what it amounts to, and when that ceases to be, chaos exists."[2]

President John F. Kennedy put together a dynamic and forceful staff that was later inherited by Lyndon B. Johnson and described as "the best and the brightest" by journalist David Halberstam.[3] Halberstam argued persuasively that major White House decisions escalating the Vietnam war during the Johnson administration could be traced directly to powerful White House staffers such as Walt Rostow, McGeorge Bundy, and Robert McNamara (who later changed from hawk to dove and resigned his position as secretary of defense to become president of the World Bank).

It was during the Nixon years that the White House staff, controlled by H. R. (Bob) Haldeman and John Ehrlichman, arrogantly wielded power around Washington in the name of the president. The Nixon White House staff was dubbed the "Palace Guard," because of its reputation for preventing direct access to

[1]Harry S Truman, *Memoirs: Volume 1, Year of Decisions* (Garden City, New York: Doubleday, 1955), p. 228.

[2]Ibid.

[3]David Halberstam, *The Best and the Brightest* (New York: Random House, 1972).

the president by cabinet officers and other top officials. Like Truman, Nixon recognized the need to delegate power, but unlike Truman, he did not recognize the critical importance of retaining absolute control over his own staff. Many of the acute embarrassments to the White House that occurred during the Nixon administration, including possibly the Watergate break-in itself, might have been avoided had the president been less optimistic about the system of broad delegation of powers that he established in the White House.

Regardless of who is president, the tendency of those on the White House staff is to aggrandize their personal power. White House staffers continually seek to be in the good graces of the president, which not only may involve backroom intrigue among different individuals and groups of staffers, but also tends to mute honest criticism of the president if he embarks on what an ambitious staffer feels to be the wrong course of action. In the following selection George Reedy, a longtime associate of Lyndon B. Johnson, both on Capitol Hill and in the White House, provides a succinct personal account of the way in which the institution of the presidency affects staffers. Reedy was Lyndon Johnson's press secretary in 1964–1965, after which he returned to private life, only to be summoned back to the White House in 1968 as a special adviser to the president on domestic matters. When Johnson was in the Senate, Reedy served with him at various times, both as a staffer on the committees Johnson chaired and as a member of the senator's personal staff. Reedy's thesis is that the atmosphere of the White House tends to breed "blind ambition," to borrow John Dean's phrase, on the part of staffers, even though their personalities might not have revealed this trait before they entered the White House.

19 George E. Reedy
THE WHITE HOUSE STAFF: A PERSONAL ACCOUNT

The most frequently asked question of any former presidential assistant is whether he misses the White House. My answer is a heartfelt no!

It is an institution which can be regarded with a far higher degree of approbation from the outside — where reverence softens the harsh lines of reality — than from the inside. Like any impressionistic painting, it improves with distance. . . . The factor that I have missed in most of the works on the presidency I have read is the impact of the institution on individuals. The literature on the subject seems to assume that the White House somehow molds the man and his assistants into finer

From George E. Reedy, *The Twilight of the Presidency*, pp. xii–xvii. Copyright © 1970 by George Reedy. All rights reserved. Reprinted by permission of Harry N. Abrams, Inc.

forms and that the major problem of government is to assure channels through which these forms will have full expression. It is virtually taken for granted that the proper objective of a study of our chief executive is to identify those inhibiting factors which frustrate his efforts to resolve national problems and to devise mechanisms which will remove those frustrations. This is a type of study which should be continued on a priority basis. The frustrations are many and could be catastrophic.

But the analysis is inadequate. It ignores the fundamental reality of society, which is that institutions are manned by individual human beings and that government — regardless of the managerial flow charts produced by the behavioral scientists — is still a question of decisions that are made by people. The basic question is not whether we have devised structures with inadequate authority for the decision-making process. The question is whether the structures have created an environment in which men cannot function in any kind of a decent and humane relationship to the people whom they are supposed to lead. I am afraid — and on this point I am a pessimist — that we have devised that kind of a system.

To explain this, I must start with a highly personal reaction. The trouble with the White House — for anyone who is a part of it — is that when he picks up a telephone and tells people to do something, they usually do it. They may sabotage the project, after they have hung up the phone. They may stall, hoping that "the old son of a bitch" will forget about it. They may respond with an avalanche of statistics and briefing papers in which the original purpose will be lost and life will continue as before. But the heel click at the other end of the wire will be audible and the response — however invalid — will be prompt. There will be no delay in assurance, however protracted may be performance.

This is an unhealthy environment for men and women whose essential business is to deal with people in large numbers. It is soothing to the ego, but it fosters illusions about humanity. It comforts the weary assistant who may have gone round the clock in his search for a solution to an insoluble problem, but it paves the way for massive disillusionment. And for the very young, the process is demoralizing. It creates a picture of the world which is ill adapted to that which they will face once the days of glory come to an end. There should be a flat rule that no one be permitted to enter the gates of the White House until he is at least forty and has suffered major disappointments in life.

My own heart is back in the Senate, where I spent so many years of my adult life either as a newspaperman or a staff assistant. This is not because the people at the other end of Pennsylvania Avenue are any better in terms of character, wisdom, or goals. It is simply that their egos must face daily clashes with similarly strong egos who stand on a par and who do not feel any sense of subordination. In the Senate, no course stands the remotest chance of adoption unless a minimum of fifty-one egotistical men are persuaded of its wisdom, and in some cases the minimum is sixty-seven. These are preconditions under which even the most neurotic of personalities must make some obeisance to reality.

The inner life of the White House is essentially the life of the barnyard, as set forth so graphically in the study of the pecking order among chickens which every freshman sociology student must read. It is a question of who has the right to peck whom and who must submit to being pecked. There are only two important differences. The first is that the pecking order is determined by the individual strength and forcefulness of each chicken, whereas in the White House it depends upon the relationship to the barnyard keeper. The second is that no one outside the barnyard glorifies the chickens and expects them to order the affairs of mankind. They are destined for the frying pan and that is that.

The White House does not provide an atmosphere in which idealism and devotion can flourish. Below the president is a mass of intrigue, posturing, strutting, cringing, and pious "commitment" to irrelevant windbaggery. It is designed as the perfect setting for the conspiracy of mediocrity — that all too frequently successful collection of the untalented, the unpassionate, and the insincere seeking to convince the public that it is brilliant, compassionate, and dedicated.

There are, of course, men who seethe inwardly over this affront to human dignity — most of whom either go smash or leave quietly, their muscles set rigidly to contain an indescribable agony. There are, of course, the warm and relaxed permanent White House staff members, secure in their mastery of the essential housekeeping machinery of the mansion and watching with wry amusement and some sympathy the frenetic efforts to shine forth boldly of those who have only four years out of all eternity to grab the brass ring. But the men of outrage are few and for some reason avoid each other after they slip out the side door. There are experiences which should not be shared. A reunion would lead only to a collective shriek.

It is not that the people who compose the menage are any worse than any other collection of human beings. It is rather that the White House is an ideal cloak for intrigue, pomposity, and ambition. No nation of free men should ever permit itself to be governed from a hallowed shrine where the meanest lust for power can be sanctified and the dullest wit greeted with reverential awe. Government should be vulgar, sweaty, plebeian, operating in an environment where a fool can be called a fool and the motivations of ideological pimpery duly observed and noted. In a democracy, meanness, dullness, and corruption are entitled to representation because they are part of the human spirit; they are not entitled to protection from the harsh and rude challenges that such qualities must face in the real world.

It is not enough to say that the White House need not be like this if it is occupied by another set of personalities. It is not enough to point out that I may subconsciously be exaggerating the conditions which I de- scribe in overreacting to the reverence that has characterized most stud- ies of the presidency. The fact remains that the institution provides camouflage for all that is petty and nasty in human beings, and enables a clown or a knave to pose as Galahad and be treated with deference.

Is my reaction purely personal disappointment or shaped by service in a specific White House in a specific administration? Obviously, no man can be truly objective about an experience so central to his life and so vital to all his goals and his aspirations. All I can say is that I am fully aware of the treacherous nature of one's sensory mechanisms in survey- ing the immediately surrounding universe. I have taken this factor into account and tried to allow for it in every possible way. . . . I believe that what I am saying is more than the conclusion of one man in a unique set of circumstances.

The thirty years I have spent in Washington have been punctuated with a number of telltale incidents. I have observed, for example, that former White House assistants are reticent about their experiences. When pressed for a description they invariably resort to words like "richly rewarding" and "fulfilling" — the clichés that men always use when they wish to conceal, rather than to convey, thought. And their congratulations to newly appointed assistants begin always with per- functory "best wishes" and then shift to heartfelt friendly tips on how to survive. Only once have I felt a genuine flash of fire. It came from one of the top "assistants with a passion for anonymity" of the Roosevelt days. I described to him White House life as I saw it and his response — which was passionate — was: "Don't worry! That's the way it has al- ways been and that's the way it will always be!"

I have a feeling that Camelot was not a very happy place. Even the gentle language of Malory does not fully cloak hints of intrigue, corrup- tion, and distrust — reaching as high as Guinevere. And the "Table Round" seems better adapted to boozing in a vain effort to drown disappointment than to knightly discourse on chivalrous deeds and weighty matters of state.

In fact, Malory makes virtually no effort to describe Camelot as a seat of government. King Arthur was presumably beloved by his subjects because he was wise and valiant. But how did he handle roadbuilding, public charity, or the administration of justice? Such questions had to wait several hundred years for the advent of Mark Twain, whose entire- ly fictitious (and wholly irreverent) account was probably much closer to the reality than that produced by the original sources.

It is this aspect that gives cause for concern. The psychological ease of those who reside in Camelot does not matter except to the individuals themselves. But the type of government that Camelot produces affects every individual and, ultimately, can determine the character of the society in which we all must live.

It is my highly pessimistic view that Camelot will no longer suffice — however effective it may have been in the past. As a rallying point for men who would beat off dragons and ogres, it was superb. As a device to lead us through the stresses of modern life, it is wholly inadequate. And one of the few historical principles in which I still retain faith is that an inadequate government will either fall or resort to repression.

There is no reason to believe that the United States is exempt from the forces of history. We have no special writ from the Almighty which will substitute for normal human wisdom. There is no evidence that such wisdom is being applied effectively to the overwhelming problems that beset us nor is there any light on the horizon. And while it may seem premature at this point, we may well be witnessing the first lengthening of the shadows that will become the twilight of the presidency.

TRADITIONALLY, POLITICS AT the top levels has been a man's world. Before the women's movement began in the 1960s it was rare indeed to find women in Congress, the Cabinet, at the top levles of the administration and the bureaucracy, or in the courts. The situation had not greatly improved by 1986, when there were only twenty-two congresswomen, two female senators, and very few women in top positions in the other branches. President Reagan made a major "breakthrough" when he nominated Sandra Day O'Connor to fill a Supreme Court vacancy. But the Reagan administration did not seem to differ from its predecessors of both parties in making only token appointments of women to top-level jobs, reserving virtually all of the most powerful positions for men. Women have had little, if any, influence, particularly on the White House staff, as the following behind-the-scenes glimpse of 1600 Pennsylvania Avenue reveals.

20 Lois Romano
WOMEN IN THE WHITE HOUSE

Some say the message was delivered five years ago, as clear and as penetrating as the January air — before the Reagan team even moved into the White House.

It came from the inaugural committee in the form of a suggested dress code for the inaugural ceremony, circulated among Ronald Reagan's soon-to-be senior staff: "Gray oxford stroller jacket . . . gray striped trousers . . . gray vest . . . gray striped tie . . . black oxford shoes."

Not a word of counsel to women. "Perhaps they figured we would know how to dress, but I'm telling you, then and there we should have known where we were heading," says one woman, a former senior White House aide, who received the memo. "The White House is the ultimate power, and women have to fight like hell to get it. It's almost impossible to rise to it, and for sure, no one is going to give it to you."

"There's very much a barefoot-and-in-the-kitchen mentality in the White House," says Joanna Bistany, a former White House aide who is a vice president of ABC. "Nancy Reagan prefers to deal with men, and that certainly has the effect of setting a pace."

"Many of the people in this White House come out of the financial world," says Linda Chavez, who resigned as deputy assistant for public liaison last month to run for the Senate from Maryland, and who generally speaks highly of her former colleagues. "So you're dealing by and large with men unfamiliar with dealing with women."

For a time, it seemed as if Ronald Reagan was making some headway on the "women's issue." Reagan was, after all, the first president to appoint a woman to the Supreme Court, and the much-ballyhooed gender gap that was to be his downfall in 1984 never did materialize at the polls.

But chief of staff Donald T. Regan's impolitic remarks before the Geneva summit — women, he said, "are not going to understand throw-weights or what is happening in Afghanistan or what is happening in human rights" — brought to the surface again what insiders and outsiders describe plainly as quiet sexism in the White House.

"They seem to hang onto the men — like [former Labor secretary Raymond] Donovan and [Attorney General Edwin] Meese — and give them hugs when they mess up," says Democratic Representative Pat Schroeder of Colorado, a longtime critic of the administration's attitudes toward women. "I can't think of one bad thing Jeane Kirkpatrick or Margaret Heckler did, and yet they are gone."

"Every woman over there should ask for Regan's resignation," says Kathy Smith, a Republican whose term as chairman of the National Women's Political Caucus recently ended. "These guys are a throwback to cave men. . . ."

Most of the two dozen or so women and men close to the White House who were interviewed for this article tactfully said Regan's remarks were "regrettable." Yet, many of the same people privately refer to the chief of staff and the five men he brought to the White House with him last March as "The Boys Club."

Regan did not return phone calls for this story, and many of those interviewed would talk only on the condition that their names not be used. Some, however, made unsolicited calls to express their views. The White House also provided specially compiled fact sheets comparing male-female ratios among Reagan administration appointments with the ratios in the work place as a whole. (The administration comes out behind — 26 percent to 30 percent — in "executive, administrative, and managerial positions," and ahead — 80 percent to 77 percent — in "administrative support and clerical positions.")

And one White House spokesman called periodically to ask: "How are we doing so far?"

When it comes to gender politics, of course, Reagan's men aren't much different from the presidential staffs that preceded them.

"I worked in the Nixon White House and there simply were no women in positions of power and influence," says Patrick Buchanan, director of White House communications, who — along with former national security adviser Robert C. McFarlane — received high marks from White House women for his efforts to hire and promote them.

"Now when you come back here, there are a lot more women in positions of influence and authority."

Ask the women who work there and most will agree that there is little overt sexism at 1600 Pennsylvania Avenue — that the White House treats women no worse than corporate America, or the media for that matter. "You have to ask yourself, compared to what?" says Karna Small, deputy assistant to the president for public affairs. "Compared to the corporate world? The answer is no."

But there are problems these women don't often articulate, at least not for the record — problems much more subtle and nagging. They range from a series of little frustrations and humiliations, the kind men go crazy over but that women keep quiet about for fear of being called shrill, to the fact that it is nearly impossible for a woman to become part of the Reagan inner circle.

Among the small complaints: Up until December, there were no hours scheduled for women in the White House athletic facility. Now, at the insistence of Chavez and Deborah Steelman, now an associate director of the Office of Management and Budget, women can work out one hour a day. Two years ago, then-chief of staff James A. Baker, 3d, evicted the unisex hairdresser installed by Jimmy Carter. Now, there is only the barber, Milton Pitts.

A much more serious problem is access. Last year, Chavez asked to attend some Cabinet Council meetings, issue-oriented gatherings of some Cabinet members and staff. According to one source familiar with the incident, Cabinet Secretary Alfred Kingon, an aide that Regan brought to the White House, delayed acting on her request. Thinking she had been excluded because of her sex, Chavez wrote Kingon, telling him she was attending whether he liked it or not.

Chavez plays down the matter today. "You can't constantly be looking for slights," she says. "I am always willing to give the person the benefit of the doubt. I didn't get invited because it was an oversight. If an oversight happens too many times, then you have serious problems."

When deputy assistant Pam Turner was recommended for the job of deputy assistant to the president for legislative affairs, with responsibility for the Senate, there was much resistance. The official seeking her appointment, Kenneth Duberstein, then head of congressional liaison, told friends that he took "unmitigated grief" from men who thought only a man could talk to U.S. senators.

Turner ultimately got the job, but Becky Norton Dunlop was not as fortunate. Dunlop, a respected former deputy assistant for personnel, was passed over for promotion when her boss, John Herrington, left to become Energy secretary. The personnel job instead went to Robert Tuttle, one of Dunlop's subordinates, who is the son of Holmes Tuttle, a close friend of the president's.

"There's a tendency on the part of some people to view women in high positions as being interested in some issues more than others," says Jim Cicconi, a former aide to Baker, who now practices law. "That's something the White House has to overcome. It's no accident that women are always appointed to the public liaison job." The Office of Public Liaison is not considered a major policy-making office. Charged with improving White House relations with women, minorities and religious groups, it is often dismissed as something of a hand-holding operation.

Even Karna Small, who feels that she has been treated well since she joined the Reagan team, acknowledges that women are treated differently — for better or worse.

"I remember before I came to the NSC [National Security Council], always fighting the idea that they would have periodic briefings exclusively for women appointees. I said, 'No, you don't understand. Women want to be part of the team, not separated. They want to be known for their expertise.' "

"I said, 'What are you going to do? Have a briefing just on abortion issues and family tax plans and serve tea and crumpets?' "

Opinion seems divided on whether White House women were better off before Regan and Baker switched jobs in March 1985.

"There is now an old-fashioned chauvinism here indicative of the board-room mentality," says one mid-level male, referring to Regan's corporate career at Merrill Lynch, Pierce, Fenner & Smith, Inc. "People who come from Wall Street are from a culture where women don't have a role, or have a token role, like one woman on a board."

Others close to the White House say things weren't very different under Baker. But there is one added thorn, they'll tell you: The new corporate-style "pyramid" structure that Regan has designed, with himself at the pinnacle, seems to work against the advancement of women.

When the triumvirate — Baker, Meese, and Michael K. Deaver — ruled the White House, women such as Margaret Tutwiler, one of Baker's top assistants, could at least come within striking distance of the Oval Office. But Regan has surrounded himself only with men.

Also, under Regan there are fewer "assistants to the president" — the highest ranking staff job — and none who are women. The title, among other things, confers admission to the important morning senior staff meeting. After last April, when Regan downgraded the top job in the Office of Public Liaison from "assistant" to "deputy" after Faith Ryan Whittlesey's departure, no women attended the meetings — for the first time since 1977. But Christopher Hicks, a Regan associate who is deputy assistant for administration, says, "He didn't downgrade the position because a woman held the job."

It was only after a critical story ran in *The Wall Street Journal* last September that Chavez was invited to attend. "It's true that I was invited that week," says Chavez. "But it is also true that prior to the August trip to California, I had put in a request to go and I was told it was being considered."

Not surprisingly, women who have left the administration talk more freely about their working lives.

Joanna Bistany was one of those White House women who had power without portfolio. She carried the lowest commission, special assistant to the president, but as chief assistant to then-White House communications chief David Gergen, she controlled the flow of people and paper into his office. Still, that didn't prevent others from viewing her as a secretary.

"One night we were working quite late, and there was a crisis in the Mideast," she recalls. "Dave and I were frantically trying to pull a statement together, when Al Haig came flying in and said to me, 'Here! Type this quick.' "

"Fortunately, Dave reacted very quickly — I must say he is gender blind — and said to Haig, 'We'll have our secretary do it.' "

But Bistany echoes other former female aides and top officials who say that blatant male chauvinism was not their primary complaint. Women, she says, simply have a hard time advancing to power positions in the White House, and an even harder time keeping the momentum once they do.

"It's just very hard to get ahead there for a woman," she says. "It's pretty subtle but you just know it. There's a tendency for them not to take you quite as seriously."

"If you happened to have a mentor," says Judy Buckalew, who worked for Whittlesey, "you would be able to participate in top policy-making sessions — [but] only because you were given access because of a male. . . . That was the case with Jim Baker and Margaret Tutwiler, and Bud McFarlane and Karna Small. Those women were in high-powered meetings because those men allowed them to be there."

Buckalew, now vice president for government relations of the International Association of Financial Planners, says, "You not only had to fight your way through the male bodies," but "when the women got some semblance of power, you had to fight them, too. Margaret [Tutwiler] had a classic queen bee syndrome. She would not let another talented woman near Jim Baker."

Tutwiler, who followed Baker to the Treasury Department, declined to be interviewed.

The three most prominent women to leave the administration have been Environmental Protection Agency Administrator Anne M. Burford, U.N. Ambassador Jeane J. Kirkpatrick, and Heckler, secretary of Health and Human Services. Heckler did not return phone calls for this story, but Kirkpatrick and Burford are outspoken in their opinions of White House attitudes.

Kirkpatrick is considered the only woman to achieve insider status in the Reagan administration, but when her name was suggested for national security adviser, White House aides told reporters that she was too "temperamental" for the job. Soon afterward, Kirkpatrick began to lash back publicly, saying "sexism is alive" in the Reagan administration.

"The two most-used words to describe women are temperamental and unstable," she says. "Both words have been used against me. I pointed out that my life history did not seem to support these charges. I have been married to one person 31 years, and I have had one job at Georgetown [University] most of that time. I even lived in one house, and my children have gone to one school. That is hardly the life of an unstable person."

Her experience was not unique, she says. "A good many women have a lot of trouble with this administration. When Liddy Dole was in the White House [Dole also held the public liaison job], the rumors flew fast about the dissatisfaction with the job she was doing. And when Faith Whittlesey took that job, the rumors flew fast again. Anne Burford got a raw deal: She took the positions they asked her to, and then was left on a limb. And I found the Margaret Heckler situation dismaying. . . ."

About her departure, Kirkpatrick says, "There were a lot of stories indicating I was an ambitious job seeker. I never sought a job in my life. I never asked for a job. I never talked to the president about other jobs. I do think that is what they do to women."

Burford, still bitter about being forced to resign in 1983 from the scandal-plagued EPA, says the "administration cannot deal with strong women."

Jim Baker, she says, "is the all-time biggest chauvinist I have ever encountered in my professional life. . . . I voiced concern with him once over an executive privilege order, and he said, 'Now Anne, are you going to be a prima donna over this?' I had to sit down. . . . They call him assertive. They call me bitchy."

"If I were a man, they would have never put me out on a limb and then sawed me off," says Burford. "I do think I would have been a lot better off if I weighed 200 pounds, looked like Ma Kettle, and wore

Army boots. I wore purple silk dresses and I'm sure that threw them off."

Whittlesey, now ambassador to Switzerland, also left the administration under duress. But her sex, she says, was only part of her problem.

"They certainly leaked about me," she says, "and I thought it was a combination of sexism and ideology. It's hard to distinguish completely — but you have to look at the leaks about the men, too — Meese, Clark, Buchanan. . . . I think that in any group of men today, there are going to be strains when a single woman enters what otherwise is an exclusively male preserve."

Will there ever be a White House that is *not* a male preserve? The history of the Carter staff, as well as that of Reagan's suggests the day may not come soon.

The Carter administration offered, at least at first glance, a more laid-back and collegial environment. But while Jimmy Carter was quick to name a woman — Midge Costanza — to a senior White House position (again as public liaison chief) the Carter White House's record on appointments was at best average. In fact, according to figures compiled by the Office of Personnel Management, the Reagan administration (in its first four years) appointed a slightly higher percentage of women — 64 percent compared with 61 — to political jobs. And soon after her appointment, Costanza found herself banished to a basement office because the Georgians didn't like her aggressive personality.

Costanza left and was replaced by Anne Wexler, a savvy, no-nonsense political operative who is often cited as one of the first women who was really given entree to a White House inner circle. "Well, it depends how tight you drew the circle," says Jody Powell, Carter's press secretary. "If it was three or four — no. But if it was five or six — yes, Anne was absolutely there."

The White House, Powell adds, "is tougher for women to crack because of the personal-staff nature of the place. . . . The president surrounds himself with people he has known and worked with for a while. That in itself limits an entry by an outsider in any case. And it makes it a lot tougher on women."

But others don't see any problems.

"I have been here from the beginning, and I have felt very much a part of the team," says Paula Dobriansky, who at 30 is the director of European and Soviet affairs for the National Security Council. "The doors have been opened, and I know my advice has been taken seriously and heard."

"I'm a complainer by nature," says Elizabeth Board, a special assistant to the president who left NBC a little over a year ago to direct the White House television office under Buchanan. "And I have never had a better boss — or better work. . . . I have gotten more respect here than I have ever had. . . . And I really am very sensitive to that."

Among those who are less than completely satisfied with their lot, there is a conviction that over time, as more women enter politics, things will change. And, indeed, one can hardly imagine a female White House aide saying in 20 years, "I just feel so protected by all those men" — as one did for this story. Or a male aide responding to a question about one of his colleagues: "Gosh, I just don't know many of those girls over there."

Most observers agree that the White House is not a place for women with thin skins.

"I came here after having been visible and after having a reputation of being fairly hard-nosed and down-to-business," says Chavez, "and I think the reputation that I was not a shrinking violet has probably stood me well here. In a sense, maybe women need that reputation more than men do because they have the opposite assumption to work against. . . . Some of it has to do with the nature of working your way up. Women are more recent entries to the world of politics. . . ."

"But you're seeing a lot more now, and the more you see, the more the men in power will get used to working with women. It's just going to take time. That's all there is to it."

THE
CONGRESS

Chapter Five

Congress is a fascinating amalgam of individual characters, personalities, and styles, which help to shape the institution. Personality is particularly important as it affects congressional leadership, both of party leaders and of committee chairmen. Different personality types in positions of power within Congress develop contrasting styles that influence the way Congress operates For example, the Senate under the majority leadership of Lyndon B. Johnson operated very differently than it did under Mike Mansfield. Johnson's active-negative character was evident in the Senate as in the White House. His personality compelled him to seek control over the Senate, which he managed through knowledge of the strengths, weaknesses, and needs of his colleagues, skill in manipulation of institutional procedures, and an extraordinary ability to persuade others. Each senator became a challenge to Johnson, who sought personal loyalty above all else. The aggressive and dominating style of Lyndon Johnson as majority leader of the Senate was similar to, but much more flamboyant than that of his mentor, House Speaker Sam Rayburn, and it stemmed from different personal needs.

In sharp contrast to Johnson's style as majority leader was the style of Mike Mansfield, who was elected majority leader in January 1961, and served until his retirement at the end of the Ninety-fourth Congress in 1976. Mansfield's style was, to say the least, more muted than Johnson's. He treated each senator with great respect and as an equal. No attempt at a personal cult of leadership was evident during Mansfield's tenure. Johnson was highly effective as a personal leader, whereas Mansfield's effectiveness was as a team player. The contrasting personalities of Johnson and Mansfield go a long way toward explaining differences in Senate operation during their periods of leadership. Under Mansfield, senators were far freer to pursue their own legislative interests without fear of retaliation if they happened to disagree with the majority leader. Mansfield's style became the model for his successor, Robert Byrd. Howard Baker too led by consensus, not by command, in a Senate that would no longer tolerate LJB's system of unilateral control.

Personality is as important in the House as in the Senate in determining who runs for positions of party leadership, and what their styles of leadership will be. Sam Rayburn, Speaker of the House for seventeen years, enforced discipline in the House. Like Lyndon Johnson in the Senate, Sam Rayburn knew every member of the House, their constituencies, and their needs and aspirations. He was able to use this information to consolidate his power as Speaker. Again like Johnson, Rayburn operated on a highly personal basis in the House. The House was his constituency, as the Senate was Johnson's, and he did not hesitate to involve Republicans as well as Democrats in his decisions as Speaker. The election of John McCormack as Speaker of the House in 1962 brought about profound changes, primarily because of the contrasting personalities of Rayburn and McCormack. Robert L. Peabody says:

> Peaceful succession brings on more incremental change, but the impact of such *different personalities* as Rayburn and McCormack on the Office of the Speaker was considerable. McCormack's style was both more institutional and partisan than Rayburn's. He called more meetings to discuss legislative strategy and involved the Majority Leader and Whip to a much greater extent than Rayburn did. . . .
> The telephone was one of McCormack's most effective weapons — "I'd call the Devil if I thought it would do any good." In contrast, Rayburn operated on a more independent and personal basis. He preferred the intimacy and informality of after-the-session gatherings of the "Board of Education." The Whip organization was used less frequently and Rayburn almost never called a party caucus beyond the opening meeting.[1]

Both Rayburn and McCormack, although differing in their personalities and styles, provided effective leadership to the House. Carl Albert, of Oklahoma, became Speaker in 1971, and his personality and style were criticized as weak and ineffective. Peabody points out that "One reason he easily advanced to the Speakership was summed up in a widely affirmed statement — 'Nobody's mad at Carl.' "[2] Being a "nice guy" is usually a reflection of inability to make hard decisions that inevitably antagonize others.

After an extensive analysis of congressional leadership, Peabody concluded:

> Of the twenty variables highlighted in this analysis, the most pervasive and continuing influence upon leadership's selection for party office has been exerted by the personality and skill of the candidate and, especially, of the incumbent. Every leader in Congress, as in other organizations, brings to office a unique set of characteristics: age, ambition, education, health, personal

[1]Robert L. Peabody, *Leadership in Congress* (Boston: Little, Brown, 1976), p. 309. Italics added.

[2]Ibid., p. 155.

232

skills, prior political and professional experience — in sum, a personality. Not only does this personality affect the opportunities he may have to obtain a leadership position, they also, in part, influence the extent to which he can maintain office and perhaps even alter the scope and potential of a given party position. A leader's personality, his strengths and liabilities, also is the single most important variable that affects his ability to withstand or succumb to a challenge.[3]

Personality is also a factor in the selection of committees and in the functioning of committee chairmen. The Senate Government Operations Committee (renamed the Governmental Affairs Committee in 1977), under the chairmanship of Senator Joseph McCarthy from 1953 until 1955 operated very differently than it has at any other time. The personality and the style of Senator McCarthy were responsible for this difference. The Senate Foreign Relations Committee under the chairmanship of Senator J. William Fulbright from 1959 until his defeat in 1974 was quite different than it became in 1975 under the chairmanship of Senator John Sparkman of Alabama.

South Carolina Republican Strom Thurmond runs the Senate Judiciary Committee in an entirely different way than did his predecessor, Massachusetts Senator Edward Kennedy.

Weak chairmen, strong chairmen, chairmen who seek the limelight, and those who use chairmanships for "grand-standing," all have contrasting personalities and styles. The committee system is an important institution of Congress, and the way it functions largely depends on the personalities of committee members. Committees are used to advance the goals of their chairmen and key members, who are attempting to gain power and status within and without Congress. Thus the legislative work of committees is often undertaken as much to serve personal ambition as to respond to constituents' needs; legislators use the committee hearing and investigation process for personal aggrandizement,as well as for legislation.

Beyond Capitol Hill personality is also a key factor in determining the way in which representatives and senators relate to their constituents. Personal choice and preferences determine the amount and kinds of electoral responsibilities that will be delegated to staff, how much time a candidate will spend in his or her district, the nature of constituent contacts — whether in large or small groups, or one-on-one — and what type of media will be emphasized. Political campaigning always reflects the character and style of the candidate.

[3]Ibid., p. 498.

P OLITICAL SCIENTIST RICHARD F. Fenno, Jr., lists three incentives that guide to varying degrees the behavior of members of Congress; (1) reelection; (2) power and influence *within* Congress; (3) good public policy.[1]

Member goals are not mutually exclusive, but members usually do pursue one more than the others. Junior House members, for example, who have not yet secured their electoral bases, divert more time, energy, and resources to winning reelection than to climbing the congressional ladder of power. But once members of Congress can count on electoral support, which House members usually do after they have served several terms, they can divert more time to their Washington careers. A House member in his second term observed, "I haven't been a congressman yet. The first two years, I spent all of my time getting myself reelected. That last two years, I spent getting myself a district so that I could get reelected. So I won't be a congressmen until next year."[2] Being a congressmen means, to most members, being free to pursue internal power and influence without having to worry about constituency pressures.

Members of the House and the Senate as well can take either the *committee* or *party* and *leadership* routes to power. The first involves seeking the most prestigious committees, such as the House Ways and Means, Appropriations, and Rules committees, and the Senate Foreign Relations, Judiciary, Finance, and Appropriations committees. It is difficult and sometimes impossible for junior congressmen and senators to obtain seats on these committees. They often have to wait years before they can get on the panels of their choice.

Moreover, junior members may prefer what are called *reelection committees,* such as Agriculture, Interior and Insular Affairs, Banking, or Finance and Urban Affairs, which have jurisdiction over matters of more direct and special concern to their districts. Of course, congressmen can and have used their positions on the more prestigious committees, particularly Appropriations, Finance, and Ways and Means, to boost their reelection prospects by tending to constituency interests and claiming credit for benefits flowing to their districts. But these and the other influential committees represent and serve the broader memberships of the House and the Senate, diminishing the capacity of any single committee member to give priority in committee deliberations to interests of his or her district.

While most members seeking internal power take the committee route, a select, and in some cases, a chosen few rise to the top through service to their congressional parties. In this arena House members who set their sights particularly high aim to become Speaker, which is not only one of the most powerful positions in Congress but in the entire government. It is a long journey to the Speakership. The majority party determines who will fill the position but chooses only someone who has performed effectively in lower-party leadership posts. The House majority leader often succeeds to the Speakership, having been elected by the party to the next

---

[1]See Richard F. Fenno, Jr., *Congressmen in Committees* (Boston: Little, Brown and Company; 1973); and *Homestyle* (Boston: Little, Brown and Company, 1978).

[2]Richard F. Fenno, Jr., *Homestyle op. cit.*, 215.

highest position. The party caucus chairman and the chief whip then may compete to become majority leader. The chairman of the Rules Committee, who occupies what is essentially a party-leadership position, may also join the fray if he or she is particularly ambitious. Of course no one is excluded from running for party posts, although generally the party leadership track is confined to those who have chosen it over the committee route to power.

The following portrayal of Washington State Representative Thomas S. Foley, whose fifth congressional district is centered in Spokane, reveals how a quietly effective Democrat from a traditionally Republican district has successfully taken the party leadership track to power. Foley's success was not easily predictable. First elected in 1964, he did not solidify his electoral base back home until 1982 when the voters gave him a 64 percent margin, followed by an even greater electoral victory in 1984. A political "accident" and fortuitous circumstance made him chairman of the Agriculture Committee in 1974 when the Democratic Caucus, in an unprecedented move, deposed the long-time committee chairman Bob Poage along with two other chairmen it considered to be unresponsive to the newly-emerging liberal party majority. House liberals liked Foley, whom they had previously chosen to be chairman of their intra-party caucus, the Democratic Study Group. Foley worked closely with the leadership during the 1970s, and Speaker Thomas P. (Tip) O'Neill appointed him to the majority-whip post after the 1980 defeat of John Brademas, the incumbent occupant of the position. At the opening of the 100th Congress in 1987 Foley is a likely successor to Majority Leader Jim Wright who will run for the Speakership vacated by the retirement of O'Neil.

21 Janet Hook
THOMAS FOLEY: RISING TO THE TOP BY ACCIDENT AND DESIGN

As House Majority Whip Thomas S. Foley tells it, his first campaign for Congress was a model of cordiality. No mud was slung; indeed, the candidates sometimes exchanged compliments in that 1964 campaign. After winning the election, Foley held a reception for the man he beat, eleven-term incumbent Republican Walt Horan.

It was an appropriate initiation for Foley, whose temperament and tactics have led him throughout his career to shun confrontation and seek consensus.

The Washington Democrat's skill at brokering compromises, both across party lines and among House Democrats, has earned him wide respect. It also has helped spare him a contest as he seeks to climb another step up the leadership ladder.

From *Congressional Quarterly Weekly Report,* Vol. 44, No. 10, pp. 549–552 (March 8, 1986). Reprinted by permission.

After five years as Democratic whip, Foley is running without apparent challenge for the job of majority leader in the 100th Congress. The current majority leader, Jim Wright Democrat of Texas, is widely expected to succeed House Speaker Thomas P. O'Neill, Jr., when the Massachusetts Democrat retires after this year. (See Table 2.)

House Democrats will choose their new leaders in December, after the 1986 congressional elections. As of now, Wright and Foley seem assured of victory.

A Paradoxical Choice

In one sense, Foley's ascent to the No. 2 leadership job is predictable: It is the obvious step up from the post he now holds. But in other ways, Foley is an implausible candidate to have risen to the top levels of party leadership.

He is an urbane, intellectual Democrat representing Washington's conservative, largely rural 5th District — not an ideal match that one would expect to survive eleven elections.

Foley shows little taste for aggressive politicking for advancement and seems uncomfortable with the self-promotion of campaigning.

Although he has had a hand in crafting many major pieces of legislation, his name is rarely found on a law. While he does not shun publicity, neither does he seek it.

"Tom's influence is a subtler kind of influence," says Philip R. Sharp Democrat of Indiana. "It's not always front-page influence, not always high visibility. That's one of the things that generates a broader base of trust for Tom."

As whip, Foley has functioned largely behind the scenes, corralling votes for the leadership and keeping his finger on the pulse of House Democrats. Among Foley's tools are a broad knowledge of the workings of the House, a prodigious memory, and a gift for explaining complex issues.

"He knows so much about both sides of a question he can argue both sides ferociously," says Pat Williams, a Montana Democrat.

Although Foley's thoughtful, evenhanded style is generally regarded as his greatest strength, he is sometimes criticized for being too cautious. "Tom Foley has too many hands," as one quip has it. "He's always saying on the one hand and on the other hand."

Foley's conciliatory, pragmatic approach can frustrate members looking for a party leader to yell "Charge!" He would rather help the troops pick their way through enemy lines than seek to overpower the opposition.

Foley is aware of criticism that he is not partisan enough, but he is unperturbed. "The best partisan ship is not necessarily the most obvious or most strident," he said.

"I'm not going to be a nineteenth-century opposition-basher," he added. "I don't think that's my style and I don't think it's effective. It doesn't attract people who weren't already knee-jerk supporters. The task is to convince people who are subject to being influenced or persuaded."

A Wright–Foley Team

As Majority Leader, Foley would be the Democrats' point man in floor debate, and would join the Speaker in setting the legislative schedule, and serving as a party spokesman.

Leadership sources say Wright and Foley work well together, despite differences in style. Foley's cool temperament and nonconfrontational manner contrast sharply with Wright's often feisty, combative partisanship.

"Wright will shoot from the hip, he'll give the rousing speech," says one Democrat. "Foley's is the more thoughtful, careful approach."

Wright as Speaker would likely be the leading public spokesman for House Democrats. But some members say that Foley would be as good, if not better, at presenting the Democratic Party's case to the public.

"Foley has not been tagged as someone who carries with him the party of the past," says California Democrat Leon E. Panetta. "He

Table 2. House majority leaders, 1899–1986, and the years they served as leader. Asterisks (*) indicate leaders who subsequently became speaker of the House.

Sereno E. Payne, R-N.Y. 1899–1911	William B. Bankhead, D-Ala. 1936*
Oscar W. Underwood, D-Ala. 1911–1915	Sam Rayburn, D-Texas 1937–1940*
Claude Kitchin, D-N.C. 1915–1919	John W. McCormack, D-Mass. 1940–1947, 1949–1953, 1955–1962*
Franklin W. Mondell, R-Wyo. 1919–1923	Charles A. Halleck, R-Ind. 1947–1949, 1953–1955
Nicholas Longworth, R-Ohio 1923–1925*	Carl Albert, D-Okla. 1962–1971*
John Q. Tilson, R-Conn. 1925–1931	Hale Boggs, D-La. 1971–1973
Henry T. Rainey, D-Ill. 1931–1933*	Thomas P. O'Neill, Jr., D-Mass. 1973–1977*
Joseph W. Byrns, Jr., D-Tenn. 1933–1935	Jim Wright, D-Texas 1977–19—

bridges the gap between Wright and his supporters and the younger members in the party who are looking for some change of direction."

However, some liberals worry that while a Wright-Foley leadership team may improve the party's media image, there would be no strong voice at the top for their wing of the party. "There is no strong liberal in there to make up for the loss of Tip," says one Democrat. "Foley's a good spokesman, but what do they have to say?"

Liberal interest groups have given higher ratings to both Wright and Foley in recent years. Foley's rating from Americans for Democratic Action rose from 55 percent "correct" in 1981, when he became whip, to 80 percent in 1984. In 1985, his rating dipped to 75.

Eclectic Tastes

If some liberals would like Foley to move left, his opponents back home say he is too liberal for his district, which cast 60 percent of its votes for Ronald Reagan in 1984.

Indeed, Foley's continuing electoral success seems improbable for several reasons. Although he is one of the House's leading experts on farm programs, he lacks the folksy style one might expect of a member who represents a largely rural district.

He is as comfortable quoting Shakespeare as commodity prices, he knows a smattering of Japanese, and uses it on nearly annual trips to Japan.

Although he has no major source of income outside his congressional salary and speaking fees, Foley has expensive tastes in contemporary art, modern furniture and high-tech stereo equipment that might seem out of place among his wheat-farming constituents.

"In the past, I've suggested that he loosen up and go hunting, fishing, or pose [for photographs] with a cow, but he's always a three-piece-suit kind of guy out here, too," says William F. Mullen, a professor at Washington State University at Pullman who has been a county campaign coordinator for Foley in the last several elections.

While Foley often holds town meetings with voters when he visits the district, he does not revel in campaign glad-handing. "He doesn't like to ask people to vote for him," says Mullen. "He prefers talking issues."

Rising by Accident and Design

Foley's rise through the House Democratic ranks came about through a combination of low-key determination and fortuitous circumstances.

A lawyer, Foley came to the Capitol in 1961 as counsel to Democratic Senator Henry M. Jackson of Washington, then chairman of the Interior Committee. It was Jackson who encouraged Foley to run for Congress two years later.

Foley dragged his heels for months and did not file as a candidate until the last possible date in the summer of 1964. Like many other Democrats that year, he was helped to victory by President Johnson's landslide triumph over Barry Goldwater.

Foley describes his early years in Congress as a series of "accidental advances," fueled by such factors as the retirement of more senior members of committees to which he was assigned.

Foley chaired the liberal Democratic Study Group (DSG) in 1974, at a time when the DSG was spearheading a drive to open up committee proceedings and weaken the seniority system. Foley was active in the campaign for such changes, but he was clearly a reformer — not a radical.

He backed a change in House rules that allowed secret-ballot elections of committee chairmen, but he opposed a 1975 move to oust the aging chairman of the Agriculture Committee, Texas Democrat W. R. Poage. Poage was defeated nonetheless, and Foley — as the next most senior Democrat on the panel — was chosen chairman.

"[Foley] was thrust into the chairmanship over the political body of a guy he respected and worked with," recalls Arizona Democrat Morris K. Udall. "It was a real test for Tom, and he handled it in a classy kind of way."

Foley recognized from the first that Poage's ouster and his own elevation signaled lasting changes in the seniority system. He said at the time:

"People think of me as chairman as if we were back in the days when chairmen ruled as well as reigned. It isn't that way anymore. The newcomers may pay a certain amount of respect to the leadership, but they're not going to defer to my judgment."

Foley says his first deliberate step onto the leadership ladder was his election as chairman of the Democratic Caucus in late 1976 — the year that O'Neill became Speaker, and Wright won an upset victory in the race for majority leader.

In that stormy majority leader's contest, Foley supported the leadership bid of Wright's rival, Phillip Burton, a California liberal who was viewed with distrust by O'Neill.

Nonetheless, Foley soon won the trust and respect of the two more senior Democrats. When Indiana Democrat John Brademas, the majority whip, was defeated in his 1980 re-election bid, O'Neill and Wright named Foley to the post. Dan Rostenkowski, an Illinois Democrat, then chief deputy whip, was in line for it, but he chose instead to take the chairmanship of the Ways and Means Committee — which had been opened by the defeat of Oregon Democrat Al Ullman.

In a logical extension of some of the democratizing reforms Foley helped put in place in the 1970s, House Democrats last year decided to make the whip an elective post, beginning with Foley's successor.

Performance as Whip

As majority whip, Foley, more than his predecessor, has practiced what one member called the "politics of inclusion." He has expanded participation in the whip's organization, thus increasing the number of people with a stake in leadership decision-making. Last year, he increased the number of deputy and at-large whips.

Foley also has made heavy use of task forces to ease passage of important, complex bills and to get junior members involved in the process.

Whip meetings are not always harmonious. When key elements of the party are unhappy about a leadership decision, the dissent is clear at the weekly whip gatherings, usually attended by more than 50 Democrats.

For example, at a February 27 whip's meeting, Foley was the sounding board for bitter complaints from urban liberals about leadership plans to bring up legislation (HR 4188) to ease the effects of the Gramm-Rudman-Hollings budget-cutting law on milk price supports. Liberals maintained that the dairy industry should not be protected from the across-the-board cuts that faced all other programs.

O'Neill claimed he was "blindsided" by the Agriculture Committee's decision to report the bill, despite the fact that Foley is vice chairman of the committee. Foley, who supported the bill, was taken by surprise by the depth of opposition from urban members, aides said. After the volatile whip's meeting, the leadership pulled the dairy bill from the schedule.

Close Calls Back Home

Foley remains demure about the majority leader's race. He has canvassed all House Democrats, but refuses to report the results. "I'm continuing to talk to people," he says, "and am very, very encouraged by the results."

A decade ago, Foley learned the hard way the perils of overconfidence in a campaign. In 1976, he stopped campaigning a month before the election after his GOP opponent died in a plane crash. But the Republicans came up with another candidate, and through vigorous last-minute campaigning held Foley to 58 percent of the vote.

The message seemed to be that Foley was vulnerable, and he faced serious challenges in the next two elections: He garnered only 48 percent of the vote in a three-way contest in 1978 and 52 percent in 1980.

Since then, Foley seems to have surmounted his political problems at home. In 1984, he was reelected with 70 percent of the vote. Although Republicans have charged Foley is out of touch with his district and more interested in national issues, his constituents apparently appreciate the value of having a representative in the upper ranks of the House leadership.

Still, some members are wary of electing as party leaders members who might — like Brademas — be dumped by the voters in part because they are linked with party positions that are unpopular in their districts. One member critical of Foley's cautious style attributes it in part to insecurity about his conservative district.

"It is a definite disadvantage for us to have as a majority leader someone who has to look over his or her shoulder at his or her constituency," this liberal Democrat said. "You like to have your leaders fearless."

But Foley says the days of very close elections are probably behind him now. And he dismisses any interpretation of his caution as being linked to concerns about political vulnerability at home.

"To the extent that I'm cautious, I want to be cautious and I don't propose to change that," he said. "I have a mental habit of wanting to think through a policy or position."

Crossing Lines on Agriculture

Foley's nonconfrontational approach allows him to cross party lines to forge compromises. "He is trusted [by many Republicans] because he seems in his present role to be less political, until he needs to be, than the others" in the Democratic leadership, says Washington Republican Sid Morrison.

Foley has worked most openly and consistently on a bipartisan basis in the Agriculture Committee, where farm-state interests tend to divide more along regional than party lines.

Although Foley had to give up the Agriculture chairmanship when he became whip in 1981, he has continued to play a major role in shaping farm legislation. He still chairs the Subcommittee on Wheat, Soybeans, and Feed Grains — the panel of most interest to his many wheat-growing constituents.

His bipartisan approach had put Foley at odds with some Democrats on the Agriculture Committee during the panel's consideration of the 1985 farm bill. The dissenters wanted to stake out a clearly Democratic farm policy. "The farm bloc is politically the most volatile bloc in 1986 and 1988," says Kansas Democrat Dan Glickman. "We needed more counterpoint to the president.

Foley backed a price-support proposal that drew the strongest opposition from fellow Democrats rather than from Republicans. The plan, which lowered price supports while maintaining high income subsidies for farmers, was in part a reflection of the interests of Foley's district. Price supports in effect set a floor on prices, and many of Foley's export-dependent farmers favored lowering supports to make their crops more competitive on world markets.

Foley initially objected to alternatives pushed by Berkley Bedell of Iowa and other committee Democrats. They wanted to allow wheat and feed grain farmers to decide in a referendum whether to accept sharp government production controls in exchange for higher price supports.

However, Foley surprised his adversaries and cast a crucial committee vote to include a version of the referendum in the bill sent to the floor. He swallowed his misgivings, an aide said, to ensure broader support from committee Democrats and to head off a potential mutiny on the floor.

The bill that finally passed the House, however, reflected Foley's original preferences. While he gave referendum supporters their chance on the floor and voted against a GOP amendment to strike the provision, he offered only a mild defense of the concept. The referendum was killed when the House approved the GOP amendment.

Gramm–Rudman Role

Foley's role in negotiations over the Gramm-Rudman-Hollings law exemplified his consensus-building *modus operandi*.

He was never a prime mover or enthusiast for the legislation. Rather, he helped House Democrats decide how to make the best of what many saw as a bad deal. He played a key role in reshaping the legislation along lines more acceptable to his colleagues — and more painful for Reagan and the Republicans.

The budget-balancing bill originated in the Senate as an amendment to "must" legislation raising the ceiling on the national debt. While the measure was still in the Senate, Foley was asked by O'Neill to chair a task force of House Democrats to monitor the legislation and begin developing a response. That task force brought together Democrats from as far apart on the political spectrum as liberal Henry A. Waxman of California and conservative Marvin Leath of Texas.

House leaders first had to decide whether to try to defeat the bill, pass it unchanged, or seek improvements.

Foley was the prime proponent of the strategy ultimately followed by the Democrats: Send the bill to conference with the Senate, thus buying time to analyze the measure, and come up with alternatives and changes to improve it.

Initially he was at odds with many House Democrats — both opponents and proponents of the budget-balancing measure — who wanted an immediate House vote on the Senate-passed bill. Several senior committee chairmen wanted to meet the issue head-on and try to kill the bill. But Foley told them that was not a realistic option, citing whip counts indicating that Democrats did not have enough votes to defeat the bill.

"It would have been disastrous to rush out and have an up-or-down vote on the issue," says Foley.

"Foley, more than anyone else, understood there was no gain to be made by pretending it could be stopped," said one leadership aide.

However, some Democrats still believe the leadership conceded too much to supporters of Gramm-Rudman-Hollings by basing their strategy on the assumption that passage of the bill was inevitable. "I think we should have had a bold stroke early, and undercut the need for Gramm-Rudman," says Williams. "It was a mistake to amend Gramm-Rudman to make it better."

But Waxman says he was persuaded by Foley's assessment.

"He turned to us and said, 'We're going to get Gramm-Rudman. What kind of Gramm-Rudman is it going to be?' " said Waxman. "It was a clear statement of political reality and a convincing reason for us to work together."

House leaders, including Foley, point with pride to the display of party unity House Democrats ultimately showed on the issue. After the first round of conference negotiations over the Senate measure broke down, the House passed an alternative version of its own with only two dissenting Democratic votes.

The House alternative protected certain poverty programs against automatic cuts and made an important change in the timing of the mandated deficit reductions. It ensured that the first round of cuts would be felt before the 1986 elections, when the Republicans must defend 22 Senate seats.

Political Fallout

It remains to be seen whether House Democrats' role in shaping the Gramm-Rudman-Hollings law will, in the end, be a political asset or a liability. Foley's view is that incumbents of both parties will share the praise — or blame — for Congress' performance on the budget this year.

Given his pivotal role in the Democrats' strategy for handling the new budget law, Foley's standing among his colleagues could be affected by the political fallout from the measure between now and the time Democrats choose their next majority leader.

But for now, Foley's success in brokering a unified House Democratic position seems to have raised his stock even among those most antagonistic to the budget-balancing measure.

"Foley showed he could lead in a moment of crisis and pull together diverse elements of the party," says Waxman. "But members are going to be looking not only at how leadership candidates performed in the past, but by what happens to the Democratic Party this year."

GEORGIA SENATOR SAM Nunn, the subject of the following selection, has had a meteoric political career that says a great deal about the nature of political power in general, and particularly in the Senate. He comes from good political stock, being the grandnephew of former Georgia Congressman Carl Vinson, who served from 1914–65 and chaired the prestigious House Armed Services Committee from 1949 to the end of his congressional career (except for a two-year interruption when the Republicans controlled the House). After he was first elected in 1972, Nunn made the military his political bailiwick, inheriting former Senator (1933–71) Richard Russell's Armed Services Committee seat. Nunn aspired to become, as Russell had been, a powerful Armed Services Committee chairman.

As a freshman Senator, Nunn immediately set out to become a recognized expert on military affairs. He concentrated talented staff resources in this area, did his homework, and soon gained the respect of his colleagues and national recognition as the capable chairman of the Manpower and Personnel Subcommittee of Armed Services. The subcommittee was created for Nunn in 1974, and he used it effectively to build his reputation for power and expertise. Nunn, who captured 80 percent of his state's vote in 1984 at a time when Ronald Reagan was sweeping Georgia and the nation, is free to devote most of his time and energy to the pursuit of his Washington career. The following selection illustrates how his style, personality, and politics have made Nunn a major force in the Senate and in the national political arena as well.

22 Fred Barnes
FLYING NUNN: THE DEMOCRATS' TOP HAWK

Here's a story you won't hear about many Washington politicians. In early 1982 the Democratic Party decided to have its best and brightest in Congress respond to President Reagan's State of the Union address. They would appear on prime-time national television just after Reagan's talk. To speak on defense, there was only one choice: Senator Sam Nunn of Georgia, a respected figure in military affairs, though a good bit more hawkish than most congressional Democrats.

Greg Schneiders, then working for Senate Democratic leader Robert Byrd, called Nunn. Senators were falling all over themselves to get a spot on the Democratic response, but Nunn was leery. The plan was to give him 90 seconds on the air. "I can't say anything in a minute and a half that makes sense about defense," he complained. Schneiders told

From *The New Republic*, April 28, 1986. Reprinted by permission.

him a summary statement was all that was needed. "Well, let me try," Nunn said. A few days later, he got back to Schneiders. "I've been working hard on this," he said, "and I don't see how I can do it responsibly in 90 seconds. Why don't you let someone else do it?" And so another senator got the national TV exposure.

Sam Nunn, 47 years old, achieved his prominence in the Senate in the most prosaic fashion. He worked for it, painstakingly and unobtrusively gaining detailed knowledge on defense and a few other issues. Others have followed the glitter path: TV appearances, ghostwritten books, a blizzard of press releases, speech after speech on the rubber-chicken circuit. That can bring fame. But it doesn't bring influence. Nunn and Senator Joseph Biden of Delaware were both elected to the Senate in 1972. Both are now well-known nationally. But Nunn, the workhorse, has considerable influence in the Senate. Biden, the show horse, doesn't.

Nunn, in fact, is the most influential Democrat in the Senate — maybe in Congress. He is neither a striking presence (hair brushed over a bald spot) nor a powerful orator (flat speaking style). But he is smart and breathtakingly knowledgeable. Without his backing, the Reagan administration has little chance of getting its way in military and foreign matters. If he had opposed the 1981 sale of AWAC planes to Saudi Arabia, the deal surely would have died. If Nunn had wished, he could have restricted the number of MX missiles to fewer than 40. Now he is in a position to keep the MX total capped at 50, unless the administration satisfies his request for a new basing mode. Nunn often demands a price for his support. Before he agreed to vote for military aid to the *contras* in March, he forced Reagan to promise a new effort to bring the anti-Sandinista rebels under firm control of democratic, civilian leadership. Should the Reagan crowd decide it wants to build more than 100 B-1 bombers, it is probably going to have to persuade Nunn first. If it hopes to take Star Wars beyond the research-and-development phase, it's going to need Nunn's assent. And he's far from convinced that Reagan's dream of a missile-thwarting shield makes sense.

But influence in Washington is one thing, and influence in the Democratic Party another. For more than a decade, Nunn ignored the party altogether, as if it were an embarrassing relative. Two years ago, as the party neared a disastrous presidential defeat, Nunn changed his tactic. Now he is working to pull the Democratic Party to the right, making it less liberal, and thus more acceptable in the South. The goal is a party more or less hawkish on defense and foreign issues, pro-business in economic affairs, and tolerant of diversity, especially of conservative views, on social issues. In other words, a party along the ideological lines of Nunn himself.

"I used to consider myself to the right of center, and I still do," Nunn says. "But the spectrum has shifted since I've been in the Senate, and I suspect I'm somewhat in the middle now. There are a good number of people in that category, anywhere from slightly left of center to slightly right of center. Many of us have concluded that the national Democratic Party has to have leadership, in terms of substance and perception, that clearly is identified in the middle, if it's got a chance of becoming a party that can compete for the presidency. I don't have any personal ambition beyond being in the Senate. I do want to be part of a party that has a chance to compete in the future for the White House and certainly for control of the Senate. We might be able to control the Senate without much [ideological] movement. But we'd be greatly strengthened if we had a much more coherent — scratch the word coherent — a much more *appealing* agenda." Translation: unless the party jettisons its liberalism and isolationism, it won't attract votes in the South, the pivotal region, and can forget about winning back the White House.

Plots to revive the Democratic Party are as common as UFO sightings and usually no more connected to reality. But Nunn also founded the Democratic Leadership Council, which is trying to yank the party rightward. Former Virginia Governor Charles Robb, Representative Richard Gephardt, and Arizona Governor Bruce Babbitt usually get the credit (or blame, from liberals). But it was Nunn whose telephone call brought the group together. Nunn, Senator Lawton Chiles of Florida, and a dozen other moderate or conservative Democrats in the Senate already had begun conferring anxiously about the drift of the party.

"Most of us had been running away from the Democratic Party for years," says Chiles. "But we were beginning to see you couldn't enjoy the luxury of that anymore. Maybe some of us would survive, but there wasn't going to be a Democratic Party behind us in our state." Nunn had heard that Robb was eager to draw together moderate and conservative forces in the party. Nunn scarcely knew Robb, but in early fall 1984 he called with an invitation to confer, in private, with his Senate group. The result was the formation of the DLC early last year, over the strong objections of Democratic national chairman Paul Kirk.

Nunn's involvement was surprising, given his past indifference to party affairs both nationally and in Georgia. He is also notoriously cautious. In 1984 he balked at endorsing his friend and Senate ally John Glenn for the Democratic presidential nomination, and in the end offered public praise but no endorsement.

In Georgia, Nunn's alliances have frequently shifted. As a young state representative, he supported Jimmy Carter for governor, once objecting that Carter was running too conservative a campaign. But in 1972 he challenged David Gambrell, the man Carter had appointed to a vacant Senate seat. Nunn had hoped to run for the House, but reapportionment had gone awry and an appropriate district hadn't been created. In the Senate primary he stayed to the right of Gambrell, campaigning as the antibusing candidate and linking Gambrell to Democratic liberals like George McGovern. Nunn had the backing of segregationist Lieutenant Governor Lester Maddox. He also was endorsed by Julian Bond, the black state legislator. Once Carter was president, Nunn was perfectly willing to cross him. In 1979 Nunn became a major thorn in Carter's side by refusing to back SALT II.

Even in his new role as a party activist, Nunn is insufficiently partisan for some Democrats. Last year, while Georgia Democrats were scouring the state for candidates to run against Republican senator Mack Mattingly, Nunn told Greg McDonald of the *Atlanta Journal-Constitution* that he wouldn't actively campaign against Mattingly and complimented his GOP colleague. Nunn later claimed that his remarks had been misinterpreted. At a press conference he vowed to support the Democratic nominee, and he spoke favorably of all four primary candidates, including liberal representative Wyche Fowler.

Nunn's aloofness from party politics and his reputation as a respected expert on defense made his participation in the DLC all the more significant. "Nunn is the central figure," says Al From, the executive director of the DLC. "The two things we have to show are that this party can make the economy strong and the country strong. Nunn is Mr. Strength." Robb, the DLC chairman, says, "It's because we got the Sam Nunns of the world that people are excited." In Dallas, businessman Jess Hay sponsored a successful DLC fund-raiser in March simply because Nunn was willing to attend.

Despite his reputation as being tepidly partisan, Nunn has proved to be the DLC's chief Reagan-basher. Before the group's initial foray to Florida a year ago, DLC leaders were queasy about criticizing Reagan, figuring it might backfire with the moderate and conservative Democrats they aimed to attract. Nunn was undeterred. He sharply attacked Reagan for muddled defense policies. He is also the most outspoken about the council's goal. "We're trying to make the national party competitive again, so it will be a help rather than a hindrance," he said in Raleigh, North Carolina, last October. "We're trying to make it safe for state and local officials to identify themselves with the national party and survive," he declared in Greensboro, North Carolina.

There is a Nunn model for other Democrats to emulate, but it's not quite what you think. Nunn is pro-defense, and he's for spending cuts and economic growth. And on some important but secondary issues, Nunn offers bold leadership — raising the standards of the all-volunteer Army, reorganizing the Pentagon, signaling European allies that they've got to carry more of their weight in NATO. But on major defense and foreign policy issues, his strategy is often not to stake out a solid position, but to stay flexible in hopes of shaping a compromise. This leaves Nunn in the position of supporting mushy compromises that he's not wild about. He winds up as both a supporter and critic of Reagan on the same issue. Conservatives say his backing is too weak, and liberals grouse that he's sided with Reagan again.

Take the MX. Nunn has been a part of every compromise that has kept the missile alive for the last ten years. He believes the United States needs an invulnerable, land-based, intercontinental missile, which the MX is supposed to be. So he agreed last year to raise the number of MXs to 40. "Had Sam opposed any more MXs, it would have been hard for any Democrats to have supported it," says Republican senator William Cohen of Maine. "As it was, it passed by one vote." After going along with 40, Nunn gave in to unrelenting White House pleas, delivered by his friend Bud McFarlane, then Reagan's national security adviser, and raised the number to 50.

Despite this, Nunn is harshly critical of the way the Reagan administration plans to deploy the MXs — in hardened Minuteman silos, not spread around the barren reaches of a Western state, as the Carter administration planned. "We're ending up without the kind of land-based, hard target, kill capability that the military has described for some time as being absolutely essential. . . . The strange thing is one of the primary cases the Reagan administration made against the Carter basing mode was that it depended on an arms-control agreement. The Soviets could saturate it [without one]. That's true. But that's the position we're in with every proposal they've got. For every one of [the proposals], if you don't have some arms-control agreement, there's a theoretical saturation capability." Yet Nunn voted for 50 MXs.

Or take aid to the contras. In a speech in April 1985 to the Coalition for a Democratic Majority, Nunn advocated "a policy that continues pressure on the Sandinistas while moving American promotion of military action in that region to the back burner." In June he voted for humanitarian aid to the contras, saying it "should facilitate negotiations both within the Contadora framework and between the United States and the Sandinistas." Nunn was critical of the administration for imposing economic sanctions against Nicaragua awkwardly. This April Nunn went after the contras. "It is unclear who is in control of the contra organization," Nunn said. "Is it the civilian leadership or is it the former National Guard officers who make up most of the senior military leadership?" He also cited reports of human rights abuses by the contras, saying they "raise many disturbing questions which must be answered."

What, then, was Nunn to do about the administration's request for military aid to the contras? He arranged an exchange of letters with

Reagan. Nunn said aid should be given through civilian contra leaders, the contras should be built into a genuine democratic movement, reports of human rights violations should be investigated, and a kind of Contra University established at which reading, writing, health care and economic skills would be taught. Reagan responded affirmatively on all counts. Part of the deal was that Nunn must then go along with Reagan's assurances. He did, and voted for military aid. Once again, he went Reagan's way with noisy misgivings.

Finally, consider Star Wars. Nunn votes for billions for Star Wars research, yet he is all but scandalized by Reagan's promoting of it as a "shield" that can make nuclear weapons obsolete. "What that does is cause the framework of the program to be so broad that it's going to be hard to narrow it down to a viable alternative that replaces deterrence. That's what he's talking about. It causes the scientific community to be shooting in a very broad fashion and is very injurious to a sound program. . . . I think it is a political plus with the general public, and probably a political plus in the short term. But in the long term, it's a real trap, not for this president, but for the one who has to go before the American people and say, 'Oops. I realize Reagan said we're going to protect Peoria, but now let me tell why we've got to protect the missile fields in Montana.' Somebody's going to have a hard job."

No one doubts Nunn's sincerity in raising doubts about Reagan's defense schemes and then voting for them. The question is whether it is good politics for Democrats. At the least, Nunn can be accused of being a me-too Democrat, regularly backing Reagan proposals, with qualifications. It may be an honest approach, but it isn't a bold or exciting one.

Where does all this leave Nunn today? "He is the person who, as a Democrat, can speak for defense," says Chiles. "And he's not locked into the stereotype of just wanting to throw money at defense." That's worth something. But it doesn't make Nunn presidential material, though Robb has prodded him to run in 1988. Nunn says this is the furthest thing from his mind, but Robb insists Nunn is "weakening" and is now willing to discuss it.

Still, that is probably a waste of time. On the scale of one to ten, one being most liberal and ten being most conservative, Nunn puts himself at six or seven. He says most Southerners are the same. He says Reagan talks like a nine, but governs like a seven. But most Democrats aren't quite that conservative, and the Democrats who dominate the presidential primaries and caucuses are even less so. Besides, Nunn has something in his record to antagonize nearly every Democratic constituency. Feminists are angered by his vote in favor of a constitutional amendment banning abortion. His support for right-to-work upsets labor. His vote for a Jesse Helms bill to cut ten percent from social programs across the board alarms numerous constituencies.

But as a vice presidential nominee, Nunn would attract far less opposition. Why? Democrats are desperate to win in 1988, even if it means accepting a nonliberal running mate. In this sense, Nunn may be the right person, and liberal activists aren't ruling him out. "The worst thing that can happen to liberals, labor, feminists right now is to say that anybody is unacceptable because of this or that vote," says Joanne Symons, the political director of the American Nurses Association. "I really would like to see Nunn picked [for vice president]," says Richard Murphy of the Service Employees Union. "He's an honest conservative Democrat. I don't think he's anti-union by any means."

Nunn demurs. Putting a Southerner on the ticket won't help the Democrats much in winning the South, he says. "I don't think it solves the basic problem. You have to have a philosophy in the ticket itself that is compatible" with the South. Besides, Nunn has something else in mind for himself — chairman of the Senate Armed Services Committee. Naturally, there are skeptics who question what Nunn really wants. The assumption in the political community is that any politician who courts national prominence wants to be president.

Several days after the Philippine election, Nunn sent a scorching letter to Reagan, saying that Cory Aquino was the rightful winner and that Ferdinand Marcos should be abandoned at all cost. It was a new issue for Nunn, and the release of the letter prompted fresh speculation about a presidential bid. In truth, it was the old Nunn at work. The letter was influential in the Senate. It touched off a stampede among Democrats of all stripes to denounce Marcos. It also brought the TV networks and print reporters to Nunn's door. But he didn't grant a single interview.

LYNDON B. JOHNSON, A MEMber of the Senate freshman class of 1948, was majority leader from 1955 until 1960, when he was elected vice president. His experience in Washington predated his Senate career; he had been a congressional staff member in 1931 and at the age of twenty-eight had defeated seven other candidates in a special election to fill the seat of the tenth Texas congressional district left vacant by the death of the incumbent representative.

Johnson was a consummate politician from the very beginning of his stay in Washington. He embraced the New Deal, and became a favorite of President Franklin D. Roosevelt; he even supported the president's ill-fated court-packing plan, which was opposed by many of Roosevelt's Washington supporters.[1]

While still a congressman, Johnson ran and was defeated in a special election for a Senate post vacated by the death of incumbent Senator Morris Sheppard in 1941. Johnson continued to serve in the House (with a brief leave in 1942 to serve as a naval reserve officer) until, with John Connally as his campaign manager, he defeated archconservative Governor Coke Stevenson in the Democratic primary in 1948 by 87 votes out of almost a million cast. Since there was essentially no Republican opposition in Texas at that time, the election in the Democratic primary was tantamount to victory in the general election held in November.

When Johnson became majority leader the "Johnson era" began in the Senate. The "Johnson system" of power reflected his personality and style: He unhesitatingly rewarded his friends, from whom he demanded loyalty, and punished his enemies. His formal powers as majority leader were minimal. His chairmanship of the Democratic Steering Committee, for example, did not automatically guarantee him personal control over Democratic committee assignments. But Johnson exerted such control. He developed an informal network of power, and a dazzling style that came to be known as "the treatment."

---

[1] In 1937 Roosevelt recommended legislation to Congress under which he would be given authority to appoint one new Supreme Court justice for each justice over seventy years old. At the time there were six septuagenarian justices, so that Roosevelt could easily have "packed" the court with his own appointments.

23 Rowland Evans and Robert Novak
THE JOHNSON SYSTEM

To build his Network, Johnson stretched the meager power resources of the majority leader to the outer limit. The mightiest of these was his influence over committee assignments. Still, it was not comparable to the absolute power enjoyed by Nelson Aldrich, a half century before. As chairman of the Democratic Steering Committee, Johnson steadily widened the breach in rigid seniority rules, working delicately with a surgical scalpel, not a stick of dynamite.

In January 1955, his ally and adviser, Clinton Anderson, pressed his claim for an overdue assignment on either Foreign Relations or Finance. Each committee had one vacancy. But former Vice President Alben Barkley, who had just returned to the Senate as a "freshman" from Kentucky in the 1954 elections, asked for the Finance Committee — a request that could scarcely be denied. A further complication was the still unresolved problem of Wayne Morse, the Oregon maverick who had bolted the Republican party in the 1952 campaign and, after two years in the political wilderness as an "Independent," now joined the Democratic caucus in 1955. Morse's decision was vital to Johnson. It provided him with the narrow one-vote margin he needed to cross the bridge, incalculably important in terms of power, from Minority Leader to Majority Leader. Thus, it was incumbent upon Johnson to give Morse a good committee assignment, and Morse wanted Foreign Relations.

Johnson duly explained these facts of life to Anderson, who agreed not to insist (as he well could have) on either Finance or Foreign Relations. But Johnson remembered his old friend's personal loyalty and, on a 1956 speaking engagement in New Mexico, he publicly — and unexpectedly — promised that Clint Anderson would become the next chairman of the Joint Atomic Energy Committee. That post, because of New Mexico's Los Alamos atomic installation, would solidly enhance Anderson's prestige. To make good his promise, Johnson was required to jump Anderson over none other than Richard Russell, who outranked Anderson on the joint committee.

The Foreign Relations maneuvers temporarily drew the sharp-tongued Morse to Johnson, in sharp contrast to a year earlier. In January 1954, Morse had told an ADA Roosevelt Day Dinner in Texas: "Johnson has the most reactionary record in the Senate. Look at his voting record. If he should ever have a liberal idea, he would have a brain hemor-

From *Lyndon B. Johnson: The Exercise of Power* by Roland Evans and Robert Novak. Copyright © 1966 by Roland Evans and Robert Novak. Reprinted by arrangement with New American Library, New York, New York.

rhage. . . ."[1] But a little more than a year later, ensconced on the Foreign Relations Committee, Morse gently confided to the Senate: "During the past year, I have been the beneficiary of one kindness after another from Lyndon Johnson. I consider him not only a great statesman but a good man."

And as chairman of the Joint Atomic Energy Committee, Anderson was even more pleased than he would have been on Foreign Relations. The only grumbling over Johnson's ingenious shuffling came from Russell, who had not agreed in advance to step aside for Anderson. But the grumbling was private and soft, not public and bitter. Lyndon Johnson could count on Dick Russell not to make a public fuss about such matters.

Two years later, Anderson was the center of far more devious committee maneuvers by Johnson. After the presidential election of 1956, Estes Kefauver of Tennessee and John F. Kennedy of Massachusetts, who had competed on the national convention floor at Chicago for the vice-presidential nomination the previous summer, were competing again — this time for a single vacancy on Foreign Relations. Johnson, who had backed Kennedy against Kefauver at Chicago, was not trying to bring Kennedy closer to his orbit. He was determined to have the vacancy go to Kennedy over Johnson's old foe, Kefauver. But how to get around Kefauver's four-year seniority bulge over Kennedy? In December 1956, long before Congress convened, Johnson telephoned Anderson with a most curious question: "How are you getting along with your campaign for the Foreign Relations Committee?"

Anderson was puzzled. Could Johnson have forgotten that his "campaign" had ended two years earlier? But Johnson persisted.

"This may be your chance," he said.

Before Anderson could reply that he had his hands full as chairman of Atomic Energy, Johnson rushed on.

"You have seniority now over Jack Kennedy," Johnson explained. "But if you don't claim it, Estes Kefauver may get there first."

Johnson's ploy suddenly came through to Anderson. Both Anderson and Kefauver were members of the Class of '48 and therefore had equal seniority. If they both applied for the one vacancy on the Foreign Relations Committee, Johnson could throw up his hands in the Steering Committee, declare a standoff — and give the vacancy to Kennedy. Anderson went along with this neat strategy, and Kennedy was given the seat, just as Johnson wanted.

Johnson's use of power to influence committee assignments cut both

---

[1]Johnson retaliated in kind: "Texas doesn't need any outsiders to come in and tell them [sic] how to vote. I don't think Texas will pay any more attention to him than the Senate does." In those early days of his leadership, Johnson was far more ready to engage fellow senators in a war of words than he would be later.

ways. "Good" liberals, such as Humphrey, could be prematurely boosted into the Foreign Relations Committee, and a "bad" liberal, such as Kefauver, could be made to cool his heels for years. A "bad" liberal such as Paul Douglas could be barred from the Finance Committee for eight long years, while five fellow members of the Class of '48 (Kerr, Long, Frear, Anderson, and Johnson himself) and one from the Class of '50 (Smathers) were finding places there.[2] Senators who dared to function too far outside the Johnson Network waited long to get inside the prestige committees.

In these clandestine committee maneuvers, Johnson seldom exposed his hand. But in the routine committee shifts, he enjoyed wringing out the last drop of credit. One evening in early January 1955, shortly after the committee assignments for the Eighty-fifth Congress had been settled and announced, Johnson invited a couple of friends into his majority leader's office in the corner of the Capitol for a political bull session over Scotch and sodas. Nothing relaxed him more than these feet-up, hair-down chats. They invariably lasted well into the night and they invariably ended in long, often hilarious LBJ monologues, full of ribald yarns and racy mimicry.

Suddenly, he interrupted himself. "My God," he said, "I forgot to call Senator Stennis and congratulate him." Stennis had been valuable to Johnson a month earlier in the McCarthy censure fight, and now had just landed a coveted seat on the Appropriations Committee — thanks to Lyndon Johnson. Johnson reached over, cradled the phone between his shoulder and chin, and dialed.

Mrs. Stennis answered the phone, and the conversation commenced. "Ma'm, this is Lyndon Johnson, is your husband there? . . . He isn't? . . . Well, I must tell you, Ma'm, how proud I am of your husband and how proud the Senate is, and you tell him that when he gets home. The Senate paid him a great honor today. The Senate elected your husband to the Appropriations Committee. That's one of the most powerful committees in the Senate and a great honor for your husband. I'm so proud of John. He's a great American. And I know you're proud of him, too. He's one of my finest Senators. . . ." Accompanying this monologue were nods and winks in the direction of Johnson's fascinated audience.

Johnson went on to tell Mrs. Stennis how the Steering Committee had selected her husband unanimously for the Appropriations spot and how the full Senate had unanimously concurred, but implicitly he was

---

[2]This extraordinary treatment of Douglas also reflected Johnson's desire to keep the Finance Committee free of Northern liberals opposing special tax advantages for the oil and gas industry. But if Douglas had been a "good" liberal in the Humphrey mold, Johnson could have shaved a point, since the Finance Committee was already so stacked in favor of the oil and gas industry.

belaboring the obvious — that it wasn't the Steering Committee or the full Senate that really was responsible. It was LBJ.

Johnson quietly commandeered other bits and pieces of Senate patronage that previous majority leaders ignored. To cement his budding alliance with Senator Margaret Chase Smith, for instance, he arranged for a special staff member of the Senate Armed Services Committee to be appointed by her and to be responsible to her alone, even though she was a Republican on the Democratic-controlled committee, and only a fourth-ranking Republican at that.

Although in the past, office space for senators, a source of sometimes intense competition, had been distributed by strict seniority as a routine housekeeping chore of the Senate's sergeant-at-arms, Johnson quickly perceived its value as a weapon of influence and fitted it into his growing system of rewards and punishments. When Paul Douglas lost that top-floor Capitol office to Johnson in 1955, the Senate took notice. It was a dramatic sign of the consequences of a lack of rapport with the majority leader. Johnson skillfully exploited the gleaming New Senate Office Building in 1958, with its spanking new suites, as an inducement for help on the floor. Senator Mike Monroney of Oklahoma, sometimes troublesome for Johnson, was brought into line on one bill with the award of a handsome corner suite that Johnson knew Monroney coveted.

Johnson also kept his ears open to discover which senator — or senator's wife — was really anxious to go on which senatorial junket abroad. At a cocktail party early in 1957, Johnson was chatting with the wife of Frank Church, the young, newly elected liberal Democrat from Idaho. Mrs. Church innocently revealed that she had always wanted to see South America. Knowing that Frank Church might become a valuable addition to the Johnson Network, the majority leader saw to it that he was named to the very next delegation of senators to visit South America.

Even before that, however, Frank Church had reason to be grateful to Lyndon Johnson. Bitterly opposed by the Idaho Power Company and other private-power interests because of his public-power stand, Church was hard-pressed for funds in his 1956 campaign for the Senate. He sent an S.O.S. to the Senate Democratic Campaign Committee in Washington. Senator Smathers, chairman of the campaign committee, was dubious about pouring money into what seemed a hopeless cause in a small mountain state. But Johnson and Bobby Baker argued Church's cause, and their wishes prevailed.

De facto control of the campaign committee's funds was one of Johnson's least obvious but most effective tools in building his Network. He controlled the distribution of committee funds through both its chairman — first Earle Clements and later George Smathers — and through its secretary, Bobby Baker. More often than not, the requests for campaign funds were routinely made to Baker, and the money was physically distributed by him. Johnson further tightened his control when Clements was named the committee's executive director after his Senate defeat in 1956. Johnson got the most out of the committee's limited funds (at the time a mere four hundred thousand dollars) by shrewdly distributing them where they would do the most work. In the small mountain states like Idaho, a ten-thousand-dollar contribution could change the course of an election. But in New York or Pennsylvania, ten thousand dollars was the merest drop in the bucket. Johnson and Baker tried to reduce contributions to Democrats in the industrial Northeast to the minimum. Since senators seldom bite the hand that finances them, these westerners were naturally drawn into the Johnson Network, while the Eastern liberals tended to remain outside.

But this ingenious stretching of the majority leader's limited stock of patronage could not by itself explain the brilliant success of the Johnson Network. The extra, indeed the dominant, ingredient was Johnson's overwhelming personality, reflected in what came to be known as "The Treatment."

The Treatment could last ten minutes or four hours. It came, enveloping its target, at the LBJ Ranch swimming pool, in one of LBJ's offices, in the Senate cloakroom, on the floor of the Senate itself — wherever Johnson might find a fellow senator within his reach. Its tone could be supplication, accusation, cajolery, exuberance, scorn, tears, complaint, the hint of threat. It was all of these together. It ran the gamut of human emotions. Its velocity was breathtaking, and it was all in one direction. Interjections from the target were rare. Johnson anticipated them before they could be spoken. He moved in close, his face a scant millimeter from his target, his eyes widening and narrowing, his eyebrows rising and falling. From his pockets poured clippings, memos, statistics. Mimicry, humor, and the genius of analogy made The Treatment an almost hypnotic experience and rendered the target stunned and helpless.

In 1957, when Johnson was courting the non-Senate Eastern liberal establishment, he summoned historian and liberal theoretician Arthur Schlesinger, Jr., down from his classroom at Harvard. Wary at the prospect of his first prolonged meeting with Johnson (whom he suspected of disdaining the liberal cause), Schlesinger had in his mind a long list of questions to ask Johnson. Never known for shyness, Schlesinger was nevertheless on his guard when he entered Johnson's Capitol office and sat in front of the great man's desk.

The Treatment began immediately: a brilliant, capsule characterization of every Democratic senator: his strengths and failings, where he fit into the political spectrum; how far he could be pushed, how far pulled; his hates, his loves. And who (he asked Schlesinger) must oversee all these prima donnas, put them to work, knit them together, know when to tickle this one's vanity, inquire of that one's health, remember this one's five o'clock nip of Scotch, that one's nagging wife? Who must find the hidden legislative path between the South and the North, the public power men and the private power men, the farmers' men and the unions' men, the bomber boys, and the peace lovers, the eggheads and the fatheads? Nobody but Lyndon Johnson.

Imagine a football team (Johnson hurried on) and I'm the coach, and I'm also the quarterback, I have to call the signals, and I have to center the ball, run the ball, pass the ball. I'm the blocker (he rose out of his chair and threw an imaginary block). I'm the tackler (he crouched and tackled). I'm the passer (he heaved a mighty pass). I have to catch the pass (he reached and caught the pass).

Schlesinger was sitting on the edge of his chair, both fascinated and amused. Here was a view of the Senate he had never seen before.

Johnson next ticked off all the bills he had passed that year, how he'd gotten Dick Russell on this one, Bob Kerr on that one, Hubert Humphrey on another. He reached into his desk drawer and out came the voting record of New Jersey's Clifford Case, a liberal Republican. You liberals, he told Schlesinger, are always talking about my record. You wouldn't question Cliff Case's record, would you? And he ran down the list and compared it to his voting record. Whatever Johnson had on those two lists, he came out with a record more liberal than Case's.

Johnson had anticipated and answered all of Schlesinger's questions. The leader rolled on, reiterating a theme common to The Treatment of that time. He'd had his heart attack, he said, and he knew he'd never be president. He wasn't made for the presidency. If only the good Lord would just give him enough time to do a few more things in the Senate. Then he'd go back to Texas. That's where he belonged.

Breathless now, ninety minutes later, Schlesinger said good-bye and groped his way out of Johnson's office. Eight years later, he was to record his impressions. Johnson had been "a good deal more attractive, more subtle, and more formidable than I expected." And, he might have added, vastly more entertaining.

The Treatment was designed for a single target or, at most, an audience of three or four. In large groups, what was witty sounded crude, what was expansive became arrogant. It was inevitable, then, that when Johnson allowed The Treatment to dominate his "press conferences" a sour note entered his relations with the press. Reporters en masse didn't like being on the receiving end of The Treatment. Johnson's failure to understand that annoyed the press, which in turn made Johnson increasingly wary and suspicious. Unable to tame the press as he tamed so many senators, he foolishly took offense at routine questions, and was quick to find a double meaning in the most innocent point raised by a reporter. Although Senate reporters and Washington's top columnists were captivated in their *private* sessions with Johnson in his office or at the LBJ Ranch, his press conferences were fiascoes. They simply could not be harnessed to The Treatment. . . .

EDWARD M. KENNEDY AND Robert C. Byrd have fundamentally different personalities, which have shaped their respective Senate careers. Each, like most of his colleagues, has sought power and status on Capitol Hill. But the route to power each has selected reflects a different background, character, and style. Kennedy is a star and has embraced an individualistic style; through the astute use of the committees he chairs he has sought to put the Kennedy imprint upon legislation, investigations, and committee reports. Kennedy's style represents the "new Senate," in which individual senators are more independent of their colleagues. They seek power not so much through the traditional emphasis upon collegial cooperation, but by gaining personal recognition among colleagues for hard work on committees, specialized knowledge, and legislative accomplishments. There remains an important collegial aspect to these efforts, but in the modern Senate an increasing number of members tend to focus on the separate worlds of their committees more than upon the collective demands of the institution.

Robert Byrd, in contrast to Kennedy, adopted a collegial style of operation; he sought positions of leadership in the Senate body rather than emphasizing his individual power through committees. Because of his service to fellow senators, Byrd was elected majority whip and majority leader. His personality is more muted than that of Kennedy, his style less flamboyant and aggressive. As the following selection makes clear, each has made an important contribution to the Senate.

24 Laurence Leamer
ROBERT BYRD AND EDWARD KENNEDY: TWO STORIES OF THE SENATE

The Capitol is the greatest public building in America. Visitors can sit in the House and Senate galleries, climb the broad staircases, roam the marble halls, and ride the elevators. They can go almost anywhere they choose. Yet hidden within the Capitol are offices and nooks and gathering places that are private. On the House side of the Capitol, down a back staircase from the House floor, stands an unmarked door. Behind the door is a dark room shrouded in drapes, with an old desk and a few chairs casually arranged. Here Speaker Sam Rayburn's "Board of Education" used to meet each afternoon over bourbon and water to talk politics. Fifteen years after Rayburn's death the star of Texas is still there, painted in ornate style on the far wall.

Excerpt from *Playing for Keeps in Washington* by Laurence Leamer. Copyright © 1977 by Laurence Leamer. Reprinted by permission of Doubleday & Company, Inc.

On the Senate side of the Capitol there are fifty-four private rooms used by senators. Some are no more than rude accumulations of government-issue desks, chairs, and paintings. Others are exquisitely decorated with antiques, political memorabilia, ornate telephones. The largest office is a three-room suite that can be reached by going down a narrow staircase just off the main corridor. These are the offices out of which Bobby Baker, the assistant to Senate majority leader Lyndon Johnson, operated. Baker had worked there until he was convicted of abusing his position and sent to prison.

These are the rooms that Edward "Ted" Kennedy of Massachusetts claimed as his own in 1969 when he was elected Democratic whip, the number-two position in the Democratic leadership. Then the offices had all the sweaty urgency of a political boiler room. The suite was full of Kennedy people. The phones rang constantly. Journalists hurried in and out. Now and again Kennedy came bursting in for a few minutes before rushing off somewhere else. There was always something happening. There had never been anything quite like it in the Senate.

In 1971 Robert C. Byrd of West Virginia defeated Kennedy and took over the suite. From all appearances, Byrd did not think the suite a grand prize but more a gift kept for occasional use. The doors might stay locked for days. Byrd decorated the rooms with just enough pictures and artifacts so that the suite became indisputably his. On the wall he put mounted whips that Senator Joseph Montoya of New Mexico had given him and a copy of a *Parade* magazine story about himself ("Senate Whip Bob Byrd: From Poverty to Power").

On the wall of the outer office hung pictures of the fourteen men who had served as Democratic whip. From Jay Hamilton to Hubert Humphrey, from Morris Sheppard to Russell Long, from Lister Hill to Lyndon Johnson, the first twelve faces looked forth with the fleshy, canny confidence of the professional politician. But Kennedy and Byrd were different. Kennedy's picture had the perfect looks of a Hollywood publicity glossy. Byrd, for his part, looked half-embarrassed, as if in the act of allowing himself to be photographed he was giving away something that he did not want to give away.

As much as Kennedy and Byrd were different in appearance from the twelve men who preceded them, so were they different from each other. They were two of the most powerful men in Washington. They did not like each other. They did not like each other's politics. In their distinct ways they symbolized what power had become in the modern Senate.

Senator Robert Byrd walked down the main corridor of the Capitol, down a narrow staircase, and unlocked the door to the whip's office. Many senators travel with a flotilla of aides, but Byrd almost always walks alone. He is a little man with a chalk-white face and black-and-white streaked hair swept back in a high pompadour. He looks like a wary sparrow, with a face that could be found up most any hollow in Appalachia, the face of a man who had missed some basic nutrient. It belonged to the man who was on the verge of becoming the Senate majority leader — the most powerful and prestigious position in Congress.

Byrd is a man of religious intensity, both public and private, the personification of the self-made man, a man of deep, unfathomable ambition, beyond perhaps anyone else's in the Senate. He sought power, wooed power, lived with and for power. . . .

The Senate that Byrd was sworn into in January 1959 was still dominated by Southerners like Lyndon Johnson of Texas and Richard Russell of Georgia. A conservative might believe that a certain lassitude and the petty corruption of privilege were merely the exhaust fumes given off by the Senate as it made its stately way through history. Senator Thomas Dodd of Connecticut, for instance, had an elderly retainer known as the "judge" who slept blissfully at a desk outside the senator's office.

The Senate had not yet spread out into the nearly completed New Senate Office Building. Donald R. Matthews, an academician, was finishing work on a book on the Senate, *U.S. Senators and Their World*. He broke Senate offices down into two general types: the bureaucratic and the individualistic. In the bureaucratic offices, "the senator has delegated considerable nonroutine responsibilities to his staff, established a fairly clear-cut division of labor and chain of command." The individualistic offices were "vest pocket operations in which the senator has delegated only routine tasks and in which the staff has little influence and less authority."

Byrd was arriving in the Senate as it was going through a profound evolution. The old Senate, the Senate of "individualistic" offices, had just been portrayed in *Citadel: The Story of the United States Senate*, a book by William S. White. White wrote of the U.S. Senate as "an institution that lives in an unending yesterday where the past is never gone, the present never quite decisive, and the future rarely quite visible. It has its good moments and its bad moments, but to the United States it symbolizes, if nothing else at all, the integrity of continuity and wholeness." This Senate was an institution where, when a man was sworn in, he assumed a mantle of dignity and honor. It was honor enough for any man to be in this body.

When the *Citadel* came out, Senator J. William Fulbright noticed that for a few days some of his colleagues attempted to play senator, walking the halls of Congress as if they were wearing togas. On January 15, 1957, Lyndon B. Johnson had a luncheon for the six new Democratic senators.

He gave the six freshmen autographed copies of *Citadel* and he told them that they should think of the book as a kind of McGuffey's *Reader*.

Johnson knew that White's Senate was not his, but he may have found a certain comfort in that mythical body. To White, the Senate was a great conservative body, the naysayer and watchman of democracy. But what gave the Senate its greatness were individual senators with individual ideas. They worked in the body of Congress to transform their ideas into legislation that would affect the nation. When Johnson had come to Washington, George Norris of Nebraska was still in the Senate. For years Norris had studied how to protect the land and the people. He had prepared his bill for the Tennessee Valley Authority, and he had defended it as if it were a part of his very being, which in a sense it was. Robert Wagner of New York was in the Senate too. For years he worked on the great legislation of the New Deal, including the labor bill that bears his name. Bob La Follette and Robert Taft were also in the Senate in those years. What these senators had in common was an organic relationship between what they believed, the people they served, and what they did and said to achieve their ends.

When Robert Byrd entered the Senate, he accepted the life of the Senate as the central reality of his being. "Over the years he has cloaked himself in what he perceives to be senatorial dignity and aura," said one of Byrd's former aides, "but even when he arrived, there really was very little dignity left and the aura was gone."

Byrd allied himself with Lyndon Johnson of Texas and more closely yet with Richard Russell of Georgia. Those who watched Byrd often thought him great only in petty things. But to a man who revered the Senate as much as Byrd, there were no petty duties. In 1960, during an all-night civil rights filibuster, Byrd talked for a record twenty-one hours. Five years later in another filibuster, he talked for fifteen hours. Byrd was always ready to volunteer for the KP duty of legislative life. The Senate was based on rules and precedents. And Robert Byrd, alone of his generation, was willing to learn the rules and the precedents. He studied them until he knew them as did no one else and then he studied them some more.

Byrd performed duties, great and small, for senators of every persuasion, North and South, Democrat and Republican. He helped colleagues whenever he could. When he had helped, he sent them notes saying that he had been glad to be of service. These he filed away. In 1967 he was elected Secretary of the Democratic Conference, the number-three position in the Senate Democratic leadership. Four years later he defeated Ted Kennedy and became senate whip, the number-two position in the Senate Democratic leadership.

As a Senate leader, Byrd worked even harder. He knew the Bible, the book of Senate rules and the book of precedents, and these were just about the only books he figured he would ever have to know. He had read the 900-page collection of precedents cover to cover, two times, and late at night at home he was reading it for the third. When the Senate was planning to go into closed session on matters of national security, he would go over Rule 35 once again. When there was going to be a vote on cloture, he would read the rule on cloture. Byrd knew the rules and he knew the precedents and could make them turn upside down and dance on their heads. It was *his* Senate now, and he left the floor rarely.

The Washington Monument splits the window of his vast inner office in the Capitol. Senator Byrd speaks quietly, the twang of the hills in his voice: "The Senate is a forest. There are ninety-nine animals. They're all lions. There's a waterhole in the forest. I'm the waterhole. They all have to come to the waterhole. I don't have power but I have knowledge of the rules. I have knowledge of the precedents. I have knowledge of the schedule. So I'm in a position to do things for others."

"Now the majority leader is the dispatcher, the engineer, the fellow at the head of the engine who's looking out from the dark night at the headlight down the railway, pulling on the throttle a little harder, pushing on the throttle a little, or leveling off a little, moving it along. Or he determines to move over on this sidetrack or that sidetrack. This legislative organism, with its power, has to have direction. It has to have a leader, but he doesn't have the power. He's the umpire, the referee. He doesn't have any more of that raw power than any other senator has."

"The president, he has power. He's the chief executive of this country. The presidency of the United States should in reality seek the man. Someone said that. That's the way it ought to be. People ought not to be persuaded by a person's pretty teeth, by his smile, or by the way he cuts his hair — by his charisma. That's misleading. That's not to say that a person with pretty teeth and a pretty smile and a handsome build and charisma may not have the ability. But they don't necessarily go together either."

Talking about pretty teeth and a pretty smile and the cut of a man's hair, Robert Byrd could have been sketching a caricature of Edward Kennedy. Byrd and Kennedy were the two Janus faces of the Senate, Byrd often looking backward to a past that had never been, Kennedy looking forward to a future that might never arrive. They approached their work as differently as two men in the same profession possibly could. They also had different conceptions of power and how to use it.

Edward Moore Kennedy walked down the center aisle of the Senate to be sworn in as the junior senator from Massachusetts on January 9, 1963. He had the accent and bearing of the Kennedys, but was a big, brawny fellow with a rousing, friendly manner that suggested an Irish politician of a half century past. He was the scion of a family that seemed destined to dominate American political life in the last decades of the twentieth century as had the Adams family in the first decades of the nation's history. . . .

Kennedy fit unobtrusively into the traditional role of the freshman senator. One morning he went around to see Senator James Eastland of Mississippi, chairman of the Judiciary Committee and champion of the old Senate. He drank bourbon with the senior senator and Eastland discovered that the Kennedys were not all alike. He went around to see Senator Richard Russell of Georgia, Robert Byrd's patron, and he went to the Senate prayer breakfast, too — once at least — and led his colleagues in prayer.

While Kennedy might act out such old-fashioned rituals of the Senate, he was still the most modern of freshmen. A decade later, James Macgregor Burns, a biographer of Kennedy, would call him a "presidential senator." Kennedy was a presidential senator not only in the sense that he had become the sole bearer of the Kennedy legacy and heir apparent to the White House. He was presidential in the way he went about being a senator. He launched a frenetic, permanent presidential-like campaign within the very Senate.

In the favored analogy of his staff, Senator Kennedy stood at the center of a circle of aides who flowed in and around him. The Kennedys had always had a special talent for acquiring and using people whose talents met the needs of the moment. They attracted members of that natural aristocracy of the able and the ambitious. These aides were perhaps no more talented than those around other contenders for the ultimate prize in American politics. But in the livery of the Kennedys, they seemed to serve with extraordinary energy and devotion, and in the end they were, in one way or another, rewarded in kind.

One of those who was there when Kennedy entered the Senate was Milton Gwirtzman, now a Washington lawyer.

"From the beginning Kennedy knew how to use his staff," Gwirtzman observed. "Even in his first term he had that lineup outside his office. There were perhaps six professionals then and Kennedy used them as a multiplier." To a Borah or Taft or Wagner, the idea of a senatorial multiplier would have been absurd. It would, indeed, have been impossible, for until the Legislative Reorganization Act of 1946, most senators had only a clerk and a secretary.

Kennedy was one of the first senators to employ his staff so systematically that he helped create a new definition of "senator." Kennedy not only used the half dozen or so aides who were his natural due, but he subsidized two others. Gwirtzman, for one, left the staff in 1964 but for the next six years was paid $18,000 a year by the Park Agency, a

Kennedy family conduit, for speeches and advice. Kennedy, moreover, had a press secretary. That itself was a relatively new position on the Hill: a media-savvy specialist who measured success in newsprint and television time, not merely in a product called legislation.

Kennedy understood how to develop his staff so that they would serve him. He did not want any one Super Aide around him who might become for him what Ted Sorensen had been for Jack. He did not want an alter ego. What he did want was a group of people who could work on their own, self-motivated young men ambitious for themselves and for him, men whose competitiveness with one another might sometimes spill over into jealousies, but whose energies and ideals could be channeled into furthering Senator Ted Kennedy and his career.

In those first years in office, Kennedy did not draw on his name. He did not use his power in ways that were memorable or important. He had a quotation from Machiavelli as his maxim: "Power not used is power saved." Machiavelli, however, was writing about power that had once been used. Kennedy was hoarding a commodity whose worth he could not know until he used it. He was acting as if even he accepted the common definition of himself as the last and the least of the Kennedys — the kid brother.

During the day Kennedy abided by all the rituals of egalitarianism: bantering with aides, employing the ersatz intimacy of first names. However, if an aide stepped over a certain line, visible only to Kennedy, that aide learned to regret it. By day they might be members of a team but not in the evening. It was simply understood that if you worked for Ted Kennedy you did not go to social gatherings that he attended. You learned to treat his family in a special way. An aide had taken a phone call from Rose Kennedy in Hyannis Port one day. "Your mother called," the aide said when Kennedy returned to the office. "You mean *you* talked to *my* mother?" Kennedy said. If politics was one world, and social life another, then the family was yet a third and the most exalted of Kennedy's worlds. Here the subordinates were not allowed to trespass, even for a moment.

On that November afternoon in 1963 when President John F. Kennedy was assassinated in Dallas, Ted Kennedy was performing that most thankless of tasks foisted on the freshman: presiding over a nearly empty Senate. When he learned of the shooting and he finally reached his brother on the telephone, Robert Kennedy told him, "You'd better call your mother and your sisters." In their division of the duties of mourning, it fell to Ted Kennedy to comfort the family.

By that next June, Kennedy had prepared his public face. His party back in Massachusetts was preparing to nominate him for his first full term in office. Kennedy, however, was still on the floor of the Senate waiting to vote on the civil rights bill. It was so typical of his life to have a dozen people, a dozen decisions, a dozen proposals backed up waiting for him.

Kennedy finally left Washington for Massachusetts by private plane, accompanied by Senator Birch Bayh of Indiana and his wife Marvella, and aide Ed Moss. It was no kind of weather to be flying in a private plane, but Kennedy lived in a world of days that were scheduled too tight, cars that were driven too fast, planes that were flown when they shouldn't have been. On the approach to the airpost outside Springfield, the plane crashed. The Bayhs were injured, the pilot was dead, Moss would die soon afterward, and Kennedy had cracked ribs, a punctured lung, and three damaged vertebrae.

Kennedy spent the next six months in bed. . . .

While still in the hospital, Kennedy won reelection in Massachusetts with 74.4 percent of the votes. In New York, his brother Bob defeated Kenneth Keating for a Senate seat by a much closer margin. Afterward his brother had come up to visit in the hospital. The two Kennedys had posed for the photographers. "Step back a little, you're casting a shadow on Ted," one of the photographers said to Bob Kennedy.

"It'll be the same in Washington," Ted Kennedy said laughing.

During the nearly four years that the two Kennedys served together in the Senate, Ted Kennedy largely deferred to his brother and to his leadership. In 1965 he took over the chairmanship of the Subcommittee on Refugees and Escapees. This was his first chairmanship, the natural legacy of the seniority system. It was a moribund subcommittee concerned largely with refugees who had fled Communist Europe. But it represented more staff and an area that he could now legitimately make his own.

Ted took the subcommittee and expanded its mandate to the refugees of Southeast Asia. He used it as his ticket of admission to the issue of Vietnam. He went to Vietnam and the papers were full of the poignant testimony of human suffering. . . .

It was not until after the murder of his brother Bob in 1968 that Ted Kennedy, the senator, began to fully emerge. In his time of mourning he had gone sailing for days on end, and drinking, and carousing. Then in August in Worcester he had given a speech important enough to be televised nationally. He told his audience that he had been at sea. But he said, "There is no safety in hiding. Not for me, not for any of us here today . . . like my brothers before me, I pick up a fallen standard." He went on to talk about the Vietnam war and all it had cost in money and blood. He proposed that the United States unconditionally end the bombing and negotiate a peace. . . .

The next office Kennedy did seek was one that his brothers would never have considered. In January he defeated Russell Long, that son of Louisiana, and son of oil, to become majority whip. The whip had a series of thankless bureaucratic duties such as rounding up senators and arranging schedules. He was, nonetheless, the number-two leader in the Senate. Kennedy set out to make the whip more than that. He brought in some of his own academic and other expert advisors to forge a cohesive policy for the Democrats. Senators, however, are a jealous and self-protective group. A hundred different policies were better than one, if the one came stamped with the mark of a particular senator. Worse yet, Kennedy simply did not perform the mundane, pesky tasks of the whip as they were supposed to be. Bored by them, he foisted such chores as he could onto his staff.

Kennedy was drinking heavily. At times his face had the florid look that showed him a full-blooded member of the race of Irish drinkers. Then in July on vacation he had gone over to Chappaquiddick Island to attend a party for some of Bobby Kennedy's "boiler-room girls." He had left with one of them, Mary Jo Kopechne, and the next morning the police had found her body in Kennedy's overturned Oldsmobile off a bridge on a dirt road on Chappaquiddick Island.

Kennedy, according to his own statement, had dived down to try to get her out and then he had left and gone back to his friends to get help. He had not contacted the police until the next morning. The Kennedys, whatever else one said about them, had always showed the grace under pressure that Hemingway had called the mark of courage, the mark of a man. The private Kennedy had failed that night, as those around him failed. "It was in part a failure of staffing," one of his aides said. "He had no one with him to tell him he was crazy."

Within hours Kennedy had left the island. He retreated into that flimsy story; he made a televised public statement prepared by Ted Sorensen, Gwirtzman, Richard Goodwin, and Burke Marshall and then backed into legal refuges, the power of wealth and position, and the sympathy that people of Massachusetts had for him and for his family. . . .

Until that night at Chappaquiddick, Kennedy had appeared an inevitable choice for the 1972 presidential nomination. But that was all over. When Kennedy returned to the Senate, Mike Mansfield, the majority leader, as goodhearted a man as was to be found in that body, noticed Kennedy pausing for a moment in the cloakroom. "Come here," Mansfield said encouragingly. "Come here, right back where you belong." To the last of the Kennedys, it was a phrase not without its ironies. . . .

INDIVIDUAL STYLES AND IN-stitutional norms have affected at different times the way the Senate works. Most senators agree that in the 1980s the body is far less collegial than in the past, when it took years of hard work and skillful political maneuvering for a member to gain the respect of his or her colleagues and rise to a position of power. Senior committee chairmen and party leaders dominated the body, determining what legislation would be developed and scheduled for floor debate. They also controlled committee assignments and other internal matters. Whether or not the Senate was a club, as journalist William S. White described it in his 1956 book, *Citadel: The Story of the United States Senate,* it clearly was an institution in which members knew — and for the most part respected — each other just as they supported the deliberative processes that had evolved over the years.

The Senate began to change in the 1970s. An inner core of senior members remained, but retirements and a growing number of successful electoral challenges to incumbents brought an influx of newcomers. Institutional norms of behavior that arose from collegiality, which had already begun to crumble in the 1960s, appeared to vanish in the 1980s as each senator, regardless of seniority, sought an equal share of power. The following selection describes how one freshman senator made a major impact not only in the institution, but on public policy. His name became a household word in 1986 with the passage of the Gramm-Rudman-Hollings bill that imposed mandatory spending cuts upon the federal government.

25 Jacqueline Calmes
THE TEXAS TORNADO: SENATOR PHIL GRAMM

Phil Gramm was a loser. At least that's what Gramm remembers his older brother calling him as he left to learn discipline at military school. But he also recalls some fraternal advice that followed.

"I want you to go to your first class and I want you to watch everybody walk into class," the brother said. "And I want you to say to yourself, 'I am the smartest person in this room, and before this semester is over, everybody in this room is going to know it.' "

Now 43, Gramm seems to have followed that advice — from Georgia Military Academy all the way to the U.S. House and Senate. Exhibiting energy, intellect, ego and ambition, and apparently undeterred by any need to be well liked, the Texas Democrat-turned-Republican has earned the kind of fame and stature most legislators only dream about. And he has done so in less than a decade.

From *Congressional Quarterly Weekly Report,* Vol. 44, No. 11, pp. 611–615 (March 15, 1986). Reprinted by permission.

Few members ever see their names on a law. Gramm's is already on two landmark statutes: the 1985 Gramm-Rudman-Hollings balanced-budget law, which radically overhauled the nation's spending policies, and the 1981 Gramm-Latta law implementing President Reagan's economic program of domestic budget cuts and defense-spending hikes.

What makes the feat all the more incredible is that in a clubby institution where success often rests on good relations with other members, Gramm is among the least popular.

"I've told him, 'Phil, you are your own worst enemy', " says Republican Trent Lott of Mississippi, the House minority whip.

"He's not a popular guy," Lott added. "He's a little brash. He doesn't stand in line and wait his turn. I grant you all that. But he gets results."

Predictably, many of Gramm's harshest critics are Democrats who resent his 1981 betrayal of their budget strategy to Reagan's camp and his much-publicized 1983 party switch. But some Republicans also say privately they are put off by a man they describe as arrogant, egocentric, and just plain mean.

"I never take these criticisms that are made from time to time personally," Gramm says. "People who can't debate the issues tend to engage in personal attacks. And I always take it as a sign of weakness."

"I get in battles to win because I think the battles are important. The people of Texas . . . elected me to win. And I do that."

A fellow Texan, Democratic Representative Marvin Leath, says, "I tell my colleagues who get quite distraught with him at times, 'You can feel however you want to about Phil. You can love him or hate him, or you can tolerate him, whatever. But when you're dealing with him, there are two things you've got to remember: Number one, he's smarter than you are. Number two, he's meaner than a junkyard dog.' "

An Aggie Goes to Washington

Given Gramm's image as a winner, it is sometimes forgotten that his political debut was a disaster.

Born and raised in Georgia, Gramm made Texas his home after earning a doctorate from the University of Georgia in 1967 and taking a job teaching economics at Texas A&M University. At 33, he dared to challenge Texas Senator Lloyd Bentsen in the 1976 Democratic primary.

He complained that Bentsen had moved leftward to court national support for a presidential campaign, and said he had become "a blatant hypocrite and a master of deceit who continues to say one thing in Texas and do another in Washington."

The incumbent dismissed Gramm as "an extremist," and held him to just 29 percent of the vote.

Instead of giving up on politics, Gramm lowered his sights.

In 1978, Democratic Representative Olin E. "Tiger" Teague decided to retire after 16 terms representing the 6th District, which stretched through east-central Texas northward into the Dallas-Fort Worth area. Gramm challenged Teague's former aide and protégé in the Democratic primary and won. That fall he easily beat a Republican, collecting 65 percent of the vote.

Focused from the Start

He arrived in Washington with a vision: a government with low taxes, minimal social responsibilities, and the world's best-stocked arsenal — all within a balanced federal budget.

Just two months after taking office in 1979, Gramm offered a preview of the strategy he would use six years later to propel Gramm-Rudman-Hollings through Congress.

That spring, Congress had to pass unpopular legislation raising the government's limit for borrowing money. Gramm joined with Lott and Democrat James R. Jones of Oklahoma to try to attach an amendment requiring a balanced budget. This time, unlike 1985, the tactic failed. But so did the debt-limit bill.

Faced with a government default, a divided House had to try again. Gramm and his allies were ready with another balanced-budget amendment, but the Rules Committee rejected it for floor consideration.

The episode spotlighted not only Gramm's preoccupation with the budget, but also his ego. One senior aide recalls that Gramm's appearance before Rules "caused quite a stir among members on the committee."

What Gramm said, according to an unofficial, unedited committee transcript, was: "I am not claiming to be the world's greatest expert on economics. But I believe I am the only member of the House with a Ph.D. in economics and [who] has had publications in the *American Economic Review* in the past decade. And I would say . . . my academic credentials are probably as good as anyone who has served in this Congress since Senator Douglas."

Later in the hearing, Rules Chairman Richard Bolling, (Missouri Democrat 1949–83), returned to Gramm's reference to Senator Paul H. Douglas, (Illinois Democrat 1949–67), a respected economist. "I don't think you would have agreed on a single thing," Bolling told Gramm.

In 1980, Gramm irritated Majority Leader Jim Wright, (a Texas Democrat), and other House leaders when he joined Republican Marjorie S. Holt of Maryland, in proposing an unsuccessful substitute for the House Budget Committee's fiscal 1981 budget. It would have transferred $5.1 billion from domestic to military spending.

But if his go-it-alone style alienated Democrats in Congress, his constituents loved it. He was re-elected in 1980 with 71 percent of the vote.

Winning Budget Seat

Gramm returned to the House with a special goal — a seat on the Budget Committee.

To that end, he easily secured the support of other Southern Democrats, who were chafing at their lack of influence over party policy. Fellow Texan Wright took up Gramm's cause. But House leaders demanded extraordinary assurances that he would be a loyalist, not a rebel.

"I will work hard to perfect a budget in committee and during floor debate," he pledged in a January 8, 1981, letter to House elders. "But as a member of the committee, I will support final passage of the budget."

"Gramm did all the right things," said M. Wendell Belew, Jr., then the Budget Committee chief counsel. "He talked to everybody. He even talked to the staff. He went out of his way to reassure people that he would support the Democratic position."

The Democratic Steering and Policy Committee nominated Gramm for Budget, but some Democrats balked. Among efforts to allay their concerns was a letter from five party leaders — Budget Chairman Jones; John P. Murtha of Pennsylvania; Richard A. Gephardt of Missouri; Tony Coelho of California; and Charlie Rose of North Carolina.

"We believe that Phil Gramm can bring new ideas and a new balance to the Budget Committee that will benefit every Democrat," they wrote.

A month later, Gramm shared one new idea with Wright. The two co-sponsored a bill that was the precursor of Gramm-Rudman-Hollings. Like the 1985 bill, it called for automatic cuts if the budget was not balanced, empowered the president to order the cuts, and even used the same esoteric terms, such as "controllable expenditures" and "sequestration." But this 1981 bill never went anywhere.

Break with Democrats

The bill marked the last time the two men would work together. Democrats soon learned Gramm was collaborating with the Reagan administration on the budget.

Gramm worked secretly with budget director David A. Stockman, a former House ally (Michigan Republican 1977–81), on a substitute budget outlining Reagan's economic program. Then he engineered its passage in the House, leading other Southern Democrats, the "Boll Weevils," into a coalition with the minority House Republicans.

The result became known as Gramm-Latta I. Democrat Gramm received top billing on the GOP document over the chief Budget Committee Republican, Delbert L. Latta of Ohio — a fact the two men were overheard to argue about.

Next came Gramm-Latta II. This "reconciliation" bill carried out many of the cuts recommended in Gramm-Latta I — $130.6 billion in savings over three years, a record still unmatched.

What particularly embittered House Democrats about the second measure was the fact that Gramm and administration supporters forced a floor vote on their version even though the Budget Committee, working with authorizing committees, had produced a bill that more than met the deficit-cutting target set in Gramm-Latta I.

To this day, many House Democrats damn Gramm as a traitor and a liar for his activities in 1981. But Wright, the man said to have the most reason to feel betrayed, will not talk.

He recoiled recently when asked about Gramm, and snapped, "I don't think that's a subject for me to comment on. There are other subjects I'd be glad to talk about. Ask me one."

Gramm vehemently denies that he betrayed Democrats' trust in 1981: "In the House for four years I was a conservative Democrat with a mandate from the people back home and a philosophy that was different from the leadership of the Democratic Party. And to have worked with the party would have been in essence to have given up on trying to achieve the objectives that I felt I had been elected to achieve and that I felt were in the national interest."

"This idea that I was put on [the Budget Committee] to represent anything other than the conservative philosophy just won't hold water," he adds. "The letter says very clearly that, number one, I preserve my right to try to perfect the budget both in committee and on the floor. But as a member of the Budget Committee, whether I win or lose, I will support final passage — which I religiously did. Only they were my budgets."

Gramm recalls Gramm-Latta I and II as "a once-in-a-lifetime chance. If I didn't get out in the lead, the job might not get done and there wouldn't be a Reagan program."

Into the GOP . . .

Throughout 1982, Gramm continued to work with Republicans on the budget. He and Vice President George Bush worked to get the final signatures on a petition forcing floor action on a proposed balanced-budget constitutional amendment; the drive succeeded but the measure failed.

In the 1982 primary, Democrats ran a candidate against Gramm — Jack Teague, son of Gramm's popular predecessor. But Gramm beat him by more than 2-to-1. Republicans then withdrew their candidate and allowed Gramm a 95 percent vote in the fall.

With Gramm back in Washington, Democrats finally took their revenge. On January 3, 1983, the Steering and Policy Committee voted 26–4 to yank him from Budget.

On January 5, in what proved to be a masterful gamble, Gramm resigned and returned to Texas to seek the vacant seat as a Republican. He withstood 10 rivals and won 55.3 percent of the vote. He was back in his seat February 22, the first Republican ever to hold it.

. . . And the Senate

Publicity from the special election laid the groundwork for Gramm's 1984 Senate race. He drew 73 percent of the vote in a four-man GOP primary, and in the fall defeated Democrat Lloyd Doggett 59 percent to 41 percent — the largest margin ever received by a Republican for a statewide office in Texas.

Once in the Senate, Gramm's agenda remained the budget, and he pursued it with characteristic zeal.

"I'll never forget it," says one senior Republican aide. "Two days after he was elected to the U.S. Senate, the phone rang. It was Gramm. He had started immediately to campaign for the Senate Budget Committee."

Gramm says he lost because the seat went to a more senior member, Missouri Republican John C. Danforth.

But Senate Republican sources say the story is more complicated. They say three senior Republicans were asked to take the Budget seat to prevent it from going to Gramm. Danforth finally accepted.

Danforth acknowledges he did not seek the seat. But he says a Budget staff suggestion that he take it was not presented as a block-Gramm tactic.

Instead of his first choice, Gramm was assigned to the Armed Services and Banking, Housing and Urban Affairs committees.

On Armed Services, Gramm has been an ardent advocate of Reagan's defense buildup. In his first year, he beat organized labor and won Senate passage of an amendment to the fiscal 1986 defense authorization bill exempting most military construction work from a law requiring workers on federal projects to be paid prevailing local wages. The provision was later dropped in conference with the House.

A fellow Armed Services member, Michigan Democrat Carl Levin, says Gramm "gets inside of issues; he's willing to look at the nuts and bolts. He feels strongly, at times too strongly, I think, about issues."

Though he is not on the Budget Committee, its work has remained Gramm's focus — sometimes to the panel's dismay. Last spring, he criticized its fiscal 1986 budget in newspaper columns. The panel grew so wary that when Gramm had a press conference to describe his stand on a White House-Senate GOP budget compromise, the committee's staff director sent an aide to listen.

Gramm's own account of his initial months in the Senate describes a man working to shed a reputation for rebelliousness and to bury an old House joke that went, "What's the most dangerous place to be? Between Phil Gramm and a TV camera."

"I thought it was important to show I could work within the system," he says. "And so I made a conscious decision during the first nine months to turn down national television, to stay away from interview shows, to work behind the scenes."

Gramm–Rudman–Hollings

This self-imposed exile ended September 25, when Gramm — with Senators Warren B. Rudman, New Hampshire Republican, and Ernest F. Hollings, a South Carolina Democrat — sponsored the bill that had been incubating since his first days in Congress. Suddenly, Gramm was back on the TV circuit.

The bill would undergo major changes during tortuous Senate debate and negotiations with the House. But when Reagan signed it into law three months later, the basic concept remained: Congress and the president had to meet annual deficit targets leading to a balanced budget, or they would trigger automatic, across-the-board cuts.

"It looked like it came out of nowhere," Gramm says of the bill. "The truth is, a lot of preparation went into it. Two months prior to its surfacing, the majority leader and Sen. Domenici [Budget Chairman Pete V. Domenici, Republican of New Mexico] were alerted to it. I met with every element at the White House . . . and I also kept the Republican leadership and the Boll Weevil leadership in the House informed about it. I think I proved in the House that I could go outside the system, but in Gramm-Rudman I think I proved in the Senate that I could work within the system."

He noted the bill's similarity to the one he co-sponsored with Wright in 1981, which he had offered again in 1982: "I felt then the time had not come — but it was going to come."

Good timing was the primary reason for the bill's success, according to numerous members and aides. Gramm drafted it last summer with an eye on an approaching deadline for legislation raising the debt limit, the same vehicle to which he, Jones and Lott had tried to add their balanced-budget proposal in 1979.

Rudman, too, was looking ahead to the debt-limit bill, and had served notice he would hold it hostage without some action against deficits. When he saw a story that Gramm was drafting a budget amendment, the two joined forces.

They knew that conservative Republicans and most Democrats would not support more borrowing without some step to reduce deficits. Senate GOP leaders had nothing to offer them. Gramm did.

"Something had to be done and it was the idea of the moment," says Louisiana Democratic Senator J. Bennett Johnson an opponent.

"He has a unique ability to reach to the central issue of every problem and articulate it in one sentence or two, in a way that people can understand," says Texas Republican Representative Steve Bartlett. "While everyone was wringing their hands . . . he said simply, 'Congress must impose limits on itself for future years.' And he came up with an enforcement mechanism to make it work."

Not all credit for the law belongs to Gramm. In fact, many sources cited his unpopularity as a major liability. During House debate in November, for instance, GOP leaders asked Senate Republicans to help get Gramm, who was visiting the chamber, off the floor. "Democrats hate his guts and some Republicans have problems, too," one said.

Lott says, "This legislation passed probably in spite of him."

Of Gramm's co-sponsors, Rudman is praised for bringing a respectability, particularly on defense issues, that Gramm lacked, while Hollings gave the product a bipartisan label.

Just as important, the sponsors had the right allies — Domenici; Majority Leader Robert Dole, Kansas Republican; Senate Finance Committee Chairman Bob Packwood, Oregon Republican, floor manager of the debt-limit bill; James C. Miller III, Reagan's budget director; and the president himself. (Miller and Gramm have been friends since their teens; Miller hired Gramm's wife, Wendy Lee, to head the budget office's regulatory arm.)

Both Dole and Domenici initially were private doubters. "In its original form, suffice to say, it wouldn't have worked," Domenici says. "I'm not embarrassed to say that I had grave reservations. But I was not alone in being skeptical. A number of us, Dole included, decided we ought to get it done only after fixing it dramatically."

Charges of Deception

Even now, some senators and aides in both parties complain that Gramm either misunderstood or misrepresented what the proposal would do, how much power it would give to the president, and its effect on farm, defense, health and veterans' programs.

"Now I don't want to get involved in speaking against a colleague, but during the debate I asked a number of questions. . . . 'What is an outlay? What is a controllable expenditure?' And I just couldn't get an answer from him," Johnston recalls. "He just gave me these half-hour 'mini-busters' on the deficits. Now that's not right. A senator has got a right to say anything he wants to on the floor, but when another senator asks a question about a bill, that senator's got a right to an answer."

When debate began October 3, Daniel P. Moynihan, New York Democrat, disdainfully revealed that costly farm programs were exempt from cuts. Gramm disagreed. But Moynihan was right, and the bill was changed.

Levin correctly argued that, contrary to sponsors' claims, the president would have unprecedented power to decide where automatic cuts would be made because the bill defined programs to be cut based on a publication of the president's Office of Management and Budget (OMB).

For example, Levin cited one OMB defense account with 253 programs; the president could pick among them, killing some and protecting others, as long as the account was reduced by the required amount.

Levin went to Rudman, who insisted that was not his intent. They agreed to a clarifying amendment. But Levin says that "very, very hard bargaining" ensued when Gramm and administration officials got involved.

On October 9, the Senate approved Levin's amendment making Congress' appropriations bills, not OMB, the source for defining programs to be cut. "But right off the bat there was some difference of opinion," Levin says.

Minutes before the amendment was adopted, Gramm explained it in a way that Levin felt was wrong. Levin and Rudman set the record straight.

Throughout debate on the bill, Gramm exasperated opponents by repeatedly insisting his proposal was "a simple idea" similar to practices in 43 states. (He included his own state in that number. However, while Texas' constitution requires a balanced budget, the state has no provision for automatic or mandatory cuts if spending exceeds revenues.)

"Is the man who was able to panic the House of Representatives in 1981 now able to panic the U.S. Senate in 1985?" asked Florida's Lawton Chiles, the Budget Committee's senior Democrat, in floor debate. "It is his heritage."

In the House, despite Democrats' animosity toward Gramm, the measure had immense political appeal. When it arrived from the Senate, House leaders assumed they could not defeat it. They called instead for a conference with senators.

As in 1981, when House Democrats refused to name Gramm to a Gramm-Latta conference, Senate GOP leaders did not include Gramm among their negotiators.

"I think it showed good judgment on Dole's part not to include Gramm on the conference because of the known hostility House members have toward him," Hollings says.

But after the first conference collapsed, Gramm was named to a second conference committee, as were Hollings and Rudman. "I wasn't on the first conference and it went nowhere," Gramm says. "I was on the second conference and we solved it."

What the Future Holds

Forecasts of Gramm's future in the Senate fall into two contrary schools. Some members predict he will thrive in a chamber where individualists have freer rein than in the House. But others bet he will trip amid its diplomatic folkways.

"I'm convinced he is a rising star in the Senate," says Senator Thad Cochran, a Mississippi Republican. "He came in at full speed. He knew the procedure, the rules, the federal government. He was comfortable here."

Domenici says Gramm is "a very individual and independent person. He has a fixed philosophy. But he is a good enough legislator to match that with being a team player."

"Diplomacy is not his strength," Illinois Democratic Senator Paul Simon says. "But my instinct is that his intelligence and hard work largely make up for it."

Hollings says Gramm is brilliant and fearless; if his ways don't always make him popular, "he doesn't mind."

"He's just too professorial. He can be impatient with the 'class' and talk down to the 'students' at times," Hollings says. "But I found working with him very enjoyable."

Still, some colleagues insist Gramm's breaches of Senate protocol threaten his future effectiveness.

He enraged Moynihan, for example, during a joint TV appearance January 19 when he called Moynihan "one of the weakest" defense supporters.

"I'm not going to have my voting record misrepresented," Moynihan snarled on the air. "You're one year in the Senate, fella. You don't do that to another senator."

Moynihan later defended his record on the Senate floor. Gramm did not apologize.

Gramm also is reputed to have a mean streak. During floor debate on the bill, one Senate Democrat marveled to another about Gramm's tenacity. The second member replied, "But you know, I've only seen two members ever be mean to an elevator operator — Wayne Hays and Phil Gramm."

A Republican Senate aide recalls that during the Gramm-Rudman-Hollings debate, Gramm grabbed him and asked a question. When the aide couldn't answer it, Gramm pushed him away, saying, "Then what the hell are you doing here?"

Senator Howard M. Metzenbaum, Ohio Democrat, says, "I think we all agree he's smart. I'm not sure what future he has in the U.S. Senate regarding his effectiveness, and I'm not one that considers myself one of the club, either. . . . He gets a little personal at times. I have disagreements with my colleagues but I try never to get personal."

A conservative Democratic senator, who asked to be unnamed, says, "He is a potentially dangerous ideologue because I feel he honestly believes his is the only course to rightness. . . . He is of a type that, unless he watches himself, he could say or do something that would end with Senate censure."

Another senator had a less dire assessment: "There is no question he is not ever going to be as effective as his abilities would permit, simply because of his personality."

But critics acknowledge that their grousing about Gramm's abrasiveness and his unwillingness to play by Washington rules is mostly the stuff of insiders that only makes Gramm more attractive to Texas voters.

"The people of North Carolina don't care a fig whether you're a prominent member of the club," North Carolina Senator Jesse Helms says. "That formula has worked pretty well for me and I think it will work well for Phil."

"He's a folk hero in Texas," Bartlett says. "He is seen as someone who was finally able to move establishment Washington from its free-spending ways."

Still, even Gramm recognizes that fallout from Gramm-Rudman-Hollings budget cuts could hurt politically. Though he does not face re-election until 1990, Texas Democrats already chortle about what one called "a Chinese water torture of daily headlines" about cuts in Texas.

"I'll guarantee you one thing. He won't back off of it," Leath says. "Regardless of the headlines, he'll be telling people he's right."

"I expect to go through Valley Forge before we get to Yorktown," Gramm tells people nowadays. But he confidently predicts economic prosperity ahead, largely thanks to his law. And if he's wrong, he says, "I'll be satisfied to go back to Texas A&M."

THOMAS P. ("TIP") O'NEILL IS the epitome of the Massachusetts politician, which according to some political observers is a unique breed. O'Neill was born in 1912, into a second-generation Irish immigrant family. His father was a Cambridge politician, and by the time Tip O'Neill was in his teens, he was actively involved in political campaigns. He was elected to the Massachusetts legislature in 1936, the same year he graduated from Boston College. He served in the state legislature until 1952, having been chosen minority leader in 1947 and 1948, and Speaker of the House from 1948 until 1952. In 1952 he ran for John F. Kennedy's vacated House seat (Kennedy was running a successful senatorial campaign against Henry Cabot Lodge, Jr.), and after a close primary win he won the general election by a large majority, which was the case in all of his subsequent elections to the House.

Tip O'Neill advanced rapidly in the House, not only because of his own consummate skill as a politician, but because he was aided by another Massachusetts politician, John F. McCormack. In 1955, McCormack, who was majority leader, appointed O'Neill to the powerful House Rules Committee. When McCormack became Speaker of the House in 1962, O'Neill served as an informal majority leader until the selection of Carl Albert. Tip O'Neill himself became majority leader in January 1971, after the untimely death of Majority Leader Hale Boggs of Louisiana, who was lost on a plane flight over Alaska. The backing of Boggs's people in the House helped to give O'Neill the majority leadership. O'Neill conducted the same kind of highly effective personal campaign for the House leadership that had always guaranteed him success with the regular electorate. Within the House, O'Neill's personal friendship with McCormack and his close working relationship with Carl Albert, both when Albert was majority leader and when he was Speaker, reflected O'Neill's effective personality and style. By the time the Democratic caucus met in January 1973 to choose its new majority leader, Tip O'Neill was unopposed. From the position of majority leader it was only one short step to the Speakership in 1977 after Albert retired. In the following selection we see why Tip O'Neill is truly a master politician; we are given a close look at his two major assets, his personality and style.

26 Jimmy Breslin
THE POLITICIAN

The hand that rocked the bureaucracy into motion was found, of a Saturday night in June 1974, wrapped around a glass.

"Will you drink a Manhattan?" Tip O'Neill asked a man joining the party.

The man thought about it.

"I asked you, will you drink a Manhattan?"

The man thought more about it. Agitation showed in O'Neill's face.

"The reason I'm asking if you take a Manhattan is that there's no bar here and it takes them too long to bring us back a drink. So I ordered two Manhattans for myself and you can have one of them if you want."

This was in the early part of the evening, when more than forty people came into the private dining room of the Wayside Inn, at Chatham, on Cape Cod, the people gathering there in celebration and admiration of the thirty-third wedding anniversary of Tip and Milly O'Neill and simultaneously the sixtieth birthday of Milly O'Neill, that number being loudly announced to all by her husband.

O'Neill was standing in a circle of people, everybody talking, O'Neill talking back to everybody, when his son Tom — who was running, successfully it turned out, for lieutenant governor of Massachusetts — placed a hand on his father's elbow. "Dad, I just want to tell you this one thing."

O'Neill, looking straight ahead, the eyes taking in the entire room — politics is for backcourt men — said out of the corner of his mouth to his son, "Hey, I can listen to five conversations at once. Just keep telling me what you want me to know."

His father went back to the group. "Chuck, is the weather really that bad? I thought Bantry was part of Cork. Cork's not supposed to be that bad. Oh, it's in West Cork? Oh, they have bright spells. That's good. Bright spells. Dick, old pal, you look good. Mary, darling! How are you? What will you have to drink, dear? Are you playing any golf, Paul? Well, I played today. You know what happened the other day out there? I'm on the third hole and there's a ball on the fairway and I don't know where the hell it came from. And here coming through the woods from the other fairway is Jim St. Clair. I said to him, 'Hey, Jim, what are you doing over here?' He just gave me this shrug and I kept going my way. Stop to talk to him? Oh, I wouldn't do that. It just so happens that we're both members of Eastward Ho. Do I know him? I'll tell you a story about

Jim St. Clair. One day a long time ago I got a call on a Sunday morning from a man whose son was arrested for drunken driving the night before. The boy was a senior at West Point. He was taking a summer course at MIT. The boy had been out and he'd had a few and the officer arrested him in Central Square for drunk driving. Well, I get a call from the father. He said the son'll be thrown out of West Point. Could I help? Well, geez, a kid goes to his last year in the Academy. I'm not going to let him get into trouble over a few drinks. Of course, I'll try to help. I told him I'd get my brother Bill, who was alive then. Practicing law, you know. Well, Bill calls the guy and the father says there's ten thousand in it if you could get my son off. My brother says, no, one thousand will be the charge, and I *cahn't* guarantee you anything but a pretty good try. The father said, no, it has to be ten thousand. My brother Bill says, no, I'll charge you a thousand. So on a Sunday morning we all come to court. I take a seat and the clerk comes up to me and says the judge wants to see me in the back. So I go back there and the judge says, 'Tip, what are you doing in here?' So I tell him the story of this West Point lad. When I finish I go outside and by now the father and the boy are in court. And with them is Jim St. Clair. During the night, it seems the father had gotten nervous after he arranged to have my brother Bill. And the father asked for the name of the biggest lawyer in Boston and they told him Jim St. Clair. So Jim St. Clair sees Bill and I starting to leave and he says to the father, 'You know, I'm not as experienced in a city court like this one. I think you're better off with Bill O'Neill here.' So the father said all right, and Jim St. Clair went off to play golf and my brother handled the case. Well, it was in Cambridge, and you got to know Cambridge. The policeman got up on the stand and my brother asked him, 'Did you know that this boy was a senior at West Point and that he is taking summer courses at MIT in order to better prepare himself to defend his country, and that he just pulled off to the side of the road on Saturday night to sleep off the exhaustion?' And the cop said, 'No, I didn't. If I had known it, I never would have allowed the court clerk to issue the summons.' Now you see, in Cambridge at the time the cop did not issue the summons. The court clerk did. So now the cop decided not to press the matter anymore. At the same time he himself didn't have to rip up any ticket or anything. It was up to the court clerk to revoke the summons. Which of course he did and the case was over. And now I'm going to show you where Jim St. Clair is so smart. Remember the father telling my brother Bill about ten thousand dollars for the case? Well, he gave Bill three hundred dollars on the first day. Now for the rest of the bill, seven hundred, it was pulling teeth to get it out of him. Anyway, Paul, old pal, you look marvelous. Hey, what about all this food? Come on now, let's eat." He began steering people toward the buffet table.

At the end of the night, on his way to the car, O'Neill led his wife into the crowded smoky taproom of the Wayside Inn. He waited until George McCue, who plays the piano, finished a song. Then he came through the tables and up onto the small bandstand. He wanted to do one thing before the evening was over.

"My name is Tip O'Neill and I fool around in politics. I just want to sing a song for my wife, Milly, on her thirty-third wedding anniversary. I want to sing the song they played on the day we were married. The name of the song is 'Apple Blossom Time.' "

George McCue began to play the song on the piano and O'Neill's barbershop voice boomed out the start of the song.

> I'll be with you in apple blossom time,
> I'll be with you
> To change your name to mine. . . .

He sang through the smoke to his wife, selling her a love song in front of strangers. You thought automatically of Nixon and his Haldeman and Ehrlichman, standing in the doorway of the amber light of the room, smirking and starting to leave, secure in the absolute belief that no such open, old-fashioned people could be dangerous. If O'Neill was Congress's idea of a leader, how could they be hurt? How could a man who sings to his wife in public ever qualify as an opponent? At the last note, O'Neill broke into a neighborhood cheer, his voice coming up from the sandlots:

"Milly Miller O'Neill! Yeah!"

The next day he went to Washington, taking with him in all his mannerisms and speech the loud, crowded life of the streets and of the frame houses of Cambridge and Boston, and the life as a politician that is much a part of the area. There is no way to understand what went on in Washington in the summer of 1974 unless you realize that what happened was because of politicians. Ask Peter Rodino what was the single most important thing he had to do to bring about the impeachment vote against Richard Nixon and watch the constitutional scholars pack around to hear his answer:

"When I was able to hold Mann, Thornton, and Flowers, then I knew it could be done," Rodino tells you. "I had to have them. Once I had them I could start to put it together."

Put it together. A vote. The basics of clubhouse politics. He had to know that he had the votes of James Mann of South Carolina, Walter Flowers of Alabama, and Ray Thornton of Arkansas. With these Southerners for impeachment, the needed Republican votes would not be impossible to obtain. Let the scholars debate the narrow versus broad interpretations of the Constitution as the most meaningful thing to come out of the impeachment. Peter Rodino knew it was the votes that did it. The politics, not the scholarship of the matter.

And, from his position, Tip O'Neill knew it was the job of causing the bureaucracy to move that enabled everything else to happen. He knew this because he was a professional politician, and you might as well know a little bit of what these people are and where they come from.

For a little island, it has caused so much pain. In 1845, there was a great potato famine in Ireland, people in remote areas trying to subsist on yellow winter grass and, finally, crazed, entering the black torture of cannibalism. Everywhere in the country there were children unable to close their mouths, the lack of calcium in their bones preventing their jaws from working. Three O'Neills — Pat, John, and Mike — left Cork City for the terrible ocean crossing to Boston, and the promise of jobs with the New England Brick Company. In Boston, the first money the brothers gathered that was not needed for food went directly into the Irish stock market — cemetery plots. The next money Pat O'Neill had — in 1855 — was spent going home to Ireland and bringing back a wife to America. A son from this marriage was Thomas P. O'Neill, Sr. He was raised to be a bricklayer. In 1900, he won a seat on the Cambridge City Council. On the day his son was born — Thomas P. O'Neill, Jr. — the father was picketing Harvard with people from the bricklayers' union. The only thing better a man from Cambridge could say about his father is that the father was elected president on the day he was born. For Harvard, until it began to grow up in the last fifteen years, always regarded the people outside its gates as leaves upon the streets.

In 1914, Thomas P. O'Neill, Sr., received the highest mark in a Civil Service test for the job of superintendent of sewers and sanitation for Cambridge. There were 1700 men on the payroll, none of them Civil Service, which meant that O'Neill was in charge of hiring and firing. His hand immediately reached out to touch more jobs. He married the executives of the Edison Cambridge Gaslight Company, a joining together worth hundreds of jobs to O'Neill, Sr. In North Cambridge, he became known as "The Governor." He ran the North Cambridge Knights of Columbus baseball team, was president of St. John's Holy Name Society and — strict Irish rather than dreaming Irish — head of the St. Matthew's Temperance Society. Nobody in his house was allowed to wear anything that did not have a union label on it. No clothes were ever thrown out — there always was a society for the needy. And all the children in the household were brought up to regard the first Tuesday after the first Monday in November as the most important day of the year. When Tip O'Neill was fifteen, he was out ringing doorbells to pull people out of their houses to vote for Al Smith for president and Charley Cavanaugh for Massachusetts state representative. Tip O'Neill, in charge of half a precinct, reported at the end of the day that only four people in his area did not vote, and they were out of town.

Tip O'Neill hung out with a large crowd of kids at a place called Barry's Corner, and without anybody mentioning the fact, O'Neill was the leader. One of them, Red Fitzgerald, remembers his mother saying that Tip O'Neill was going to be a bishop. "He never pulled a dirty trick in his life, so how could he miss?" Red Says. O'Neill always had a way to keep the crowd around him, and also be useful to them. He had a job as a night watchman at a brickyard, and he fixed up the outdoor telephone pay station with a nail into the contact so that his nightly crowd of visitors had free phone service. It was in the middle of the Depression and nobody had the nickel for a call.

By 1931, O'Neill was out of high school and earning $21 a week as a truck driver for a brick company. November of that year was cold and work was slow. O'Neill took courses at Boston College High School at night, then entered Boston College. Neither the college nor the O'Neill family publicizes his scholastic achievements, although Boston College prints his picture on its literature and considers him as perhaps the school's most important alumnus. Meanwhile, if Boston College ever were to falter, Harvard would be more than happy to claim O'Neill as its own. The matter of academic brilliance was brought up over the summer in Washington, when Peter Rodino (who never went to college) and John Sirica (scholastic background at best vague) were busy showing the nation that honesty might be important.

"The night-school students are saving the country," Mary McGrory, the writer, was saying one day. "I don't think Sirica or Rodino spent a day in a regular undergraduate school. And I'm certain that Tip did not."

"Oh, no, he went to Boston College," she was told.

"Oh, yes, but thank God it wasn't serious," Mary McGrory said.

In his education O'Neill did himself and the country a favor by not following the traditional path of entering law school before going on to politics. During the early months of 1973, a Tip O'Neill, attorney at law, trained in the deviousness and tiny facts of the law, never would have come walking into Carl Albert's office saying that Richard Nixon was going to be impeached. That was too outrageous, and also too true, for a lawyer. Tip O'Neill, attorney, would have had instilled in him by professors the knowledge that he had not a scintilla of evidence upon which to base any judgment at all of Richard Nixon's status in February of 1973. O'Neill, not being a lawyer, did not know that he was using such terribly unsure methods as instinct, a little anger, and a boxcar full of common sense.

The fact that O'Neill is not a lawyer gives singularity to his success. It always has been extremely difficult for legitimate people to get into politics because the base of the American political system has been built on the needs of lawyers. They come out of offices that are one flight over a drugstore and have gold lettering on the windows that says "Attorney at Law," and they come into the political system because time and occupation make it the place to be. Lawyers are not lashed to a normal person's work schedule. Always, a lawyer can switch his schedule around so he may attend a city council meeting at one-thirty on Thursday afternoon. Also, as the nation grew and started its sprawl at the turn of the century, the lawyers then in command drew up codes so intricate, so tangled that no citizen could ever do business with a government agency of any size, from town to federal, without the service of a lawyer. Particularly a lawyer involved in politics. Many of the rules and regulations adopted throughout the country, most still in effect today, carried with them the unwritten admonishment, "Bring Extra Money!" This, in envelopes, for sliding under the table. Corruption to benefit lawyers was built into the government structure as if it were notarized. Today in politics, at the place where most men must start, it seems to be almost solely a place for lawyers. Judges appoint referees, lawyers, for mock-auctions of foreclosed properties. The judges appoint lawyers known in the business, and politics is the business of judges. The items spiral upward to a point where you have foreclosure proceedings on multi-million-dollar mortgages and the judge appoints a referee, a monitor, again a clubhouse lawyer who receives as high as $30,000 on a million-dollar matter; receives the $30,000 for doing approximately nothing. How much of this does the lawyer keep for himself and how much does he hand back to the judge? That depends upon the bargaining ability of both. If they were to strike a poor deal, a quarrelsome deal, somebody might hear of it and a district attorney would consider the subject a prime opportunity for career advancement. Other matters between lawyer and judge can be settled in ways that almost can be traced; the judge has a son and daughter who attend expensive colleges, all bills paid from a sort of scholarship set up by a lawyer.

Because there is money to be made from the system, lawyers get into politics as a business necessity. The reasoning is that lawyers are necessary in government because government makes and deals with laws, and lawyers are best equipped for this. But laws are things to be understood and obeyed by everybody, so why should the making of laws be left to a small inbred system? The major reason for the presence of so many lawyers in government is, of course, the economics. Less than 5 percent of the lawyers in the nation ever stand on their feet in a courtroom. That is too unsure a life. A public payroll, however, is very sure. Representing a contractor who does business with government agencies — where the lawyer knows many people through his political life — also can be considered a certainty. And then the financial structure of public life makes officeholding a dream for a lawyer. Most local and state and many federal elective posts allow a person to practice law on the side. Senator Jacob Javits has a law firm on Park Avenue in New York City. State Representative Michael LoPresti has a law practice in Boston. The rewards produced by the situation cannot be counted. Therefore, at the start of a career, it bothers not a politician to have to live in the state capital for four or five months a year, at a salary of perhaps less than $15,000, because his law office in his home district is producing a living for him. But for a college teacher with ideas, or a steamfitter with ideas, it is financially impossible to serve in a state legislature. Some think or dream or even try. Always the result is the arithmetic of family bills makes politics impossible.

Left mainly to lawyers, then, the pursuit among most politicians on a local level is for the great prize: a judgeship. Judges receive excellent money, serve lengthy terms, and have short working hours and long vacations. In New York, higher courts pay up to $49,000 for terms of fourteen years. Foraging rights appear to be limitless. The scramble for a judicial vacancy becomes so intense that the entire political structure of a county can be frozen while councilmen and assemblymen and leaders push and swirl and bargain — often openly passing money about — for the judgeship.

Tip O'Neill represents the ones who came another way. If you see the system work on a local basis, you wonder how anybody worthwhile ever lasts through it and gets anyplace. But for O'Neill, there was no way he could not be a lifetime politician. Clearly, the viral containers in his genes held, who knows, a couple of thousand years of the ability to control, to calm others, to decide without being abrasive, to be affable while the insides boil. For good politicians, real politicians, are not created in law school or in bank vaults. They are born, as their fathers were born, and the father of the father before them, and then back through the ages, with this viral container of public life in the genes. Just as the ability to play a piano in concert or to write a lasting novel is present at birth.

As a senior at Boston College he ran for Cambridge City Council. His father did virtually nothing to help him, and he lost the election by a hundred and fifty votes. The arithmetic still is fresh. "I got four thousand votes," he says quickly, "and thirteen hundred of them were from North Cambridge. I should have gotten eighteen hundred votes there. That's if I pulled what I should have in wards seven, eight, nine, ten and eleven. What happened? My father said to me at the end of the election, 'You know, you never asked me for help.' The woman across the street said the same thing to me on election day. Her name was Mrs. Elizabeth O'Brien. She was an elocution teacher. She called over to me in the morning, 'Good luck, Thomas, I'm going to vote for you even though you didn't ask me.' I told her I'd known her all my life. 'Mrs. O'Brien, I used to run to the store for you. I didn't think I had to ask you.' And she said to me, 'Tom, people always like to be asked.' Well, you could of punched me right in the nose and I wouldn't of felt it."

The next time he ran he was working in a small insurance brokerage and real-estate office in Harvard Square. The insurance business can serve the same purpose as a law degree to a politician, but he never did very much with it. In the election this time, there was a candidate named Tierney who had to be beaten for a seat in the state legislature. A few days before the election, an old pro named Foley said to O'Neill, "You've done well for a beginner. I don't want you to feel bad when you lose." O'Neill began to come continually late to street-corner rallies. He was too busy working the side streets and asking housewives to vote for him.

On election night, Tierney took a hotel room, had a few drinks, then slept for an hour. He showered and changed his clothes in order to look fresh and vibrant when acknowledging the cheers later on. Tierney came to his headquarters and, whistling softly, asked to see the results from his prime area, Ward 11, Precinct 3. Eleven-three contained St. John's School, its rectory and convent. Tip O'Neill had worked the area so thoroughly he owned it. The slip of paper for 11-3 was handed to Tierney. Tierney's soft whistle stopped, as did his heart. The results from 11-3 showed O'Neill with 712 votes and Tierney with 163. Rested, showered, Tierney went out in search of a pulmotor. And in his own headquarters, a rumpled, sweaty, flushed Tip O'Neill let out the first of what were to become a lifetime of election-night laughs.

Some years later, 11-3 was given a thorough campaigning by Congressional candidate John F. Kennedy. The area is changing now, with college students moving into houses that have been cut into small apartments; but if you walk into the kitchen of a house where lifelong residents live, the woman will point to a chair at the kitchen table and tell you, "He came in here and he sat right there. God rest his soul."

One day after the 1962 Congressional elections, Jack Kennedy saw O'Neill in the White House, and he said, "Say, Tip, how did you do in 11-3?"

"You know, only thirty-four people voted against me," O'Neill said.

"And I'm sure you have the names and addresses of every one of them," Kennedy said.

In 1935 O'Neill was almost twenty-three when he won this first election. Also in that election, up in another section of Cambridge called Greasy Village, Leo Edward Diehl, twenty-two, won a seat in the legislature. He won as much by his powers of observation as anything else. One morning, at the start of the campaign, Leo was out in the streets in time to see one Father John Geoghegan driving a woman named Peggy Dolan in the general direction of Peggy Dolan's job in Boston. You would have had to cut off Leo Diehl's head to make him forget this.

Some mornings later, Leo Diehl was on the same street at the same time and here was Father Geoghegan again driving Peggy Dolan to work. Leo grunted.

It then happened that in the core of the campaign, Leo Diehl heard that Father Geoghegan was going door to door on behalf of Leo's opponent, a man named Hillis. When this news was brought to Leo Diehl, the candidate showed no outrage. He simply asked for somebody to give him a lift. As the car pulled away, everybody on the sidewalk was surprised at the calmness with which Leo received the news, very bad news for his campaign because in Cambridge a priest's word had power second only to money.

The friend driving Leo Diehl said to him. "Where are we going?"

"I want to drop by and say hello to Peggy Dolan."

Peggy Dolan was shocked by Leo Diehl's accusations. "I do not go out with Father Geoghegan! I just let him drive me to work.

"Besides," she said, "Father Geoghegan goes steady with Theresa MacNamara."

Theresa MacNamara was a local dance instructress who had danced the parish to death. Leo immediately had his friend drive over to Theresa MacNamara's dance studio.

"We do not!" Theresa MacNamara squalled. "All we do is the Texas Tommy together."

Leo Diehl persisted. Soon, in tears, Theresa MacNamara said: "He calls me Pussy Cat."

Later that night, grunting, grimacing, Leo Diehl pulled himself up the rectory steps and rang the doorbell. When Father Geoghegan appeared, Leo Diehl said, "I just wanted your permission for Theresa MacNamara to come around with me tonight and tell all the people that she's your best girl and that she wants them all to vote for me."

Father Geoghegan started to faint. He pulled himself together long enough to agree that he would make the rounds on behalf of Leo Diehl himself.

"Make sure you do," Leo said. "By the way, I don't know what's the matter with you. I'd rather jump on top of Peggy Dolan than Theresa MacNamara any day."

In January of 1936, O'Neill and Diehl entered the State House for the first time. It was the beginning of a relationship which is closer today than it ever was. And it also was the true beginning of a political career for Tip O'Neill.

There is in this country no place that could even be suggested as being anywhere near the Massachusetts State House for bone politics. Throughout the nation, the complaint with state legislatures is that they are part-time bodies. Not even that in many places. New York, supposedly so efficient, has a state legislature which meets in January and averages three days a week until the late spring. After which it is regarded as a criminal offense for the legislature not to be recessed well in advance of the closing days of the school year, thus giving legislators time to open summer houses, pack their kids' clothes for camp, and plan vacation trips. In Massachusetts, the legislators prefer to sit forever. They usually have to be driven out of the building, practically at gunpoint. If a Massachusetts legislator is removed from his game, his sport, his very life, then all that is left for him to do is return home to his wife and family, and in Massachusetts anybody can have a family but the true goal of life is to be a politician; or, true term, a Pol. It is not uncommon for the Massachusetts Pols to sit in the state house throughout the summer, arguing, spreading rumors, using the phones, and — true glory — plotting against each other.

But in this they are so right. For who would leave a building, and what possible reason could he give, where the life in its halls is dedicated to the memory of the actions of such as former governor — among other things — James Michael Curley? Ask anybody in Boston about Curley and they will grope for a place to begin; there is so much to tell. Well, in 1933 new President Franklin D. Roosevelt offered Curley the post of United States Ambassador to Poland. From the state house there came a great cry, "He'll pave the Polish Corridor." And from James Michael Curley himself, in a face-to-face meeting with Roosevelt, there came, "If Poland is such a great place, why don't you resign and go there yourself?"

THE COURTS

Chapter Six

Character, personality, and style help to shape the judiciary at all levels. A true picture of the judicial process would not be complete without a personality profile of the actors that are involved, including judges, prosecuting attorneys, lawyers for the defense, plaintiffs and defendants, and, in some cases, jurors. At the trial level the drama of the courtroom is shaped by all of the personalities that are involved. The full-fledged and celebrated criminal trial is, however, a rarity, and personality usually affects the judicial process outside of public view.

The character of judges inevitably has a profound effect on the judicial process. At the trial court level their personalities determine the way in which they run their courts. At the appellate level, and particularly on the Supreme Court, their personalities and styles determine the effect they will have on colleagues. The character of judges has been molded long before they reach the bench. Certainly it would be profitable to apply James Barber's character classification of presidents to judges. An active-positive judge would deal with cases quite differently than would an active-negative judge. The value system of the former would be better developed and more likely to affect opinions without at the same time being rigid. An active-negative judge would be opportunistic on the bench, and particularly below the Supreme Court, would always be keeping an eye out for the possibility of higher judicial or political office. The character of some judges will cause them to seek the emulation of colleagues, and others will exhibit a strongly independent and iconoclastic streak. Some judges will attempt to control everything that goes on in their courts and will seek rights of defendants who they feel deserve a break. The character of every courtroom will reflect the personality and style of the presiding judge.

The Supreme Court is unique, not only because its decisions are far-reaching, but also because it is affected more by group dynamics among the justices than other courts are. Coalitions are formed, and pressures are used to change minds. The effectiveness of the chief justice and the influence of other justices largely depends on their personalities. A strong and persuasive personality can often change colleagues' minds. The chief justice is potentially an important leader. He presides over the weekly, secret conferences of the justices, gives his opinion first, and votes last. When he votes with the majority he determines which majority justice will write the opinion. A forceful chief justice can bring unity to a divided Court, and in some cases bring about unanimity on politically crucial decisions, such as the desegregation decision in *Brown* v. *Board of Education,* decided in 1954. At that time, Chief Justice Earl Warren, who assumed office in October 1953 after the Brown case had been taken up by the Court, used his considerable powers of persuasion and his highly personal leadership style to bring unanimity to a highly divided Court.[1]

Judicial decision making, at both Supreme Court and lower levels, is a far more fluid process than is commonly known. In commenting on Supreme Court decisions in the decade that ended with the *Brown* decision, one scholar concludes on the basis of reviewing the private papers of Supreme Court justices that "hardly any major decision in this decade was free of significant alteration of vote and language before announcement to the public."[2] Justices often change their minds regardless of their seeming ideological commitment. Group pressure has its effects on Supreme Court justices as on ordinary human beings. The "Freshman effect" causes instability in voting patterns among new justices to the Supreme Court.[3] Freshman justices may follow rather than lead their colleagues during their initial period of assimilation onto the Court, although this certainly was not true of Chief Justice Earl Warren, who was a pivotal justice from the time he was appointed in 1953.

Most Supreme Court justices have had little or no prior judicial experience before joining the Court and almost without exception those justices ranked as great or near-great have been more "political" than "judicial" in their styles.[4] Many of the most effective justices from John Marshall to Earl Warren held elected or appointed political offices, and often were highly partisan politicians. This political experience helped to shape their style of operation once on the Court. The Court was viewed as a political arena, in which pressure and persuasion could be used to change the minds of colleagues on cases that had far-reaching political ramifications.

[1]See S. Sidney Ulmer, "Earl Warren and the Brown Decision," *Journal of Politics* 33 (1971):689–702.

[2]J. Woodford Howard, Jr., "On the Fluidity of Judicial Choice," *The American Political Science Review* 52 (March 1968):43–56, at p. 44.

[3]Ibid., p. 45.

[4]An interesting rating of Supreme Court justices by law school deans and professors of law, history, and political science, undertaken in 1970, may be found in Henry J. Abraham, *Justices and Presidents* (New York: Oxford University Press, 1974), pp. 289–90. Holmes and Cardozo were notable exceptions to the usual lack of prior judicial experience among justices ranked as great.

Although the Supreme Court is somewhat more cloistered than the other branches of the government, the justices do not remain in isolation from each other or from Congress, the president, and administrative officials. Conflicts between the Court and other branches is often smoothed through personal contacts. While the New Deal Court was turning down much of Roosevelt's New Deal legislation, Justice Harlan F. Stone, at an informal party, gave Frances Perkins, FDR's secretary of labor, the idea to use the taxing and spending authority of Article I to support the Social Security Act.[5] The Court is not supposed to give advisory opinions, but nothing prevents a justice from informally communicating his ideas to the president or a member of his administration. Justice Felix Frankfurter remained a close personal friend of Franklin Roosevelt after he was appointed to the Court, and Abe Fortas was a constant political adviser to President Lyndon B. Johnson. Hugo Black, who wrote the majority opinion in the 1952 *Steel Seizure* case, which held that President Truman did not have independent constitutional authority to seize the steel mills, invited President Truman to dinner to help keep the president and the Court on good terms with each other. Justice William O. Douglas was present, and he described the incident in his autobiography as follows:

> Hugo loved company and long conversations. His spacious garden in his exquisite Alexandria home was ideal for that purpose during spring and summer. He loved to entertain there; and when, during the Korean War, the Court held on June 2, 1952, that Truman's seizure of the steel mills was unconstitutional, Hugo asked me what I thought of his idea of inviting Truman to his home for an evening after the decision came down. I thought it a capital idea. So in two weeks Hugo extended the invitation and Truman accepted. It was stag dinner, and only Truman and members of the Court were present. Truman was gracious though a bit testy at the beginning of the evening. But after the bourbon and canapes were passed, he turned to Hugo and said, "Hugo, I don't much care for your law, but, by golly, this bourbon is good." The evening was a great step forward in human relations, and to Hugo Black, good human relations were the secret of successful government.[6]

As this anecdote has shown, the personalities and styles of the justices affect external as well as internal relationships.

[5]Frances Perkins, *The Roosevelt I Knew* (New York: Viking, 1946), p. 286.
[6]William O. Douglas, *Go East Young Man* (New York: Random House, 1974), p. 450.

N OWHERE IN GOVERNMENT is the impact of character and personality more important than on the Supreme Court. Each week while the Court is in session, the justices meet secretly in conference to deliberate their decisions on cases involving some of the most important issues that confront our government, such as discrimination, freedom of speech and press, the death penalty, the busing of school children, executive privilege, the separation of church and state, and abortion. The decisions of the Court take precedence over those of the president, the Congress, and the state legislatures, and the actions of the Court are unreviewable.

The scales of justice are supposed to be balanced through a rational, deliberative process that carefully and objectively ascertains the facts of individual cases and applies the law. However, the law is not readily defined objectively but requires interpretation to give it meaning. The process of judicial interpretation necessarily involves a highly subjective element. It is the subjectivity of the law that permits and even encourages judges to apply their own values and prejudices in making decisions. And, on the Supreme Court, where the justices must work in close contact with their colleagues, interpersonal relationships among "The Brethren" may influence the outcome of a case as much as the ideological orientation of the justices.

The private world of the Supreme Court, like that of the other branches of the government, is characterized by maneuvering among the justices to gain internal power and status. The highly personal and political dimension of Supreme Court decision making has generally been overlooked in the study of constitutional law. The following selection gives a behind-the-scenes view of the role of personalities in the historic Supreme Court decision that held that women have a constitutional right to obtain abortions.

27 Bob Woodward and Scott Armstrong
THE BRETHREN AND
THE ABORTION DECISION

Douglas had long wanted the Court to face the abortion issue head on. The laws in effect in most states, prohibiting or severely restricting the availability of abortions, were infringements of a woman's personal liberty. The broad constitutional guarantee of "liberty," he felt, included the right of a woman to control her body.

Douglas realized, however, that a majority of his colleagues were not likely to give such a sweeping reading to the Constitution on this increasingly volatile issue. He knew also that the two cases now before the Court — challenging restrictive abortion laws in Georgia and Texas (*Doe* v. *Bolton* and *Roe* v. *Wade*) — did not signal any sudden willingness on the part of the Court to grapple with the broad question of abortions. They had been taken only to determine whether to expand a series of recent rulings limiting the intervention of federal courts in state court proceedings. Could women and doctors who felt that state prosecutions for abortions violated their constitutional rights, go into federal courts to stop the state? And could they go directly into federal courts even before going through all possible appeals in the state court system? Douglas knew the Chief wanted to say no to both these jurisdiction questions. He knew the Chief hoped to use these two cases to reduce the number of federal court cases brought by activist attorneys. The two abortion cases were not to be argued primarily about abortion rights, but about jurisdiction. Douglas was doubly discouraged, believing that his side was also going to lose on the jurisdiction issue.

These are difficult cases, the Chief said. No one could really tell how they would come out until the final drafting was done. . . .

Brennan and Marshall counted the vote five to two — Douglas, Brennan, Marshall, Stewart, and Blackmun for striking the laws; the chief and White dissenting.

Douglas, however, thought there were only four votes to strike the laws. Blackmun's vote was far from certain. He could not be counted on to split with the Chief on such an important issue.

For his part, Blackmun was for some kind of limited ruling against portions of the laws, but he had not decided what to do. . . .

. . . The puzzle was Blackmun.

The Chief's assignment sheet circulated the following afternoon. Each case was listed on the left side in order of the oral argument, the name of the Justice assigned to write each decision on the right.

It took Douglas several moments to grasp the pattern of the assignments, and then he was flabbergasted. [Flouting Court procedure] the Chief had assigned four cases in which Douglas was sure the chief was not a member of the majority. These included the two abortion cases, which the Chief had assigned to Blackmun. He could barely control his rage as he ran down the list. Was there some mistake? He asked a clerk to check his notes from the conference. Douglas kept a docket book in which he recorded his tabulation of the votes. It was as he suspected. . . .

Never, in Douglas's thirty-three years on the court, had any chief justice tried to assign from the minority in such fashion. For two terms now there had been incidents when the Chief had pleaded ignorance, had claimed he hadn't voted, had changed his vote. Until now they had been isolated instances.

On Saturday, December 18, Douglas drafted a scathing memo to Burger, with copies to the other justices. He, not the Chief, should have assigned the opinions in four of the cases. And, Douglas added, he would assign the opinions as he saw fit.

The Chief's response was back in a day. He conceded error in two of the cases, but insisted that the voting in the two abortion cases was too complicated. "There were . . . literally not enough columns to mark up an accurate reflection of the voting," Burger wrote. "I therefore marked down no votes and said this was a case that would have to stand or fall on the writing, when it was done.

"This is still my view of how to handle these two sensitive cases, which, I might add, are quite probable candidates for reargument."

Douglas ascribed to Burger the most blatant political motives. Nixon favored restrictive abortion laws. Faced with the possibility that the Court might strike abortion laws down in a presidential-election year, the Chief wanted to stall the opinion, Douglas concluded.

Blackmun was by far the slowest writer on the Court. The year was nearly half over and he had yet to produce a first circulation in a simple business case that had been argued the first week. . . . It was the kind of case in which Douglas produced drafts within one week of conference. But in the abortion cases, Douglas had a deeper worry. The Chief was trying to manipulate the outcome.

Blackmun might circulate a draft striking portions of the restrictive abortion laws. But as a judicial craftsman, his work was crude. A poor draft would be likely to scare off Stewart, who was already queasy, and leave only four votes. Or if Blackmun himself were to desert the position — a distinct possibility — precious time would be lost. Either defection would leave only a four-man majority. It would be difficult to argue that such a major decision should be handed down on a four-to-three vote. There would be increasing pressure to put the cases over for the sort of case that Nixon had in mind when he chose Powell and Rehnquist.

Blackmun was both pleased and frightened by the assignment. It was a no-win proposition. No matter what he wrote, the opinion would be controversial. Abortion was too emotional, the split in society too great. Either way, he would be hated and vilified.

But from Blackmun's point of view, the Chief had had little choice but to select him. Burger could not afford to take on such a controversial case himself, particularly from the minority. Douglas was the Court's mischievous liberal, the rebel, and couldn't be the author. Any abortion opinion Douglas wrote would be widely questioned outside the Court, and his extreme views might split rather than unify the existing majority. Lastly, Blackmun had noticed a deterioration in the quality of Douglas's opinions; they had become increasingly superficial.

Brennan was certainly as firm a vote for striking down the state abortion laws as there was on the Court. But Brennan was the Court's only Catholic. As such, Blackmun reasoned, he could not be expected to be willing to take the heat from Catholic antiabortion groups. Marshall could not be the author for similar reasons: an opinion by the Court's only black could be unfairly perceived as specifically designed for blacks. That left only Stewart. Blackmun believed that Stewart would certainly relish the assignment, but he clearly had trouble going very far.

Blackmun was convinced that he alone had the medical background and sufficient patience to sift through the voluminous record for the scientific data on which to base a decision. He was deeply disturbed by Douglas's assumption that the Chief had some malicious intent in assigning the abortion cases to him. He was *not* a Minnesota Twin.

True, Blackmun had known the Chief since they were small children and had gone to Sunday school together. They had lived four or five blocks apart in the blue-collar Daytons Bluff section of St. Paul. Neither family had much money during the Depression. The two boys had kept in touch until Blackmun went to a technical high school.

Blackmun's seven years at Harvard, however, put the two men worlds apart. Burger had finished local college and night law school in six years and was already practicing law when Blackmun came back to clerk for a judge on the court of Appeals. Blackmun was best man at Burger's wedding, but the two drifted apart again as they established very different law practices.

Blackmun tried to tell his story every chance he got. His hands in his pockets, jingling change uncomfortably, he would explain how he had practiced in Minneapolis, where large law firms concentrated on serving major American corporations. Burger had practiced in St. Paul, across the river, in the political, wheeler-dealer atmosphere of a state capital.

"A Minneapolis firm," Blackmun would say, "will never practice in St. Paul or vice versa." Left unsaid was the disdain so obvious in the Minneapolis legal community for St. Paul lawyers.

But Blackmun was a hesitant and reserved storyteller, and he was never sure that the others got the message. Douglas, however, should have realized by now that Harry Blackmun was no Warren Burger twin.

Blackmun had long thought Burger an uncontrollable, blustery braggart. Now, once again in close contact with him, he was at once put off and amused by the Chief's exaggerated pomposity, his callous disregard for the feelings of his colleagues, his self-aggrandizing style. "He's been doing that since he was four," he once told Stewart.

Blackmun was just as aware as Douglas was of the Chief's attempts to use his position to manipulate the Court. Douglas was correct to despise that sort of thing. But this time, Blackmun felt, Douglas was wrong. When he arrived at Court, Blackmun had assumed the Chief's job as scrivener for the conference. Burger had finally given up trying to keep track of all the votes and positions taken in conference, and had asked Blackmun to keep notes and stay behind to brief the Clerk of the Court. Even then the Chief sometimes misstated the results. Blackmun would deftly field the Chief's hesitations, filling in when he faltered. When Burger misinformed the Clerk of the Court, Blackmun's cough would cue him.

"Do you recall what happened there, Harry?" the Chief would then say. "My notes seem to be a bit sporadic."

Blackmun would fill in the correct information as if Burger had initiated the request.

Part of the problem was that the Chief spread himself too thin. He accepted too many social, speaking, and ceremonial engagements, and exhibited too little affection for the monastic, scholarly side of the Court's life. As a result, Burger was often unprepared for orals or conference. Too often, he had to wait and listen in order to figure out which issues were crucial to the outcome. His grasp of the cases came from the summaries, usually a page or less, of the cert. memos his clerks prepared. The Chief rarely read the briefs or the record before oral argument.

The problem was compounded by Burger's willingness to change his position in conference, or his unwillingness to commit himself before he had figured out which side had a majority. Then, joining the majority, he could control the assignment. Burger had strained his relationship with everyone at the table to the breaking point. It was as offensive to Blackmun as it was to the others. But one had to understand the Chief. For all his faults, here was a self-made man who had come up the ladder rung by rung. Blackmun did not begrudge him his attempts at leadership.

The abortion assignment really amounted to nothing more than a request that Blackmun take first crack at organizing the issues. It was one of those times when the conference had floundered, when the briefs and oral arguments had been inadequate, when the seemingly decisive issue in the case, jurisdiction, had evaporated. The Court had been left holding the bull by the tail.

Blackmun was not so naïve as to think that the Chief had given him the abortion cases with the intention of having him find a broad constitutional right to abortion. But he was distressed by Douglas's implicit suggestion that he was unfit for the assignment or was somehow involved in a deception.

Blackmun also knew that he, after all, had a unique appreciation of the problems and strengths of the medical profession. At Mayo, he had watched as Doctors Edward C. Kendall and Philip S. Hench won the Nobel Prize for research in arthritis. He rejoiced with other doctors after their first successful heart-bypass operation, then suffered with them after they lost their next four patients. He sat up late nights with the surgical staff to review hospital deaths in biweekly meetings, and recalled them in detail. He grew to respect what dedicated physicians could accomplish. These had been terribly exciting years for Blackmun. He called them the best ten years of his life.

If a state licensed a physician to practice medicine, it was entrusting him with the right to make medical decisions. State laws restricting abortions interfered with those medical judgments. Physicians were always somewhat unsure about the possible legal ramifications of their judgments. To completely restrict an operation like abortion, normally no more dangerous than minor surgery, or to permit it only with the approval of a hospital committee or the concurrence of other doctors, was a needless infringement of the discretion of the medical profession.

Blackmun would do anything he could to reduce the anxiety of his colleagues except to spurn the assignment. The case was not so much a legal task as an opportunity for the Court to ratify the best possible medical opinion. He would take the first crack at the abortion case. At the least, he could prepare a memo to clarify the issues.

As was his custom, Douglas rushed through a first draft on the cases five days after conference. He decided not to circulate it, but to sit back and wait for Blackmun. He was still bitter toward Burger, whom he had taken to calling "this Chief," reserving "The Chief" as an accolade fitting only for retired Chief Justice Earl Warren. But Douglas broke his usual rule against lobbying and paid a visit to Blackmun. Though he would have much preferred that Brennan write the draft, he told Blackmun, "Harry, I would have assigned the opinion to you anyway."

Reassured, Blackmun withdrew to his regular hideaway, the justices' second-floor library, where he worked through the winter and spring, initially without even a law clerk to help with research.

Brennan, too, had little choice but to wait for Blackmun's draft. But in the interval, he spotted a case that he felt might help Blackmun develop a constitutional grounding for a right to abortion. Brennan was writing a majority opinion overturning birth-control activist Bill Baird's conviction for distributing birth-control devices without a license (*Eisenstadt* v. *Baird*). He wanted to use the case to extend to individuals the right to privacy that was given to married couples by the 1965 Connecticut birth-control case.

Brennan was aware that he was unlikely to get agreement on such a sweeping extension. He circulated his opinion with a carefully worded paragraph at the end. "If the right to privacy means anything, it is the right of the individual, married or single, to be free from unwarranted governmental intrusion into matters so fundamentally affecting a person as the decision whether to bear or beget a child."

That case dealt only with contraception — the decision to "beget" a child. He included the reference to the decision to "bear" a child with the abortion case in mind. Brennan hoped the language would help establish a constitutional basis, under the right to privacy, for a woman's right to abortion.

Since the last paragraph was not the basis for the decision, Stewart could join it without renouncing his dissent in the 1965 case. Brennan got Stewart's vote.

But Blackmun was holding back. The Chief was lobbying Blackmun not to join Brennan's draft. Brennan's clerks urged their boss to lobby Blackmun.

Brennan refused. Blackmun reminded him, he said, of former Justice Charles E. Whittaker, who had been paralyzed by indecisiveness. Whittaker's indecision had ended in a nervous breakdown and his resignation. Former Justice Felix Frankfurter had misunderstood Whittaker's indecision and had spent hours lobbying him. Instead of influencing him, Frankfurter had drawn Whittaker's resentment. No, Brennan said, he would not lobby Blackmun.

Blackmun finally decided not to join Brennan's opinion, but simply to concur in the result. That worried Brennan. Without adopting some logic similar to that provided in the contraception case, Blackmun would have difficulty establishing a right to abortion on grounds of privacy.

With the official arrival of Powell and Rehnquist, the Chief scheduled a January conference to discuss which cases should be put over for reargument before the new nine-man Court. Burger suggested that cases with a four-to-three vote should be reargued. His list included the abortion cases, . . .

Blackmun spent his time — apart from oral argument, conferences, and a bare minimum of office routine — in the justices' library. Awesome quantities of medical, as well as legal, books were regularly carried in. But all indications pointed toward no circulation of a first draft until much later in the spring. . . .

Blackmun began each day by breakfasting with his clerks in the Court's public cafeteria, and clerks from the other chambers had a standing invitation to join them. Blackmun would often spot a clerk from another chamber eating alone and invite him over. He seemed, at first, the most open, unassuming, and gracious of the justices.

Breakfast-table conversation generally began with sports, usually baseball, and then moved on to the morning's headlines. There was an unspoken rule that any discussion of cases was off limits. Where other justices might openly debate cases with the clerks, Blackmun awkwardly side-stepped each attempt. The law in general was similarly out of bounds. Blackmun turned the most philosophical of discussions about law around to his own experience, or to the clerk's family, or the performance of a younger sibling in school.

The clerks in his own chambers saw a different side of Blackmun which betrayed more of the pressure that he felt. The stories were petty. An office window left open all night might set him off on a tirade. It was not the security that worried Blackmun, but the broken social contract — all clerks were supposed to close all windows each night. Number-two pencils, needle-sharp, neatly displayed in the pencil holder, need include only one number three or a cracked point to elicit a harsh word. If Blackmun wanted a document photocopied, and somehow the wrong one came back, he might simply fling it aside. An interruption, even for some important question, might be repulsed testily.

The mystery of the Blackmun personality deepened. His outbursts varied in intensity and usually passed quickly. "Impatient moods," his secretary called them. But they made life more difficult; they added an extra tension.

Yet none of his Court family — clerks, secretaries, or his messenger — judged Blackmun harshly. They all knew well enough the extraordinary pressures, real and imagined, that he worked under.

From his first day at the Court, Blackmun had felt unworthy, unqualified, unable to perform up to standard. He felt he could equal the Chief and Marshall, but not the others. He became increasingly withdrawn and professorial. He did not enjoy charting new paths for the law. He was still learning. The issues were too grave, the information too sparse. Each new question was barely answered, even tentatively, when two more questions appeared on the horizon. Blackmun knew that his colleagues were concerned about what they perceived as his indecisiveness. But what others saw as an inability to make decisions, he felt to be a deliberate withholding of final judgment until all the facts were in, all the arguments marshaled, analyzed, documented.

It was a horribly lonely task. Blackmun worked by himself, beginning with a long memo from one of his clerks, reading each of the major briefs, carefully digesting each of the major opinions that circulated, laboriously drafting his own opinions, checking each citation himself, refining his work through a dozen drafts to take into account each Justice's observations. He was unwilling, moreover, to debate the basic issues in a case, even in chambers with his own clerks. He preferred that they write him memos.

Wearing a gray or blue cardigan sweater, Blackmun hid away in the recesses of the justices' library, and his office had instructions not to disturb him there. The phone did not ring there, and not even the Chief violated his solitude. Working at a long mahogany table lined on the opposite edge with a double row of books, Blackmun took meticulous notes. He spent most of his time sorting facts and fitting them to the law in a desperate attempt to discover inevitable conclusions. He tried to reduce his risks by mastering every detail, as if the case were some huge math problem. Blackmun felt that if all the steps were taken, there could be only one answer.

These abortion cases were his greatest challenge since he came to the Court. Beyond the normal desire to produce an opinion that would win the respect of his peers in the legal community, Blackmun also wanted an opinion that the medical community would accept, one that would free physicians to exercise their professional judgment.

As general counsel at the Mayo Clinic, Blackmun had advised the staff on the legality of abortions the hospital had performed. Many of them would not have qualified under the Texas and Georgia laws now in question.

Blackmun plowed through both common law and the history of English and American law on the subject. He was surprised to find that abortion had been commonly accepted for thousands of years, and that only in the nineteenth century had it become a crime in the United States. At that time, abortion had been a very risky operation, often fatal. The criminal laws had been enacted largely to protect pregnant women.

The use of antiseptics and the availability of antibiotics now made abortion relatively safe, particularly in the first few months of pregnancy. The mortality rates of women undergoing early abortions were presently lower than the mortality rates for women with normal childbirths. That medical reality was central for Blackmun. It was itself a strong medical justification for permitting early abortions.

A decision to abort was one that Blackmun hoped he would never face in his own family. He presumed that his three daughters felt that early abortions should be allowed. He claimed to be unsure of his wife Dottie's position. But she told one of his clerks, who favored lifting the restrictions, that she was doing everything she could to encourage her husband in that direction. "You and I are working on the same thing," she said. "Me at home and you at work."

By mid-May, after five months of work, Blackmun was still laboring over his memorandum. Finally, he let one of his clerks look over a draft. As usual, he made it clear that he did not want any editing. The clerk was astonished. It was crudely written and poorly organized. It did not settle on any analytical framework, nor did it explain on what basis Blackmun had arrived at the apparent conclusion that women had a right to privacy, and thus a right to abortion. Blackmun had avoided extending the right of privacy, or stating that the right to abortion stemmed from that right. He seemed to be saying that a woman could get an abortion in the early period of pregnancy. The reason, however, was lost in a convoluted discussion of the "viability of the fetus," the point at which the fetus could live outside the womb. Blackmun had added the general notion that as the length of the pregnancy increased, the states' interest in regulating and prohibiting abortions also increased. But there was no real guidance from which conclusions could be drawn. Blackmun had simply asserted that the Texas law was vague and thus unconstitutional.

The clerk realized that the opinion could not settle any constitutional question. It did not assert, or even imply, that abortion restrictions in the early months of pregnancy were unconstitutional. The result of this opinion would be that restrictive laws, if properly defined by the states, could be constitutional.

The draft seemed to fly in the face of Blackmun's statements to his clerks. "We want to definitely solve this," he had told them. But he seemed to be avoiding a solution.

In the Georgia case, he had found that the law infringed on a doctor's professional judgment, his right to give advice to his patients. Blackmun proceeded from the doctor's point of view; a woman's right to seek and receive medical advice did not seem an issue.

Blackmun's clerk, who favored an opinion that would establish a woman's constitutional right to abortion, began the laborious task of trying to rehabilitate the draft. But Blackmun resisted any modification of his basic reasoning or his conclusions. He circulated the memo to all chambers with few changes.

Stewart was disturbed by the draft. Aside from its inelegant construction and language, it seemed to create a *new* affirmative constitutional right to abortion that was not rooted in any part of the Constitution. Stewart had been expecting a majority opinion. Blackmun's memo did not even have the tone of an opinion, merely of a tentative discussion.

Stewart decided to write his own concurrence, specifying that family-planning decisions, including early abortions, were among the rights encompassed by the Ninth Amendment, which says that all rights not specifically given to the federal or state governments are left to the people. Rather than identify the rights that women or doctors have, Stewart preferred to say that states could not properly interfere in individuals' decisions to have early abortions. He circulated his memo two weeks after Blackmun's but immediately joined Blackmun's original.

Douglas saw no shortage of problems with the Blackmun draft, but Blackmun had come a long way. At least it was a step in the right direction. Though Douglas was still holding on to his concurrence, he did not circulate it. Instead, he joined Blackmun.

At the time, the Court was considering an antitrust case against a utility company, the Otter Tail Power Company, which operated in Minnesota. Douglas saw an opportunity to flatter Blackmun. "Harry, you're not a Minnesota Twin with the Chief," he told him. "I am the real Minnesota Twin. . . . We were both born in Minnesota and you were not."

Blackmun appreciated the point.

"Furthermore, Harry, I belong to the Otter Tail County regulars. You can't belong, because you weren't born there."

Douglas regaled Blackmun with stories of his father's life as an itinerant preacher in Otter Tail County, and he praised Blackmun's abortion draft. It was one of the finest presentations of an issue he had ever seen, he said.

Blackmun was ecstatic. Douglas, the greatest living jurist, had freed him of the stigma of being Burger's double. Soon, Blackmun had five votes — his own and those of Douglas, Brennan, Marshall, and Stewart. It was one more than he needed; it would have been a majority even if Powell and Rehnquist had participated.

For White the term had its ups and downs like any other year at the Court. He had been a fierce competitor all his life. He loved to take control of a case, pick out the weaknesses in the other Justices' positions, and then watch them react to his own twists and turns as he pushed his own point of view. When he could not, which was often, he took his frustrations to the third-floor gym to play in the clerks' regular full-court basketball game.

Muscling out men thirty years his junior under the boards, White delighted in playing a more competitive game than they did. He dominated the games by alternating savage and effective drives to the basket with accurate two-hand push shots from twenty feet. White consistently pushed off the clerk trying to cover him, calling every conceivable foul against the hapless clerk, while bitching about every foul called against himself. He regularly took the impermissible third step before shooting. The game was serious business for White. Each man was on his own. Teamwork was valuable in order to win, not for its own sake.

One Friday afternoon White was out of position for a rebound, but he went up throwing a hip. A clerk pulled in the ball and White came crashing down off balance and injured his ankle.

The Justice came to the office on crutches the next Monday: He would be off the basketball court for the rest of the season. He asked the clerks to keep the reason for his injury secret. The clerks bought him a Fussball game, a modern version of the ancient game of skittles. It was competition, so White enjoyed it, but it lacked for him the thrill of a contact sport like basketball — or law.

On Friday, May 26, Byron White read a draft dissent to Blackmun's abortion decision that one of his clerks had prepared. He then remolded it to his liking. The structure of Blackmun's opinion was juvenile; striking the Texas law for vagueness was simply stupid. The law might have several defects, but vagueness was not among them. The law could not be more specific in delineating the circumstance when abortion was available — it was only to protect the life of the mother.

Blackmun was disturbed by White's attack, but whether it made sense or not, it showed him that he had more work to do. The more he studied and agonized over his own memo, the less pleased he was. He needed more information, more facts, more insight. What was the history of the proscription in the Hippocratic oath which forbade doctors from performing abortions? What was the medical state of the art of sustaining a fetus outside the womb? When did life really begin? When was a fetus fully viable? What were the positions of the American Medical Association, the American Psychiatric Association, the American Public Health Association?

These and dozens of other questions plagued Blackmun. His opinion needed to be stronger. It needed more votes, which could mean wider public acceptance. A nine-man court was essential to bring down such a controversial opinion. "I think we can get Powell," he told his clerks.

One Saturday toward the end of May, the Chief paid Blackmun a visit, leaving his armed chauffeur-bodyguard in the outer office. Blackmun's clerks waited anxiously for hours to find out what case the Chief was lobbying. The Chief finally left, but Blackmun also departed without a word to his clerks. The next week, the Chief shifted sides to provide the crucial fifth vote for Blackmun's majority in an antitrust case against professional baseball (*Flood* v. *Kuhn*).

The following Saturday, June 3, Blackmun drafted a memorandum withdrawing his abortion opinion. It was already late in the term, he wrote. Such a sensitive case required more research, more consideration. It would take him some time both to accommodate the suggestions of those in the majority, and to respond to the dissenters. Perhaps it would be best if the cases were reargued in the fall. He asked that all copies of his draft memo be returned.

Douglas was once again enraged. The end of the year always involved a crunch. Of course, there was tremendous pressure to put out major opinions without the time to fully refine them. That was the nature of their work. The pressure affected them all. It was typical that Blackmun could not make up his mind and let his opinion go. Douglas had heard that the Chief had been lobbying Blackmun. This time, Burger had gone too far. The opinion had five firm votes. It ought to come down. It was not like cases with only four votes that might change when Powell's and Rehnquist's votes were added. Douglas also did not want to give the Chief the summer to sway Blackmun.

Burger was taking the position that there were now five votes to put the case over to the next term — Blackmun, White, Powell, Rehnquist, and himself. Douglas couldn't believe it. Burger and White were in the minority; they should have no say in what the majority did. And Powell and Rehnquist had not taken part; obviously they could not vote on whether the case should be put over.

The looming confrontation worried Blackmun. There were no written rules on such questions, and Douglas's apparent willingness to push to a showdown would further inflame the issue. Finally, Blackmun turned to Brennan, who was sympathetic. Obviously the opinion could not come down if its author did not want it to come down. But Brennan also wanted it out as soon as possible.

Blackmun said he understood that Douglas did not trust him, but insisted that he was firm for striking down the abortion laws. The vote would go the same way the next year. They might even pick up Powell. That would make the result more acceptable to the public. He would be able to draft a better opinion over the summer.

Brennan was not so certain of Blackmun's firmness. At the same time, he did not want to alienate him. He agreed to tell Douglas that he, too, was going to vote to put the case over for reargument. He was fairly certain Marshall and Stewart would join. That would leave Douglas protesting alone.

Douglas was not pleased by the news of Brennan's defection. But the battle was not yet over. He dashed off a memo, rushed it to the secretaries for typing and to the printers for a first draft. This time, Douglas threatened to play his ace. If the conference insisted on putting the cases over for reargument, he would dissent from such an order, and he would publish the full text of his dissent. Douglas reiterated the protest he had made in December about the Chief's assigning the case to Blackmun, Burger's response and his subsequent intransigence. The senior member of the majority should have assigned the case, Douglas said, . . .

Douglas knew a fifth Nixon appointment was a real possibility on a Court with a seventy-four-year-old man with a pacemaker; with Marshall, who was chronically ill; and with Brennan, who occasionally threatened to quit. . . .

Borrowing a line from a speech he had given in September in Portland, Douglas then made it clear that, despite what he had said earlier, he did in fact view the Chief and Blackmun as Nixon's Minnesota Twins. "Russia once gave its Chief Justice two votes; but that was too strong even for the Russians. . . . "

"I dissent with the deepest regret that we are allowing the consensus of the Court to be frustrated."

Douglas refined his draft three times, circulated it, and left for Goose Prairie.

The Court erupted in debate over whether Douglas was bluffing or was really willing to publish the document. Though sympathetic to his views, Brennan, Marshall, and Stewart could not believe that Douglas would go through with it. No one in the history of the Court had published such a dissent. The Chief might be a scoundrel, but making public the Court's inner machinations was a form of treason. And the reference to the Russian Chief Justice with two votes was particularly rough. They pleaded with Douglas to reconsider. His dissent would undermine the Court's credibility, the principal source of its power. Its strength derived from the public belief that the Court was trustworthy, a nonpolitical deliberative body. Did he intend to undermine all that?

Douglas insisted. He would publish what he felt like publishing. And he would publish this if the request to put over the abortion decision was not withdrawn.

But, the others argued, what good would it do to drag their internal problems into public view?

It would have a sobering influence on Blackmun, Douglas retorted. It would make it harder for him to change his mind over the summer.

Brennan's impatience with Douglas turned to anger. Douglas had become an intellectually lazy, petulant, prodigal child. He was not providing leadership. Douglas was never around when he was needed. His departure for Goose Prairie was typical. He was not even, for that matter, pulling his share of the load, though he certainly contributed more than his share to the tension. The ultimate source of conflict was the Chief. But Douglas too was at fault.

Finally, Brennan gave up arguing.

Blackmun then took it up, pleading with Douglas to reconsider. He insisted that he was committed to his opinion. He would bring it down the same way the next term; more research would perhaps pick up another vote.

Douglas was unconvinced. He needed time to think it over. His clerks would remain instructed to publish the opinion if the cases were put over for reargument.

But Blackmun had made his point. Douglas finally decided that he couldn't publish. It would endanger next term's vote on the abortion cases.

No longer speaking to his own clerks, whom he blamed for slow mail delivery to Goose Prairie, Douglas called Brennan and told him to have his dissent held. A memo came around to the Justices from Douglas's chamber asking for all the copies back.

The conference agreed to put over the abortion cases, but they would not announce their decision until the final day of the term. . . .

Harry Blackmun returned to Rochester, Minnesota, for the summer of 1972, and immersed himself in research at the huge Mayo Clinic medical library. Rochester and the clinic were home to Blackmun, a safe harbor after a stormy term. He worked in a corner of the assistant librarian's office for two weeks without saying a word to anyone on the Mayo staff about the nature of his inquiry.

In his summer office in a Rochester highrise, Blackmun began to organize the research that would bolster his abortion opinion. He talked by phone nearly every day with one of his clerks who had agreed to stay in Washington for the summer. . . .

The clerk who was working on the opinion began to worry that one of the other clerks, strongly opposed to abortions, might try to change their boss's mind. He took no chances. Each night he carefully locked up the work he had been doing for Blackmun. At the end of the summer, he carefully sealed the latest draft in an envelope, put his initials across the tape, and had it locked in Blackmun's desk. Only Blackmun's personal secretary knew where it was.

Powell also made abortion his summer research project. As a young lawyer in Richmond in the 1930s, Powell had heard tales of girls who would "go away" to Switzerland and New York, where safe abortions were available. If someone were willing to pay for it, it was possible to have an abortion.

Powell understood how doctors viewed abortion. His father-in-law had been a leading obstetrician in Richmond, and his two brothers-in-law were obstetricians. Powell had heard all the horrifying stories of unsanitary butchers and coat-hanger abortions.

Nevertheless, Powell came quickly to the conclusion that the Constitution did not provide meaningful guidance. The right to privacy was tenuous; at best it was implied. If there was no way to find an answer in the Constitution, Powell felt he would just have to vote his "gut." He had been critical of justices for doing exactly that; but in abortion, there seemed no choice.

When he returned to Washington, he took one of his law clerks to lunch at the Monocle restaurant on Capitol Hill. The abortion laws, Powell confided, were "atrocious." His would be a strong and unshakable vote to strike them. He needed only a rationale for his vote.

In a recent lower court case, a federal judge had struck down the Connecticut abortion law. This opinion impressed Powell. The judge had said that moral positions on abortion "about which each side was so sure must remain a personal judgment, one that [people] may follow in their personal lives and seek to persuade others to follow, but a judgment they may not impose upon others by force of law." That was all the rationale Powell needed.

Brennan and Douglas worried that votes might have shifted since the previous spring. Blackmun remained a question mark, Stewart might defect, and they were not sure what Powell would do.

At conference on October 12, Blackmun made a long, eloquent, and strongly emotional case for striking down the laws. Stewart too seemed ready to join. But the big surprise was Powell. He made it six to three.

Immediately after conference, Douglas called Blackmun to tell him that his presentation had been the finest he had heard at conference in more than thirty years. He hoped the call would sustain Blackmun for the duration.

Before the end of October, Blackmun's new draft in the abortion case was circulated to the various chambers. . . .

The clerks in most chambers were surprised to see the justices, particularly Blackmun, so openly brokering their decision like a group of legislators. There was a certain reasonableness to the draft, some of them thought, but it derived more from medical and social policy than from constitutional law. There was something embarrassing and dishonest about this whole process. It left the Court claiming that the Constitution drew certain lines at trimesters and viability. The Court was going to make a medical policy and force it on the states. As a practical matter, it was not a bad solution. As a constitutional matter, it was absurd. The draft was referred to by some clerks as "Harry's abortion."

By early December, Blackmun's final draft had circulated. Stewart's and Douglas's concurrences were finished, and White's and Rehnquist's dissents were ready. There was still nothing from Burger. . . .

Stewart and Brennan thought he was stalling. The Chief was scheduled to swear in Richard Nixon for his second term as president on January 20. It would undoubtedly be embarrassing for Burger to stand there, swearing in the man who had appointed him, having just supported a sweeping and politically volatile opinion that repudiated that man's views.

At the Friday, January 19, conference, the Chief said that his schedule had been busy, and he still had not gotten to the abortion decision. Stewart figured that, having manipulated a delay until after the inaugural, Burger would acquiesce. The others wanted a Monday, January 22, announcement, three days later, and Burger said that he would have something.

Over the weekend, he wrote a three-paragraph concurrence. Ignoring the sweep of the opinion he was joining, Burger said that one law

(Texas) was being struck because it did not permit abortions in instances of rape or incest, and he implied that the other law was being struck because of the "complex" steps that required hospital board certification of an abortion. He did not believe that the opinion would have the "consequences" predicted by dissenters White and Rehnquist, and he was sure that states could still control abortions. "Plainly," he concluded, "the Court today rejects any claim that the Constitution requires abortion on demand."

The day of the scheduled abortion decision the Chief sat in his chambers reading the latest edition of *Time* magazine. "Last week *Time* learned that the Supreme Court has decided to strike down nearly every antiabortion law in the land," an article said. The abortion decision had been leaked.

Burger drafted an "Eyes Only" letter to the other justices. He wanted each justice to question his law clerks. The responsible person must be found and fired. Burger intended to call in the FBI to administer lie-detector tests if necessary.

Dutifully, Rehnquist brought up the matter with his clerks. It was harmless in this case, he said. But in a business case, a leak could affect the stock market and allow someone to make millions of dollars. None of Rehnquist's clerks knew anything about the leak, but they asked him if it were true that the Chief was thinking of lie-detector tests. "It is still up in the air," Rehnquist said. "But yes, the Chief is insisting."

Rehnquist's clerks were concerned. Such a witch hunt would be met with resistance. Certainly, some clerks would refuse to take such a test and would probably have to resign. The Chief is mercurial, Rehnquist explained. "The rest of us will prevail on him."

Brennan summoned his clerks and read them the Chief's letter. It was another example, he said, of the Chief usurping the authority each justice had over his own clerks. "No one will question my law clerks but me," Brennan said. Then in a softer voice, he added, "And I have no questions." The real outrage for Brennan was not the leak but the delay. If the Chief had not been intent on saving himself and Nixon some embarrassment on Inauguration Day, there probably would have been no damaging leak.

Marshall asked what his clerks knew about the incident. When he was assured that they knew nothing, he told them to forget it.

Douglas treated the letter as he had treated a request from the Chief the previous term that all clerks be instructed to wear coats in the hallways. He ignored it.

Powell was out of town, so one of his clerks opened the Chief's letter. The clerk had talked to the *Time* reporter, David Beckwith, trying to give him some guidance so he could write an intelligent story when the decision came down. But the delay in announcing the decision had apparently left *Time* with a scoop, if only for half a day.

The clerk called Powell and told him about the Chief's letter and his own terrible mistake in talking with Beckwith. He volunteered to resign.

That would not be necessary, Powell said. But a personal explanation would have to be given to the Chief.

Powell called Burger and explained that one of his clerks, a brilliant and talented young lawyer, was responsible. The clerk realized his mistake and had learned his lesson. The clerk went to see the Chief.

Burger was sympathetic. Reporters were dishonest and played tricks, he said. It was a lesson everyone had to learn.

Apparently never expecting to learn so much about the little deceptions of both reporters and sources, Burger pressed for all the details. It took nearly forty-five minutes to satisfy his curiosity.

The clerk concluded that Burger understood, that he was being a saint about the matter. Burger wanted a memo detailing exactly what happened. The clerk would not have to resign.

Later, the Chief met with top editors of *Time* in an off-the-record session. He labeled Beckwith's efforts to get inside information at the Court improper, the moral equivalent of wiretapping.

Blackmun suggested to his wife, Dottie, that she come to Court to hear case announcements on Monday, January 22. He did not tell her why. As Blackmun announced the decisions, Powell sent a note of encouragement to Blackmun's wife. Powell suspected they were about to witness a public outcry, the magnitude of which he and Blackmun had not seen in their short time on the Court.

"I'm very proud of the decision you made," Dottie later told her husband.

After the abortion decision was announced, Blackmun took congratulatory calls through most of the afternoon. But former President Lyndon Johnson died that same day, and the news of his death dominated the next morning's newspapers.

Blackmun was unhappy that the abortion decision did not get more attention. Many women, especially the poor and black, would not learn of their new rights. But the outcry quickly began, led by the Catholic Church. "How many millions of children prior to their birth will never live to see the light of day because of the shocking action of the majority of the United States Supreme Court today?" demanded New York's Terrence Cardinal Cooke.

John Joseph Cardinal Krol, of Philadelphia, the president of the National Conference of Catholic Bishops, said, "It is hard to think of any decision in the two hundred years of our history which has had more disastrous implications for our stability as a civilized society."

Thousands of letters poured into the Court. The guards had to set up a special sorting area in the basement with a huge box for each justice.

The most mail came to Blackmun, the decision's author, and to Brennan, the Court's only Catholic. Some letters compared the justices to the butchers of Dachau, child killers, immoral beasts, and Communists. A special ring of hell would be reserved for the justices. Whole classes from Catholic schools wrote to denounce the justices as murderers. "I really don't want to write this letter but my teacher made me," one child said.

Minnesota Lutherans zeroed in on Blackmun. New Jersey Catholics called for Brennan's excommunication. Southern Baptists and other groups sent over a thousand bitter letters to Hugo Black, who had died sixteen months earlier. Some letters and calls were death threats.

Blackmun went through the mail piece by piece. The sisters of Saint Mary's hospital, the backbone of the Mayo Clinic, wrote outraged letters week after week. He was tormented. The medical community and even his friends at Mayo were divided. Blackmun encountered picketing for the first time in his life when he gave a speech in Iowa. He understood the position of the antiabortion advocates, but he was deeply hurt by the personal attacks. He felt compelled to point out that there had been six other votes for the decision, besides his, that the justices had tried to enunciate a constitutional principle, not a moral one. Law and morality overlapped but were not congruent, he insisted. Moral training should come not from the court but from the church, the family, the schools.

The letters continued to pour in. Every time a clergyman mentioned the decision in his sermon, the letters trickled in for a month from members of the congregation. The attack gradually wore Blackmun down. At breakfast with his clerks, when the discussion turned to the decision, Blackmun picked up his water glass reflectively, turning it slightly on edge and staring into it in silence.

The criticism also drew Blackmun and Brennan closer. Blackmun wrote Brennan a warm thank you note: "I know it is tough for you, and I thank you for the manner in which you made your suggestions."

Brennan tried to cheer up Blackmun. Doing the right thing was not often easy, he said. The one thing in the world Brennan did not want known was his role in molding the opinion.[1]

Blackmun did not cheer up easily. The hysteria on each side of the

[1]When the clerks later put together bound volumes of the opinions Brennan had written that term, they included the abortion opinions, and on page 156 they wrote, "These cases are included with Justice Brennan's opinions for the October term 1972 because the opinions for the Court were substantially revised in response to suggestions made by Justice Brennan."

issue convinced him that any decision would have been unpopular. However, the deepest cut came when the state of Texas filed a petition for rehearing that compared Blackmun's conclusion, which held that a fetus was not a person, to the Court's infamous 1857 decision that said that Dred Scott, a slave, was not a citizen or person under the Constitution. Blackmun thought that comparing his opinion with the Court's darkest day of racism was terribly unfair. And, after all, it had been Stewart who had insisted on that part of the opinion.

Months later, Blackmun gave a speech at Emory Law School in Atlanta. He was chatting with students and faculty when a petite young woman with black curly hair ran up the steps to the stage. She squeezed through the group, threw her arms around Blackmun and burst into tears. "I'll never be able to thank you for what you have done. I'll say no more. Thank you."

The woman turned and ran from the room.

Blackmun was shaken. He suspected that the woman was probably someone who had been able to obtain an abortion after the Court's decision. He did not know that "Mary Doe," the woman who had filed one of the original suits in Texas under a pseudonym, had just embraced him.

T ECHNICALLY JUDGES ARE SUP- posed to apply the law to the facts in deciding cases and contro- versies. But subjectivity inevitably enters judicial decisions. The philosophical leanings of judges, which derive from their characters and personalities, often determine how they will interpret the law and view the facts. The labels "liber- al" and "conservative" are useful in helping to explain judicial decision- making, but labels often impose a simplistic framework that obscures the complexities of judicial interpretations. Illustrated in the following account of the dispute over the role of the Supreme Court between Ronald Reagan's Attor- ney General, Edwin Meese, and Su- preme Court Justice William J. Brennan, Jr., are the personal factors and political philosophies that shape individual per- spectives on the appropriate role of the judiciary.

28 Stuart Taylor, Jr.
MEESE V. BRENNAN: WHO'S RIGHT ABOUT THE CONSTITUTION?

An activist jurisprudence, one which anchors the Constitution only in the consciences of jurists, is a chameleon jurisprudence, changing color and form in each era.

The Constitution . . . is a mere thing of wax in the hands of the judiciary, which they may twist and shape into any form they please.

If the policy of the Government upon vital questions affecting the whole people is to be irrevocably fixed by decisions of the Supreme Court, the instant they are made . . . the people will have ceased to be their own rulers.

The Court . . . has improperly set itself up as . . . a super-legislature . . . reading into the Constitution words and implications which are not there, and which were never intended to be there. . . . We want a Supreme Court which will do justice under the Constitution — not over it.

Sounds like Ed Meese, doesn't it? Well, the first quotation is the attorney general's. But the second comes from Thomas Jefferson, the third from Abraham Lincoln, and the fourth from Franklin D. Roosevelt. When Meese assails government by judiciary, he is in good company.

Meese has denounced major Supreme Court rulings of the past 60 years and called for judges to look to "the original meaning of con-

From *The New Republic*, January 6 & 13, 1986. Reprinted by permission.

stitutional provisions" as "the only reliable guide for judgment." No attorney general in the past four decades has set out so deliberately to reduce the power of the judiciary or to screen the ideological credentials of new appointees.

Champions of liberal judicial activism have launched a ferocious counterattack. Justices William J. Brennan, Jr., and John Paul Stevens retorted with pointed critiques of Meese's so-called "jurisprudence of original intention." Brennan said it was "arrogance cloaked as humility" for anyone "to pretend that from our vantage we can gauge accurately the intent of the Framers on application of principle to specific, contemporary questions." The real animus of advocates of this "facile historicism" he said, is a "political" agenda hostile to the rights of minorities.

Meese is certainly vulnerable to this sort of attack. He seems less a constitutional philosopher than a constitutional window-shopper, seeking to dress up his conservative political agenda as a principled quest for truth. His notion that judges can answer the hard questions raised by the Constitution without being "tainted by ideological predilection," simply by plugging in the intent of the Framers, is at best simpleminded and at worst disingenuous. When the Framers' intentions *are* clear, but contrary to a result Meese wants, he ignores them. While calling for restraint in the exercise of judicial power — especially enforcement of civil liberties — he pushes to aggrandize executive power.

Along the way, he has said some revealing things. "You don't have many suspects who are innocent of a crime," he told *U.S. News & World Report.* "That's contradictory. If a person is innocent of a crime, then he is not a suspect." This from a man who was himself suspected of several federal crimes until a special prosecutor cleared him last year — a man who then billed the government $720,824.49 for his defense lawyers. (He later confessed to a "bad choice of words.")

Meese also assailed as "intellectually shaky" and "constitutionally suspect" the Court's sixty-year-old doctrine that most of the Bill of Rights, originally applicable only to the national government, was applied to the states by the 14th Amendment. Eminent Supreme Court justices criticized the doctrine too, but that was decades ago. When a Supreme Court ruling has "been affirmed and reaffirmed through a course of years," Lincoln said in 1857, "it then might be, perhaps would be, factious, nay even revolutionary, not to acquiesce in it as a precedent."

Nevertheless, the standard liberal retort to Meese is superficial. It caricatures his position as more extreme than it is. It ignores the long and honorable history of political attacks on judicial usurpation of power. Most important, its scorn for the "original intention" approach begs the question of where — if not from those who wrote and ratified the Constitution and its amendments — unelected judges get a mandate to override the will of the political majority by striking down democratically enacted laws.

For all his fumbling, Meese has spotlighted some of the real problems with the freewheeling judicial activism sometimes practiced by people like Brennan. Among these is a tendency to "find" in the Constitution rights (such as abortion rights) and social policies that can honestly be found neither in the language of the document, nor in the records left by those who wrote it, nor in any broad national consensus that has evolved since then. This is bad constitutional law even when you like the policies, as I sometimes do.

Meese deserves credit for bringing the deepest questions of constitutional law out of the law journals and into the newspapers. He surely has a political motive. But liberals who believe in democracy (anybody out there after two Reagan landslides?) should welcome the debate.

Too often liberals have taken the elitist view that ordinary voters are the natural enemies of civil liberties, and that only judges can be trusted to protect them. It is a shortsighted approach. As Justice Robert Jackson said four decades ago, "Any court which undertakes by its legal processes to enforce civil liberties needs the support of an enlightened and vigorous public opinion." Today most people confine their thinking about the Constitution to whether they like the policies the Court has decreed. The larger question of when courts should displace the ordinary policy-making role of elected officials gets little attention from anyone but law professors. Meese has begun to remind the public that in enforcing constitutional rights, federal judges are by definition restraining majority rule.

Within proper limits this is a noble function. Those who wrote the Constitution and its amendments saw them as bulwarks against oppression of minorities by a tyrannical majority. They specified certain fundamental rights shared by all Americans. They created special protections for minorities, especially blacks. They laid down these principles in majestic generalities meant to have continuing relevance in a changing society — freedom of speech, equal protection of the laws, due process of law. The federal courts — precisely because they are not answerable to the voters — are the logical bodies to enforce these rights against the majority.

Here, however, lies a difficult dilemma to which no wholly satisfactory solution exists. The Constitution being what the judges say it is, how can the judges be prevented from usurping the powers of elected officials and making political decisions? Meese's admonition to stick to original intent is only a starting point. The Constitution does tell judges to enforce certain broad principles such as "freedom of speech," but if these principles are to be enforced at all in a changing society, judges must supply much of their meaning.

The trouble is that judges of all political stripes have gone beyond applying the Constitution's principles to new circumstances. They have written their own moral and political values into it, pretending to have found them there. Sometimes they have "interpreted" the Constitution to forbid things explicitly allowed by its language.

Take Brennan, a hero to liberals — deservedly so — and Meese's principal foil in the current debate. In his speech belittling "original intention" theorists, Brennan denied writing his own views into the Constitution. "It is, in a very real sense, the community's interpretation that is sought," he said. "Justices are not platonic guardians appointed to wield authority according to their personal moral predilections."

But he gave these words a hollow ring when he explained why he always votes to strike down death penalty laws. He said they violate "the essential meaning" of the Eighth Amendment's prohibition against cruel and unusual punishment by denying "the intrinsic worth" of the murderers who are executed. Now, Brennan knows perfectly well that those who wrote that amendment had no intention of banning the death penalty, which was common at the time and was explicitly recognized in the Fifth and 14th Amendments.

So whence comes his mandate for invalidating the death penalty? "I hope to embody a community striving for human dignity for all, although perhaps not yet arrived," he explained. Translation: my moral convictions on this issue are so strong I would override the laws adopted by the people's elected representatives any way I could. Brennan admitted that most of his fellow countrymen and justices think the death penalty constitutional. As Judge Robert Bork has put it: "The truth is that the judge who looks outside the Constitution looks inside himself and nowhere else."

Well, what's so bad about that? If elected officials don't have the decency to end the death penalty (or antiabortion laws, or minimum-wage laws, or whatever else offends you), why shouldn't the judges do it?

The most important answer is that judicial legislation erodes democratic self-government. It converts judges into an unelected and illegitimate policy-making elite. Indeed, its more radical exponents evince a deep antipathy for the democratic process. But as Felix Frankfurter said, "Holding democracy in judicial tutelage is not the most promising way to foster disciplined responsibility in a people."

Defenders of judicial activism like to point out the vagueness of the

Constitution's words and the futility of the quest for consensus on original intention. "And even if such a mythical beast could be captured and examined, how relevant would it be to us today?" asks Harvard law professor Laurence Tribe. He dismisses as a dangerous fallacy the notion that judges can be significantly restrained by the Constitution's text or history. The Supreme Court, he says, "just cannot avoid the painful duty of exercising judgment so as to give concrete meaning to the fluid Constitution."

Well, perhaps. But why can't the Court do something many law professors barely deign to discuss? When the Constitution's language and history provide little or no guidance on a subject, why can't it leave the law-making to legislatures? Those who work so hard to prove that the Constitution cannot supply the values for governance of modern society seem to think it follows that judges must do it, with a little help from their friends in academia. But their argument rebounds against the legitimacy of judicial review itself. Bork poses a question for which they have no good answer: "If the Constitution is not law — law that, with the usual areas of ambiguity around the edges, nevertheless tolerably tells judges what to do and what not to do — . . . what authorizes judges to set at naught the majority judgment of the American people?"

The activist approach of amending the Constitution in the guise of interpreting it goes hand in hand with a certain lack of candor about the enterprise. A judge who acknowledged that his goal was to strike down democratically adopted laws by rewriting the Constitution would risk impeachment. So we hear a lot about "finding" in the Constitution rights that had somehow gone unnoticed for more than a century.

There is no reason to suppose that unelected judges, using theories concocted by unelected law professors, will make better policies over time than elected officials. Nor that they will make more liberal policies. Judicial activism is not a game played only by liberals. Conservative judges rode roughshod over progressive and New Deal legislation for several decades ending about 1937. "Never . . . can the Supreme Court be said to have for a single hour been representative of anything except the relatively conservative forces of its day," Robert Jackson wrote in 1941.

Franklin Roosevelt changed that, ushering in an era of liberal judicial activism. Now the tables are turning again. Reagan and Meese are filling up the lower federal courts with conservatives and hoping to do the same with the Supreme Court. "I dream of a conservative Supreme Court striking down most federal legislation since the New Deal as unconstitutional," writes conservative columnist Joseph Sobran. Liberals may soon rediscover the virtues of judicial restraint, and find themselves urging a Reaganized judiciary to practice what Meese has been preaching.

Brennan and other liberal activist judges deserve the applause they have won for thrusting upon the nation some policies that were also triumphs of constitutional principle. Desegregation is one example. Protection of the rights of poor criminal defendants is another.

But liberal activism has gone to dubious extremes. Take the case of the man who approached a policeman in Denver and said he'd killed someone. The policeman told him about his rights to remain silent and have a lawyer. The man said he understood and proceeded with his confession, leading police to the scene where he said he had killed a 14-year-old girl. The sometime mental patient later told a psychiatrist that the voice of God had ordered him to confess. The Colorado Supreme Court threw out the confession on the ground that it was compelled by mental illness, and therefore involuntary. If he is ever tried, neither the confession nor, presumably, the other evidence ("fruits" of the confession) will be admissible. And he may go free.

Such judicial excesses are giving constitutional rights a bad name. Ed Meese is not alone in his outrage at judges who free criminals on the basis of technical rules that protect only the guilty, especially where they have little to do with deterring police abuse. The more this sort of thing happens, the greater the danger that the considerable public backlash may build to radical reaction.

There will always be cases in which judges must let criminals go free, and must defy public opinion, to vindicate the constitutional rights of innocent and guilty alike. Their ability to do so suffers when they squander the reservoir of goodwill they need for such occasions. "Liberty lies in the hearts of men and women," Learned Hand wrote. "When it dies there, no constitution, no law, no court can save it."

Judicial creation of new constitutional rights can also be mistaken even when much or most of the public approves. The best example is *Roe* v. *Wade*, the 1973 decision creating a constitutional right to abortion and striking down all state antiabortion laws. Abortion is one of the toughest moral issues around. If I were a legislator I might vote (with misgivings) to allow free access to abortion in the early stages of pregnancy, as the Supreme Court did. But the Court is not a legislature, and there is no plausible basis in the Constitution for it to take this issue away from the states, some of which had already legalized abortion before *Roe*.

Justice Harry Blackmun's opinion "found" a right to abortion within the vague, general "right to personal privacy." He said these rights were in the Constitution somewhere, though he was not sure where — probably the 14th Amendment's generalized protection of "liberty," maybe the Ninth Amendment. Blackmun (appointed by Richard Nixon) made no pretense that the Framers of these amendments intended to legalize abortion. History shows clearly that they did not. They were not thinking about abortion at all, although it was a familiar practice, illegal in some states, when the 14th Amendment was adopted. Nor do the words of the Constitution provide a shred of support for the detailed regulations the Court has drafted over time to curb state regulation of abortion.

Right-to-lifers are not the only people who deplore *Roe* v. *Wade*. Many liberal scholars — defenders of the pioneering Warren Court decisions so despised by Meese — have said the Burger Court went too far down the road of naked judicial legislation in that case. Among them are Archibald Cox, now retired from Harvard Law School, Dean John Hart Ely of Stanford Law School, and Dean Benno Schmidt of Columbia Law School, soon to be president of Yale. The abortion issue poses an excruciating clash between two moral imperatives: a woman's right to personal autonomy and protection of the unborn. Why every detail of local, state, and national policy on such a fundamental moral issue should depend on the personal philosophies of five or six judges escapes them, and me.

The disregard for the written Constitution that *Roe* v. *Wade* embodies is also a two-edged sword. President Reagan said in his debate with Walter Mondale that an unborn child is a living human being "protected by the Constitution, which guarantees life, liberty, and the pursuit of happiness to all of us." Well, there he goes again, quoting the Declaration of Independence and calling it the Constitution. But he was close enough: the 14th Amendment says no state may "deprive any person of life, liberty, or property, without due process of law." For those who believe a fetus is a "person" and abortion is murder, as Reagan does, it is possible to conclude that judges should strike down any state law that allows it. Farfetched? Well, what if a state excluded homosexuals or handicapped children from the protection of its murder laws?

None of this means Meese's own approach to constitutional interpretation is adequate. It isn't. For starters, there is little evidence he has given the subject much thought. Beyond the high-sounding, platitudinous stuff about the Framers in the speeches his aides have written for him, he has had little specific to say about what he thinks their intentions were, or how broadly these intentions should be read. There is enormous room for disagreement here. The most important constitutional phrases, like "equal protection of the laws," are sweeping, vague, and only dimly illuminated by history.

Meese has tiptoed away from some of the few specific things he has said, including his attack on the doctrine that most of the Bill of Rights applies to the states through the 14th Amendment. It appeared in the written text of his July 9 speech to the American Bar Association. For some reason he omitted this point when he read the speech aloud.

Moments afterward, reporters bearing tape recorders asked Meese whether he thought the Court had gone too far in applying the Bill of Rights to the states. "No," he responded. "I, well, I think this is something that's been done in 1925 and since, and so I don't think, ah, ah, I think, I do not have any particular quarrel at this stage of the game with what the Court has done in the intervening 60 years." Will the real Ed Meese please stand up?

Meese has stuck to his guns in denouncing as "infamous" major decisions upholding the rights of criminal defendants. One of his least favorites is *Mapp* v. *Ohio* (1961), which extended to the states the "exclusionary rule" barring use of evidence seized in violation of the Fourth Amendment. Meese has said *Mapp* helps only "the guilty criminal," and has suggested abandoning the exclusionary rule in state and federal cases alike.

But Meese seems to have forgotten *Boyd* v. *U.S.*, which Justice Louis Brandeis said "will be remembered as long as civil liberty lives in the United States." The 1886 decision was the Supreme Court's first major Fourth and Fifth Amendment ruling. Unlike modern rulings, it was explicitly based on a detailed study of the Framers' intentions. *Boyd* held that the Framers intended the Fourth Amendment's ban on "unreasonable searches and seizures" to prohibit *all* governmental attempts to obtain a person's private papers or other property — even by warrant or subpoena — and to forbid their use as evidence to convict him. Innocence or guilt was irrelevant to this determination. The Court's confident assertion that this was the Framers' intention was based on a reading of their natural rights philosophy, on eighteenth-century case law, and on the fury at sweeping British searches that helped fuel the American Revolution.

If *Boyd* were the law today, it would place far greater restrictions on police than any imposed by the Warren Court, which Meese has denounced for its "expansive civil libertarianism." The modern Court, unwilling to restrict official power so severely, has abandoned this broad vision. Its use of the exclusionary rule as a limited deterrent to police abuses is a pale remnant of the expansive rights the Court saw in the Fourth Amendment 99 years ago.

Meese's contention that the exclusionary rule helps only guilty criminals is demonstrably false. Of course, exclusion of improperly obtained but reliable evidence helps only the guilty in the immediate case at hand. But if officials knew they could search everyone indiscriminately and use any evidence they found, a lot of innocent people would be victims of illegal searches. The only way to take the profit out of police abuses is to bar use of the evidence found. This means letting some guilty criminals go free. It is one thing to say this is too high a price to pay in cases in which police inadvertently cross the line between marginally legal and marginally illegal searches. It is quite another to let officials use any and all illegally obtained evidence, as Meese would.

Meese's selectiveness in applying original intention is not limited to criminal law issues. If he really believed the Framers' specific intentions are "the only reliable guide for judgment," he would have to condemn *Brown* v. *Board of Education,* the landmark 1954 decision desegregating public schools. Anybody who did that today would be assailed as a segregationist crank. Meese recently applauded *Brown* as a case study in finding the original intention of the post-Civil War 14th Amendment. "The Supreme Court in that case was not giving new life to old words, or adapting a 'living,' 'flexible' Constitution to new reality," he declared. "It was restoring the original principle of the Constitution."

That's nice, but it's not true. The Congress that wrote the amendment had no intention of outlawing segregation, as Raoul Berger, Alexander Bickel, and others have demonstrated. The same Congress segregated its own Senate gallery and the District of Columbia schools, and rejected various desegregation bills. What the Court saw nearly 90 years later was that state-enforced segregation, relegating blacks to inferior schools and other facilities, had made a mockery of the 14th Amendment's central purpose: to put blacks and whites on an equal footing before the law. So the Court gave "new life to old words," to use Meese's mocking phrase, and threw out segregation.

The same Congress that drafted the 14th Amendment also passed some special welfare programs for recently freed slaves and other blacks in the South. These were, in modern parlance, affirmative action programs involving racial preferences for blacks — sort of like the government hiring quotas that Meese has declared in violation of the 14th Amendment. Congress specifically excluded whites from some of these programs. Among them were federally funded, racially segregated schools for blacks only — a single program that contradicts the Meese view of the 14th Amendment's original intention on segregation and affirmative action alike. These programs were passed over the Meese-like objections that they discriminated against whites and included some blacks who were not personally victims of discrimination. But Meese's Justice Department, checking its slogans about judicial restraint at the door, has urged the Supreme Court to strike down every local, state, and federal government affirmative action program in the nation that prefers black employees over whites. Right or wrong, Meese's position on affirmative action is at war with his preachings about strict adherence to original intention.

The same is true of his position on a lot of issues. Many of the powers that his Justice Department exercises daily — reaching into every community with its wiretaps, its informers, its subpoenas — would have horrified the Framers. They feared centralized power more than anything but anarchy. They sought to limit severely the national government's law enforcement powers, leaving to state and local authorities jurisdiction over the all but genuinely interstate crimes.

What would Meese do about the strong historical evidence that the Framers intended to deny the government the power to issue paper money, which they saw as a threat to propertied interests? What about their intent to bar the president from launching military expeditions without congressional approval, except to repel attacks on United States territory?

And what about the First Amendment's religion clauses, as expounded by Joseph Story, a nineteenth-century justice whom Meese sometimes quotes on original intention? "The real object," Story said, "was not to countenance, much less to advance, Mahometanism, or Judaism, or infidelity, by prostrating Christianity; but to exclude all rivalry among Christian sects." Meese buys the "infidels" part when he says the Framers would have found "bizarre" the notion that government may not favor religion over nonreligion. He ignores the rest, of course. Any official who argued today that only Christians are protected by the religion clauses would be drummed out of office, and properly so.

The broader point is that sticking to the Framer's immediate goals as closely as Meese sometimes suggests is neither possible nor desirable. If *Brown* v. *Board of Education* was right, and it was, then a "jurisprudence of original intention" worthy of respect cannot mean enforcing constitutional rights only in the specific ways envisioned by the Framers. Such an approach would doom these rights to wither with the passage of time. The Framers' central purpose of preventing abuse of minorities would be strangled by narrow-minded attention to their more immediate concerns. As for the possiblity of updating the Constitution by the formal amendment process, this takes a two-thirds majority in each house of Congress and approval by three-fourths of the states. Such majorities could rarely be mustered to deal with new threats to the rights of minorities.

New technologies such as wiretapping threaten liberties the Framers enshrined in ways that they could not have imagined. And the changing nature of society poses threats that the Framers did not foresee to the constitutional principles they established. Take libel law. Million-dollar libel suits by public officials were not prevalent in the eighteenth century, and it is fairly clear that the Framers did not intend the First Amendment (or the 14th) to limit private libel suits as the modern Court has done. But they did intend to protect uninhibited, robust, and wide-open debate about public affairs. And it seems to me proper for the

Supreme Court to effectuate that broad purpose, in this litigious era, by imposing some curbs on libel suits.

Am I slipping into the kind of judicial revision of the Constitution I just rejected? I don't think so. There is a middle ground between narrow adherence to original intention and freewheeling judicial legislation. As Chief Justice John Marshall said in a famous 1819 decision, the Constitution is not a code of "immutable rules," but rather the "great outlines" of a system intended "to endure for ages to come, and, consequently, to be adapted to the various crises of human affairs." But it is for elected officials, as he said, to do most of the adapting. Judges should invalidate democratically enacted laws only, in John Ely's words, "in accord with an inference whose starting point, whose underlying premise, is fairly discoverable in the Constitution."

This approach will often set only loose outer boundaries around the Court's options in deciding specific issues. It requires judges in close cases to draw fine lines. And it does not pretend to purge their moral and political convictions entirely from the process. But its recognition that the Constitution imposes some bounds on judicial power — limits fleshed out more clearly by the accumulation of precedent — would channel the growth of the law in a more principled and therefore more legitimate direction.

At the outer limits of legitimacy are those cases in which the justices read into vague constitutional phrases like "due process" an emerging social consensus that seems contrary to the particular intentions of the Framers. This goes beyond applying old principles to new circumstances, and gets into tinkering with the principles or creating new ones. I think the Supreme Court should do it in a few rare cases, nudging society to progress in the common law tradition of gradually evolving principles against a background of continuity.

Brown v. Board of Education was such a case. It struck at the heart of a great evil. Though departing from the particular plans of the Framers, it honored their deeper, nobler intentions. And though overriding the democratic process, it crystallized an emerging national consensus that legally compelled racial segregation was unacceptable in modern America. That is the difference between judicial activism and judicial statesmanship, and why most of the fiercest critics of judicial activism don't dare criticize *Brown* today.

But the Court should attempt to lead only where the nation is prepared to follow. The creation of new constitutional values is a slippery slope, down which the courts should not travel too far too fast. At the bottom lies the kind of uninhibited and essentially lawless judicial legislation that Bork has justly assailed. The urge to do good is powerful, the urge to court greatness intoxicating. Judges should resist the sincere, but arrogant, assumption that they know best. Brandeis's words, aimed at Ed Meese's ideological predecessors, should also be heeded by his ideological adversaries: "The greatest danger to liberty is the insidious encroachment by men of zeal, well-meaning but without understanding."

THE BUREAUCRACY

Chapter Seven

The bureaucracy is usually thought of as consisting of hordes of civil servants whose greatest interest is in job security, and who spend their lives in eight-hour days engaged in routine matters, never taking a chance, hoping to reach retirement safely. Whatever ripples bureaucrats are supposed to cause on the political scene are generally thought to go no further than the invention of ingenious ways of increasing red tape and regulations that irritate the public. Bureaucrats are seldom pictured in the grandiose terms that are used to describe presidents, members of Congress, Supreme Court justices, and the leaders of parties and pressure groups. The bureaucracy and the people that serve within it may not seem as dynamic and forceful as the charismatic leaders that populate the political scene elsewhere, but the personalities and styles of bureaucratic leaders have had a profound effect on the political system and public policy over the years.

The great size and diversity of the bureaucracy, and the many functions it performs, allows many kinds of personalities to be effective. There is greater movement into and out of the bureaucracy from the private sector than is the case with other governmental branches. The infusion of new personalities into the bureaucracy may cause changes in methods of operation and may cause different policies to be adopted or emphasized. There is a constant struggle in the administrative branch between defenders of the status quo and incoming or even permanent members of the bureaucracy who wish to innovate. The personality of bureaucrats goes a long way toward explaining such conflicts.

Contrasting personalities and styles are readily observable throughout the bureaucracy. There is the cautious bureau chief, who over the years has developed careful relations with the chairmen of the congressional committees that have jurisdiction over his agency. He will not make a move without consulting them and may have developed close personal friendships with them. Other administrative officials may pay only token attention to Congress, going to Capitol Hill only when it is absolutely necessary. Some officials may try to cultivate power relationships within the bureaucracy, whereas others may seek public acclaim and outside support. Some officials, when dissatisfied with policies that they see being implemented by the White House or by their agency, may resign in protest, making their dissatisfaction known to the press and the public. Other bureaucrats in the same position will try to change the policy from within, and if they resign will keep their discontent to themselves, knowing that in some agencies a public attack on the bureaucratic establishment will close the doors to future employment there. Differing bureaucratic personalities will result in a wide variety of styles, including playing it safe, playing an external or internal power game, becoming a bureaucratic politician, and seeking power and status through expertise. The positive and negative character attributes of administrators at all levels of the bureaucracy greatly affect government.

CERTAINLY NO ONE WOULD have predicted, when J. Edgar Hoover was born in 1895 in Washington to a family of undistinguished civil servants, that he would become one of the most powerful men in the federal bureaucracy, using the Federal Bureau of Investigation as his power base. The Bureau of Investigation within the Justice Department was created in 1906 and expanded during World War I; it was taken over by J. Edgar Hoover in 1924 when he was appointed its acting director by Attorney General Harlan Fiske Stone, who was shortly to join the Supreme Court.

Hoover had been working as a lawyer in the Justice Department, when he became an assistant in 1918 to the director of a newly created General Intelligence Division, which had been assigned the task of compiling information on alleged radicals. During this period, A. Mitchell Palmer, the attorney general, used the bureau to carry out the infamous "Palmer Raids" on radicals throughout the country. Thousands of people, particularly new immigrants, were arrested without warrants, and thrown into seamy jail cells. Most were eventually released, although some noncitizen anarchists were deported. The raids brought the Bureau of Investigation into disrespect in many quarters of the country. When President Warren G. Harding assumed office, a new director of the bureau was appointed, William J. Burns, who had once been head of the Secret Service, and had established the William J. Burns National Detective Agency in 1909 after his retirement. As a private detective he had been convicted of a misdemeanor charge after illegally entering a New York law office. Sanford J. Ungar notes, however, that to the Harding administration the conviction

seemed to be taken as a qualification rather than as a blot on his record, and it became widely known that Bureau men, under Burns's leadership, randomly wiretapped, broke into offices, and shuffled through personal files, and kept tabs on people's private lives. The most likely targets were "enemies" — persons who criticized [Attorney General] Daugherty, the Department of Justice, and the Bureau of Investigation; Senators who asked too many questions; and other competing government departments.[1]

The bureau continued to be deeply involved in political activities under the directorship of Burns, and attacks were launched on alleged radicals within and without government. When Democratic Senator Burton J. Wheeler of Montana attacked corruption in the Justice Department after his election in 1922, the bureau used every device possible to discredit him, including supplying information to the Republican National Committee on the senator's alleged radicalism, spying on his Washington home, and attempting to lure him into a compromising situation with a woman. But the bureau was not to stop there; it even aided the Justice Department in securing an indictment against Wheeler from a federal grand jury in Montana for influence peddling. The attempt by the bureau to frame Wheeler failed, and the senator was acquitted.

When Calvin Coolidge assumed the

---

[1]Sanford J. Ungar, *F.B.I.* (Boston: Atlantic-Little, Brown, 1975), p. 45.

presidency after the death of Harding, he replaced Attorney General Daugherty, who had been implicated in the Teapot Dome scandals, with Harlan Fiske Stone. Burns was forced to resign. It was Stone who chose Hoover to clean up the bureau. When Stone called Hoover into his office in May of 1924 to offer him the job, the following exchange took place:

> Hoover said, "I'll take the job, Mr. Stone, on certain conditions."
>
> "What are they?" the Attorney General asked.
>
> "The Bureau must be divorced from politics and not be a catchall for political hacks. Appointments must be based on merit. Second, promotions will be made on proved ability and the Bureau will be responsible only to the Attorney General," Hoover replied brashly.
>
> As this account has it, Stone was delighted with the terms and said, "I wouldn't give it to you under any other conditions. That's all. Good day."[2]

With that, J. Edgar Hoover became director of the Bureau of Investigation, and was to turn the FBI into one of the most politically oriented agencies of government under the guise of maintaining political neutrality at all costs, and operating solely as a highly efficient federal police force.

Hoover proceeded cautiously after taking over the Bureau of Investigation, but soon he was to involve it in extensive public relations to fortify its image. Both he and the bureau were to become invincible in the minds of both the public and Congress. The agency was always treated with extreme favoritism by most senators and congressmen. Within the bureau, Hoover tried to rule over every detail, and he was to develop a cult of personality that has never been seen in the bureaucracy before or since. In the end, J. Edgar Hoover became more powerful in many ways than the presidents he served. During the Nixon years, he single-handedly vetoed a White House-sponsored plan to establish extensive domestic political surveillance, using the FBI, because he felt that it would not serve his purposes, but the president's. Hoover had for many years used the FBI for political surveillance.

In the following selection, we see how complete Hoover's domination was. For many years the FBI was run on the basis of Hoover's supposed strengths. In this selection Ungar shows that bureau operations equally reflected Hoover's many weaknesses.

[2]Ibid., p. 48.

330

29

Sanford J. Ungar
THE KING:
J. EDGAR HOOVER

FBI Director Clarence M. Kelley came to the office of Senator James O. Eastland (D., Miss.), chairman of the Senate Judiciary Committee, one day in June 1974 for a little ceremony in which Eastland presented Kelley with the first copy of a handsome black volume in memory of J. Edgar Hoover, containing *Memorial Tributes in the Congress of the United States and Various Articles and Editorials Relating to His Life and Work.* The following exchange occurred, as Kelley sought to turn a rather stiff and formal occasion into a relaxed and social one:

KELLEY: "Senator, there's an awful lot about J. Edgar Hoover in this book."

EASTLAND: "Chief Kelley, there's an awful lot about J. Edgar Hoover that ain't in this book."

There is a treasury of jokes about J. Edgar Hoover in FBI folklore, stories that agents tell each other during long, uneventful surveillances while they wait for things to happen and that assistant directors use to cheer each other up in moments of exasperation. In one, the director is at the beach with his constant companion, Clyde Tolson. Tolson agitatedly scans the shoreline back and forth and finally says with a sigh of relief, "Okay, Boss. The coast is clear. Now you can practice walking on the water." Another tale has it that Hoover and Tolson, as they became older, decided to check into the cost and availability of cemetery plots. When Tolson reported back to him on the high price, Hoover, a notorious cheapskate, was outraged. "Never mind, Clyde," he declared. "You buy yours. But I'll just rent a crypt. I don't plan to be there for more than a few days anyway." Yet another related that whenever Tolson became depressed or dispirited, which was apparently often, the director would seek to cheer him up by saying, "Clyde, why don't you transfer somebody?" If that didn't do the trick, Hoover would escalate the suggestion: "Go ahead, fire someone." And if Tolson still complained that this didn't help, the director would add, "Fire him with prejudice" — a device that made it nearly impossible for the victim to find another job. Only then, went the story, did Tolson feel better.

Such bizarre fantasies conjure up the image of a man who regarded himself as infallible and godlike and who exercised arbitrary and sometimes inexplicable control over thousands of lives. J. Edgar Hoover had a degree of authority and prerogative seldom seen in democratic governments. The longer he stayed in power, the greater these prerogatives became and the more inconceivable it became that he might ever be removed; the phenomenon seemed at times to grow out of the medieval notion of the divine right of kings. Indeed, some suggested that, in times of trouble, the elevation of Hoover was just what the country needed, and his friend, Senator Joseph McCarthy of Wisconsin, tried more than once in the 1950s to launch Hoover-for-President boomlets.

But Hoover disavowed any such ambition. He was content to stay where he was, ruling over a limited but significant realm — an agency that he had salvaged from the depths of scandal and raised to the heights of honor and influence. The director turned away other job offers — to become national baseball commissioner or head of the Thoroughbred Racing Association. Hoover put his own distinct imprint on the FBI and then turned himself into an institution. It became a tradition — and a necessity for those who sought to advance through the ranks — to say what the director wanted to hear. By definition, it was right. It also became a tradition, as one FBI official put it, "that you do what the director says without really agreeing with him." Hoover's words and acts were converted into legends, and some of them came out sounding as stiff and unreal or as difficult to believe as those of such other authoritarian leaders as Chairman Mao Tse-tung of the Chinese Communist party. If an attorney general or a president made him angry, the director could just threaten to resign, and that was usually enough to bring the offender back into line. No president could afford to lose him.

Reflecting on the reverence that came to be accorded Hoover, Clarence Kelley, his successor, says, "His most casual remark [to a member of the FBI leadership] would be turned into a point of philosophy. They would even go out and document it and build it up, so it could aid them at a future time."

This treatment could be taken to laughable extremes. Once asked how he got along so well with the director, Sam Noisette, Hoover's black retainer who was an "honorary agent," replied, "It's easy. . . . If it's snowing and blowing outside and the director comes in and says it's a beautiful, sunny day, it's a beautiful, sunny day. That's all there is to it."

John Edgar Hoover — he abbreviated his name when he learned of a namesake who had large debts — was born the third child of an obscure family of civil servants in Washington on the first day of 1895. His father, like his father before him, worked for the Coast and Geodetic Survey, and his brother, Dickerson N. Hoover, Jr., became inspector general of the Steamboat Inspection Service in the Department of Commerce. In high school Hoover distinguished himself as a good student, a debater (overcoming an early childhood stutter and arguing, on occasion, in favor of American annexation of Cuba and against women's suffrage), and a member of the cadet corps. He had to work for anything he obtained after his high school graduation in 1913, and while studying law at night at George Washington University he had a daytime job, for thirty dollars a month, as an indexer at the Library of Congress.

After obtaining two degrees, a bachelor's and a master's of law, and passing the District of Columbia bar exam, he went to work in 1917 as a law clerk in the Justice Department. As Jack Alexander noted in a unique and intimate 1937 profile of Hoover in *The New Yorker*, from his earliest days in the department,

> Certain things marked Hoover apart from scores of other young law clerks. He dressed better than most, and a bit on the dandyish side. He had an exceptional capacity for detail work, and he handled small chores with enthusiasm and thoroughness. He constantly sought new responsibilities to shoulder and welcomed chances to work overtime. When he was in conference with an official of his department, his manner was that of a young man who confidently expected to rise. His superiors were duly impressed, and so important did they consider his services that they persuaded him to spend the period of the [First] World War at his desk.

Rise he did. By 1919, at the age of 24, Hoover became a special assistant attorney general in charge of the General Intelligence Division of the Bureau of Investigation. In that position, he was responsible for assessing the threat to the United States from communists and other revolutionaries, and the information he developed became essential background for the "Red raids" conducted by Attorney General A. Mitchell Palmer in 1920. Few of the ten thousand persons arrested and detained in the raids were ever convicted under the wartime Sedition Act, but Hoover was successful in his personal efforts before a Labor Department tribunal to have at least three well-known figures deported: radicals Emma Goldman and Alexander Berkman as well as Ludwig Martens, the unofficial representative in the United States of the new Soviet government. Hoover became an assistant director of the Bureau of Investigation under Director William J. Burns during the presidency of Warren G. Harding; but his patience and freedom from association with the Harding scandals were rewarded when after his exchange with Coolidge's new attorney general, Harlan Stone, about the need to keep politics out of the Bureau, Stone named Hoover its acting director at age 29.

Before and after he took over the troubled Bureau of Investigation in 1924, Hoover was something of a mystery man in Washington. He kept very much to himself, living in the house where he was born and caring for his mother, the descendant of Swiss mercenary soldiers and a strong disciplinarian, until her death in 1938. But although he remained close to her, Hoover apparently shunned the rest of his family. His sister Lillian fell upon hard times, but got no help from him. "J.E. was always accessible if we wanted to see him, but he didn't initiate contacts with his family," said Margaret Fennell, his niece to interviewer Ovid Demaris. Indeed, even Hoover's most persistent admirers and defenders within the FBI complained occasionally that the absence of any family devotion on his own part contributed to his lack of compassion toward or understanding of strong family men who worked for him. "Hoover couldn't have a family-type feeling toward anyone," observed one agent long stationed in New York; "a man who has never been a father cannot think like a father." The wife of a former assistant director of the FBI said that "the man just had no feeling at all for families." There was a certain paradox to this attitude, as Hoover expected his married agents to be loyal family men.

Hoover's coldness to his own family could not be readily explained by a busy schedule of other commitments and associations. For a time, especially in the 1930s, he was seen frequently with well-known writers and other friends on the New York nightclub circuit; and sometimes he went with bachelor friends to baseball games and other sports events (he was occasionally joined on excursions to watch the Washington Senators in the 1950s by then Vice President Richard M. Nixon); but Hoover generally turned away all other social engagements, unless they involved official business at the Justice Department. There was little socializing in the top ranks of the bureau itself, and relations between Hoover and his associates were intentionally kept on a businesslike level. The only woman in the director's life, it was often said, was Shirley Temple, his favorite actress and then a child. His most frequent and celebrated diversion, especially as he became older, was horse races, where he generally placed small, losing bets and sometimes presented trophies in the winner's circle.

The replacement for family, and eventually for everyone else, in Hoover's celibate life was Clyde A. Tolson, a native of Missouri who came to Washington at the age of 18 to work as a clerk in the War Department. He eventually became confidential secretary to Secretary of War Newton D. Baker and two successors, but after getting a law degree in night school at George Washington University, he joined the bureau in 1928. He originally planned to move on to practice law in Cedar Rapids, Iowa, where he once attended business college for a year. But for reasons that were never entirely clear, Tolson rose quickly and was soon working at the Director's side. Hoover and Tolson became so close that, as Don Whitehead put it in his history, "They have even reached the point where they think alike." They also came to spend a great deal of time together, including, on most days, lunch at a restaurant and dinner at one or another's home. When Hoover appeared at an official function, Tolson was invariably a few steps behind and to the right of him, almost like a courtier carrying a king's cloak. As associate director, a title Hoover finally gave him in 1947, Tolson was in effect the director's chief of staff and his mouthpiece. He chaired the bureau's executive conference of assistant directors. Many of Hoover's attitudes and opinions, his wrath or his satisfaction, were transmitted through Tolson, who, as the years went on, seemed to do very little thinking or acting on his own. Tolson would invariably write his comments on a memorandum in pencil rather than in pen, so that he could change them to conform with the director's point of view if necessary. If the executive conference voted unanimously on a matter but Hoover was later found to disagree,[1] Tolson would take it upon himself to solicit unanimity for the "correct" position, and he usually got it. Long-time bureau officials, asked to list Tolson's contributions and innovations to the service, are generally unable to come up with any. And even to those who worked for years near his office, he remained an enigma. Efforts to fraternize with him were turned away abruptly, and any other bureau executive presumptuous enough to try to join him and the director for their ritual daily lunch at Harvey's restaurant or the Mayflower Hotel risked disciplinary action or some more subtle punishment.

Tolson's only known diversion was to dream up obscure inventions, and he actually obtained patents on a few, including a mechanism to open and close windows automatically. Hoover usually agreed to try out Tolson's inventions, either in the bureau or at home.

According to the persistent gossip in Washington for decades, Hoover and Tolson were homosexuals; and — according to this interpretation — their attempt to repress and conceal their relationship helped explain the bureau's vigilant, even hysterical bias against men of that sexual orientation. In fact, any such relationship between the two was never acknowledged or discovered. As one former ranking official put it, "If it was true, they were never caught. And you know how we feel in the bureau: you are innocent until proven guilty." Another debunked the rumors about their relationship on the basis of the fact that Hoover "liked to crack jokes about sex."

Tolson was always the more sickly of the two men, and whenever he fell ill, he would move into Hoover's home to be nursed back to health by the director's servants. When Hoover died suddenly in May 1972 Tolson was grief-stricken, and after going through the formality of being acting director of the FBI for about twenty-four hours, he announced his retirement. But for a few token items and sums of money willed to

---

[1]The director's famous euphemism was to say, "I approve the minority view."

others, Hoover left all of his worldly possessions — an estate valued at half a million dollars — to Clyde Tolson. Tolson, increasingly ill, closed himself up in Hoover's home and declined to talk with anyone, even most of his former bureau colleagues. He died on April 14, 1975, at the age of 74, passing most of the fortune on to other loyal bureau folk.

From all accounts, of those who knew Hoover and those who studied him, the director was a cold and self-indulgent man. His expressions of warmth were few and far between and private — friendship with neighborhood youths whom he invited into his house; a gift of a beagle pup to replace one that died which had belonged to his neighbors in the 1950s, Senator and Mrs. Lyndon B. Johnson; offers to pay a hospital bill for one of the children of Assistant Director Cartha D. DeLoach. But according to one official who was sometimes the beneficiary of such largess from Hoover, "He extracted a pound of flesh for every ounce of generosity," especially from those who worked for him. From them he expected repayment in the form of intensified loyalty and utter obeisance. From someone like Johnson he wanted political capital; from other neighbors he seemed to require only respect and deference. Seldom did his gestures seem to be motivated simply by unselfishness or humanitarian concern toward others.

Hoover moved only once in his life — after his mother's death in 1938, from the family home in Seward Square on Capitol Hill to a large red-brick house that he bought on 30th Place in Northwest Washington, near Rock Creek Park. There he built a huge collection of antiques, art objects, and pictures, mostly of himself with other famous people. According to his neighbors, the position of each item, once settled upon, remained the same year after year. Each time a new president was elected, Hoover would move a photograph of himself with that president into a place of particular prominence in the entrance hall. Some of the art objects were fine and valuable, but others, it was discovered when they were auctioned after his death, were peculiar items like an eight-sided basket made of Popsicle sticks; a wooden stork from the old Stork Club, one of the director's favorite New York nightclubs; a salt shaker with a nude woman on the side; and other assorted bric-a-brac. Hoover's house was impeccably well kept (he had a fear of insects and germs and kept an ultraviolet light in the bathroom) and his Kentucky bluegrass front lawn was the pride of the neighborhood until it was replaced with artificial Astro Turf shortly before his death.

He was a man of habit, leaving the house and returning at precisely the same hour every day. He always ate cottage cheese and grapefruit for lunch. If he ever had serious health problems, beyond an ulcer condition, they were a carefully guarded secret; and he did not even like it to be known that in his later years he took a nap in the office for about two hours each afternoon. Hoover did not smoke, and he took only an occasional drink of bourbon, preferably Jack Daniels, with water.

His life was the FBI and there were few diversions from it. The director did have pretenses of being a religious man. (As a high school student he sang in a Presbyterian church choir and taught a Sunday school class, and at one point, according to his biographers, he considered becoming a minister.) But one man who worked closely with Hoover for many years claimed in an interview that the Bible on his desk was really just "a prop" and that the director exploited organized religion and famous preachers and evangelists for his own and the FBI's selfish purposes. Despite his extraordinary power and exposure, in the eyes of most of his associates Hoover seemed to remain a man of small dimensions who never became sophisticated or graceful. He was prejudiced and narrow-minded, overtly biased against black people ("As long as I am director, there will never be a Negro special agent of the FBI," he was often heard to say in the years before Attorney General Robert F. Kennedy exerted pressure on him to change that policy), distrustful of other minority groups, and intolerant of women in any but subservient positions. Always somewhat defensive and insecure about his own education, Hoover had a notorious distrust of people who had gone to Harvard and other Ivy League universities; he claimed that they had little knowledge of the real world. He was embarrassingly susceptible to manipulation through flattery or fulsome praise and sometimes hopelessly out of touch with the realities of changing times. He was, above all, a lonely man.

When Hoover first took over the bureau, he was little known and seldom noticed. When he was appointed to the job, *Time* magazine remarked only that he was distinguished by "an unusually accurate and comprehensive memory," but most of the press merely ignored him. It was almost five years, in fact, before he ever achieved a distinction symbolic to Washington bureaucrats, mention in the *Congressional Record*. A Democratic congressman from Texas, Thomas L. Blanton, took the floor of the House of Representatives in early 1929 to compliment Hoover for "the high character of the splendid work they are doing" at the bureau. Four years later, during a budget debate, Congressman John McCormack (D., Mass.) — later Speaker of the House and always one of Hoover's staunchest supporters — praised the bureau as "a credit to the federal government" and the director as "a brilliant young man . . . one of the finest public officials in the service of the federal government."

But before long, once he had consolidated power and genuinely improved the agency, Hoover determined to go public, to build a reputation for the bureau and to construct what came to be a cult around himself. This took the form initially of an anticrime "crusade," a zealous effort to awaken the citizenry to the threat and the consequences of lawlessness and to the need to cooperate with the authorities. The wisdom and invincibility of the "G-men" (a name that gangster George "Machine-Gun" Kelly allegedly gave the bureau agents, who had previously been known mostly as "the Feds") were trumpeted in comic strips; children wore G-man pajamas to bed and took G-man machine guns out to play. Alongside the easy, mass-appeal aspects of the crusade, however, there was also a loftier pitch for the federal police efforts, the development of a philosophy that gave the bureau coherence and lasting importance. The director came to have the image of an expert, a sage, almost of a saint come to deliver the nation from the forces of evil — even if he had never been out on the street working a case.

Hoover was hardly a scholar, nor was he a particularly literate man. He had made an early effort to "understand" the radical forces in the country, holding long arguments in his Justice Department office, for example, with Emma Goldman and others he had deported during the Palmer Raid era. But he soon abandoned any such dialogue and effort to understand and turned to the attack. Apart from the most important reports crossing his desk, he was said to read very little, and one of the best stories about the director was that not only had he not written the books published under his name, but he hadn't even bothered to read them. His letters often bordered on incoherence, especially in his last years, and sometimes what semblance of logic and rationality they had came from "corrections" mercifully made by close aides like Louis Nichols and Cartha DeLoach or Hoover's lifelong secretary, Helen Gandy. The director was notorious for his mispronunciation of words that he used often, such as communist ("cominist") and pseudo ("swaydo"), a term he generally put in front of "intellectual" or "liberal" as an expression of contempt; but it was taboo for anyone who intended to have a bright future in the bureau to correct him on such matters.

Most of Hoover's vocabulary was graphic and quotable, and some of it was crude. Criminals were generally "rats" of one form or another and those who failed to keep them in jail were "yammerheads." One of the greatest threats to the nation came from "venal politicians." Those who criticized him might be diagnosed, as columnist Westbook Pegler was, as suffering from "mental halitosis." The press, for that matter, was full of "jackals." In a speech before the Washington, D.C., chapter of the Society of Former Special Agents of the FBI in 1971, he attacked the "few journalistic prostitutes" who could not appreciate the FBI; in that same appearance, one of his last major public addresses, he insisted that the FBI had no intention of compromising its standards "to accommodate kooks, misfits, drunks and slobs." "It is time we stopped coddling the hoodlums and the hippies who are causing so much serious trouble these days," he declared; "let us treat them like the vicious enemies of society that they really are regardless of their age."

Whatever the level of the discourse, Hoover found respectable forums and outlets for his ghostwritten elegies on law and order. He appeared regularly, for example, in the *Syracuse Law Review*. His treatise there on juvenile delinquency in 1953, replete with footnotes, advised the reader:

> Of primary importance in the child's early environment is a wholesome family life. A happy home which glows with morality provides a healthy atmosphere for the growing child. During the years of accelerated character development, the child quickly learns from observing his parents. As the language of his parents becomes his language, so the cleanliness of body and soul displayed by them exerts early influence on him. The child who is confronted with parental strife, immorality, and unhappiness in the home must look beyond the family circle if he is to develop orderly, wholesome ideals. Too often the child does not find proper guidance when it is not provided in the home.

The same article advised that it was a bad idea for both parents in a family to be employed, that poolrooms and other "hangouts" bred juvenile delinquency, and warned that "law enforcement agencies in various parts of the United States are required to adhere to restrictions which hamper policy efficiency. . . . the tendency to discount juvenile crime and to assume an overly protective attitude toward the juvenile offender is dangerous." And there were generally a few words on behalf of the old virtues:

> Truthfulness is one of the strongest characteristics of good citizenship. All criminals are liars; their lives are patterned after the deceit which they reflect in both word and deed. Certainly each parent must insist of his children that they be truthful in their every word. A child should be disciplined more severely when he attempts to hide his misconduct behind a lie than when he is guilty of misconduct alone. That truthfulness can best be learned in the everyday association between the child and his parent is self-evident. Likewise the father who is caught in a lie hardly can demand the truth from his child.

Eleven years later, he was back in the same law review on the same subject, with some rather strident warnings:

> There is a growing possibility that Nikita Khrushchev will never be forced to make good his boast of burying us — we may save him the trouble by doing it ourselves through the dissipation of the youth of our country. . . . The moral deterioration in our people is another basic cause for the large juvenile involvement in criminal activity. . . . Either we solve the problem or we may well go down!

In his prime, Hoover gave frequent speeches, and he had something to say about nearly everything:

Corruption: "One of the worst degenerative forces in American life during the past fifty years has been corruption in public office. Corrupt politicians make venal politics, and right-thinking citizens know there is but one answer and one remedy. Corruption must be eradicated. . . . Few communities in the land are free from contamination of the syndicated leeches who masquerade behind the flattering term — 'politician.' " (National Fifty Years in Business Club, Nashville, May 20, 1939.)

American Home Life: "When the home totters, a nation weakens. Every day it is my task to review the histories of scores who obey only the laws of their own choosing. Always the one thing that stands out is a lack of moral responsibility and any feeling of religious conviction. . . . While we fight for religious freedom, we must also fight the license sought by the atheist and those who ridicule, scoff and belittle others who would seek spiritual strength." (Commencement exercises, St. John's University Law School, Brooklyn, June 11, 1942.)

Loyalty: "In our vaunted tolerance for all peoples the Communist has found our 'Achilles' heel.' The American Legion represents a force which holds within its power the ability to expose the hypocrisy and ruthlessness of this foreign 'ism' which has crept into our national life — an 'ism' built and supported by dishonor, deceit, tyranny and a deliberate policy of falsehood. . . . We are rapidly reaching the time when loyal Americans must be willing to stand up and be counted. The American Communist Party . . . has for its purpose the shackling of American and its conversion to the Godless, Communist way of life." (Annual convention of the American Legion, San Francisco, September 30, 1946.)

Hoover was even sought out by *Parents' Magazine* in 1940 for remarks on "The Man I Want My Son to Be." His answer:

> I would want him to be intelligent, not necessarily possessed of learning derived from reading, but equipped to face the world with a self-reliant resourcefulness that would enable him to solve, in the majority of instances, the problems of human existence. . . . I would want him to realize that nothing in life can be truly gained without paying the equivalent price and that hard, intensive work is necessary.

There were subjects, perhaps, that Hoover, with his accumulation of influence and credibility, could have profitably addressed himself to, but did not. For example, he never wrote or spoke about the need to control the distribution of handguns. Instead, in sensationalized accounts written for *American Magazine* under his byline by Courtney Ryley Cooper, with titles like "Gun-Crazy," he seemed to lend some romanticism to such groups as the "Brady Gang . . . the gun-craziest gang of desperadoes ever to fall to the lot of the Federal Bureau of Investigation to blast into extinction."

The director did not hesitate to pronounce his views on other issues of national controversy. He bitterly opposed the visit to this country of Nikita Khrushchev in 1959 (although he would later endorse President Nixon's voyages to Moscow and Peking). He frequently spoke out against the parole system, which he felt was administered by "sob sisters" with irresponsible leniency. "It is time that we approached the parole problem with a little more common sense," Hoover proclaimed in 1939; "it is time that sound practical businesslike methods supersede the whims of the gushing, well-wishing, mawkish sentimentalist. . . . The guiding principle, the basic requirement, the sole consideration in judging each and every individual case in which parole may be administered, should be the protection of the public."

Hoover often made decisions about people and chose his friends on the basis of their conformity with his own ideological attitudes. He was delighted, for example, when federal judge Irving Kaufman in New York gave death sentences to Julius and Ethel Rosenberg, who were convicted of espionage in his courtroom for the alleged leak of U.S. atomic secrets to the Soviet Union. Kaufman and Hoover became fast friends. Whenever the judge went to visit his son at college in Oklahoma, he was chauffeured by agents from the Oklahoma City Field Office; and even into the 1970s, after Hoover was gone, the FBI did special favors for Kaufman, by then chief judge of the U.S. Court of Appeals for the Second Circuit. Just a phone call from the judge to the New York Field Office, complaining about a group that was demonstrating outside his courthouse, was enough to launch a preliminary bureau investigation of the group.

With the help of his publicity-conscious lieutenants, Hoover cultivated his own image as the fearless enemy of every criminal, so effective in his job as to be loathed by them all. The director always behaved as if there were an imminent danger to his life. He would put his hat on one side of the rear-window ledge in his chauffeured limousine and then sink down in the corner of the other side, on the assumption that any would-be assassin would fire at the hat first. He and Tolson always sat against the wall in a restaurant so they could see anyone approaching them. And whenever Hoover traveled out of town, he invariably had a large retinue of agents from the nearest field office on duty to protect him. On one occasion, Hoover became alarmed over the origin of suspicious stains that appeared on the floor of his limousine. He ordered the FBI lab to do tests on the carpet. The conclusion: The stains came from a package of bones that he had taken home from a banquet for his dog. As former agent Joseph L. Schott has reported in his light-hearted memoir of life in the bureau, *No Left Turns,* after an incident in California during which Hoover was jostled uncomfortably during a left-hand turn of his car, he issued a strict order of procedure: There would henceforth be no left turns. His drivers would have to learn to chart their routes accordingly.

Occasionally the director was criticized — for example, by Senator Kenneth McKellar of Tennessee in 1936 — for having little, if any, experience himself in the investigation and detection of crime and for never having made an arrest. As one sympathetic Hoover biographer, Ralph de Toledano, puts it, after McKellar's criticism "Hoover was boiling mad. He felt that his manhood had been impugned." In response, he staged a dramatic trip to New Orleans and supposedly led the raiding party to capture a member of the "Barker gang," Alvin Karpis. Later, thanks to arrangements made by his friend, columnist Walter Winchell, he repeated the performance in New York for the capture of rackets boss Louis "Lepke" Buchalter. Such gestures grabbed headlines and calmed his critics. It was only years later that it became known that Hoover strolled into both situations after all danger was past and that he played a purely symbolic role.

Many of those who worked closely with the director privately resented his comfortable daily schedule. While he took an interest in all the important matters before the bureau, says one longtime aide, he "never lost sleep" — neither from working around the clock nor from worrying about the progress on cases. While his agents logged the required "voluntary overtime," he usually left the office on schedule at 4:45 P.M. There was a standing order not to call him at home after 9 P.M. He handled bureau affairs in a routine and businesslike manner, apparently leaving most of the stresses and strains to others. Nonetheless, Hoover showed unusual leadership abilities and maintained the undying loyalty of almost everyone in the FBI for nearly half a century. He managed to persuade underlings that he cared deeply about their careers, and there are thousands of people still in the FBI who, like Special-Agent-in-Charge Arnold C. Larson of Los Angeles, attribute their success in life to such inspirational personal advice from Hoover as "Set your goals high. Go to college. Better yourself. Don't remain a clerk forever." Anyone in the bureau who ever had a personal audience with the director remembers it in intimate detail, even if it consisted merely, as it often did, of listening to a Hoover monologue on the evils of communism or the misdeeds of politicians. There was competition among some people to the very end to offer proof of their closeness to the director; one ex-bureau official, John P. Mohr, asserts that he was the first to be notified of Hoover's death, and John J. Rooney, the New York congressman who supervised the FBI budget for many years, boasted that he was the only member of Congress at the gravesite after Hoover's funeral.

Hoover was often arbitrary and unreasonable, especially with those jockeying for his favor, but they seldom resisted his way of doing things. "There was a constant desire on your part to please him," explained one man who worked at it for some thirty years. "You wanted to obtain that praise from him, that letter of commendation, that incentive award. When you did, you had a great sense of pride in it. It gave you a feeling of exhilaration; you had accomplished something. He had an ability to keep you at arm's length, yet make you want to work your guts out for him. . . . I rebelled at the idea of working through fear, but I did it anyway. This was my niche. I have always wondered whether the fear was necessary, whether it might have been better to rule on the basis of mutual respect. But it is hard to fight success."

Working for the FBI and for Hoover meant, above all, submitting to discipline and regimentation that sometimes exceeded the military in its severity and lack of compassion. During the Prohibition era, taking a single alcoholic drink was grounds for being fired, if it were discovered. Hoover assumed the right to set standards for his agents' personal lives, and the sexual taboos, for example, were absolute. Not only would young unmarried male and female clerks be dismissed if it were learned that they had had illicit sexual relations, but the same punishment would be dealt to a fellow clerk who knew about any such indiscretion and failed to report it. The rules persisted, at least for agents, well after Hoover's death, and as late as mid-1974 Director Clarence Kelley approved the transfer and demotion to street-agent status for the special-agent-in-charge of the Salt Lake City Field Office because of his alleged amorous adventures.

Cars had to be kept bright and shiny, and agents were to wear conservative suits and white shirts — even though such uniform characteristics often gave them away and made them less effective at their work. Coffee drinking on the job was forbidden, especially at FBI headquarters, and some veterans still tell of "Black Friday," in the 1950s, when a large number of agents were caught drinking coffee in the Justice Department cafeteria after the deadline hour of 9 A.M. and severely punished. The official justification for such harsh standards was that Hoover wanted all his men to have "an unblemished reputation." As one official explained it, "The FBI name was to be so good that whenever an agent went before a jury, he would be believed."

Sometimes Hoover was simply mean; when he discovered that one agent's wife had an alcohol problem and his son was in trouble with drugs, he exiled the family to a small resident agency far away, apparently out of concern that the bureau would be embarrassed if the agent remained where he was stationed. The director was so angered when he heard that another agent had indiscreetly said he was willing to serve "anywhere but New York or Detroit" that he made a personal effort to guarantee that the man's entire career was spent in those two cities. The no-mistake concept that Hoover constantly preached caused the bureau to lose some valuable people to other agencies. William V. Broe, for example, was an up-and-coming supervisor when one minor error in a report that came to the director's attention brought him a cut in pay and a transfer. Broe decided he could not afford to accept the punishment and instead resigned and went to the Central Intelligence Agency, where he rose to one of its top positions.

One of the most-publicized disciplinary excesses involved agent Jack Shaw of the New York Field Office, who was taking graduate courses at the John Jay College of Criminal Justice under FBI auspices. Shaw wrote a letter to one of his professors, in part defending the bureau but also criticizing Hoover for concentrating on "dime-a-dozen" bank robbers and neglecting organized crime, and for a "sledgehammer" approach to public relations, among other matters; foolishly, Shaw had the letter typed in the office secretarial pool and its contents became widely known. Hoover, when the matter reached him, sent Shaw a telegram accusing him of "atrocious judgment" and transferring him to the Butte, Montana, Field Office, despite the fact that his wife was dying of cancer. When Hoover learned that the Shaw letter had been stimulated in the first place by remarks critical of the bureau by one of Shaw's professors, he also ordered that no more agents were to attend the John Jay College or any other educational institution where the FBI was not held in appropriate esteem. Shaw sued for reinstatement, and on behalf of agents' freedom of speech, but ultimately dropped his efforts to return to the bureau and settled for damages of $13,000. He eventually came back into the Justice Department after Hoover died, first working for the Office of National Narcotics Intelligence, then the Drug Enforcement Administration, and eventually the department's Office of Management and Finance.[2]

Hoover had some extraordinary fetishes. His dislike for sweaty or moist palms was rumored to be so extreme that some desperate agents with hands that tended to perspire were nearly driven to seek medical or psychiatric assistance in advance of an occasion when they were expected to shake hands with the director. Jay Robert Nash, in *Citizen Hoover*, tells of an incident in which Hoover, meeting with a new agents

---

[2]The bureau can bear a long grudge on its late director's behalf, however. When it issued passes in 1975 authorizing access to the new FBI building for certain Justice Department personnel, it excluded Shaw.

class, stared repeatedly at one man in the group who had a sallow complexion. The reason was that the man had been wounded in the face during wartime combat, and plastic surgery had been only partially successful; but Hoover didn't like his men to look that way, and so the prospective new agent, who had previously done well during the training course, was told that he had failed a critical examination. The director also instituted a stringent "weight-control program" which followed a life insurance company chart and went well beyond the actual restrictions within which men would be able to perform their jobs effectively. But resourceful individuals sometimes found their way around the rules, and on occasion the nation's number one G-man was easily fooled. Kenneth Whittaker, for example, later special-agent-in-charge of the Miami Field Office, once found himself overweight in advance of a scheduled interview with Hoover. He solved the problem by buying a suit and shirt that were too big for him — to create the impression that he had lost weight, rather than gained it — and personally thanked the director for "saving my life" with the weight requirements. In another instance a man slated to be assigned to one of the bureau's overseas offices was hesitant to keep an appointment with the director because he had gone bald since their last meeting and Hoover did not like to promote bald men. Thinking ahead, and with the help of some clever colleagues, the man wrote to Hoover saying he felt that it would be selfish and unfair to take up the director's precious time just before his annual appearance before the House Appropriations Committee. Hoover agreed and appreciated the man's sacrifice. When the agent later had to visit Hoover on his return from the overseas post, he brought the director a gift large enough to distract his attention from his offensive hairless scalp.

Gifts to Hoover — and sometimes to Tolson — were the clue to many dramatic promotions and rapid advances within the FBI ranks. One up-and-coming man had especially good luck after giving the director a custom-made Persian rug with the initials JEH woven into the center. After a time, major gifts to Hoover from the top leadership were, in effect, informally required on such occasions as his birthday and the yearly anniversary of his appointment as director. Each time his choice, usually things for the home, would be communicated through Tolson, and then the assistant directors would chip in the appropriate amount of money to try to find the item wholesale through bureau contacts. On Hoover's last bureau anniversary before his death, his forty-seventh on May 10, 1971, his aides spent almost two hundred dollars on a trash compacter obtained through an FBI friend at the RCA Whirlpool Corporation. Sometimes, if Hoover was not particularly fond of a gift, he would not hesitate to give it to someone else in the bureau, even though the recipient might have seen it the first time around. It saved him money. On one occasion, office assistant Sam Noisette was surprised and pleased to receive an expensive pair of cuff links from his boss; then he discovered that they were engraved with JEH on the back.

In order to believe that he looked good himself, the director often needed to hear that others looked bad. Some of his men played up to that need. In an FBI memorandum that became available to Justice Department officials during a court case in the 1960s, an assistant director, James H. Gale, described to Hoover a meeting with the attorney general, in this case Nicholas deB. Katzenbach — Gale wrote that the attorney general "squirmed" in his chair and "turned pale" during the discussion; when they later shook hands, the assistant director said, the attorney general's hand was "cold and clammy." On another occasion Hoover returned from a meeting at the White House with President Truman and was furious — the director had quoted a passage from the Bible and Truman had insisted he was misquoting and had corrected him. Back at the bureau, Hoover wanted the matter researched. As it turned out, the director was wrong; but his aides twisted the context and presented their findings to Hoover so that it was the president who seemed foolish.

Others found different routes to favor with the director. One, Robert Kunkel, spent years as a clerk under the tutelage of Hoover's influential secretary Helen Gandy; she was generally considered to be responsible for his becoming an agent and, eventually, a special-agent-in-charge (although he also gained some leverage by giving good stock market tips to the director). John F. Malone, long the special-agent-in-charge in Los Angeles and later the assistant-director-in-charge in New York, is another bureau executive who became close to Hoover, in part because of the friendship he developed with bandleader Lawrence Welk, whose television program was one of the director's favorites.

Even those who admired Hoover's style and tolerated some of his excesses had difficulty with his more irrational and extreme acts. He tended, for example, to go overboard in trying to correct abuses or avoid controversy. After the Central Intelligence Agency was exposed in the late 1960s for having funded the National Student Association and other university groups, the director for a time withdrew authorization for anyone in the FBI to contact anyone on any campus, a ruling that made it difficult for agents to handle some routine inquiries. Eventually he relented. When Hoover declared in 1969 that agents were forbidden to fly on Trans World Airlines, because a TWA pilot had criticized the FBI's handling of a hijacking crisis, agents simply ignored the order because, as aides had tried to point out to Hoover, there were some air routes covered only by TWA. (In connection with the same incident, Hoover wrote to the president of the airline and, apparently drawing upon confidential files, told of the pilot's earlier "difficulties in the Air Force.")

When Hoover was dissatisfied with the cooperation of the Xerox Corporation in the investigion that followed the theft and distribution of documents from the bureau's Media, Pennsylvania, Resident Agency, he sought to have all Xerox photocopying machines removed from all FBI offices and replaced with another brand; that plan was canceled only when assistant directors persuaded him that the change would be cumbersome, time-consuming, and expensive.

It required considerable bureau resources to build and nourish the desired public interest in Hoover. A "correspondence section" handled the replies to incoming mail that sought personal information about the director, ranging from his favorite recipe for apple turnovers to how he ate his steak and what color neckties he preferred. Sometimes the correspondence was handled in a laughable, almost cynical way. Once, for example, a two-page letter was drafted explaining why Hoover's favorite hymn was "When the Roll Is Called up Yonder." When the director saw the draft, he changed his mind and ordered up a new one giving his choice as "Rock of Ages." The correspondence section merely substituted the name of one hymn for the other and sent the letter out, with the explanation for the choice left the same.

One of the major occasions for pronouncements of wisdom from the director was his annual trip to Capitol Hill to justify the bureau's budget request before the House Appropriations Committee. (He testified only occasionally before the parallel Senate committee.) The transcripts of these sessions read smoothly and show Hoover first giving an eloquent statement and then responding with impressive clarity to every question posed by his congressional interrogators. Bureau officials familiar with the closed-door committee meetings, however, say that quite a lot of work went into sprucing up the public version of the transcripts; one told it this way: "There would be serious mistakes every time he appeared, especially before the House committee. The director would recite the facts concerning particular cases, and he might have them all wrong, even providing false information about individuals. Sometimes he would be completely off base, especially when he attempted to answer the congressmen's questions. . . . So we would always get the record back the next day, and we would work almost around the clock for three or four days to straighten it out. The job was controlled by John Mohr in the Administrative Division. We would take out the garrulous crap and replace it with perfect language and grammar. When the record came out [publicly], it would be beautiful; it had to be, because Hoover would issue it to everyone on the FBI mailing list. . . . The congressmen were proud to be part of it all, and most of them probably didn't even notice the difference."

But some of the Hoover statements were impossible to take out or doctor up, especially if some of the legislators had immediately latched on to them for their own purposes. The story is told of the occasion in the late 1940s when the director was asked how much crime cost the country each year and he answered, off the top of his head, twenty-two billion dollars. Back at headquarters later, in trying to justify the figure, the best anyone could come up with was eleven billion. But the public record was left to stand, of course, since Hoover's word was assumed to be gospel. That figure was used blindly for years until finally someone wrote in and asked why, in light of the increase in crime, its cost to the nation never changed. From that time on, the bureau began raising the estimate slightly each year.

These slips and quirks were not publicly known, however, and even had they been revealed, they would have posed no serious threat to Hoover's position. He had himself locked securely in place and employed foolproof techniques for keeping himself there. One was to let it be widely known, or at least believed, that his men in the field were collecting juicy tidbits about political figures, unrelated to pending cases but submitted for Hoover's personal interest and, if necessary, his use. Francis Biddle, one of President Franklin Roosevelt's attorney generals with whom Hoover got along well, wrote in his memoirs that the director, in private sessions with him, displayed an "extraordinarily broad knowledge of the intimate details of what my associates in the cabinet did and said, of their likes, their weaknesses and their associations." Such information was stored in special locked file cabinets in Hoover's inner office. Access was permitted to only about ten Hoover lieutenants through Miss Gandy. The director's personal files included some political dynamite — allegations about the extramarital affairs of President Roosevelt and his wife Eleanor, the inside story about an undersecretary of state believed to be a homosexual and his alleged attempt to seduce a porter during a train ride to Tennessee, incidents from Richard Nixon's years as vice president, and the early escapades of John F. Kennedy. The files grew thicker and more significant all the time, because whenever someone entered the running for president, Hoover would have any records on him in the bureau's general files pulled out, updated, and transferred to his office. What use Hoover made of any particular file is a matter of speculation; but what is now clear is that the implicit threat to use them was always there. It was one way of instilling in politicians a special kind of loyalty toward the FBI: fear of what Hoover might have on them and could choose to reveal. What became of each of Hoover's controversial private files after his death is still a subject of some mystery and concern. Miss Gandy and Tolson are each believed to have taken some with them when they left the bureau, and others were moved into the office of W. Mark Felt, who became acting associate director under Acting Director L. Patrick Gray, 3d, and were later inherited by Associate Director Nicholas Callahan.

Many of the files are unaccounted for and were probably shredded before Hoover died or shortly after.

Attorney General Edward H. Levi, testifying before the House Judiciary Subcommittee on Civil Rights and Constitutional Rights on February 27, 1975, announced an inventory of the 164 files that had been made available to him from the associate director's office. Classified as Official and Confidential material or marked OC, they included "many routine, mundane and totally innocuous materials," Levi said; but he also acknowledged that at least forty-eight of the folders contained "derogatory information concerning individuals," including members of Congress. It seemed clear that some of the most important OC files were missing — and that there was probably another entire set of delicate Hoover files, perhaps labeled Personal and Confidential, that were missing and were never made available to the attorney general at all. Miss Gandy later admitted destroying the "personal" files.

Another of Hoover's successful techniques was to calculate carefully his relationships with those in power. As one former associate noted, the director had "many of the attributes of a genius. He could identify people's foibles and weaknesses and play upon them cleverly." He was not particularly fond of the Kennedy brothers, but the brother he liked least was Robert, who sought to assert unprecedented control over the FBI when he became his brother's attorney general. (One irritant, according to those in the Justice Department in the early 1960s, was Kennedy's personal comportment; Hoover felt that he desecrated the hallowed halls of the Justice Department by strolling around in his shirtsleeves and by bringing his dog to the office.) Hoover knew of, and exploited, Lyndon Johnson's distrust of Robert Kennedy, and immediately after John Kennedy's assassination the director virtually suspended communication with the attorney general. He replaced a Kennedy intimate, Courtney Evans, as White House liaison with a Johnson favorite, Cartha D. DeLoach. Hoover's antennae were excellent and helped him move quickly to keep up with any realignment of power.

Whatever the complaints about Hoover, most observers generally praised him for keeping the bureau honest and above the temptation of corruption to which so many other law enforcement agencies succumbed. But it has become clear that the director himself did not measure up to the rigorous standards of honesty and avoidance of conflict of interest that he set for others. In an agency where a man could be severely disciplined for taking an office car home overnight without special permission, it was a little difficult to reconcile and justify the fact that the director had five bulletproof limousines, each worth about $30,000, at his service — two in Washington and one each in Los Angeles, New York, and Miami — and that he regularly used them for personal business, like trips to the racetrack or on his vacations with

Tolson. The vacations, in Florida or southern California, were never officially called vacations but "inspection trips" — meaning that Hoover would drop in at a field office or two each time and shake hands. That was enough for him to charge the whole trip to the government.

In Miami Hoover stayed free at a hotel owned by Meyer Schine, who admitted in congressional testimony that he also had ties with big-name bookmakers. (Schine's son, G. David, was counsel to Senator Joseph McCarthy's investigating subcommittee, along with Roy Cohn.) In La Jolla, California, his stays at the Hotel Del Charro were at no cost, courtesy of the owners, millionaire Texas businessmen Clint Murchison and Sid Richardson. Sometimes they had elaborate parties in La Jolla in Hoover's honor, flying in specially prepared chili from Texas for the occasion; the bills that were never presented to Hoover and Tolson ran into the thousands of dollars. Murchison and Richardson gained control of a nearby racetrack that Hoover frequented; some of the profits from it were supposed to be channeled to a newly established charitable foundation, but prominent members of the foundation board soon quit when they found that this was not happening. Both of these Hoover friends came under investigation in the mid-1950s in connection with a controversial proxy fight to win control of the New York Central Railroad, and it was learned years later that Richardson, who had extensive oil holdings, made payments to Robert Anderson while Anderson was serving as President Eisenhower's secretary of the treasury and was in a position to influence national oil policy. By means that were never publicly known, Hoover himself amassed substantial oil, gas, and mineral leases in Texas and Louisiana — they were valued at $125,000 at the time of his death — alongside his other valuable investments. All the while the director was growing rich, he never hesitated to accept free accommodations wherever he traveled.

His annual visit to the West Coast became one of the most important events on Hoover's calendar. If the invitation to stay at the Del Charro did not arrive on schedule, the SAC in San Diego was asked to nudge it along. One year the field office there was sent into a frenzy because it had neglected to stock the hotel's freezer with the director's favorite ice cream. When he asked for it upon arrival, the SAC had to call the ice cream manufacturer to open his plant at night in order to satisfy Hoover's needs. A stenographer from the field office was then dressed up as a waitress and dispatched to the Del Charro to serve the ice cream to Hoover and Tolson.

The director eagerly used the extensive and sometimes expert facilities of the bureau for his own personal whim and benefit. He was reluctant, ostensibly for security reasons, to permit outside workmen in or near his home, so it was the FBI laboratory that performed such duties as building a porch or installing new appliances. The lab was sent in on one occasion because Hoover was impatient with how long it took his television set to start up. The problem was solved by rigging the unit so that it was always on; he just had to turn it up to get the picture. Unknown to Hoover, this just meant that the tubes burned out and had to be changed often — at government expense. Sometimes the lab's assignments nearly resulted in disaster, as on the occasion Hoover decided that he wanted a new toilet installed. But the director did not like the new one, because it was too low, and he demanded the old one back. Fortunately, the technicians were able to reclaim it from a junk heap after a search.

In his earliest days at the bureau, Hoover had steadfastly and emphatically declined to profit from the G-man boom, turning back the honoraria when he gave speeches and declining to endorse cigarettes or other commercial products. But as time passed he became avaricious. When the Freedoms Foundation, a conservative organization based in Valley Forge, Pennsylvania, twice gave him its gold medal and five-thousand-dollar award, it called ahead to the director's aides, pointing out that it was customary for the recipient of the award to donate the money back to the foundation. Both times Hoover refused and said he intended to keep the money for himself. Perhaps the most profitable transactions, however, involved the books published under Hoover's name, especially the enormously successful *Masters of Deceit,* subtitled *The Story of Communism in American and How to Fight It.* The book was written primarily by agent Fern Stukenbroeker, a bureau researcher on subversive groups, but the substantial royalties were divided five ways — one-fifth each to Hoover; Tolson; Assistant-to-the-Director Louis B. Nichols; William I. Nichols (no relation to Louis), editor and publisher of *This Week* magazine, who helped to market the book; and the FBI Recreation Association — which permitted the director to contend that the profits were going to the hard-working FBI personnel. Hoover aides urged that Stukenbroeker be rewarded for his efforts with an incentive award. Hoover balked, but agreed after a dispute; however, he knocked the amount down from five hundred dollars to two hundred and fifty. Later, when Warner Brothers wanted to launch a television series about the FBI, Hoover's condition was that the film studio purchase the movie rights to *Masters of Deceit.* His price was seventy-five thousand dollars. As the deal was being closed, the director suddenly got cold feet and worried whether he would be subjecting himself to criticism. He sent Cartha DeLoach to President Johnson to discuss the situation, and Johnson gave his confidential approval. The television series, with Efrem Zimbalist, Jr., as the star, got off to a successful start. Hoover pocketed the money and later left it to Clyde Tolson.

When J. Edgar Hoover died suddenly on May 2, 1972, the news was initially kept from the agents for about three hours; the day began like any other in the bureau, early and busily. When the word finally came out, it was greeted with a combination of shock and relief. Some felt comfort, for Hoover's sake, that he had died painlessly and in the job rather than suffering the indignity of replacement after forty-eight years; others looked ahead to the opportunity, at last, for a review and reconsideration of the FBI and its roles. Many were oblivious to the turmoil Hoover was leaving behind, and few sensed the trouble ahead.

That night, hundreds of agents and former agents, some traveling from far away, gathered at a funeral home in Washington to pay their respects to the director. One who came from out of town later recalled the scene this way: "They had washed his hair, and all the dye had come out. His eyebrows, too. He looked like a wispy, gray-haired, tired little man. There, in the coffin, all the front, all the power, and the color had been taken away."

The next day his body lay in state in the rotunda of the United States Capitol and Hoover was eulogized by Chief Justice Warren E. Burger as "a man who epitomized the American dream of patriotism, dedication to duty, and successful attainment." A day later, in the National Presbyterian Church, President Nixon added his own tribute: "He was one of those individuals who, by all odds, was the best man for a vitally important job. His powerful leadership by example helped to keep steel in America's backbone and the flame of freedom in America's soul." He was buried not at Arlington National Cemetery but, in accordance with his instructions, at the Congressional Cemetery in the Capitol Hill section of Washington, with members of his family.

On the first anniversary of Hoover's death — a day that one can imagine Hoover would have wanted to be elaborately noted — there was no ceremony because the FBI was in disarray. On the second anniversary, Director Clarence M. Kelley led the assistant directors in a solemn, private wreath-laying ceremony at the director's grave. For the faithful, that made things seem a little better again.

F BI DIRECTOR J. EDGAR HOO-
ver became a legend in his own
time. He was the paradigm of the
bureaucratic politician, building an
empire that transcended and circum-
vented the formal lines of authority that
placed the FBI under the attorney general. Presidents did not attempt to fire
Hoover, as some of them would have
like, nor did powerful members of Congress call for the director's resignation.
They did not love Hoover, but feared
him and respected his power.

The bureaucracy is highly political at
every level, but especially at the top.
Those who make the bureaucracy a lifelong career must play a particularly
astute political game if they want to
maintain and expand the power they
have attained. Civil Service laws protect
the lowly bureaucrat, but not the
ambitious one who has achieved a
policymaking position by moving up
from within the bureaucracy.

Outside political appointees, such as
cabinet secretaries, must also be skilled
in making their voices heard at the
White House, on Capitol Hill, and within their own departments. Unlike their
bureau chiefs and many of their principal aides, however, cabinet secretaries
usually have a firm base outside of the
bureaucracy to which they happily return if trouble overwhelms them. When
President Jimmy Carter fired Joseph Califano, his secretary of Health, Education
and Welfare, Califano simply returned to
his prosperous Washington law practice
where he reportedly makes $1.5 million
a year, a sharp contrast to his $60,000
per year salary as secretary. There are
others like Califano, such as Caspar
Weinberger, Reagan's defense secretary,
and John Connally, former Texas governor and treasury secretary under Nixon, who move in and out of government
with ease, all of the time maintaining
their reputations for power.

By contrast with the Califanos of the
political world, those who have chosen
to make the bureaucracy a permanent
career must construct barriers against the
winds of political change, or learn to
bend with them. Those who stay in power often use their entrepreneurial talents
to build empires that are immune from
outside attack. Others learn to serve, or
appear to serve, their master of the moment. The entrepreneurs, such as J.
Edgar Hoover and Admiral Hyman Rickover, often become public figures because of their ability to cultivate and manipulate the press. But there are largely
invisible bureaucrats as well who es-
chew publicity and remain in power by
making themselves indispensable to
their chiefs.

The following selection depicts both
the entrepreneurial, often flamboyant
holders of bureaucratic power, and
those that quietly stay at the top by effectively adjusting to constant political
change.

30 Jonathan Alter
THE POWERS THAT STAY

What's hard, at the political level [of the bureaucracy], is *staying* in — figuring out how to avoid these four-year dry spells when all you can do is write op-ed pieces, agonize over lunch dates, and decide which boring law firm or think tank to bide your time in while waiting for a chance to get back to the action. The real survivors don't have to worry that they're not so terrific at picking *which* obscure former governor will win the Iowa caucuses. Why sweat it? They're still in.

How does this group of high-wire performers do it? Well, most of the survivors themselves aren't of much help beyond a grunt or two and the startling revelations that they "worked hard" or "just outlived 'em." Like other great con men, they can't ever admit their secrets, for if they do — confessing to "gambits" and "techniques" — it's a good bet they've just taken the first step toward permanent retirement. That's because success in this slippery game is determined by whether they have come to believe their own cons, and whether they've so adroitly melded their personalities, instincts, and accomplishments that they fool everybody, even themselves.

But taking that as a given, there are basically two ways of surviving in the goverment: Call them "ring kissing" and "empire building." Ring kissing is based on the model practiced by low-level civil servants and other prostrate subordinates throughout American society, but at the high levels we're talking about, it must be perfected to an art form. This requires that the aspiring survivor perform all sorts of tasks that convince his superiors (and potential future superiors) that he is indispensable. By making the boss look good, or by simply doing the boss's bidding, the imaginative ring kisser can collect a government check practically forever.

Empire building, by contrast, doesn't require the help of superiors at all. In fact, the best empire builders have prevailed over active opposition from presidents, cabinet secretaries, and others who would prefer they hang up their spikes. They survive by carving out independent power bases that are stronger than normal lines of authority, and by developing constituencies on Capitol Hill and in the press that help them to pursue their own goals. Because these goals are their own and not simply a divining of what the boss wants, the empires often take on a momentum that translates into longevity for the people who build them.

Ring kissers, you may have guessed, are by far the more common breed. In fact, most government officials planning a career in survival are only dimly aware that another model exists. This is their loss, for the very greatest of Washington players — the sultans of survival — have rejected supplication as a technique. The career of Hyman Rickover certainly testifies to that. He served in the navy for more than sixty years, at least half of them under chiefs of naval operations who would have preferred he stay submerged for good after one of his sea trials. Or consider J. Edgar Hoover. Almost every president and attorney general he served under during his forty-eight-year career as director of the FBI disliked him, but when he left the bureau, it was on his back. These masters may have been exceptions, but the skills they plied contain some useful lessons about how to complete lengthy service in the U.S. government — and how to do it without acting like a toady.

Shanghai Log Cabins

To get a sense of the real difference between the two kinds of survival, let's look at a few examples of people who fall into the ring-kissing category, who fit the conventional image of how a "Washington survivor" is supposed to behave.

The man believed by himself and some others to be Washington's "ultimate survivor" is Joseph Laitin, a public affairs officer who survived at a high level from Kennedy to Johnson to Nixon to Ford to Carter. Laitin's aim was to serve his "client," as he put it, the point being that clients tend to appreciate good service and respond with job security. His biggest client was Lyndon Johnson, and his idea of serving him — in fact, the principal Joe Laitin accomplishment of the years he spent as deputy White House press secretary — was to feed the president gossip. When LBJ went to the ranch, he'd call Laitin frequently at about 11 to hear scuttlebutt on reporters traveling to Texas. Johnson felt particularly unfriendly toward one reporter for the old New York Herald Tribune, and Laitin was only too happy to regale the boss with tales of the reporter's after-hours activities. "At first I told true stories about him," Laitin has proudly recounted on several occasions, "but then I began making them up. I think the president knew I was making them up, but he loved it just the same."

That story, pathetic as it is, has been trotted out for years as testimony to Laitin's uncanny ability to survive. Of course, "serving the client" can also take the form of genuinely helping the boss, and Laitin was good at that, too. So good, in fact, that the Ford and Carter White Houses got angry at him because he made his clients, James Schlesinger under Ford and Michael Blumenthal under Carter, look good in the press at the expense of the president.

Take the time Treasury Secretary Blumenthal flew out to the Far East for meetings. As assistant secretary for public affairs, Laitin went too, fulfilling the classic survivalist dictum that you should always travel with the boss. (The logic, now a bit dated, being that if you and the chief happen upon certain naughty diversions, it makes it hard for him ever to fire you.) Anyway, Laitin, employing his gift, suddenly insisted that Blumenthal visit Shanghai, where the new treasury secretary had lived as a boy after escaping Nazism. "That's your log cabin," Laitin told him. Blumenthal made the trip and came away with enormous publicity, not to mention respect for Laitin. Was Laitin providing good information to the public about economic issues? That didn't matter to Blumenthal. Was the large section of the department for which he was responsible well run? That didn't matter either.

So Laitin, like countless other ring kissers, could hardly be blamed for sensing that all that really matters in surviving is pleasing those above you. As for subordinates, according to this model of survival they aren't especially relevant. That explains why reporters tend to like Laitin as a person and as a professional (in part because he leaked a lot), while a number of former subordinates show a decided lack of enthusiasm on the subject of their old chief. If Laitin was known around press haunts as a guy who never forgot the name of an important reporter or government official, at Treasury he spent so much time on the phone and out to lunch that he is said not to have known even the names of two of the secretaries in his own office. A few years earlier, while at the FAA, he walked into the office of one of his top staffers one day and the secretaries remarked that they had never even *seen* him before. But why should they have? Laitin wasn't building an empire; he was building a reputation — for service to superiors.

As you can imagine, such reputations don't often depend heavily on a person's beliefs. Like most public affairs officers — indeed, like most ring kissers who bounce from agency to agency — Laitin was not much of a policy man. To come across as one is considered bad form for survivors choosing this mode, the obvious reason being that the more closely associated you are with a particular policy, the worse off you'll be when administrations change. (The new guard can usually tell the difference between those who make policy and those who just mouth it.) On the other hand, if you don't identify with the administration at least partially, you could be out *before* the next election. So there's a balance to be struck.

A man who has spent the better part of a lifetime striking that balance is Dwight Ink, who for thirty years was a top manager at a half-dozen different agencies. Ink was a competent manager as managers go, but his greatest skill, according to several people who worked with him, was appearing neither too partisan nor too facelessly neutral. The latter is the way most career civil servants play it, and that's why few rise to be superbureaucrats at a political level. Ink was different. Whether he was at the AEC, or HUD, or OMB he could subtly — and without really saying anything — convey a sympathy with the prevailing political ideology, then just as effortlessly shed those few calculated ounces of conviction when bosses or administrations changed.

"If he knew what the secretary wanted, he'd help you get it," recalls Charles Haar, a Harvard law professor who was an assistant secretary of HUD in the late 1960s when Ink was assistant secretary for administration. "But he'd never move anything too fast; the instinct was for more paper, more copies, more dotted i's and crossed t's rather than for getting something done." The reason for that, as Haar and others have noted, is that getting something done too fast might have put him in a vulnerable position, and that kind of vulnerability is what the ring-kissing survivalist fears most.

Like many other administrators who endure for years, Ink is smart, hard-working, and competent; that's his reputation, and it's one reason he gets tapped so frequently. The problem with the definition lies with that word "competence." More often than not, the word has come to mean a peculiarly calibrated type of bureaucratic performance that doesn't have much to do with commitment to goals. While sometimes sharing and acting upon the boss's goals, subordinates too often substitute for genuine aims the kind of "managerial" efficiencies that so many administrators mistakenly believe can be separated from issues of policy.

Thus, just as Joe Laitin never cared much about the politics of his clients as long as they sold briskly and reflected well on the salesman, so Dwight Ink never cared much about the prevailing philosophy of government as long as it allowed him to "do the job," whatever that meant. Given that, it was no big surprise when Ink accepted Reagan's offer last year to come out of retirement and coordinate the dismantling of the Community Services Administration, snuffing out some of the very same programs he once helped create while working at HUD. It wasn't that Ink had decided on long reflection that the programs didn't work. He simply did what good ring kissers believe they are supposed to do. He did what he was told.

Wind Sniffing

Now, in some ways it's a little unfair to single out Laitin and Ink. After all, they simply responded to the same ground rules for survival that most other upper-level bureaucrats, including many still in the government, subscribe to. Take William Heffelfinger of the Department of Energy. Reagan is planning to put DOE out of its misery, and Heffelfinger, as assistant secretary for management and administration, will do the bulk of the honors (the secretary, James Edwards, is a deferential sort of tooth puller). The fact that Heffelfinger held a similar job under Carter when the department was *created* passes in Washington without notice. After all, the standard response goes, these are bureaucrats we're talking about, and they're supposed to be "professionals."

Heffelfinger's hard-nosed — many call it brutal — style of management is said to be the only reason he survives at all. A congressional subcommittee learned in 1978 that during his many earlier government incarnations he had falsified his resume by adding degrees and awards he never received, and had destroyed public documents, among other vices. When a man can undergo a full-scale congressional investigation and still get reappointed — and the reason he can get the new job is that he has a reputation for cracking the whip and otherwise pleasing whoever is boss — the legend of this route to survival grows stronger. This is true despite the fact that Heffelfinger does not appear to act like a timid ring kisser. He yells and screams and tries to be a "tough" manager who gets things done. Depending on whom you talk to, that may even be true. The point, though, is that he furthers the impression that the best strategy for getting ahead in the government is to do others' bidding rather than your own. Heffelfinger may have missed out on other survivalist secrets — a clean nose, for instance — but he remembered the one about sniffing the wind to catch the drift of one's superiors.

The current master of that art is Frank Carlucci, a hard-working, bright, former foreign service officer, ambassador, deputy director of the Office of Economic Opportunity, deputy director of OMB, deputy CIA director, and now deputy secretary of defense. Carlucci's legendary budget-cutting abilities, like those of his current boss, Cap (nee "the Knife") Weinberger, were dulled considerably once it became clear what *Weinberger's* boss — the president — really thought about defense spending. The quickness of Carlucci's response to Reagan's concerns about leaks testifies to this uncanny meteorological ability that is so often believed to be essential for ring-kissing survival. Carlucci embraced and implemented the order that lie detector tests be administered to senior defense officials. And like the good soldier he is, went first.

Ultimately, the lie detectors may prove far more destructive to Reagan than the leaks. As high-ranking Carter administration officials can attest, nothing so quickly breaks down basic loyalty to a president as this particular brand of faith in one's trustworthiness. But more to the point, the lie detectors prove once and for all that Carlucci belongs among the ring kissers. He apparently considers it a productive day's work to have humiliated colleagues and subordinates in order to keep the boss happy.

Persuasion by Polar Water

Of course in his heart of hearts, Frank Carlucci probably doesn't like ring kissing very much. In his line of work, ambition is not easily sublimated, and people who know him say that his will to survive is developing into a will to conquer. What Carlucci may be learning is that conquering can assure surviving, and that it makes some sense to develop empire-building skills, which in Washington means contacts in the press and on the Hill. These contacts are not meant to make your boss look good (the survival technique of a Laitin) but to make *you* look good, and to hell with your boss.

The greatest empire builder of recent years is Admiral Hyman G. Rickover, who as a captain after World War II came up with an idea — nuclear submarines — and in the next thirty-five years proceeded to shape almost every aspect of the U.S. Navy: training, technology, surface ships, and so forth. The way he did it is a fascinating story, but equally interesting is the way he got away with it without losing his job.

It was in 1952 that Rickover first realized the classic ring-kissing route wouldn't work for him. He had already beaten the odds and made great progress on the development of the first nuclear submarine (it was eventually finished many years ahead of schedule), but that year a navy selection board passed him over for promotion from captain to rear admiral for the second time. Whether it was because of his Jewish background or simply that he already nettled navy brass, his career appeared over. Up to then, two rejections meant automatic retirement.

But Rickover was smart enough to know that if he could create enough interest outside the navy, he might have a fighting chance after all. In part because he had a sexy project (though it really wasn't much more newsworthy that year than a lot of what goes on in government today), he caught the attention of the press, particularly a young Pentagon correspondent for *Time* named Clay Blair. Blair knew a good story when he saw one, and Rickover knew how to be cooperative — he even lent the use of his office and his wife's editing skills for the book Blair eventually wrote about him. In later years, once safely ensconced, Rickover shunned reporters. But when it counted he played them masterfully, especially those journalists like Edward R. Murrow whom he knew could endow him with some of their own respectability.

Meanwhile, he wasted no time meeting the right people on the Hill. The year before the promotion controversy he happened to have been seated on an airplane next to a young politician named Henry Jackson. They became friends, and along with Representative Sidney Yates, Jackson led the charge that forced the navy to make Rickover a rear admiral, notwithstanding the selection board's decision. Rickover reached the mandatory retirement age for all navy personnel in 1963, but until last year (when at age eighty-one he almost sank a submarine while at the controls) he continually had been granted special two-year extensions, a biennial event that caused untold teeth gnashing among his superiors.

Why did Congress admire Rickover so much? Part was clever flattery. He took members on submarine rides, wrote them hundreds of hand-written notes while on historic sea trials (who wouldn't save a letter with the dateline, "At Sea, Submerged"?), and brought back "polar water" as gifts for their offices. But most important, according to his recent biographers, Norman Polmar and Thomas B. Allen, was a peculiar "chemistry" he developed with many congressmen that made them believe they actually were involved with the building of the world's first nuclear-powered submarine and, later, with the creation of a nuclear navy. That chemistry — a critical element in any kind of empire build-ing — is really just the reflection of an ability to accomplish goals.

The fact that Congress and the press respond best to tangible achieve-ment — as opposed to loyal ring kissing — has not always been a posi-tive thing for the country. Just because reporters and congressmen can see it, touch it, and report it back home, doesn't mean the rest of us need it, as Rickover's success in winning support for a poorly conceived weapon like the Trident submarine suggests. But if this kind of con-gressional behavior can bring us bad weapons and wasteful pork barrel projects, it can also bring out the best in government employees — the desire to create and produce, and the understanding that if you do a good enough job in those areas, forces outside the bureaucracy will help you survive.

Rickover should be particularly inspirational to budding empire builders because he proves that rank plays no role in such survival. He was a *fourth-echelon* officer (as deputy commander for nuclear propul-sion, Naval Ships System Command, he reported to the chief of naval materiel, who reported to the chief of naval operations, who reported to the president). That's not to say he didn't use what position he did have, but in Rickover's case this meant an additional position *outside* of the navy, at the Atomic Energy Commission (and later at the Department of Energy).

Many powerful survivors have donned two hats before — Richard J. Daley was both mayor of Chicago and chairman of the powerful party committee that slated candidates for mayor of Chicago — but Rickover elevated it into an art form. Admiral Elmo Zumwalt, who despised Rickover for upstaging him when Zumwalt was chief of naval op-erations, recalls that when a navy request irked Rickover, his standard practice was to reply on AEC stationery, which allowed him to distribute the copies of his position to congressional friends without going through the navy chain of command.

It was that chain of command that drove Rickover to distraction.

Acting solicitous toward Congress and the press was one thing, the point being that it helped you accrue more autonomy for yourself. But performing like that every day for your boss was quite another (although Rickover expected it of *his* much-abused staff). "What was fatal to [General Wilhelm] Keitel [chief of Hitler's combined general staff] was not his weaknesses," Rickover lectured a congressional committee during one of his more than 150 formal appearances on the Hill, "but his virtues — the virtues of a subordinate." Among such regrettable virtues, Rickover believed, was a conception of the chain of command as something that entitled a bureaucrat to someday win perquisites. As far as he was concerned, such niceties had nothing at all to do with power and survival.

So where Frank Carlucci tends to want the best office space available, Rickover worked for thirty years out of a converted ladies room with no rug and flaking yellow plasterboard; where William Heffelfinger dines most afternoons at the likes of Le Provencal, Rickover had canned soup, cottage cheese, and skimmed milk at his desk; and where Joe Laitin, while assistant secretary of defense, bragged that he sat ahead of the generals in a motorcade, Rickover rarely wore a uniform and was indifferent to the idea of a fourth star. After all, he reasoned, what did organization charts have to do with building and keeping an empire?

Passport to Perpetuation

Now, not everybody in the government can, or should, think like Hyman Rickover. If they did, we'd have a country of anarchists and ulcers. But the fact remains that in almost any realm — military or civilian — chain of command tends to impede action. The best empire builders recognize this and risk angering others in the hierarchy who believe individual initiative is a threat. Their power *and* their survival depend on a base outside the normal line of authority.

The greatest practitioner of this art was J. Edgar Hoover. When Hoover took over the FBI in 1924, it was a weak, corrupt, politicized, highly ineffective agency. When he died in 1972, the same thing might have been said. But in between, the FBI was, in the words of Victor Navasky, editor of the *Nation* and hardly a Hoover admirer, the "least corruptible, most sophisticated investigative agency in the world." Hoover revolutionized the science of crime detection — *legitimate* crime detection — by sponsoring innovation in lab work and training and by creating a high standard of performance for his agents.

The point is not to absolve this racist redbaiter of his crimes — against Martin Luther King, Jr., Jean Seberg, and the Constitution in general — but simply to make it clear that Hoover could not rely solely on his survivalist wits. If his cagey bureaucratic abilities had not been underlain by a strong conviction on the part of outsiders that he was doing something good, he wouldn't have made it.

But accomplishment, as any government official should know, takes you only so far. Like Rickover, Hoover undertook a major effort to cultivate the press, particularly columnist Walter Winchell, and the Congress, particularly Representative John J. Rooney, who for twenty-five years oversaw the FBI's budget. Equally important, he cultivated a public image, by using gimmicks like the Ten Most Wanted List and a long-running television series. Efrem Zimbalist, Jr., may be reluctant to star in the TV version of "The FDA" (co-starring special agent James Beard?), but that doesn't mean heads of government agencies less dramatic than the FBI cannot borrow some of the imagination Hoover used to create a public constituency for his programs.

You don't have to be as famous as Rickover or Hoover in order to use such skills. Consider the case of a woman named Frances Knight, who ran the passport office at the state department for more than twenty years, largely over the objections of most of the secretaries of state she saw come and go. These men resented her fiefdom but were essentially powerless to do anything about it. (Finally, in 1977, the state department succeeded in turning the passport office into what the career people always wanted — a place to let foreign service officers punch their tickets while waiting for another overseas assignment.)

Knight was controversial, but she realized that controversy, because it keeps the press interested, can be the stuff of survival, even for those in seemingly modest positions. She also understood that the press and Congress respond best if they are fed and cared for. When Drew Pearson called one Christmas Eve to say he needed fifteen passports right away, she hustled down to the office. When a congressman had a problem with a constituent's passport, she took care of it within hours, an ability that members of Congress still recall with awe.

These survival skills, applied on the Hill and in the press, should not necessarily make us feel more cynical about the way the government works. As it happens, Knight often would extend the same service to anyone (airline clerks at international terminals across the country had her home phone number). But even if she hadn't, such cultivation of outside sources of power isn't objectionable in itself. What *is* objectionable is the use of such networks solely for the purpose of surviving. When the aim instead is survival as a way of accomplishing admirable goals — even if the goal is simply running an efficient passport office — well, then even the most dubious survival techniques can be put to good use.

To demonstrate the point, let's look at the most base and contemptible of those techniques, namely, Hoover's use of blackmail. The conversation with a congressman usually went something like this:

"Hello, congressman. Edgar Hoover here. Terribly sorry to hear about this unfortunate matter."

"What do you mean?"

"Well, we've had some reports that have come into our field office in your district. Frankly, I personally find them very difficult to believe. The whole thing just doesn't sound like you. But I just wanted to alert you to the fact that some reports have indeed been filtering into the bureau."

"What reports?

"Believe me, congressman, this matter will be kept in strictest confidence between us. I've instructed the field office to route all the details of your case straight to the director."

Whatever the congressman's little embarrassment — a drunken visit to a whorehouse, a son who happened to be a homosexual — Hoover knew how to use it to his advantage. The strategy, which didn't have to be employed too often to be effective, worked equally well with presidents. Hoover's reappointment was John Kennedy's first order of business after his election, and even after a feud broke out between Hoover and his nominal boss, Robert Kennedy (during which the director instructed tour guides at the FBI building to point out that he had become head of the bureau the year before the attorney general was born), JFK never even considered his removal. How could he? Hoover knew certain, uh, *details* about Kennedy's personal life. If William Sullivan, long-time number three man at the bureau, is to be believed, Hoover used this strategy even on Nixon of all people, after he and Bebe Rebozo were spotted in the company of a particular Chinese woman during trips to Hong Kong in the mid-1960s. By the early 1970s, Nixon, once a big Hoover booster, wanted him fired too, but like other presidents, he subscribed to Lyndon Johnson's memorable judgment that given the permeability of the administration's tent, it made more sense to have Hoover inside pissing out.

Honorable Blackmail

It doesn't require a deep sensitivity to fine moral distinctions to see that Hoover's form of persuasion constituted the most reprehensible form of survivalism imaginable. But if you think about it a moment, you might realize that Hoover's blackmail, *sans* the prurient details, can be surprisingly instructive, especially to people who, unbelievable as it sounds, want to do good with their government service.

Suppose you hope to improve your program or agency, and that such improvement demands a certain level of performance from your boss. To the extent that you let the boss know that you are cognizant of what is wrong in this program or agency, and to the extent that he knows you care enough to do something about it, you have created in him a dependency not unlike that felt by presidents toward Hoover. This assumes, of course, that the boss is aware that you have attended to the fundamental empire-building duties of making contacts on the Hill and in the press that might allow you to make good on the implied threat of revelation, and it assumes that you have the guts to use those contacts. If the boss believes that you really are willing and able to go public, then he's more likely to want you inside his tent. That means you now have a powerful ability to pursue your own vision of how your agency or program should be run. Your boss, respecting this new power, will provide you more autonomy, which, assuming you maintain those essential outside contacts, could be the beginning of your own empire.

But what's remarkable is that even if you have no designs on an empire — even if you like your boss so much that you might be characterized as a ring kisser — you still can play a form of this game. In fact, the most effective user of constructive blackmail is the person who admires his superior, who wants to believe the best about him, who hopes that the boss soon realizes that his subordinates and all of the people who believe in his program will be disappointed if he doesn't shape up. What this really involves is a genuine, sincere version of what Hoover was disingenuously saying on the telephone to that congressman. It is an unconscious, unspoken way of playing not on the boss's fear of being exposed, but on his sense of guilt — guilt that he will disillusion those who share his goals.

Naturally, the only way the ring kisser can inspire that very positive form of guilt is if he does indeed share those goals. And if he does share them, he might not be such an objectionable ring kisser after all. Harry Hopkins (FDR's aide) and D. B. Hardeman (Sam Rayburn's aide) are examples of this better breed. Because they believed in what their bosses were trying to do, they shared in their bosses' accomplishments. Conversely, when ring kissers do not believe in what their superiors are trying to do — when they are simply determined to outlast them — then they do not share in their major accomplishments, except in the sense that they feel a little battered for having endured the long ride. Joe Laitin showed a keen sensitivity to this point when he admitted to the *Los Angeles Times* last year after his luck finally ran out that "I can't point to one thing I've accomplished, but my blood is all over this town for fighting for what I believe is right." What was "right," of course, was simply survival itself.

So the determining factor is not which strategy you choose to employ, but what you want to employ those survivalist techniques *for*. If survival is an end in itself, then none of the gambits are worthy of our respect. On the other hand, if survival is used as the means to genuine accomplishment, then ring kissing, currying favor with Congress and the press, even blackmail have their place when done constructively. That doesn't make all survival techniques equal in morality or even in plain tastefulness, but it can hook them to some larger purpose. The best survivors — the ones we all should learn something from — have made this essential connection.

To the Student:

Part of our job as educational publishers is to try to improve the textbooks we publish. Thus, when revising, we take into account the experience of both instructors and students with the previous edition. At some time your instructor will be asked to comment extensively on *Behind the Scenes in American Government: Personalities and Politics,* but right now we want to hear from you. After all, though your instructor assigned this book, you are the one who paid for it.

Please help by completing this questionnaire and returning it to Political Science Editor, College Division, Little, Brown and Company, 34 Beacon Street, Boston, Massachusetts 02106.

School _____ Course Title _____

Instructor's name _____

Other books assigned _____

		Liked best			Liked least	Didn't read
1.	Boyd, The Front Runner	5	4	3	2	1	_____
2.	Morganthau and Martz, What Makes Mario Run?	5	4	3	2	1	_____
3.	Roberts, Congressman Jack Kemp's Run for the Presidency	5	4	3	2	1	_____
4.	Taylor, Jack Kemp and Richard Gephardt: Image-Building in Iowa	5	4	3	2	1	_____
5.	Cannon, Ronald Reagan: A Political Perspective	5	4	3	2	1	_____
6.	Royko, The Boss	5	4	3	2	1	_____
7.	Thomas, Influence Peddling in Washington	5	4	3	2	1	_____
8.	Watson, PAC Pilgrimage Becomes Candidates' Ritual	5	4	3	2	1	_____
9.	Hunt, The Washington Power Brokers	5	4	3	2	1	_____
10.	Mayer, The Reverend Jerry Flawell and the Tide of Born Again	5	4	3	2	1	_____
11.	Whitehead, For Whom Caddell Polls	5	4	3	2	1	_____
12.	Peterson, Political Consultants: The $2 Million Men in the $11 Million Race	5	4	3	2	1	_____
13.	Powell, The Right to Lie	5	4	3	2	1	_____
14.	Katz, Pressing Matters: An Interview with White House Correspondent Sam Donaldson	5	4	3	2	1	_____
15.	Hays and Rowe, Reporters: The New Washington Elite	5	4	3	2	1	_____
16.	Weisman, Ronald Regan's Magical Style	5	4	3	2	1	_____
17.	Barber, The Reagan Presidency: Character, Style, and Performance	5	4	3	2	1	_____
18.	Seaberry and Swardson, On Maneuvers with Jim Baker	5	4	3	2	1	_____
19.	Reedy, The White House Staff: A Personal Account	5	4	3	2	1	_____
20.	Romano, Women in the White House	5	4	3	2	1	_____
21.	Hook, Thomas Foley: Rising to the Top by Accident and Design	5	4	3	2	1	_____
22.	Barnes, Flying Nunn: The Democrats' Top Hawk	5	4	3	2	1	_____
23.	Evans and Novak, The Johnson System	5	4	3	2	1	_____
24.	Leamer, Robert Byrd and Edward Kennedy: Two Stories of the Senate	5	4	3	2	1	_____
25.	Calmes, The Texas Tornado: Senator Phil Gramm	5	4	3	2	1	_____

(over)

	Liked best			Liked least		Didn't read
26. Breslin, The Politician	5	4	3	2	1	_____
27. Woodward and Armstrong, The Brethren and the Abortion Decision	5	4	3	2	1	_____
28. Taylor, Meese v. Brennan: Who's Right About the Constitution?	5	4	3	2	1	_____
29. Ungar, The King: J. Edgar Hoover	5	4	3	2	1	_____
30. Alter, The Powers That Stay	5	4	3	2	1	_____

1. Are there any authors or political figures whom you would like to see represented?

_____

2. Did you find the editor's introductions helpful? _____

3. Will you keep this book for your library? _____

4. Please add any comments or suggestions. _____

_____

_____

5. May we quote you in our promotional efforts for this book? Yes _____ No _____

Date _____ Signature _____

Mailing address _____

_____

_____